120 年前的
西方媒体观察

万国报馆 编著

生活·讀書·新知 三联书店

图书在版编目（CIP）数据

甲午：120年前的西方媒体观察／万国报馆编著．—北京：生活·读书·新知三联书店，2014.8 （2015.3重印）
ISBN 978－7－108－05055－7

Ⅰ．①甲… Ⅱ．①万… Ⅲ．①中日甲午战争－史料 Ⅳ．①K256.306

中国版本图书馆CIP数据核字（2014）第122596号

责任编辑 唐明星
装帧设计 康 健
责任印制 卢 岳
出版发行 生活·讀書·新知 三联书店
（北京市东城区美术馆东街22号 100010）
网 址 www.sdxjpc.com
经 销 新华书店
印 刷 北京市松源印刷有限公司
版 次 2014年8月北京第1版
2015年3月北京第2次印刷
开 本 787毫米×1092毫米 1/16 印张22.25
字 数 40千字 图400幅
印 数 10,001－15,000册
定 价 68.00元
（印装查询：01064002715；邮购查询：01084010542）

中日甲午战争大事记
（1894—1895）

1894年
（清光绪二十年，日本明治二十七年，朝鲜高宗三十一年）

2月15日，朝鲜东学党起义。

6月2日，日本内阁会议决定向朝鲜派兵，并解散众议院。

6月7日，中日两国相互照会出兵朝鲜。

6月22日，日本外相向中国公使递交第一次绝交书。

7月16日，日英《通商航海条约》签订。

7月17日，日本召开御前会议确定对华开战。

7月23日，日本军队占领朝鲜王宫，扶植大院君执政。

7月25日，日本海军在黄海丰岛海面偷袭中国海军舰艇和运兵船，击沉高升号运兵船，中日甲午战争首开战事。

7月29日，日本陆军和清军在朝鲜成欢开战，次日日军占领牙山。中日甲午战争陆战爆发。

8月1日，中日两国宣战，中日甲午战争正式开战。

9月16日，日军攻克清军据守的平壤，朝鲜清军全线溃败，退回鸭绿江中国一侧。

9月17日，北洋舰队在黄海大东沟海域与日本联合舰队展开大规模海战，日本联合舰队获胜，就此掌握了黄海制海权。

10月23日，日军渡过鸭绿江，进攻中国本土。

11月21日，日军第二军占领旅顺后为报复中国军队此前的抵抗，屠杀旅顺全城，几乎杀尽旅顺中国军民，仅36位抬尸人生还。

1895 年

（清光绪二十一年，日本明治二十八年，朝鲜高宗三十二年）

1 月 20 日，日军山东作战军在威海荣城龙须半岛附近的荣城湾登陆，基本未遇抵抗。

2 月 1 日，中日两国全权代表在广岛会谈。

2 月 2 日，中日两国全权代表会谈破裂。在攻克威海卫南北帮炮台后，日军第二军主力当日最终攻克威海卫防御圈，占领威海卫。

2 月 12 日，北洋舰队在刘公岛向日本海军投降。

2 月 19 日，清政府任命李鸿章为和谈全权代表。

3 月 16 日，日本任命参谋总长小松宫彰仁亲王为征清大总督。

3 月 23 日，日军比志岛支队在台湾澎湖列岛登陆。

3 月 24 日，日本人小山六之助开枪行刺李鸿章，导致李鸿章身负重伤。

3 月 30 日，中日签订停战条约。

4 月 17 日，中日在日本马关春帆楼签订《马关新约》，即《马关条约》。条约的签订标志着中日甲午战争结束。

4 月 23 日，俄、德、法三国对日进行干涉。

5 月 4 日，日本内阁决定放弃要求中国割让辽东半岛。

5 月 10 日，日本天皇任命曾督战黄海海战的日本海军军令部长桦山资纪为台湾总督。

5 月 29 日，日军在台湾北部登陆。

10 月 21 日，台南陷落，中国军民在台湾有组织的抵抗结束。

目　录

序一　超越东亚　观察甲午 / 马勇　1

序二　百年甲午的新闻解读 / 童兵　5

前言　1

一　东亚的火药桶：朝鲜　1

二　西方势力在东亚　23

三　洋务与维新　63

四　沉没的“高升”　113

五　黄海悲歌：不沉的“致远”　123

六　中国陆军的惨败　157

七　旅顺屠杀真相　207

八　威海卫的陷落　223

九　战争中的生与死　247

十　《马关条约》：中国之辱　269

十一　故国有所思　281

十二　媒体在战争中的作用　315

后记　西方的画报　333

致谢　338

序一

超越东亚　观察甲午

马勇

120年前发生的甲午战争，是人类历史上的重大事件。这场战争不仅将近代中国的历史截然分为前后两个时期，使中国被迫放弃先前30多年洋务新政，踏上激进主义变革不归路。而且，由于这场战争，使国际政治格局重新洗牌，原先在国际政治中基本上不发挥功能的日本一跃成为一个值得注意的因素。日本的崛起，直接得益于这场战争。

对于这场战争，在中文学术界，中国始终处于话语强势，欲说还休。这是因为中国毕竟是战败一方，朝野对此都有各自的追悔与反省。朝廷后悔先前几十年没有像日本那样彻底改造自己的体制，适应时代；民间知识界由于各自立场也对这场战争予以不同的解读。有的以为，甲午战争的失败说明满洲人自私，他们不可能引领中国走向现代。因此，中国现代化有待于推翻清廷，赶走满洲人。这就是孙中山的排满革命。有的认为，中国的失败主要是因为在军事体制、指挥系统上太落后、太陈旧，因而中国应该像日本那样重造一支现代化军队。于是，当战争还没有结束时，中国政府就接受这样的劝告，下决心请德国人帮助训练一支现代化新军，十年生聚，报仇雪耻。还有人认为，中国的失败主要是因为没有抓住过去几十年的发展机遇，全面改造中国社会结构、组织系统、教育体制、社会管理，没有充分、放手发展自由资本主义，因而等到战后，中国政府确实在很大程度上释放社会，释放资本，重建全新的现代教育，全面仿行日本过去几十年走过的路。

应该说，过往一百年，中国人对甲午战争过程、影响、意义的认识，是全面的、深刻的，中国也确实在此后岁月中汲取了这场战争的教训，一切归零，从头开始，改变自己。1895年后的中国，不三年，面貌大变，一个充满活力的新兴经济体，重新展示了对世界资本的吸引力，中国终于踏上了一个全新的发展道路。

甲午战争不只是中日之间的战争，中国的话语强势实质上只是“知耻而后勇”，是失败者的沉痛反省。不过，这场战争不仅关涉中日，关涉东亚，也关涉世界格局的演变，因而在回望历史的时候，我们仅仅知道中国人怎样认识这场战争，是远远不够的，还应该知道日本人怎样说，毕竟日本也是这场战争的重要一方。仅仅知道中日两国的说法、看法，仍然是不够的，还应该知道朝鲜人怎样想、怎样说，毕竟这场战争是为朝鲜前途而战，朝鲜人的看法不管是否从根本上影响了这场战争，毕竟也是重要的一方，他们的看法不论从中国立场上看是对还是错，我们都无法忽视。

至于列强，也对这场战争给予各自不同关注、影响、解读，是甲午战争之所以如此的一个重要因素。而且这场战争中有些事件，比如丰岛海战、高升号沉没，比如中日讲和，三国干涉还辽，本身就是因为列强的介入而发生、而改变，如果我们不清楚列强的想法、看法、说法，我们就很难真正认清这场战争，我们可能依然处在民族主义悲情中。

好在世界进入了数字化时代，人们不仅比较容易地获取中文史料、中文研究成果，研究者、爱好者只要有心，就可以在非中文世界获取更多史料、更多研究成果。这些非中文史料、研究成果，极大地丰富了近代中国历史的表达，东西洋各国不同说法、看法，对我们既有的看法、说法提供一个或多个修正视角。

历史研究说到底就是盲人摸象，已经消逝的过去，史料中歧义互见的矛盾陈述，研究者的探究，当然都有助于对历史事件、历史人物的认识。但说到底，历史没有办法复制，没有办法像自然科学那样重复试验，历史学主要还是凭借研究者的主观判断，因而所有的研究，都只是在不断接近历史真相。为了描绘一个完整的、立体的“历史大象”，现代历史学主张“上穷碧落下黄泉，动手动脚找东西”，只要将不同史料、不同看法完整呈现，人们自然会从这些矛盾、复杂的陈述中理出一条脉络，描绘出一个事件的各个侧面。

作为一个影响世界进程的甲午战争，中文史料的发掘比较充分，非中文文献还有相当提升空间。这个原因非常复杂，有工具方面的原因（语言），也有政治方面的障碍（意识形态）。如今的中国已与两个甲子之前完全不同了，多侧面解读甲午战争，已近乎完全可能了。这部根据当年西方出版的数十种画报编辑的《甲午——

120 年前的西方媒体观察》，超越东亚，重新审视、观察甲午，给我们提供了那个时代最直观的形象，在平实无华的叙事中为我们提供了观察甲午战争的多样性视角。这部作品的原创性毋庸置疑，相信一定会在不久的未来加进与丰富近代中国历史的表达，为近代中国历史叙事重构提供一些基础性的资料。

历史认识无止境，史料发掘无止境。一切有机会、有能力、有兴趣的有心人，都应利用自己的优势，在全世界任何可能的角落，不断扩充近代中国的历史资料。尤其是利用全球化优势，深度挖掘非中文世界有关近代中国的史料，从西方文献记载中重新发现一个不一样的近代中国。

2014 年 6 月 8 日

序二

百年甲午的新闻解读

童兵

这是一部以图为主、文图并茂的大书。万国报馆借用几百幅出自西方记者之手的摄影作品和画师的速写，呈现和评述发生在120年前的一场大战——区区小国战胜堂堂天朝，告诉120年后的我们一个事实：甲午战争的失败，不仅是洋务运动的悲哀，北洋水师的惨败，也是中国政治腐败的必然下场，是资本主义新政对封建统治残局的胜利。

这部大书用它简洁的文字和生动的图片告诉读者一个真理：眼见的血淋淋的事实胜过空洞乏力的说教，日本新生的资本主义体制最终战胜保守没落的清王朝。其中，社会制度的对立，采取完全不同的新闻政策。在整个甲午战争中，日本政府实行公开透明的新闻政策，开动全部宣传机器为战争服务，他们允许外国武官观战，欢迎外国和本国记者随军采访。用日本政府首脑的话说，利用媒体攻势取得国民舆论的支持，就等于拿下了战争的一半胜利。而清政府呢？仍然是一贯的保守封闭态度，拒绝外国记者采访，不让外国武官观战，结果把战局的报道权、成败的评价权全部让给了国际社会和日本媒体。

不同的新闻政策，得到完全不同的舆论支持。日本军队进入中国之后，到处烧杀掠夺，而他们却通过西方媒体胡吹如何仁义道德、如何救济苦难的中国百姓。对此，连李鸿章本人都不满意中国报纸的表现。他在接受《纽约时报》记者专访时批评中国报纸的“编辑们不愿将真实情况告诉读者”，“由于不能诚实地说明真相，我们的报纸就失去了新闻本身高贵的价值，失去了广泛传播文明的可能”。西方记者由于深入战场，了解战局，也就对中国有了更为真切的认识。《哈珀斯周刊》的一则评论指出，中国并非一个整体，“犹如冰川一般向敌人开去”，“实际上中国像一个百孔千疮的沙袋，当重物击来，它四处飞散。”这个对甲午战争期间中国的评价，应该说是非常准确和十分深刻的。

甲午战争前 20 年，有 100 多位传教士在上海参加在华基督教传教士大会。会上经过激烈争议，形成一个共识：中国如同巨人那样正从长眠中醒来，摇撼着古老的枷锁，擦揉着蒙眬的双眼，审视着自己所处的地位，感到自己要赶快行动起来。为此，西方要抓紧利用好三种媒介：布道坛、课堂和报刊。而报刊的普及和发展，需要经济的大力发展和政治的高度开放，但清王朝的闭关锁国既定政策，始终不会给报刊自由成长的任何雨露和阳光，最终导致甲午战争的惨败，而中国这位巨人也始终未能站立起来。

十分感谢作者以图文并茂的精彩形态向读者生动地展示了当时社会的真实面貌，让 120 年后的我们有机会看到甲午战争背后种种鲜为人知的真相，并由此引发人们去思考那场战争留给今人种种不解的问题。我们相信，对这些问题的现代剖解，将有益于我们强化道路自信的意识和有力地推进中国现代化进程。

祝贺这部大书的出版。它的出版，不仅是对甲午战争120周年的纪念，不仅是对那场战争背后的诸多社会本质的反思，也必将推动我们正在努力的振兴中华繁荣华夏的中国梦的实现，中国这位历史巨人一定会出现在世界的东方。

是为序。

2014年5月26日

前　言

2014 年是甲午战争爆发 120 周年。对于这场战争的反思随着更多的史料挖掘而日益深刻和全面。在甲午战争史料挖掘中，笔者选取的角度是：西方媒体对于甲午战争的关注和报道。我们对媒体报道的收集集中在 1850 年至 1900 年，共收集了英国、法国、美国、俄罗斯、日本等国的十几种报刊近 300 个版面，在这些报刊中以周刊为主，也有日报和月刊，图文报道之外还有大量的述评，报道角度非常丰富。

120 年前的今天，逐渐敞开大门的东亚各国正经历着航海全球化、商贸全球化和战争全球化的洗礼，新闻通讯的全球化也伴随着电报和摄影术的使用而渐渐普及。虽然新闻照片还只是初露端倪，印刷手段仍旧以木版铜版多种印制手段并行，世界上还未出现统一的通讯社报道模式，但西方媒体采用的图文报道已经趋近于今天报刊杂志的编排版式：前线记者的文字描述配备以现场素描师的场景再现或照片临摹，在后方编排而成。前线的文稿已经有一部分通过电报传输，但绝大多数文字报道和所有的画稿和图片依然通过商船、邮轮传递。

不断崛起的近代报刊，力求在中、日、朝三国历史变革的十字路口通过自己的视角从各自国家利益出发不断探求三国变革对世界格局的改变，以及对本国利益的影响。美国《哈珀斯周刊》指出，西方列强对这次朝鲜事件和 20 年前有完全不一样的反应，比起 20 年前的冷漠，这次的事件成为西方各国的关注焦点。这是因为事件背后，两大东亚最有实力的对手之间的争斗很可能会带动欧洲列强一直克制着的敌意激发出来，从而引起世界范围的战争。

在这个报刊的收集过程中，有一个现象也引起了我们的注意和思考。在中国人看来，甲午战争是一场侵略战争，但翻看这些西方报道，却难以看到西方媒体对中国的同情。这其中的原因是什么呢？是日本还打响了一场没有硝烟的战争：媒体战。

战争期间，日本邀请了 114 名随军记者参与报道，还有 11 名现场素描记者、4 名摄影记者。日本对朝鲜进行战略包围时，甚至秘密聘请了一个美国专家作为国家宣传战的总指挥，这个人就是美国《纽约论坛报》的记者爱德华・豪斯（Edward House）。豪斯很熟悉西方媒体的运作方式，在他有计划的包装下，西方媒体对中国与日本分别代表着野蛮与文明的认识，形成了一种潮流与共识。比如纽约《先驱报》说，日本在朝鲜的作为将有利于整个世界，日本一旦失败，将令朝鲜重回中国野蛮的统治。这是当时世界最典型的看法。亚特兰大《先进报》说，美国公众毫无疑问地同情日本，认为日本代表着亚洲的光荣与进步。当时美国公众中有一种说法，把日本称为“东方美国佬”，觉得跟日本人很有认同感，实际上是媒体包装出来的。

今天，再回头看 120 年前西方媒体对于东亚局势的观察，丰富了我们对于历史的思考角度。

在整理和翻译这些报道版面的时候，我们遵循的原则是原版呈现，原文翻译。选择原版呈现可以让读者清晰看到：120 年前，当时的编辑们是如何处理与甲午战争相关的新闻的；尽可能真实再现当时西方媒体对战争的观察，同时，不同媒体对同一事件或同一新闻人物的报道同时呈现也可以看到不同国家的立场和观点。

在这些报道中，不难看出，西方媒体对甲午战争的极大关注，仅在我们所收集的资料中，就可看出战争期间，至少有 20 个封面报道，专题性的报道也在百篇左右。

本书所呈现的报刊以图片类报刊为主，同时兼容了一些周刊，即使是以图片报道为主的媒体，除去对战争过程的关注，也对战前的东亚局势、各国在东亚的利益进行了大量的文字报道和新闻分析。当时的报道有几种来源，一个是特派记者的前线特稿，一个是当时派出的插画师提供的文字稿件，还有一个来源是向当时派驻东亚的军队指挥官、外交人员约稿。因此，这些稿件角度丰富、写作风格多样，具有很强的可读性。本书配合一些图片对某些报道原文做了选译，对新闻事件和新闻人物进行了简要的背景介绍。还需说明一点，本书的外文图说均为直接抄录原报纸的图说；其中一些外文的词汇用法、人名与地名等与今天的用法有不同的，一律尊重原貌，未做改动。

本书在编排上，基本上按照战争的时间顺序，兼顾重要新闻事件和新闻人物。各媒体对战前的东亚局势观察也是一个重要角度，尤其是对于中国的洋务运动、日本的明治维新的关注，提供了非常有价值的报道内容。而朝鲜，对于西方媒体来说，也是一个全新的观察。当时的媒体还对中日两国的军事实力投入了极大的关注，对陆军和海军的分析报道也成为重要的一个部分。围绕这些内容，全书分为十二个章节。而最后一个章节，是有关“舆论战”的内容，这场没有硝烟的战争是甲午战争观察中最有特点的一个环节，到今天，也是令人思考的内容。

尽管编者在收集整理的过程中反复考证、多方求教，但毕竟只是历史爱好者，难免会有偏颇遗漏，也万分期待专家们的斧正，给予我们更多的学习机会。同时也欢迎广大读者与我们交流碰撞，共同思考。

一　东亚的火药桶：朝鲜

又出事了：一个新的东方问题爆发了，这一次，是棘手而又隐晦的远东问题。在干预这个问题的过程中，万一欧洲外交出手过重，天晓得谁会引导这次事件的走向？事情最后会发展到哪一步？

中国和日本在拼命较劲，同1884年一样（1884年朝鲜的甲申政变）。如今，朝鲜不仅是导火线，而且是流血冲突的关键所在。最新从上海传来的电报告知我们这场事变的序幕。但在1884年，中日之争结束时并没有武装冲突，最后双方签订了正式条约（指1885年中日《天津条约》——编者注）。当时，敌对双方差不多势均力敌。而今天，日本确立其海洋舰队优势已有多年，它断定，展示其辉煌军事力量的决定性时机已经到来。

理论上，朝鲜是清朝的藩属国。事实上，它依附于日本贸易。1876年，尽管有中国的反对，日本还是迫使其开放了三个重要港口，它们是：靠日本海的元山、釜山，以及靠黄海、位于汉城西南方的仁川。每年，通过这三个通商口岸，价值1400万（法郎）的货物从长崎出口，进入朝鲜。但朝鲜仍然是个“隐士之国”。这个国家渴望和其他国家保持距离，甚至是和中国。它反对任何对传统习俗的改变。朝鲜国王高宗李熙正是这股保守势力的代表。他与代表中国的直隶总督李鸿章达成共识。而一直在推进变革的日本在朝鲜的宫廷中也有自己的代理人，不是别人，正是高宗李熙的父亲大院君。在这两股势力的争斗中，动荡发生了。

即将上演的武装对抗，无论其结局如何，最终都会为欧洲揭开这个神秘国度的面纱。

——1894年8月4日　法国《插图报》

THE ILLUSTRATED LONDON NEWS

REGISTERED AT THE GENERAL POST OFFICE FOR TRANSMISSION ABROAD.

No. 2884.—VOL. CV. SATURDAY, JULY 28, 1894. WITH SUPPLEMENT SIXPENCE. By Post, 6½d.

THE IMPENDING WAR BETWEEN CHINA AND JAPAN: NATIVE MARKET NEAR SEOUL, COREA.

1894 年 7 月 28 日《伦敦新闻画报》

中日战争迫在眉睫：朝鲜汉城附近的市场

The impending war between China and Japan: native market near Seoul, Corea.

一副版画清晰描绘出三国关系，朝鲜作为清朝藩属国，以其独特的地理位置，像楔子一样夹在中国、俄国、日本之间，是列强踏入远东的最后一块神秘封地。

1894 年 7 月 28 日《伦敦新闻画报》

朝鲜宫女（疑似闵妃——编者注）
Attendant on the King of Corea.
明成皇后（1851.10.19—1895.10.8），名闵兹映，是朝鲜王朝高宗的王妃、纯宗的母亲。在近代朝鲜历史中又被称为闵妃。她是骊兴闵氏外戚集团的核心人物。1895 年 10 月 8 日，她被日本浪人残杀于汉城乾清宫，史称“乙未事变”。死后谥号明成皇后。

1894 年 11 月《哈珀斯周刊》这样写道：“在朝鲜的王宫中，王后是真正的国王，是宫中掌握实权的最高统治者，她丈夫倒是好像在朝鲜其他地方做国王似的。宫中全体人员，不论男女，全部由她任命，在她的恩赐下，这些人获得了在宫中的位置。他们深知哪怕违背国王，甚至激怒国王，也要比不尊重王后安全得多。他们会主动向她汇报宫中所有的八卦，在没有请示她之前，王宫围墙之内绝对不可能发生任何事情。”

“因为害怕被革命，国王和王后整夜不睡，过着昼夜颠倒的生活。”

VIEWS OF COREA.

The singular and sequestered nation of Mongolian race inhabiting the large peninsula of Eastern Asia between the Chinese "Yellow Sea" and the Japanese islands in the North Pacific Ocean cannot be regarded as savage, but is probably the least tinged with modern civilisation, certainly the most remote from European progressive influences, of any equally large community on earth, having for ages past rejected all foreign commercial intercourse and resisted the ideas and customs of its powerful neighbours. The Coreans, estimated in number at nearly nine millions, are quite distinct in race from the Mantchu Tartars, as well as from the Chinese and the Japanese; their spoken language is akin, in some degree, to that of Japan and the Loo-choo Islands, but they use the Chinese written signs for things and thoughts without knowing Chinese words; and they have some tincture of Buddhism, also of the Lao-tse religion of China. Their political institutions, however, are different from the Chinese, involving an hereditary privileged aristocracy and priesthood, together with an absolute monarchy. The King is a well-meaning, inoffensive, but very weak-minded man, completely under the thumb of the Queen, whose family is all powerful, while the Crown Prince is said to be mentally imbecile. Hence the recent intervention of Japan, demanding certain administrative reforms, as there are some two or three thousand Japanese traders or industrialists settled at the south-eastern extremity of Corea. The chief ports and towns of Corea are situated on its western side, fronting China. The capital city, named Seoul, the King's residence, is some twenty-five miles inland from the port of Chemulpo, of which we present some views.

CONSULATE HILL AND HARBOUR, CHEMULPO.

PALACE GROUNDS AT SEOUL: KING'S AUDIENCE-HALL IN THE BACKGROUND.

A COREAN GENERAL.

THE KING AND CROWN PRINCE OF COREA.

THE BRITISH CONSULATE-GENERAL, SEOUL.

1894 年 8 月 4 日《伦敦新闻画报》

（此报在纽约出版的时间比伦敦晚两周，故纽约版出版时间为 1894 年 8 月 18 日—— 编者注）

1 仁川的领馆山和海港

2 汉城的皇家园林，背景中的是国王的听政殿

3 一位朝鲜将领

4 朝鲜国王（高宗李熙）及其子（王世子李坧，即后来的太子、朝鲜皇帝纯宗 ——编者注）

5 汉城英国总领事馆

1 Consulate hill and harbour, Chemulpo .

2 Palace grounds at Seoul, King's audience-hall in the background.

3 A Corean general.

4 The King and crown prince of Corea.

5 The British consulate-general, Seoul.

这个奇怪、封闭的种族生活在中国黄海和日本群岛之间的半岛上，他们虽然不能被视为野蛮民族，但可以算是离现代文明最远的、受欧洲改良精神影响最小的地方。长年以来，他们拒绝与外界通商、交往，甚至抵制周边强大邻国正在进行的改革。这 900 万朝鲜族人与他们的邻居——满族女真人、中国人和日本人都不同，他们的语言发音与日本和琉球群岛相近，但用中文书写，受佛教和中国道教的影响。他们的政治制度与中国不尽相同，贵族和僧侣阶层可以世袭，君主享有绝对权力。国王虽善良，却非常软弱，被王后支配，后党专权。据传，太子也是个弱智。最近，日本对朝鲜干涉的目的是要求朝鲜进行政体改革，在朝鲜东南部靠近日本的港口，有 2000—3000 名日本侨民经商；但朝鲜的主要港口坐落在西部面向中国的方向。朝鲜的都城是汉城，距离海港仁川 25 英里左右。

——《朝鲜一瞥》（选译），1894 年 8 月 4 日《伦敦新闻画报》

Le Petit Journal

TOUS LES JOURS
Le Petit Journal
5 Centimes

SUPPLÉMENT ILLUSTRÉ
Huit pages : CINQ centimes

TOUS LES DIMANCHES
Le Supplément illustré
5 Centimes

Cinquième année | LUNDI 13 AOUT 1894 | Numéro 195

LES ÉVÉNEMENTS DE CORÉE

Agitation à Séoul

LES AFFAIRES DE CORÉE. – Vue de Séoul.

1894 年 8 月 4 日《插图报》

朝鲜局势，汉城远眺

Les affaires de Corée.—Vue de Séoul.

左图：

1894 年 8 月 13 日《小日报》封面

朝鲜局势，汉城的骚动

Les Événements de Corée.Agitation à Séoul.

184 THE ILLUSTRATED LONDON NEWS AUG. 11, 1894

SKETCHES IN COREA.

The war that has been suddenly commenced, on land and on sea, between the rival empires of China and Japan, for dominion or control over the peninsula which lies a few hundred miles to the east of the Gulf of Pekin, and to the west of the island realm of the Mikado, whatever may be its naval and military victories for the one or the other of those two considerable rival Powers, will probably terminate the domestic independence of the feeble Corean nation. No one who is acquainted with the disposition of that unwarlike people seems to think it likely that the Coreans will fight on either side, unless it be under the compulsion of a foreign conqueror, but they must be alarmed and annoyed by this disturbance of their careless existence. They are genial and kind-hearted, but extremely lazy, and in this respect present a marked contrast to the restless Japanese and the industrious Chinese. Their pipes are over a yard long, and the people smoke from early childhood all day long, whatever work they are supposed to be doing. How they manage to support these huge pipes in their mouths is a mystery, as the leverage exerted is tremendous. It may be remarked that their clothes are not sewn together, but are glued at the seams with rice paste; for a Corean tailor would never be at the pains of stitching. Persons of the upper and middle classes wear a large conical black hat, which is transparent, being made of plaited horse-hair, of much the same texture as the seat of a cane-bottom chair, and plaited quite open. The beauty of this hat is that it excludes neither air, sun, nor rain. The people feed largely on crushed beans and bacon or fish. They dwell in huts or cabins built of hardened mud, and every family

ENTRANCE TO THE KING'S PALACE, SEOUL.

COREAN OFFICIALS IN COURT DRESS.

HIGH COREAN OFFICIAL AND CHILDREN.

KI-SANG, OR COREAN DANCING WOMEN.

keeps a pig. The Buddhist priests are forbidden, on pain of death, to enter Seoul, owing to their once having stirred up a rebellion in that city. Only a small proportion of the people are Buddhists. This religion, as practised in Corea, is of a very debased type. The lower orders of the people, with the exception of those who are Buddhists, believe only in the powers of evil, and have no conception of a beneficent deity. The devils are supposed by them to inhabit certain withered trees; and in order to propitiate them, passers-by throw stones at the tree, or tie pieces of coloured rag to its branches, and, when in trouble, they place offerings of rice and wine in a little house put up at the foot of the tree. The "Ki-Sang," or Corean dancing-women, are usually the wives of Court retainers, and are employed to amuse the guests at official dinners. In Corean dancing, the feet are scarcely moved at all, the body swaying to the music. This dancing is not ungraceful, and closely resembles that of the Japanese. The Court dress of an official personage of high rank is rather costly. The badges in the front of the robes are of fine embroidery, very dark blue in colour, and are made of thick silk gauze. The most curious part of this Court dress is the belt, which stands out two inches from the body all round, and is supported by tags made of wood, covered with leather, and ornamented with tortoiseshell, jade, or gems, according to the owner's dignity. The hat is of camel's-wool felt, and is surmounted by red and blue feathers and a button of the appropriate colour. The chin-strap is composed of jade beads, and is made a great deal too loose. Coreans have the habit of going about with their mouths open in order to keep their hats on. The Corean army, except the palace guards at Seoul, has only swords and bows and arrows, and is of no account as a military force. It is to enforce certain demands of administrative reform in Corea that Japan has sent troops into that country, which act of intervention has been opposed by China as an infringement of some ancient Chinese claims of sovereignty, long practically in abeyance.

1894年8月11日《伦敦新闻画报》

1 汉城王宫入口	1 Entrance to the King's Palace, Seoul.
2 朝鲜官员的朝服	2 Corean officials in court dress.
3 朝鲜高官和子嗣	3 High Corean official and children.
4 舞姬	4 Ki-Sang, or Corean dancing women.

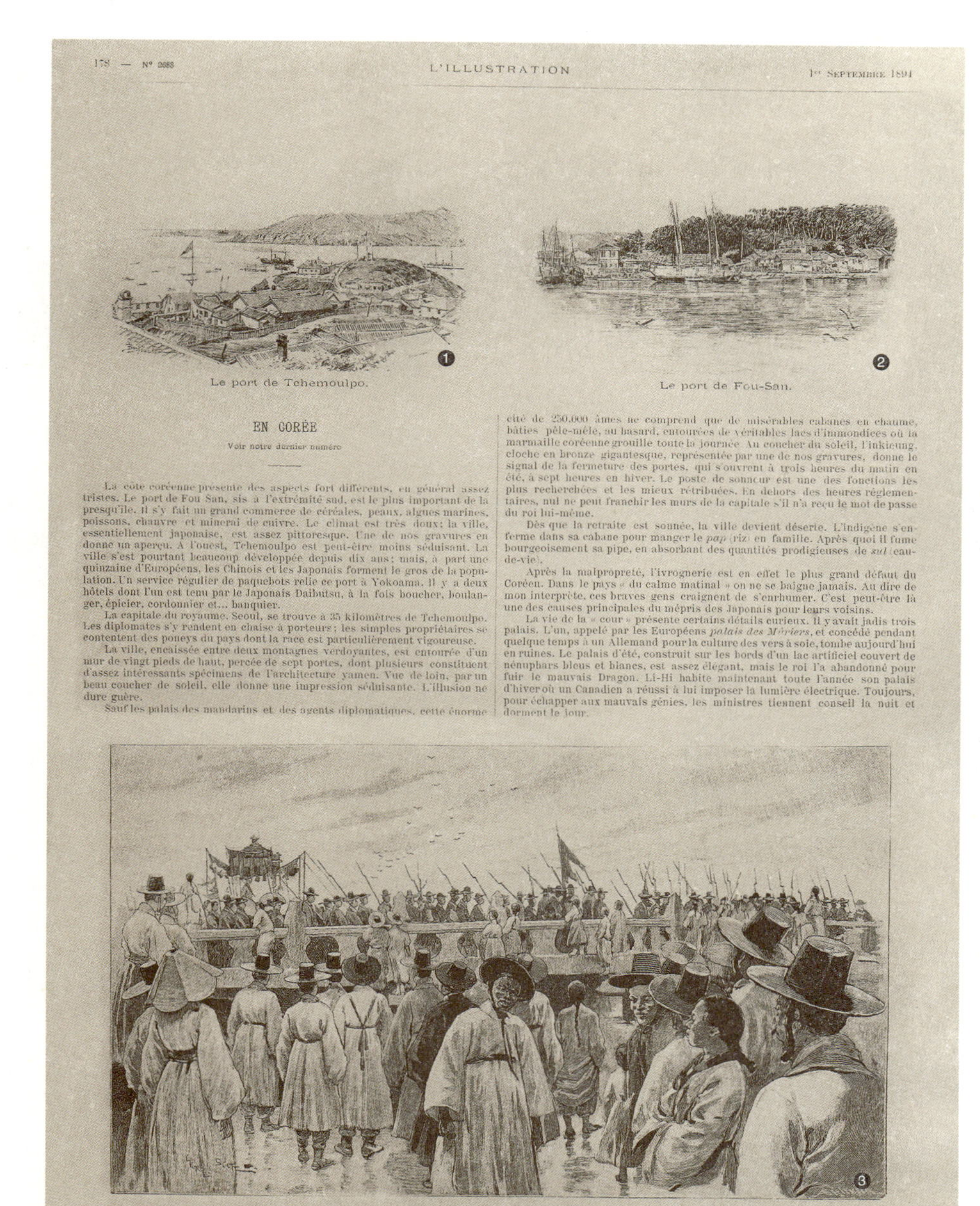

178 — N° 2688　　L'ILLUSTRATION　　1er Septembre 1894

Le port de Tchemoulpo.

Le port de Fou-San.

EN CORÉE

Voir notre dernier numéro

La côte coréenne présente des aspects fort différents, en général assez tristes. Le port de Fou San, sis à l'extrémité sud, est le plus important de la presqu'île. Il s'y fait un grand commerce de céréales, peaux, algues marines, poissons, chanvre et minerai de cuivre. Le climat est très doux; la ville, essentiellement japonaise, est assez pittoresque. Une de nos gravures en donne un aperçu. A l'ouest, Tchemoulpo est peut-être moins séduisant. La ville s'est pourtant beaucoup développée depuis dix ans; mais, à part une quinzaine d'Européens, les Chinois et les Japonais forment le gros de la population. Un service régulier de paquebots relie ce port à Yokoama. Il y a deux hôtels dont l'un est tenu par le Japonais Daibutsu, à la fois boucher, boulanger, épicier, cordonnier et... banquier.

La capitale du royaume, Seoul, se trouve à 35 kilomètres de Tchemoulpo. Les diplomates s'y rendent en chaise à porteurs; les simples propriétaires se contentent des poneys du pays dont la race est particulièrement vigoureuse.

La ville, encaissée entre deux montagnes verdoyantes, est entourée d'un mur de vingt pieds de haut, percée de sept portes, dont plusieurs constituent d'assez intéressants spécimens de l'architecture yamen. Vue de loin, par un beau coucher de soleil, elle donne une impression séduisante. L'illusion ne dure guère.

Sauf les palais des mandarins et des agents diplomatiques, cette énorme cité de 250.000 âmes ne comprend que de misérables cabanes en chaume, bâties pêle-mêle, au hasard, entourées de véritables lacs d'immondices où la marmaille coréenne grouille toute la journée. Au coucher du soleil, l'inkieung, cloche en bronze gigantesque, représentée par une de nos gravures, donne le signal de la fermeture des portes, qui s'ouvrent à trois heures du matin en été, à sept heures en hiver. Le poste de sonneur est une des fonctions les plus recherchées et les mieux rétribuées. En dehors des heures réglementaires, nul ne peut franchir les murs de la capitale s'il n'a reçu le mot de passe du roi lui-même.

Dès que la retraite est sonnée, la ville devient déserte. L'indigène s'enferme dans sa cabane pour manger le *pap* (riz) en famille. Après quoi il fume bourgeoisement sa pipe, en absorbant des quantités prodigieuses de *sul* (eau-de-vie).

Après la malpropreté, l'ivrognerie est en effet le plus grand défaut du Coréen. Dans le pays « du calme matinal » on ne se baigne jamais. Au dire de mon interprète, ces braves gens craignent de s'enrhumer. C'est peut-être là une des causes principales du mépris des Japonais pour leurs voisins.

La vie de la « cour » présente certains détails curieux. Il y avait jadis trois palais. L'un, appelé par les Européens *palais des Mûriers*, et concédé pendant quelque temps à un Allemand pour la culture des vers à soie, tombe aujourd'hui en ruines. Le palais d'été, construit sur les bords d'un lac artificiel couvert de nénuphars bleus et blancs, est assez élégant, mais le roi l'a abandonné pour fuir le mauvais Dragon. Li-Hi habite maintenant toute l'année son palais d'hiver où un Canadien a réussi à lui imposer la lumière électrique. Toujours, pour échapper aux mauvais génies, les ministres tiennent conseil la nuit et dorment le jour.

SEOUL. — Promenade du roi.

1894 年 1 月 9 日《插图报》

1　仁川港	1　Le Port de Tchemoulpo.
2　釜山港	2　Le Port de Fou-San.
3　汉城，国王出行	3　Séoul.—Promenade du Roi.

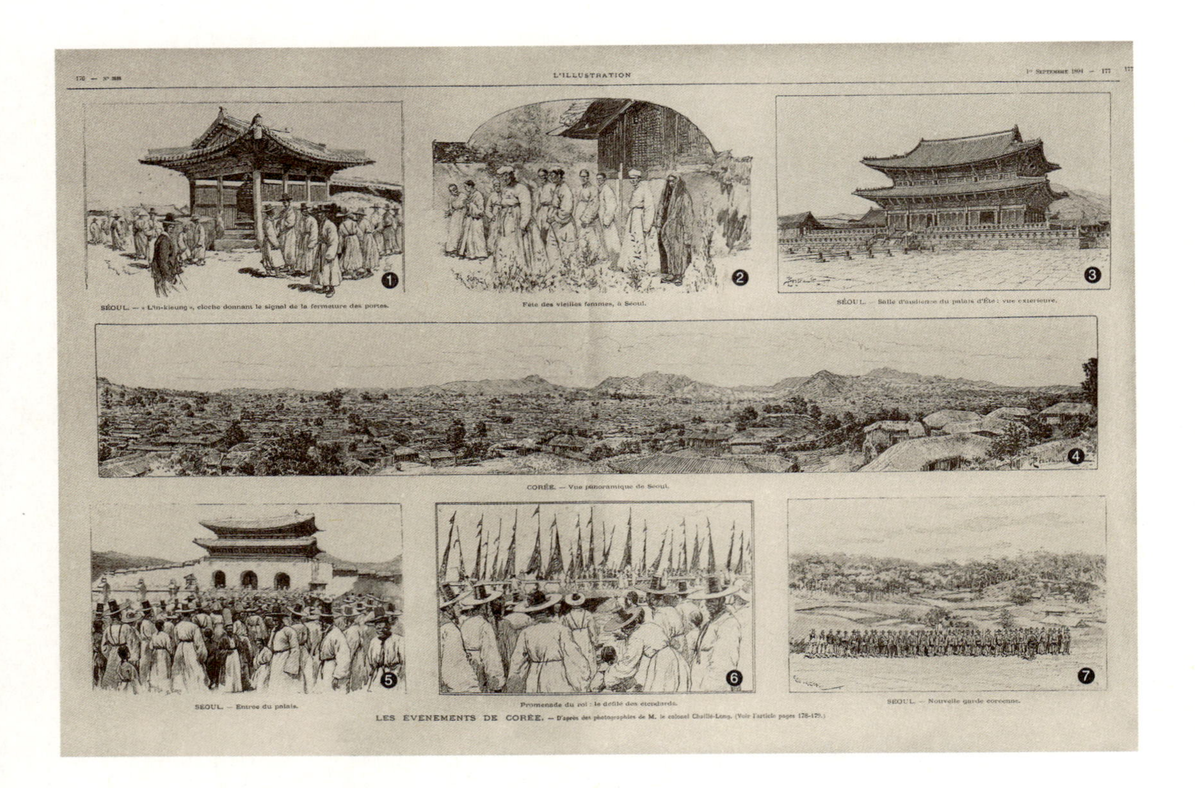

1894年1月9日《插图报》

1 汉城，“音阙”大钟，关城门的信号钟

1 Séoul— “L'in-kieung”, cloche donnant le signal de la fermeture des portes.

2 汉城的老年妇女节

2 Fête des vieilles femmes, à Séoul.

3 汉城，夏宫的朝政殿外景

3 Séoul—Salle d'audience du Palais d'Été: vue extérieur.

4 朝鲜，汉城全景

4 Corée—Vue panoramique de Séoul.

5 汉城，王宫入口

5 Séoul—Entrée du Palais.

6 国王出行——军旗飘飘

6 Promenade du Roi: le défilé des étendards.

7 新军

7 Séoul—Nouvelle garde coréenne.

沙叶龙（Chaillé-Long，美国驻朝鲜公使——编者注）撰写稿件并提供图片，所有版画图片均基于沙叶龙上校的摄影作品制版。

事实上，酗酒是继肮脏之后朝鲜最严重的缺点。在这个“早晨静悄悄的”国家里，人们从不洗澡。据我的翻译说，这些老百姓们害怕得感冒。这也许就是日本人鄙视他们这个邻居的原因之一。

每次接见都是《官报》报道关注的话题。因为朝鲜有一份每日出版的官方报纸，对国王的颂扬占据大幅版面，但他们也会在这份报纸上公布税务官的任命及各行政部门的举动。此外，朝鲜国王李熙早就明白新闻媒体的威力，他懂得想要引导舆论导向，无论是褒是贬，只要在报刊上创建一个专栏即可。

朝鲜军队其实并不存在。管制六个城门军队的长官们是地方的文官，自己招募土匪做属下，有的甚至还以此收贿。因为感觉到必须要有一支更正规的卫队，朝鲜国王请求华盛顿的总督于1888年派遣了三名可供调遣的美国军官。他们建立了一所面向贵族们开放的军校；但是这个军事使团的团长米奇第（Mickdye）上校，一名十分英勇的、曾有段时间效力于（埃及的）伊斯梅尔总督（Khédive Ismail）的士兵，还什么都没能组织起来。其实，朝鲜人几乎没什么军事气概，而日本军官们已经组建起一支拥有六到八支部队的皇家卫队，配备了雷明顿步枪；除去以上提及的土匪，这就是朝鲜军队的全貌。其军服是蓝色上装，配白色裤子和红布带镶边的黑色帽子，穿起来既不好看又不方便。

有一天，国王李熙曾想把他的军队的指挥权交给我，可我谢绝了这份美差。

——沙叶龙《在朝鲜》（选译），1894年1月9日《插图报》

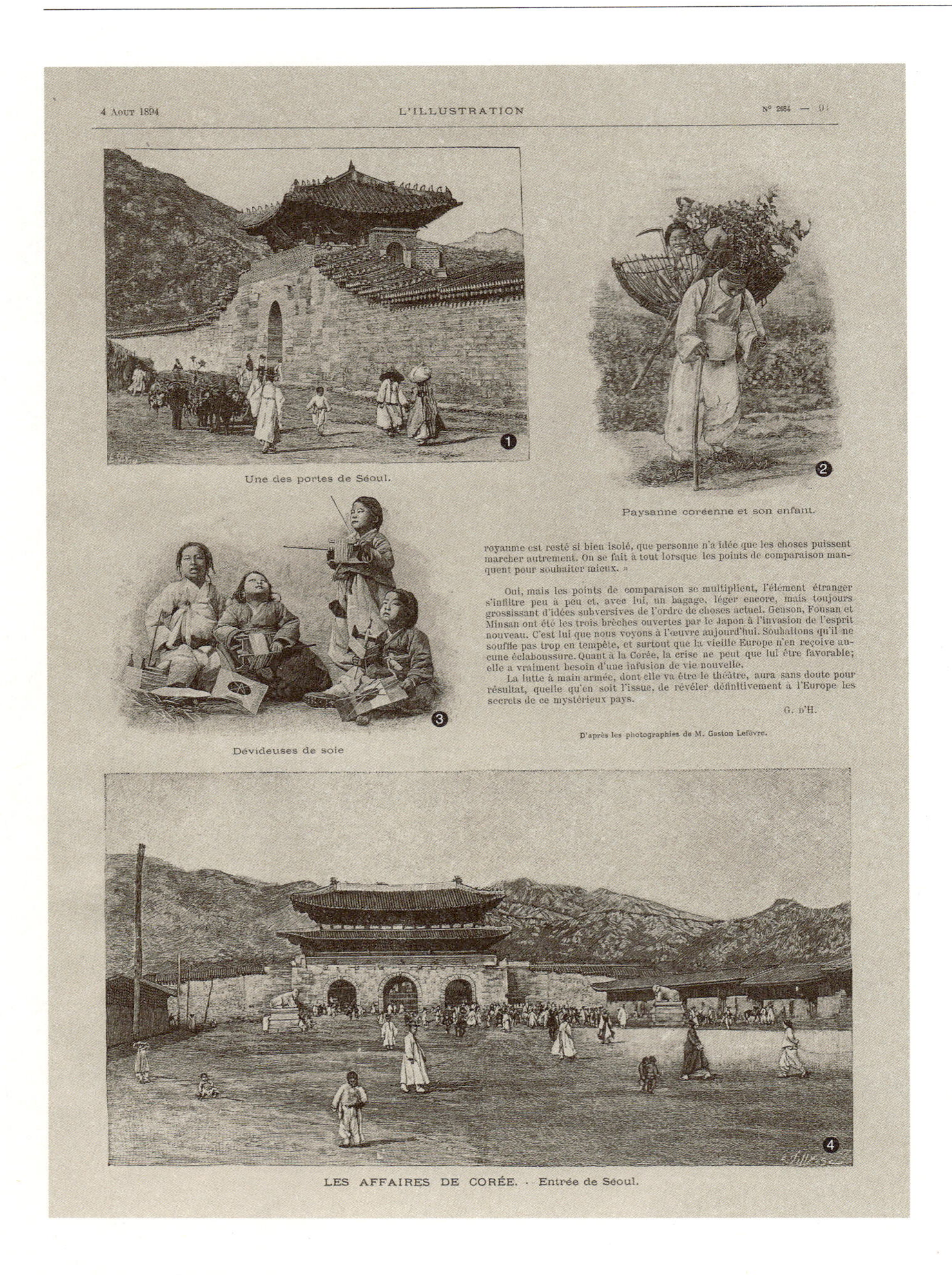

4 Aout 1894 L'ILLUSTRATION N° 2684 — 91

Une des portes de Séoul.

Paysanne coréenne et son enfant.

royaume est resté si bien isolé, que personne n'a idée que les choses puissent marcher autrement. On se fait à tout lorsque les points de comparaison manquent pour souhaiter mieux. »

Oui, mais les points de comparaison se multiplient, l'élément étranger s'infiltre peu à peu et, avec lui, un bagage, léger encore, mais toujours grossissant d'idées subversives de l'ordre de choses actuel. Genson, Fousan et Minsan ont été les trois brèches ouvertes par le Japon à l'invasion de l'esprit nouveau. C'est lui que nous voyons à l'œuvre aujourd'hui. Souhaitons qu'il ne souffle pas trop en tempête, et surtout que la vieille Europe n'en reçoive aucune éclaboussure. Quant à la Corée, la crise ne peut que lui être favorable; elle a vraiment besoin d'une infusion de vie nouvelle.

La lutte à main armée, dont elle va être le théâtre, aura sans doute pour résultat, quelle qu'en soit l'issue, de révéler définitivement à l'Europe les secrets de ce mystérieux pays.

G. d'H.

D'après les photographies de M. Gaston Lefèvre.

Dévideuses de soie

LES AFFAIRES DE CORÉE. - Entrée de Séoul.

1894年8月4日《插图报》

1 汉城的一个城门
2 朝鲜农民和孩子
3 正在缫丝的孩子们
4 汉城的大门

1 Une des portes de Séoul.
2 Payasnne coréenne et son enfant.
3 Dévideuses de soie.
4 Entrée de Séoul.

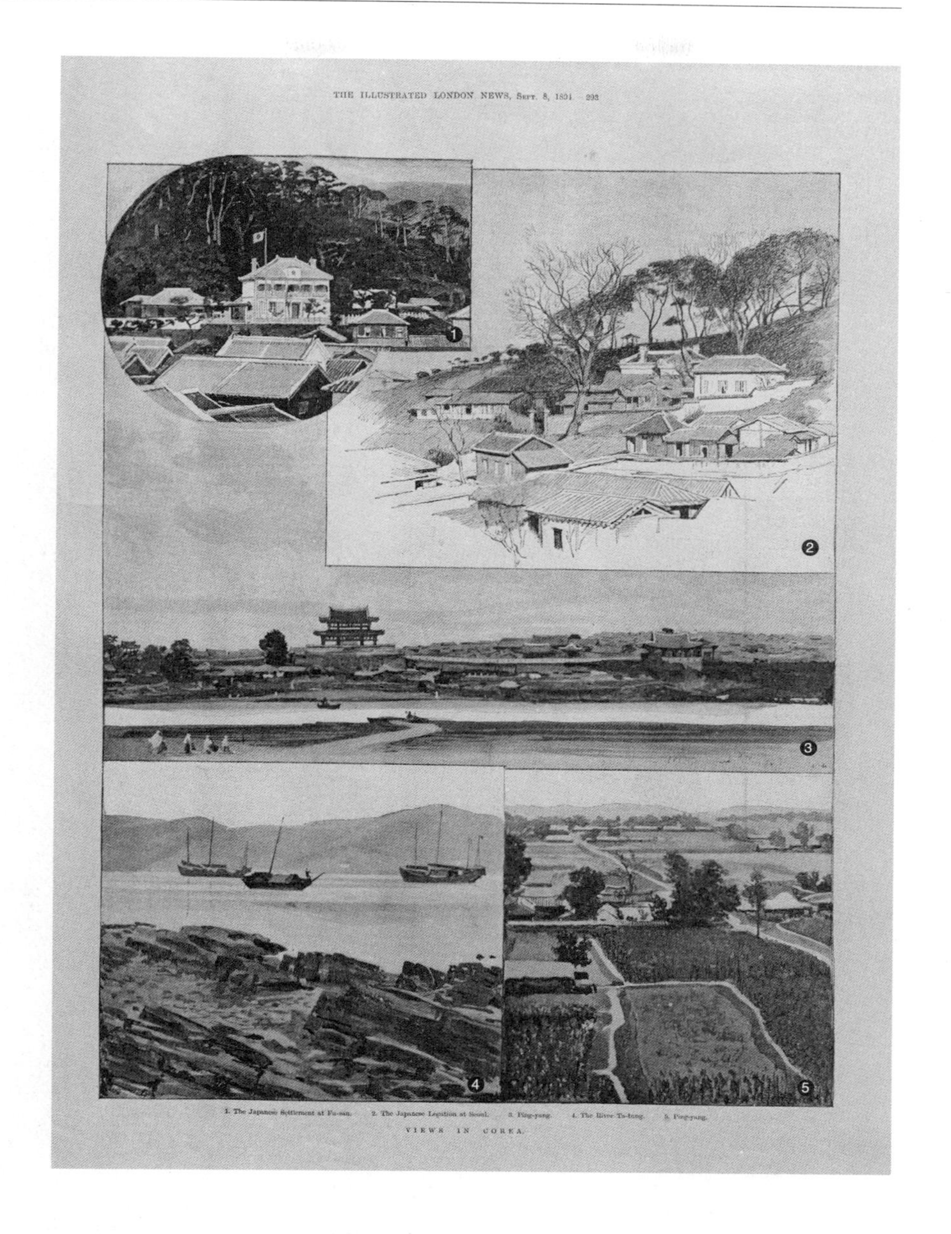

THE ILLUSTRATED LONDON NEWS, SEPT. 8, 1894 293

1. The Japanese Settlement at Fu-san. 2. The Japanese Legation at Seoul. 3. Ping-yang. 4. The River Ta-tung. 5. Ping-yang.

VIEWS IN COREA.

1894 年 8 月 25 日《伦敦新闻画报》

朝鲜景色

1 日本侨民在釜山聚居区

2 汉城的日本公使馆

3 平壤

4 大同江

5 平壤

Views in Corea.

1 The Japanese settlement at Fu-San.

2 The Japanese Legation at Seoul.

3 Ping-Yang.

4 The River Ta-Tung.

5 Ping-Yang.

COOLIE.
BOY PEDDLERS.
KOREAN SOLDIERS.
A CABINET MINISTER, HIS SON, AND DANCING-GIRLS.
A KOREAN LADY AND MAIDS.
TAI-WUN-KUN, THE KING'S FATHER.
A PALACE WOMAN, SEOUL.
AN OFFICIAL IN COURT DRESS.
KOREA—A NATION OF MOURNERS.—DRAWN BY G. W. PETERS FROM PHOTOGRAPHS.—[SEE PAGE 11.]
13

1895 年 1 月 5 日《哈珀斯周刊》

1 朝鲜苦力
2 街上的儿童小贩
3 朝鲜士兵
4 朝鲜的一位内阁大臣和他的儿子以及舞伎的合影
5 朝鲜妇人和她的女仆
6 国王生父兴宣大院君
7 汉城的一位宫女（疑似闵妃——编者注）
8 一位着朝服的官员

1 Coolie.
2 Boy peddlers.
3 Korean soldiers.
4 A Cabinet Minister, his son, and dancing-girls.
5 A Korean lady and maids.
6 Tai-Wun-Kun, the King's father.
7 A palace woman, Seoul.
8 An official in court dress.

朝鲜，以其顽固的与世隔绝和自给自足，拒绝与西方国家友好来往，拒绝交流带来的一切利益，这使它获得了“隐士王国”的名号。不过，十年之前，在我国的引领之下，它终于进入了世界大家庭。

朝鲜人的生活环境很肮脏，这使身着白色朝鲜国服的人们与其脏兮兮的环境形成了极大反差。长期穿白色衣服并不是朝鲜人天生干净整洁，而是遵循中国丧礼习俗的规定。根据规定，有人不幸身故时，所有的亲戚为了纪念死者，必须要穿上一尘不染的白色衣服 1000 天，表达深深的哀悼。如果这个不愉快的国家失去其主权，每个人都有义不容辞的责任，用这样的方法来悼念他们的祖国。

说来也巧，在朝鲜，将近一个半世纪以前，一个国王驾崩后，他的子民们开始穿起表达悲哀的白色丧服。两个继承人，在各自执政的三年和六年里，被农民们毫不留情地残杀了，结果，这个受难国的人民连续十年穿着白色丧服。在这场旷日持久的哀悼终止之日，一些智者认为：从十年的哀悼中可以得出这样的结论，如果人们再在喜庆之日着各色鲜艳服饰，会再次导致像近期发生的让人惊恐担忧的皇室贵族高死亡率，因此，全国人民应该衣着简朴；整个国家的人民再也不穿这些无用花费得来的衣物。所以，在这种观点，以及衰弱的经济与对死神来临的恐惧心理之下，朝鲜人民成了永久的默哀者。不管这种说法正确与否，朝鲜人民的确长期穿着白色丧服，除了被加冕的官员，所有人都如此。

——《朝鲜——哀悼者之国》（选译），1895 年 1 月 5 日《哈珀斯周刊》

1894 年 10 月 27 日《图片报》

朝鲜街头正在吃饭团的乞丐

Beggars in the street eating rice.

1894 年 8 月 25 日《伦敦新闻画报》

英国医生兰迪斯和他在朝鲜仁川开办的英语夜校（夜校招收通商口岸的日本和中国侨民——编者注）

Dr. Landis and his school at Chemulpo, Corea.

1894 年 10 月 27 日《图片报》

朝鲜刑法的执行——釜山窃贼被警察施以棍刑

The administration of justice in Corea: a thief being flogged by the police at Fusan.

棍刑使用棍棒的粗细与所犯罪行呈正比，犯人被剥下一部分衣服，脸朝地面趴在板凳上受刑。不过如果他能付给警察一些钱，会好过很多。被判处极刑的罪犯就这样往往被打得皮开肉绽、粉身碎骨，直至死亡。

The thickness of the stick is in proportion to the crime committed. The malefactor is strapped face downwards on to a bench and part of his clothing removed. If he has money the criminal may send for it to give to the police, who will then let him off more easily. Prisoners condemned to capital punishment are flogged to death with very thick sticks, which lacerate the flesh and generally break several bones.

HARPER'S WEEKLY

THE HARA-KIRI OF YENYA HANGUWAN.

THE art and literature of Japan have found many interpreters, but her drama, her wonderful stage, which Mr. Percival Lowell has said, in his charming book on Korea, is one of the finest the world has produced, still waits for some loving hand to unfold its wonders.

It is a perfect storehouse of history, and on its boards old Japan moves again with a vividness that is startling and a realism that needs no libretto. Its tragedies leave little to the imagination, and its comedies and farces are easily understood and some of them very funny.

The theatres are barnlike structures, with unpainted and little-adorned interiors. The stage is at one end of the auditorium, which is divided into squares, like a great checker-board. On both sides, at right angles to the front of the stage, are the *hana-michi*, or flower-paths. They are raised above the floor. The broader one, and the path most frequently employed, is about three feet in width. It is used by the players for entrance and exit, and is really a part of the stage itself, for much of the acting takes place upon it, and in the skilful hands of the Japanese it is most effective.

The costuming is excellent, the scenery fair, and the acting in the main natural and good. The theatre is essentially the amusement of the people, and consequently, of all Japanese art, it is the least tinctured with foreign imitation.

In the plays are preserved the quaint customs and curious manners of by-gone days. They represent scenes of daily life, the myths and legends of the country or of the feudal times. Of all the figures of old Japan which the stage has preserved, the most striking is the *samurai*, the man of two swords, who occupies in Japanese romantic story the place filled by the knights of old in the legends of European chivalry. He was the backbone of the feudal system, and the military class to which he belonged ruled Japan. He was the logical outcome of that system. From it was evolved for his guidance a code of conduct of the most intricate character and of etiquette of the greatest nicety, which, though it may be to our minds somewhat fantastic and strained, had for its basis an ideal of honor which was no mean conception. Patriotism in its Western sense was unknown. There was no common country, no unified nation. The lives of the castles and the camps centred about the clan. Loyalty to the clan chief was the soul of the samurai, and individual rights and liberties were sunk in the intensity of the feeling. This fealty was called *yamato damashii*, and its spirit pervaded the entire history and romance of old Japan. It found expression in the old clan wars and in the thousand feuds and fights of the ancient time. In these modern days it survives in the form of a most intense, unreasoning patriotism.

The motive of a large part of Japanese romantic story is found in the deeds of these knights of the far East, and of all the tales of the olden time none is more well known than the true story of the Forty-seven Ronins. The record of their deeds is enshrined in the hearts of the Japanese people, because it embodies to them the very essence of loyalty, which they call *chiushin*. This word, combined with *kura* (*gura*), a storehouse, gives the title to the most popular play on the Japanese stage—*Chiushingura*—which is founded on the story of the Forty-seven Ronins, and which is the apotheosis of the samurai.

The scene from the play which is the subject of the illustration is the last act of the master of the devoted ronins (literally wave-men, or retainers without a master), the *hara-kiri* of Yenya Hanguwan, the Asano Takumi no Kami of the original story.

The tearful and sorrowing retainers have, with bowed heads, come to see the last of their beloved master. All the preparations have been made with the precision and nicety which characterize this ancient and marvellous ceremony, no jot or tittle of which is omitted in its stage counterfeit.

Two straw mats six feet square have been laid, and over them is drawn a white cloth. At the corners are placed little tubes of wood, and in them sprigs of green bamboo. In front is a low stand of unpainted wood. The condemned man enters. He is attired in spotless white.

Gravely he kneels upon the mats, and, with unmoved face, listens to the sentence of self-inflicted death as read by the commissioner, a court noble, who is present as the representative of the authorities. When this is done a favored retainer moves with noiseless step to the front and lays upon the little wooden stand the fatal knife, carefully wrapped from point to hilt in soft white paper, and as silently glides away. The condemned noble bares the body about the waist, takes the knife, and raising it reverently to his forehead, calls upon the commissioner to witness his obedience. The handle is then firmly grasped in the right hand. The point of the blade is fixed touching the skin on the left side just below the rib, the edge inwards. The left hand is then placed over the right. With one strong effort the keen blade is driven home, a mighty sweep to the right across the abdomen, and the man has disembowelled himself, falling forward dead.

The samurai, who has witnessed this awful deed, walks down the *hana-michi* with stately step and grave Buddha-like face, to bear to his master his testimony of the dead man's obedience.

EUSTACE B. ROGERS, U.S.N.

KIM OK KIUN, THE KOREAN.

LAST spring a Korean noble of high degree lay dead upon a Shanghai street, murdered by a fellow-countryman. Had his schemes been successful in 1884 it might have saved his country her present humiliation, but failing, he started the train of events which has brought on a war of which the possibilities are immeasurable. This was Kim Ok Kiun. Born in 1851, he sprang from a noble family of pure Korean descent of great antiquity, and connected with the family of the King. He was a man of ability, courage, and ambition, of unusually active mind and ready resource. He had watched with keen interest the progress of Korea's neighbor and ancient enemy, Japan, and in 1873, with one companion, So Kwang Pom, he secretly went to that country—the first Koreans of noble birth who had gone, in these later days, elsewhere than to China.

On their return to Korea the fugitives went boldly to the King and told him what they had seen. But it was too soon for any forward movement.

In 1876, China consenting, a treaty was made with Japan. On May 9, 1882, the treaty with the United States was signed, the first ever made by Korea with a Western nation. Others soon followed, and the little kingdom emerged from its long seclusion. But the struggle had barely commenced. The numerous and powerful Min family, to which the Queen belonged, dominated the government. The Tai-wen Kun, father of the King, who had been deposed some years before on account of his fanaticism and cruelty, was a man of considerable energy and ability, was still active, and the leader of the "foreigner-haters," a wing of the conservative or pro-Chinese party, whose backbone was the clan of Min. Opposed to them were a few noble families who wished to shake off the bonds of Chinese conservatism and adopt Western methods and ideas. They made up the progressionist or liberal party, and were pro-Japanese.

The opening of the country was not a national movement, and it met with the most violent opposition from the people. It succeeded because it was advocated by a few of the more powerful of the noble families, but principally because China wished it; and the Min family were, in consequence, all obedience, thereby earning the enmity of the Tai-wen Kun, who thought they had joined the party of progress, and he waited like a tiger for a chance to pounce upon them.

In July, 1882, it came. On the 23d a mob incited by his agents attacked the Mins. Min Thai Ho, a leader of his family, was left for dead in a ditch; his son, Min Yong Ik,

KIM OK KIUN,
The Korean Friend of the Japanese.

fled to the mountains, and thence to Japan, disguised as a Buddhist priest. Poison intended for the Queen was taken by a maid personating her, who died. The Japanese legation was attacked. The minister, Mr. Hanabusa, with great courage, cut his way through the mob at the head of his men, and retreated to the palace to claim the protection of the King. The gates were closed. It was night, and nothing remained but a return through the hostile city. Pursued by a howling mob, stoned and fired at from the house-tops, the brave little band marched through Seoul's crooked streets, out into the country, and on to Chemulpo, where twenty-six survivors found safety on a British war-ship. Sixteen were left dead on Korean soil. The party proceeded immediately to Japan. On August 16th Mr. Hanabusa re-entered the Korean capital at the head of a Japanese regiment. Korea apologized and paid an indemnity. While these events were taking place, Kim Ok Kiun was hurrying to Korea from the Japanese capital, whence he had been summoned. Arriving at Chemulpo, he proceeded in disguise to Seoul, finding the Tai-wen Kun, his deadliest enemy, in possession. He returned to the coast, and reported the condition of affairs to the Chinese general. On August 25th 3000 Chinese troops marched into Seoul, so suspicious was China of Japan's warlike preparations. The Tai-wen Kun was kidnapped and forcibly sent to China.

Two years passed by without further outbreak. A mission had been despatched to the United States, at the head of which was Min Yong Ik.

HONG TJYONG OU,
Murderer of Kim Ok Kiun.

Our government sent the embassy back to Korea in the United States steamship *Trenton*. They returned to Seoul in June, 1884. Kim Ok Kiun returned about the same time, after two years' study in Tokyo. The liberals were active and hopeful, but it was soon apparent that a reactionary movement had set in. Min Yong Ik, of whom great things were expected, seemed to have lost the progressive ideas he had imbibed in foreign lands, and to be returning to Chinese methods. The arrival of the Chinese troops in 1882 had resulted in a new agreement with Korea, which bound her more closely to China, and welded more tightly the chains of her vassalage. Just what this agreement was has never been divulged, but of its existence there is little doubt. It was strongly fostered by the Mins. And Korea presented the singular spectacle of a revolution moving backward. The liberal leaders were in despair. They had looked hopefully upon the American treaty, and now everything seemed to be drifting out into the boundless sea of Chinese conservatism. Kim Ok Kiun and So Kwang Pom were at the head of the party, and it was soon apparent to them that at any moment they might lose their heads. The expedient most natural to an Oriental is a conspiracy, and one was formed, with Kim at its head. The time chosen for its consummation was the occasion of a banquet on the evening of December 4, 1884, in the new post-office building. A false cry of fire caused the inmates to rush forth. Min Yong Ik was wounded and left for dead.

The conservative ministers summoned to the palace were assassinated on reaching there. A new ministry was formed with Kim at the head. Unfortunately the Japanese troops were called to the palace, ostensibly to defend the King. On the 6th they were attacked by a thousand Chinese soldiers under the command of Yuen, the Resident. The Japanese, with admirable discipline and courage, repulsed all assaults, and retreated to Chemulpo in perfect order at the close of that day. This ended the new government. Kim Ok Kiun and two of his fellow-ministers fled to Japan. The third met his death bravely, preferring to die for his principles rather than escape.

Japan was in arms at once, and war was only averted by the fact that Korea and China acceded to her demands. The former apologized and paid an indemnity. The treaty with the latter bound both countries to withdraw their armed forces from Korea, except eighty men, who could be retained for the defence of the legations, and it was agreed that neither would send troops into Korea without the consent of the other, which agreement Japan now claims China has violated.

The leaders of the *émeute* of 1884 have stated that their action was urged on them by fear that the Mins would cut off their heads, also that their plans had the approval of the King. This has been fiercely denied, but the writer was informed by Lieutenant G. C. Foulk, U.S.N., who was at the time in Seoul, lived for years in Korea, and was thoroughly well informed concerning the country, that the King was at heart a progressionist, and that he did give countenance to Kim's conspiracy in 1884.

We need not follow Kim through the years of his exile in Japan. Twice his extradition was demanded and resolutely refused. Several times his life was attempted. Japan sent him to her southern possession, the Bonin Islands. Here he introduced new methods of agriculture, sent for American plants and agricultural implements, and succeeded in producing great economic changes among the wild inhabitants. At last Japan, in a soft-hearted mood, permitted his return.

On June 18th a Korean named Li Itsu Shoku was on trial in Tokyo for instigating the assassination of Kim and attempting to murder, on Japanese soil, another Korean exile. His testimony under oath showed that he had come to Japan to murder Kim and others if he could not abduct them; that he had met Hong Tjyong Ou in Japan and induced him to murder Kim. It was shown how Kim was persuaded to go to Shanghai by false representations, and how the prisoner supplied Hong with arms and money. The rest is known. The bloody work was undoubtedly instigated by the Mins. Kim's body was sent to Korea, where it was exposed in Seoul. It was then cut into eight pieces, and these fragments distributed in as many different provinces of the kingdom.

While the writer was preparing this article he received a letter from a friend who had known Kim Ok Kiun well during his exile, and he considers it of sufficient interest to be quoted almost entire. It is as follows:

"Kim was thirty-three years old in 1884, when I first saw him, a man of great dignity, genial, pleasant, and fond of story-telling. At that time he only spoke Korean; later on he learned Japanese, and spoke it fluently, but not English. He was very fond of giving entertainments.... He adopted American ideas at once, wanted to buy jewelry and be as foreign as he possibly could. While detained at the Bonin Islands he became so homesick that his health failed very rapidly, and to save his life the Japanese had to bring him to Japan. For some time he lived in Yezo, under guard; finally the Japanese removed their protection, and then, for safety, he cut his hair, wore Japanese dress, and lived under the name of Iwata, known to very few. In May, 1892, when I was in Tokyo, he came in disguise to see me. He had grown so sad, so pathetic-looking, that it made me feel melancholy.

"At the time of the rebellion in 1884 he had a wife and four children, I believe three girls and a boy, because I remember he regretted that he had not more sons. I have seen in a newspaper article that his family were beheaded after his assassination, but I am sure this is not true. I always understood that his wife, children, father, and other relations were beheaded at the time of the revolution of 1884. A Korean friend confirmed that report. Kim belonged to the same family that the King does, and there has always been great rivalry between the Kims and the Queen's family, the Mins. I believe Kim had the King's confidence and encouragement, while the Queen was against him, in his efforts to open the country. Kim was very ambitious as well for his country as for himself, but unfortunately with all his advanced ideas he tried the Chinese instead of the Western, method of making himself a hero. He was the brightest man Korea has ever produced, and if he had pushed his ideas more slowly, and had won over the Queen's party, the result would have been very different both for him and for his country...."

EUSTACE B. ROGERS, U.S.N.

SUNDAY AFTERNOON IN CHINATOWN.

LOS ANGELES is termed the Chicago of California because of its rapid growth and business progress. It has now a population of over 65,000, and, like every California town, possesses a proportion of Chinese inhabitants. A stroll through the Chinese quarter will reward the searcher for the unusual and interesting on any week-day, but on Sunday afternoons perhaps one of the strangest sights of all may greet the eye. On the corner of one of the little side streets, whose every flavor is of the flowery Celestial Empire, amidst the strange signs and gayly-colored lanterns, may be seen a group of sombrely clad Chinamen, standing about a comrade who diligently pedals a cheap melodeon. Their shrilly pitched tones rise together singing Christian hymns in their comical English, and as if to add further strangeness to the scene, sweet-voiced American girls are grouped with them, joining in the out-door service of song. Most of the worshippers, or rather, singers, amongst the Chinese appear to be of the poorer class. The wealthy men are usually merchants or proprietors of some business. They never mingle with the crowd, but clad in silken blouse and flowing trousers, pass by without glancing even at their countrymen. Prominent church members of various denominations are banded together in an effort to convert and better the condition of the Chinese in California. But it is slow work, for a Chinaman generally thinks the older a bad custom is the wickeder it is to give it up.

1894年8月18日《哈珀斯周刊》

1 金玉均——日本人的朝鲜朋友

2 洪钟宇——杀害金玉均的刺客

1 Kim Ok Kiun. The Korean friend of Japanese.

2 Hong Tjyong Ou. Murder of Kim Ok Kiun.

金玉均（1851—1894）：朝鲜资产阶级改良主义政党“开化党”领袖，1884年发动“甲申政变”，被驻朝清军镇压，流亡日本。十年后，他离开日本到上海时，被闵妃派来的刺客洪钟宇枪杀。

——编者

今年春天，一位地位显赫的朝鲜贵族在上海街头被其同胞杀害。这名朝鲜人曾于1884年谋划发动政变，倘若政变成功，他的祖国可能不至于遭受今日之耻辱；然而，他失败了，一连串的事端接踵袭来，朝鲜陷入了一场迷茫的战争（指1894年爆发的中日甲午战争——编者注）。他就是金玉均。金玉均于1851年出生于一个与王室有联系的朝鲜世袭贵族家庭。他志向远大，有着过人的胆识与才华，思维活跃，足智多谋。他一直怀着浓厚的兴趣密切关注着朝鲜的近邻及宿敌——日本的发展，并在1873年，与同伴徐光范偷访日本（史料记载，金玉均与徐光范首次赴日应该是在1881年——编者注），成为那个时代的朝鲜贵族中，最先出国（除中国外）的人。

1884年，金玉均发动“甲申政变”失败，逃离朝鲜，他的妻子和四个孩子都留在了朝鲜，我想应该是三个女儿和一个儿子，因为我记得他曾因没能再有一个儿子而颇感遗憾。我曾经看到一篇报纸报道，他的家人在他遇刺后被杀，但我知道这不是真的，因为我知道，他的妻子、孩子、父亲以及其他亲属都早在1884年政变失败时就已惨遭杀害。我的一位朝鲜朋友帮我确认，的确存在以上那篇报道。金与国王在族谱上属于同一个家族，于是，他与王后的闵氏家族之间始终存在着激烈斗争。我相信金获得了国王的信任与鼓励，但是他坚持不懈打开国门的举动却招致闵妃的强烈不满。金的雄心壮志并不只是为了国家，也是为了他自己。但遗憾的是，他虽然掌握了很多先进理念，但他依然试图借助中国的方法而非西方的方法，让自己成为一个英雄。他是朝鲜有史以来最伟大的人物，如果他能更温和地推进自己的理念，如果他能争取到后党的些许支持，不论是对这个国家，还是对他本人，都可能是一个截然不同的局面。

——《金玉均的故事》（选译），1894年8月18日《哈珀斯周刊》

296 Supplément Littéraire Illustré du "Petit Parisien"

LA GUERRE ENTRE LA CHINE ET LE JAPON

LI-HUNG-CHANG
GÉNÉRALISSIME DE L'ARMÉE CHINOISE

MUTSUHITO
EMPEREUR DU JAPON

LE GÉNÉRAL EN CHEF
DES TROUPES CORÉENNES A SÉOUL

1894 年 9 月 9 日《小巴黎人》

1 李鸿章——中国军队元帅

2 日本明治天皇

3 朝鲜军队统帅（高宗李熙——编者注）

1 Li-Hung-Chang. Généralissime de l'armée chinoise.

2 Mutsuhito. Empereur du Japon.

3 Le Général en Chef. des troupes coréennes a Séoul.

1894 年 9 月 1 日《伦敦新闻画报》

获（美国）战争部军事情报司司长许可刊发

Reproduced by permission of the Director of Military Intelligence, War Department.

朝鲜邻国简图

图上标明了电报线、海底电缆线、铁路线和运河，下划线城市为中、日、韩三国的条约港。——编者注

Outline Map of Countries adjoining Korea.

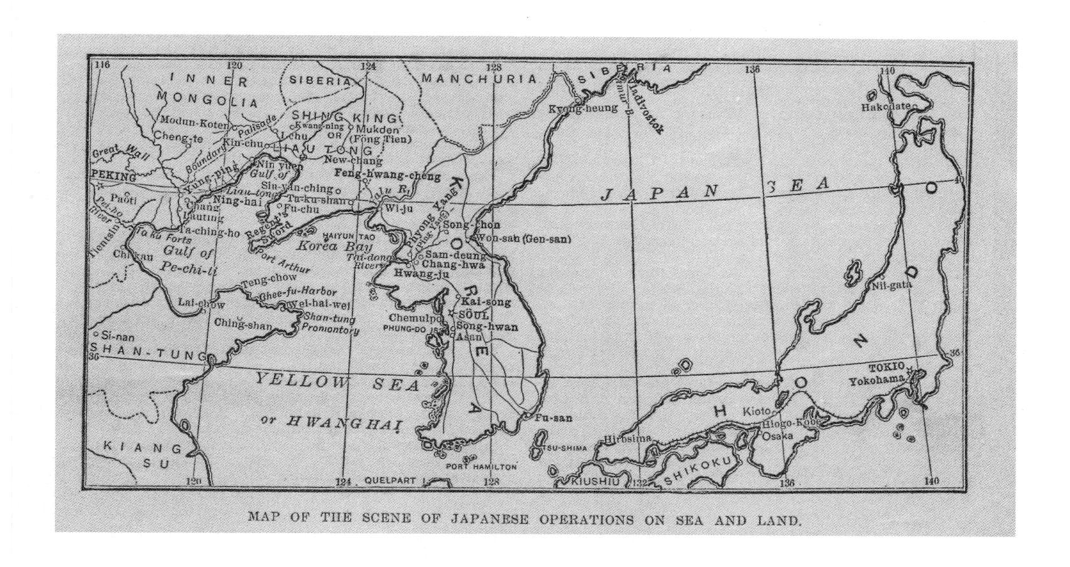

1894 年 11 月 24 日《哈珀斯周刊》

日本水、陆两方面军事行动区域图

Map of the scene of Japanese operations on sea and land.

结 语

日本虽然自称渴望和平，但它却一直谋划战争，它有野心，而中国则是它的世代仇敌。不久前，日本被国内的纷争所困扰，它希望国外的战争能带来国内的安宁。诚然，中国是保守、反改良的，它希望拖延和阻止（朝鲜的）发展，可是，如果朝鲜落入日本人的手中，鬼都不知道谁能救它！让我们为朝鲜祈祷，但愿它在走出战争的创伤之后，即便不能受到保护，在别国的帮助下，也能够崛起、独立。

——美国驻朝鲜前公使奥古斯丁·赫德（Augustine Heard）撰文
1894年9月　美国《北美评论》

中国和日本已经为朝鲜——这个双方都声称属于自己的保护国大打出手。对峙的缘由是这个国家糟糕的管理，出兵的借口是保护各自的侨民，而真相却是日本再也按捺不住的、欲与中国试比高的迫切心情。如果只是这两个国家兵戎相见，我们不难预料战争的结果：中国首先会被社会组织更先进、武器装备更精良的日本打得遍体鳞伤，可在这之后，它会倚仗自己数以百万计的兵源拖垮日本。然而事情远没那么简单：我们不知道其他国家会在哪个阶段卷入这场战争。俄国的战舰每年都会被符拉迪沃斯托克的冰雪封在港口里长达数月，它一直觊觎朝鲜的不冻港；英国则扬言只要俄国先下手，巨文岛就是它的；而美国也一直宣称它在朝鲜有商业利益需要保护……

天晓得这场战争将带给我们什么，总之，那边有乌云，一大片乌云。

——1894年8月13日　法国《小日报》

二　西方势力在东亚

在过去这些年中，俄国每向太平洋地区派遣一艘战舰，英国的传统做法是立刻派出两艘同等当量的舰船跟至同一水域。同时有报道称，法国方面也采取了海军行动，而且对俄国的处境表示极大同情。

如今，正如世人有目共睹，俄国又把贪婪的目光瞄准了朝鲜的元山港，也有人称其为拉扎雷夫港。这一港口得天独厚、易守难攻，距离西伯利亚也不远。更重要的是，这里四季温度适宜，长年不结冰。可忽然之间，形势出现了一百八十度急转弯。一个朝气蓬勃、充满新兴力量的强国瞬间出手，以迅雷不及掩耳之势推翻了中国在朝鲜的世代统治。并由此在朝鲜取得了有如英国在埃及的统治地位。当然，它会把朝鲜主权独立的旗帜高高举起，但是，根据历史上的经验而判断，这种临时性占领很可能会逐渐演变成一种长期的盘踞。当这一残酷的现实摆在面前之后，俄国忽然感到前所未有地陷入一步死棋，并因此而陷入愤怒和绝望。

如果这一明显的局势能够长期存在下去的话，英国的外交官应该能一直幸灾乐祸地偷着乐下去，因为英国在朝鲜根本没有多少商业利益可言。因此，英国更加希望能看到一个新兴的、开化的日本驱走俄国，把自己的领域范围扩大到朝鲜半岛上去，从此断绝俄国人在这片土地上谋利的念头。

——亚瑟·李（Arthur H. Lee）撰文《俄国在远东的利益》
1894 年 10 月 20 日　美国《哈珀斯周刊》

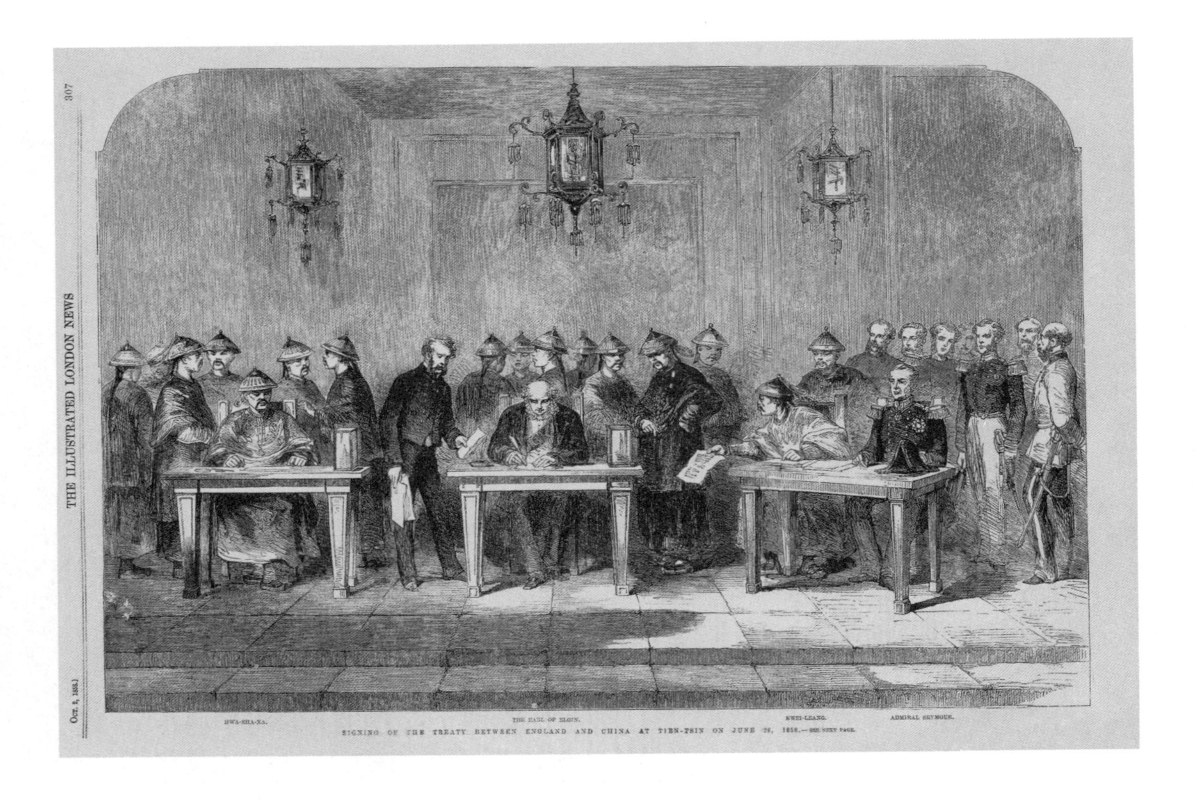

1858 年 10 月 2 日《伦敦新闻画报》

1858 年 6 月 26 日，中英《天津条约》签署现场

Signing of the Treaty between England and China at Tien-Tsin on June 26, 1858.

前排人物有：

花沙纳（Hwa-Sha-Na）、额尔金伯爵（The Earl of Elgin）、桂良（Kwei-Leang）、西摩尔元帅（Admiral Seymour）

1857 年，英国联合法国，派出远征军到中国，攻占了广州。1858 年 4 月，又北犯大沽。英、法、美、俄四国专使向清政府递交了照会，限令于 6 日内答复他们的侵略要求。在英方代表的一再威逼下，桂良等人终于屈服，被迫接受英国的条件。6 月 26 日，桂良、花沙纳与英国代表额尔金正式签订了中英《天津条约》。

1884 年 8 月 30 日《图片报》

中法战争——在天津签订条约

The war between France and China—Signing the Tientsin Treaty.

1862 年，法国开始大举入侵当时的清朝藩属国越南。到 1884 年，李鸿章在天津与法国代表福禄诺签订《中法会议简明条约》，承认法国完全占领越南，并同意撤回余部驻越清军。但签约不足十天，法军再次发起进攻，清军被迫还击，中法战争全面爆发。此图描绘的就是当时的签约场景。（本图取自中国《点石斋画报》）

LE VILLAGE DE DONG-DANG ET LA FRONTIÈRE DE CHINE

LA COMMISSION DE DÉLIMITATION. — POUR LES NOMS, VOIR CI-DESSUS L'ARTICLE

1886 年 9 月 11 日《插图报》

1 中国边境上的东塘村

2 勘界委员会官员合影

第一排左起：直隶候补道李兴锐，广东督粮道王之春，法国总理勘定边界事务大臣、前外务部侍郎、法国代表团团长浦理燮，广西巡抚李秉衡，广西勘界事务大臣、总理衙门大臣、鸿胪寺卿邓承修

第二排左起：法国代表团书记员德兰达，法国战争部代表、参将官狄塞尔，中国代表团翻译李周天，中国代表团顾问赫德（中国海关总税务司罗伯特·赫德兄长），副领事、汉学家海特斯，法国海洋部代表、海军陆战队上尉卜义内，泰国、老挝和印度支那区域探险家倪思医生

1 Le village de Dong-Dang et la frontière de Chine.

2 La Commission de Délimitation.

1885 年，中法战争之后，中国与法国签订《中法新约》，承认法国对越南的保护权，中法两国派人到中越边界共同勘界，从此越南正式脱离了与清朝的宗属国关系。

1894 年 8 月 4 日《伦敦新闻画报》

中日战争：一个朝鲜客栈

The war between China and Japan: a Corean rest-house.

图中版画再现中日两国在朝鲜的表现，英国人似乎在倾听三国声音，各国都想插手朝鲜事务，事实上在十天前该文章发表时，战争就已爆发，8 月 1 日中日两国正式宣战。

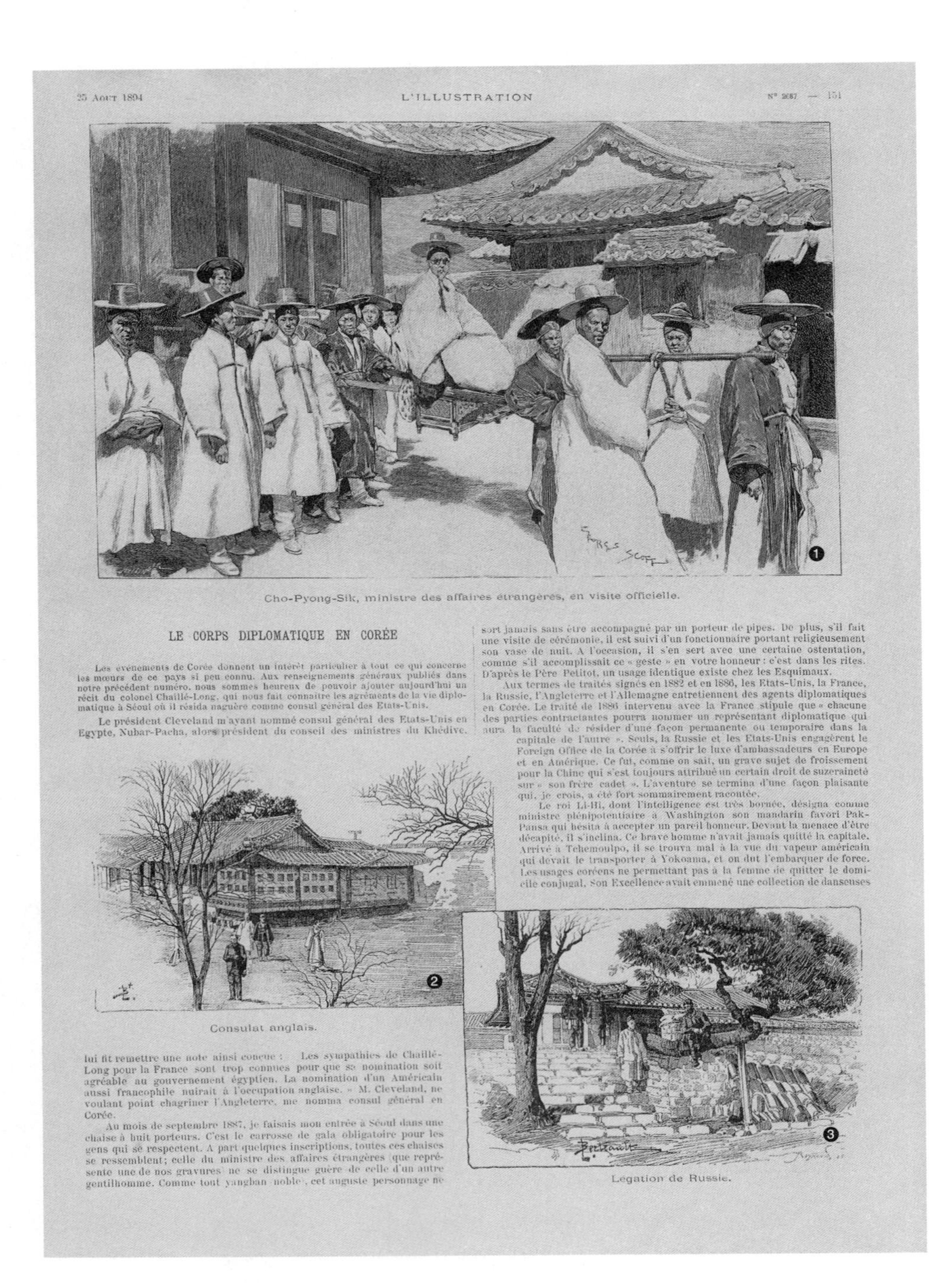

25 Aout 1894 L'ILLUSTRATION N° 2687 — 151

Cho-Pyong-Sik, ministre des affaires étrangères, en visite officielle.

LE CORPS DIPLOMATIQUE EN CORÉE

Les événements de Corée donnent un intérêt particulier à tout ce qui concerne les mœurs de ce pays si peu connu. Aux renseignements généraux publiés dans notre précédent numéro, nous sommes heureux de pouvoir ajouter aujourd'hui un récit du colonel Chaillé-Long, qui nous fait connaître les agréments de la vie diplomatique à Séoul où il résida naguère comme consul général des Etats-Unis.

Le président Cleveland m'ayant nommé consul général des Etats-Unis en Egypte, Nubar-Pacha, alors président du conseil des ministres du Khédive, lui fit remettre une note ainsi conçue : « Les sympathies de Chaillé-Long pour la France sont trop connues pour que sa nomination soit agréable au gouvernement égyptien. La nomination d'un Américain aussi francophile nuirait à l'occupation anglaise. » M. Cleveland, ne voulant point chagriner l'Angleterre, me nomma consul général en Corée.

Au mois de septembre 1887, je faisais mon entrée à Séoul dans une chaise à huit porteurs. C'est le carrosse de gala obligatoire pour les gens qui se respectent. A part quelques inscriptions, toutes ces chaises se ressemblent; celle du ministre des affaires étrangères (que représente une de nos gravures) ne se distingue guère de celle d'un autre gentilhomme. Comme tout yangban (noble), cet auguste personnage ne sort jamais sans être accompagné par un porteur de pipes. De plus, s'il fait une visite de cérémonie, il est suivi d'un fonctionnaire portant religieusement son vase de nuit. A l'occasion, il s'en sert avec une certaine ostentation, comme s'il accomplissait ce « geste » en votre honneur : c'est dans les rites. D'après le Père Petitot, un usage identique existe chez les Esquimaux.

Aux termes de traités signés en 1882 et en 1886, les Etats-Unis, la France, la Russie, l'Angleterre et l'Allemagne entretiennent des agents diplomatiques en Corée. Le traité de 1886 intervenu avec la France stipule que « chacune des parties contractantes pourra nommer un représentant diplomatique qui aura la faculté de résider d'une façon permanente ou temporaire dans la capitale de l'autre ». Seuls, la Russie et les Etats-Unis engagèrent le Foreign Office de la Corée à s'offrir le luxe d'ambassadeurs en Europe et en Amérique. Ce fut, comme on sait, un grave sujet de froissement pour la Chine qui s'est toujours attribué un certain droit de suzeraineté sur « son frère cadet ». L'aventure se termina d'une façon plaisante qui, je crois, a été fort sommairement racontée.

Le roi Li-Hi, dont l'intelligence est très bornée, désigna comme ministre plénipotentiaire à Washington son mandarin favori Pak-Pansa qui hésita à accepter un pareil honneur. Devant la menace d'être décapité, il s'inclina. Ce brave homme n'avait jamais quitté la capitale. Arrivé à Tchemoulpo, il se trouva mal à la vue du vapeur américain qui devait le transporter à Yokoama, et on dut l'embarquer de force. Les usages coréens ne permettant pas à la femme de quitter le domicile conjugal, Son Excellence avait emmené une collection de danseuses

Consulat anglais.

Légation de Russie.

1894 年 8 月 25 日《插图报》

1 朝鲜外交部长、交涉通商事务督办大臣赵秉式在外事活动中

2 英国领事馆

3 俄国公使馆

1 Cho-Pyong-Sik, ministre des affaires étrangères, en visite officielle.

2 Consulat anglais.

3 Légation de Russie.

qu'il eut l'audace d'imposer à la haute société américaine comme ses épouses légitimes. Puis, un beau jour, il décampa à l'improviste pour revenir à Séoul. Le résident chinois lui fit refuser l'entrée de la ville, et il fut contraint d'abriter sa disgrâce dans une cabane... en dehors des fortifications. Un autre mandarin, M. Cho, désigné pour représenter la Corée en Europe, alla jusqu'à Hong-Kong, et le gouvernement chinois eut assez d'influence pour l'obliger à rebrousser chemin.

En général, les membres du corps diplomatique entretiennent des relations assez cordiales et multiplient les dîners officiels pour tromper la monotonie de l'hiver. Ils admettent dans leur cercle les missionnaires protestants, tous pères d'une nombreuse famille, qui vivent sur un très grand pied.

Les palais des légations sont, avec ceux des mandarins, les seules habitations coréennes offrant quelque confortable. La légation de Russie, le consulat anglais, le consulat allemand, sont bâtis à l'européenne; la légation des Etats-Unis est une maison coréenne plus ou moins bien adaptée aux exigences de la civilisation américaine; la résidence des commissaires du Céleste Empire est du plus pur chinois. Quant au commissariat de France, il était, et il est encore installé dans une masure indigène.

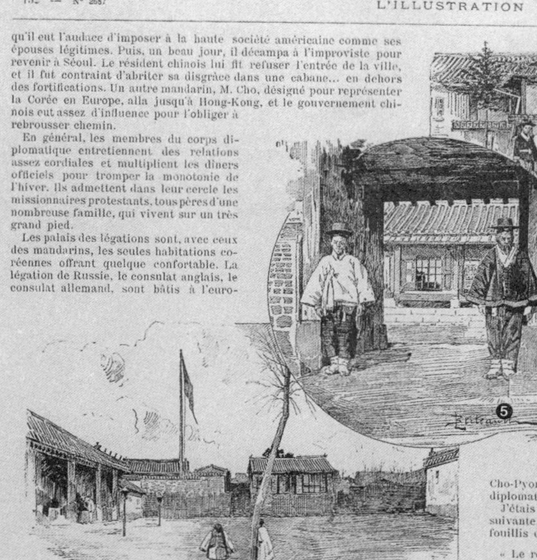

Consulat allemand.

1. Résidence des commissaires chinois. — 2. Légation des États-Unis.

Le chargé d'affaires de Russie, M. Waeber, a été pendant quelque temps le seul diplomate marié, et la grâce de Mme Waeber ajoutait un grand charme à ses réceptions. Le résident chinois, Yuan-Sie-K'ai, le chargé d'affaires du Japon, M. Kondo-Masuki et Mme Kondo, le commissaire de France, M. Collin de Plancy, assisté de M. Guérin, donnaient aussi des dîners fort appréciés, nous reposant des menus peu variés des chefs japonais qui n'arriveront jamais, même avec les recettes du *Pot-au-Feu*, à comprendre les beautés de la cuisine européenne.

Le ministre des affaires étrangères de Corée, Cho-Pyong-Sik, convie aussi de temps à autre les membres du corps diplomatique à sa table.

J'étais depuis quelque temps en Corée lorsque je reçus l'invitation suivante, dont le texte était encadré par une femme émergeant d'un fouillis de chrysanthèmes :

« Le rouge pâlit, le vert devient plus foncé, la séduisante couleur « du printemps est venue. C'est la saison de joie. Voulez-vous me faire « le plaisir de vous joindre à moi et à mes amis pour jouir de la fête « que je donne cet après-midi?

« Cho-Pyong-Sik ».

Mon interprète, me montrant quelques fleurs, me fit remarquer l'évolution de leurs couleurs, indice du changement de saison.

M. Cho-Pyong est un homme fort aimable, d'environ soixante-cinq ans. Son âge lui donnait un grand prestige : « Votre Excellence semble plus vieille

SÉOUL. — Un déjeuner diplomatique chez le ministre des Affaires étrangères.

4 德国领事馆

5 中国特使官邸

6 美国公使馆

7 汉城——外交部长在家中设午宴款待各国驻朝鲜使节

4 Consulat allemand.

5 Résidence des commissaires chinois.

6 Légation des États-Unis.

7 Séoul.—Un déjeuner diplomatique chez le ministre des affaires étrangères.

25 Aout 1894 L'ILLUSTRATION N° 2687 — 153

Fête donnée par le ministre des Affaires étrangères : le danseur de corde.

8 外交部长家的堂会——绳索舞

Fête donnée par le ministre des affaires étrangères: le danseur de corde.

这组报道是朝鲜交涉通商事务督办大臣赵秉式宴请在朝鲜的外交使团的情景。

报道中采用的宴会厅照片是由美国驻朝鲜总领事沙叶龙中校拍摄的。他这样描述了当时的场景：每位外国使节坐于一名舞姬和翻译之间。我们通过翻译来对话，我们平时只会说几句市井俚语，在如此高规格的宴会上显然无法使用；可和我们邻座的朝鲜人甚至会当着我们的面吐痰。赵秉式先生高效地关注着宴会服务的品质，向周围的宾客轮番致意，并暧昧地抚摸他的女邻桌。我随身携带了照相机，在宴席结束时把它对准宴会厅。赵秉式先生发现我的举动时，请我考虑到他的体面，容许他撤出了舞姬。这就是《插图报》转载的第 7 幅图片上没有女人的原因。

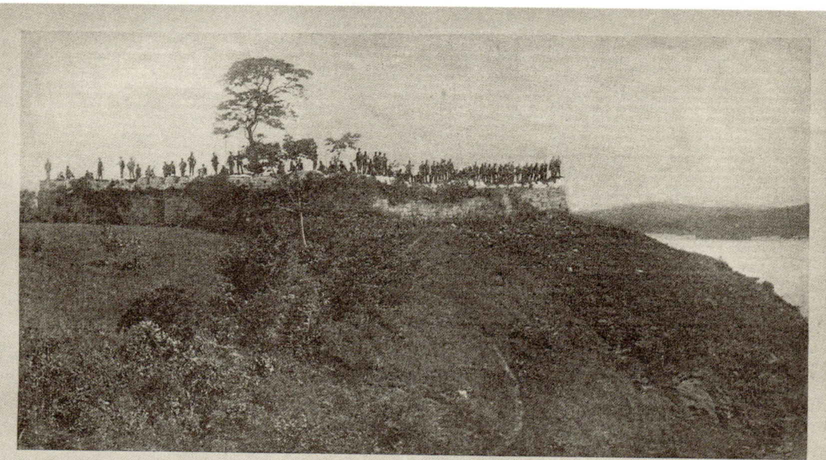

FORT MONOCACY CAPTURED BY THE UNITED STATES FORCES ON THE MORNING OF JUNE 11, 1871.

OUR NAVY IN KOREA.

BY CAPTAIN W. S. SCHLEY, U. S. N.

THE purpose of this paper is to recall an event in the history of our navy through which the last one of the exclusive empires of the East was brought into the fellowship of our Western civilization.

Some twenty-eight years ago an American schooner, named the *General Sherman*, visited the coast of Korea, that peninsula projecting in a southerly direction from Manchooria, and lying between the Yellow Sea and the Sea of Japan. This vessel was loaded with a cargo of Yankee notions, and the purpose of her captain was a peaceful exchange of these commodities with the Koreans. At the time of her visit this empire was not in touch with the outer world, but in some form or other maintained communication with the Chinese, whose language they understood, and according to the best available information at that period, Korea was reputed to be a tributary empire of China. Whatever their relations, whether distant or close, tributary or independent, amicable or unfriendly, the first authentic information which reached our government came through the Chinese authorities, and was, in substance, that the crew of the *General Sherman* had been assaulted and murdered, and that the vessel had been burned by the natives on the west coast of Korea. Neither the time nor the circumstances of this outrage, nor the precise locality where committed, were communicated, if they were known.

An examination of the map shows the peninsula of Korea projecting southerly between the empires of China and Japan, and lying directly in the route of commerce between two empires whose ports were open to the trade of the world. In the usual course of commercial interchange, with the frequent bad weather of those seas, it was to be expected that wrecks would occur to vessels caught near the Korean littoral. Every principle of justice required that trading should be regulated by treaty, and that those who were unfortunate in falling upon these coasts through stress of wind and weather should be regarded and cared for humanely, and the helpless returned to the protection of their government whenever opportunity should occur. Circumstances had so shaped matters that the time had come in the affairs of Korea, lying, as she did, directly athwart the route of the world's trade, when she must in time and in turn wheel into line as a protector of those whom misfortune had cast upon her shores, and give up forever her older practice of slaughtering them.

Towards the fall of the year 1869 Rear-Admiral John Rodgers, an officer of brilliant reputation throughout the country, was ordered to command the United States Asiatic Squadron. His prompt action in the operations of his squadron afterwards, which this paper aims to recall and recite, sustains the wisdom of his selection for the duties of this important command.

The earliest available diplomatic correspondence on the subject of communicating with Korea took place between Consul-General George F. Seward at the port of Shanghai, China, and the Honorable William H. Seward, then Secretary of State, and dated October, 1868. In this communication the Consul-General set forth the advantages that would probably occur to the trade relations of the United States if a general commercial treaty could be made with the Korean government. While there was some question in his mind whether the results of this intercourse might not introduce ideas and work changes that might tend to overthrow the then existing order of things in Korea, he yet thought that the balance of advantages would be such as to justify the attempt. His long experience at a most important post of duty, and his complete familiarity with Eastern politics, enabled him to set forth in a most excellent state paper the importance of this expedition to Korea.

The Consul-General was under the impression that the first object of the mission to that country ought to be to inquire into the loss or destruction of the schooner *General Sherman*, and if it was found true that the crew had been wrongfully treated, as reported, then indemnity should be required. The reasons for this suggestion become apparent when he states that "It cannot be well to let pass uninvestigated a matter which there is every reason to believe may have been a very grave outrage on a vessel and persons sailing under our flag," and his fuller meaning will be comprehended better when it is borne in mind that at that period there was a strong anti-foreign feeling throughout the East. If the foreign powers permitted the wrongs of their subjects to go unredressed, an obvious and unfavorable change immediately took place in the demeanor even of the working coolies towards foreigners. Their anti-foreign swagger and insolent parade in the foreigners' presence indicated what the feeling was among the upper classes.

It was therefore of the first importance to our interest and standing in the East at that time to investigate this *Sherman* outrage on the coast of Korea, and the writer is satisfied that the result which Admiral Rodgers accomplished in 1871 in storming and capturing the forts on the island of Kang Hoa largely increased the prestige and safety of foreigners in all treaty ports of the Eastern empires. It surely put an end to that savage unrest which culminated in the massacre of helpless, innocent, foreign missionary women at Tien-Tsin in 1870. In effect, it was a reminder to all the Eastern nations that treaty stipulations would be insisted upon, while it gave assurance to those domiciled in the East that they and their interests would be guarded by their governments so long as they conformed strictly to the stipulations of existing treaties.

It was intended to charge Rear-Admiral Rowan with this duty, but the difficulties of far-off situations, considered with the tedious delays of diplomatic communications in affairs that have to be worked over and over again in the absence of overt acts to excite attention, or to arouse sufficient enthusiasm at home to justify resort to corrective aggressive action, resulted in the expiration of service of this officer on that coast, and his relief was ordered. The choice of his successor in Rear-Admiral John Rodgers could not have been happier. No officer of the navy stood higher in public esteem. None more amply deserved the honors won, and surely no one had more modestly or more worthily worn them. Completely equipped in his profession, sound in judgment, rare in tact, modest in manner, gentle and just by nature, but most determined and fearless in standing for and defending his country's rights.

The squadron assigned to the Asiatic station under his command was composed of the following vessels, namely: United States steam-frigate *Colorado* (flag-ship), 52 guns; corvette *Alaska*, 16 guns; corvette *Benicia*, 16 guns; gunboat *Monocacy*, 10 guns; gunboat *Ashelot*, 10-guns; gunboat *Palos*, 4 guns; gunboat *Millet*, 1 gun; store-ship *Idaho*, 4 guns.

Toward the middle of the year 1870 this fleet had arrived in the waters of the Asiatic station. Indefinite rumors spread throughout the ships that their destination in the near future was to be the coast of Korea. Very naturally the conclusion was at once formed in the mind of every one, by those curious processes of reasoning which are so often used to fix a desired result first, and then afterwards to adjust the progressive steps which lead up to it, that Korea was to be the objective point of this fleet, and that its mission would be, first, to inquire into the outrage upon the *Sherman* and her crew; this concluded, to make a commercial treaty with the government of Korea. Just how these things were to be brought about without a collision was not clear in the mind of every one, but it was not essential to consider this part of the programme except as a matter of speculation at this time.

The rumors of the squadron's destination in time reached the shore at most of the treaty ports in China and Japan, where the matter was much discussed at the clubs and in the homes of foreigners. In all these discussions it was a little curious to listen to the various opinions about Korea. Not a soul had the faintest idea of the country, its productions, or its people; no white man had ever visited it, except clandestinely, yet scores of people knew the whole situation. The country was said to abound in wealth, the scenery to be grandly picturesque; the roads were said to be almost impassable, the inhabitants to be giants in stature, their strength reputed to be herculean, their ferocity that of the tiger, their arms the latest possible inventions, and their marksmanship was said to rival that of William Tell; their resources were without limit, and their courage—well, that was only equalled by the historic defence at Thermopylæ. Such were the stories that met one on all sides.

The United States force at this station was admirably appointed, equipped, and commanded. Most of its officers and many of its men had served in the great rebellion, only ended some five years previously. They were living in the very presence of a number of heroes who had come up under the circumstances of its service. Its commander-in-chief was a distinguished figure, and one of the foremost of this number. They believed in themselves, and they knew if the Koreans could fight, that they themselves were not novices in arms. Above all, they loved their flag, and with the chance to defend it abroad as they had done at home, there came no thought to any one of them that they would fall short of the inspiring examples of such men as Barney in the *Hyder Ally*, of Decatur at Tripoli, of Downs at Qualla Battoo, of Hunter at Alvarado, of Perry at Tabasco, of Cushing in Albemarle Sound, of Mackenzie in Formosa, and a score of others whose deeds of valor in defence of home, of flag, and of country have enriched the naval literature of our republic. It was not difficult to forecast the result if, perchance, diplomacy should fail and a resort to force become necessary. In obedience to the commander-in-chief's orders this fleet assembled in the port of Nagasaki, Japan, during the early part of the month of May, 1871.

The arrival of the flag-ship *Colorado* at the port disclosed the fact that the Admiral was accompanied by Hon. Frederick F. Low, Minister Plenipotentiary and Envoy Extraordinary to China, his secretaries of legation, Mr. Drew and Mr. Cowles, and two Chinese, who subsequently served as interpreters. All these officials observed the utmost secrecy as to the purposes and future movements of the fleet. To the more thoughtful the indications definitely set at rest the rumors of the year preceding. Korea was, after all, the objective point. This belief was strengthened by the fact that a retrospective glance over the squadron general orders showed a preference for battalion and artillery drills. Whenever two or more ships came together signals were frequent to land both infantry and artillery with the greatest expedition. The prevalent unrest of the Chinese at that time, together with the frequent outbreaks and riots at the treaty ports, was held sufficient to account for these preparations. While they were sufficient to justify this activity, they served at least to mask the real purpose of the Admiral. No squadron was ever better prepared to vindicate the honor of our country, or to protect its citizens and its commerce in the far off East.

Near the middle of May the squadron sailed from Nagasaki, Japan. Clearing this port and gaining a good offing, a course was followed to the westward and northward. The second day out the coast of Korea was in sight. All uncertainty about the squadron's destination now vanished. The only point still obscure was the precise locality to which it was bound. This was only decided when near the entrance of the Salee River, where the squadron came to anchor.

As the coast was wholly unsurveyed, except in the most general way some years before by the French squadron under Admiral Rose, and as the charts provided the ships merely gave the supposed outlines of the coast, uncertain location of its bays, and doubtful positions of its estuaries, with no soundings at all, it became necessary to anchor the squadron each day in positions determined to be safe by running surveys made the day before. This task was committed to the navigating officers of the several vessels, and the little steam-launches of the squadron were placed at their service, so that work might begin soon after sunrise and continue until sunset each day. In this way several days were taken up in reaching the final anchorage of the squadron off Isle Boisee, at the entrance to the Salee River, this locality being selected by the Admiral on account of its proximity to Seoul, the capital, and as a point most favorable to open diplomatic correspondence with the authorities of the empire.

The presence of such a formidable force in their waters and at the very gates of their empire, carrying a flag unknown to the masses, created consternation and alarm. Beacon fires were lighted upon every prominent hill-top in sight of the anchorage, with the purpose, doubtless, of signalling the squadron's arrival throughout the empire. The next day, from a town on the mainland west of the anchorage

779

❶

1894 年 8 月 18 日《哈珀斯周刊》

1　1871 年 6 月 11 日晨，被美国军队攻占的朝鲜德津堡（莫诺卡西堡）

Fort Monocacy captured by the United States Forces on the morning of June 11, 1871.

LOWER FORT IN POSSESSION OF BLUEJACKETS AND MARINES.

2　在美国水兵和海军陆战队员控制下的朝军碉堡

Lower fort in possession of bluejackets and marines.

HARPER'S WEEKLY

the peninsula to the river, north of this promontory, and isolating it from the line of rifle-pits and other defences along the hill-tops beyond the ravine. These defences were intended to hold an enemy in check until the defending forces around this promontory could have time to retreat safely into the citadel from the outlying defences.

In one angle of this quadrangular-shaped citadel a large tent was erected, and from a tall bamboo pole a few feet in front of it floated a large yellow flag containing some characters, which, our interpreters afterwards stated, were intended to indicate the headquarters of the commanding officer. In another angle of this fortification a number of thatched bamboo sheds were constructed, no doubt as quarters for the soldiers. On the walls of the forts and along the slopes of the hills near these fortifications large groups of men were collected, but it was not imagined their purpose was hostile; it was thought to be merely curiosity.

On a bold bluff, to the right going up the river, and on the mainland of Korea, another small fort was so placed as to converge its fire upon a point of the river, making a cross-fire with the batteries opposite on the peninsula, which was, in fact, the island of Kang Hoa.

When the surveying vessels had reached this vicinity the groups of men already observed suddenly disappeared, and a signal gun was fired from the citadel. Only a moment elapsed, when a furious fire was opened upon the surveying vessels from the forts situated on both the mainland and the island of Kang Hoa. A perfect storm of missiles struck about the ships and launches, but fortunately did no harm, as the guns had been ranged upon points in the channel during low water, while the increasing tide allowed the vessels to pass over a different route from that contemplated by the artillerists in laying their guns. The surveying vessels instantly opened their batteries upon the forts, and the engagement became general until they passed completely above them, silencing their guns in passing. An incident of much interest in this attack upon the ships was the heroic behavior of Master Seaton Schroeder, in command of the steam-launch of the corvette *Benicia*. Earlier in the day, at a point below the forts, while sounding out the channel, the lead line in some manner fouled the launch's propeller; some time was taken to clear it, and this delayed the little steamer until all the other vessels had gone by the forts. It was an ugly position for a little steam-launch with only one small howitzer mounted in her bow, but Schroeder's orders were to go up with the other vessels, and this was sufficient; without hesitation he pointed her up the river, and passed the forts under a perfect cyclone of projectiles. It was an instance of heroic determination to obey his orders, and in so doing he doubtless counted upon the boldness of his manœuvre to disarrange the enemy's fire. This did happen, for his party escaped without material damage. In any other service in the world his reward would have been promotion at least one grade.

The passing of these forts was not without severe damage to the *Monocacy*, as she ran upon a submerged rock in sweeping a turn around the promontory, and seriously injured her bottom plating. When she returned to the anchorage of the squadron below, she was obliged to run on to the mud flats abreast the fleet to repair a serious rent in her bottom plates. She was sent to Shanghai, China, after the operations closed, and at this writing is still an efficient cruiser on the Asiatic station.

After the vessels had succeeded in passing the forts, they turned about to repass them. This time, however, they were the aggressors, and did not wait for the enemy's fire, but began a tremendous bombardment of each fort as it came within range. The reverberation of the heavy guns was heard on board the vessels below, and from positions aloft the smoke of battle could be seen rising up over the hills about the fortifications. Occasionally a shell that had struck the ramparts was seen to burst in the air above them, but the fire of the enemy during this attack was feeble, and was mainly from the guns that had not been fired at the vessels on their way up.

The forts were only repassed when they had ceased to show any further resistance. The cannonade by our vessels was furious and destructive, and it awakened some of the rec-

THE KOREANS ON BOARD SHIP

INSIDE FORT DU COUDE AFTER THE HAND-TO-HAND FIGHTING.

781

3　朝鲜人在船（美国科罗拉多号旗舰）上

4　江华岛上广城堡内白刃战后的景象

3　The Koreans on board ship.

4　Inside Fort du Coude after the hand-to-hand fighting.

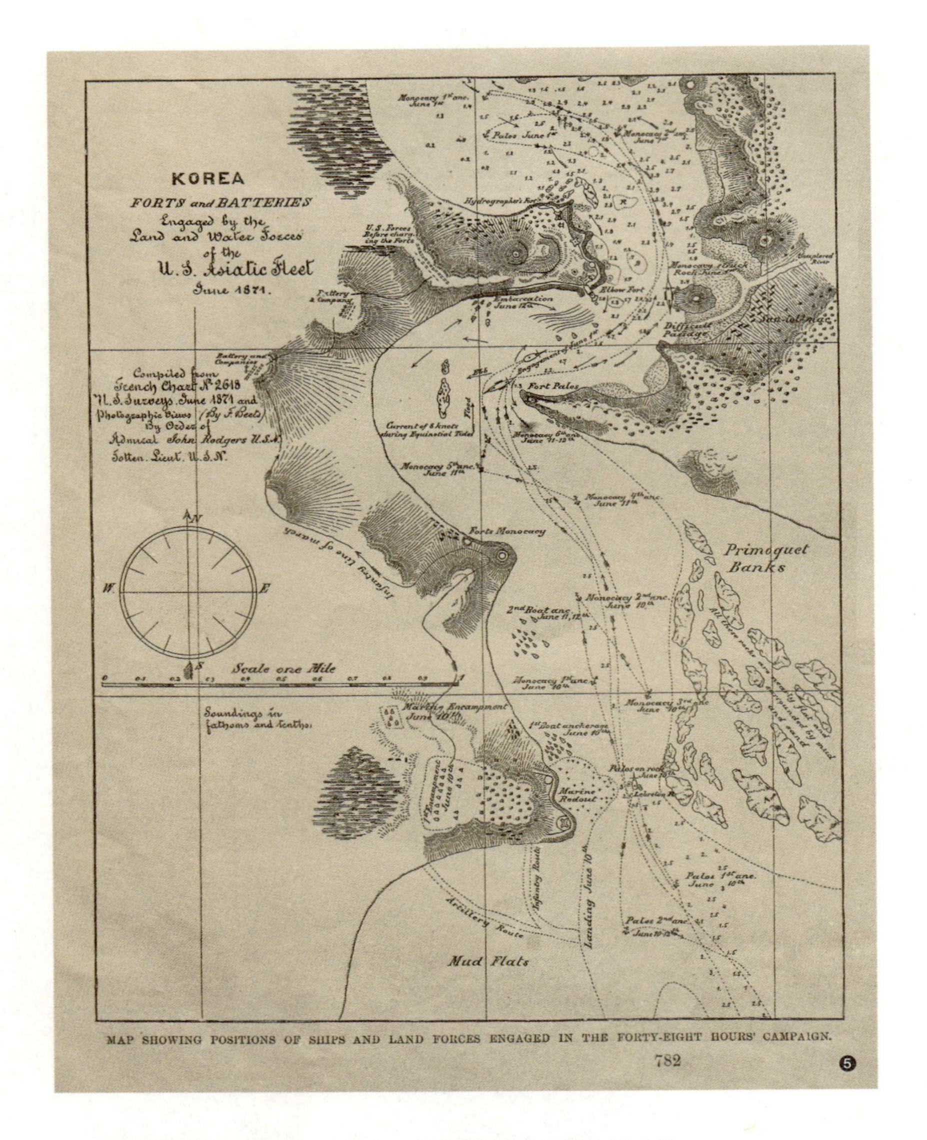

5 一张美军绘制的48小时战役图，图上标明了参战陆军及海军的位置

Map showing positions of ships and land forces engaged in the forty-eight hours' campaign.

以上这组报道来自1894年8月18日的《哈珀斯周刊》，标题是《我们的海军在朝鲜》，文章回顾了历史上美国海军两次进入朝鲜的经过。一次是1866年8月的“舍门将军号事件”，一次是1871年的“辛未洋扰事件”。20多年后，当朝鲜再次成为西方关注的焦点时，这两次战争也重新回到了人们的视野中。

版画：1853 年 6 月 6 日美国佩里将军到达琉球国首里城（今冲绳那霸）时的场景

Com. Perry's visit to Shui, Lew Chew.

马休·卡尔布莱斯·佩里（Matthew Calbraith Perry，1794—1858），美国海军将领，因率领黑船打开锁国时期的日本国门而闻名于世。

1852 年 11 月，美国派遣佩里舰队远征日本，于 1853 年 5 月中途停靠琉球那霸港，意图打开琉球国门。佩里舰队在此后一年多的时间里，先后五次访问琉球，要求琉球开国。琉球当局多次向日本、中国清朝求助，日本当时表示琉球是个遥远的国家，日方无权决定其港口开放权，清朝处于鸦片战争新败，虽积极交涉但力不从心，皆无法对琉球实施有效保护。1854 年 3 月，《日美和亲条约》签订，日本开国。1854 年 7 月，佩里与琉球政府用中英两种文字签订《琉美修好条约》，开放其港口。

在日本神奈川县横须贺市的久里滨，有一座佩里公园，这是当年佩里率领黑船登陆的地点。为了感谢这位促使日本开放的美国将军，日本人竖立了一座佩里登陆纪念碑，上有前日本首相伊藤博文的亲笔手书：“北米合众国水师提督伯理上陆纪念碑”。

THE GERMAN CLUB, YOKOHAMA.

THE BUND, KOBÉ.

YOKOHAMA.

THE UNITED CLUB AND CLUB HOTEL, YOKOHAMA.

THE "HUNDRED STEPS," YOKOHAMA.

NAGASAKI BAY, JAPAN.
Pappenberg Island in the Distance.

NAGASAKI HARBOR ON A FOURTH OF JULY.
American and Japanese Fleets saluting.

LIFE IN THE FOREIGN SETTLEMENTS OF JAPAN.—[SEE PAGE 1234.]

1894 年 12 月 29 日《哈珀斯周刊》

西方侨民在日本租界中的生活

1　横滨的德国俱乐部
2　神户的外滩
3　横滨
4　横滨的联合俱乐部和会所
5　横滨元町百段（西方侨民居住区）
6　日本长崎湾，远景为高鋅岛
7　停靠在长崎港的美国和日本舰队在美国国庆日放礼炮

Life in the foreign settlements of Japan.

1　The German club, Yokohama.
2　The Bund, Kobé.
3　Yokohama.
4　The united club and club hotel, Yokohama.
5　The "Hundred Steps"，Yokohama.
6　Nagasaki Bay, Japan. Pappenberg Island in the distance.
7　Nagasaki Harbor on a Fourth of July. American and Japanese fleets saluting.

美国海军总出纳官尤斯塔斯·罗杰斯（Eustace B. Rogers）为《哈珀斯周刊》撰写了这篇报道：居住在通商口岸之外的日本人怀着无比的好奇，礼貌地称呼外国人为“异人君”或“老外先生”，他们观察着外国人那些在他们看来十分怪异的行为，并且乐此不疲。不管是外国人的年龄、生活习惯，还是各种嗜好，都可以成为他们探听与议论的主题。

他还写到一个有意思的细节：在横滨，除中国人以外，共有 1605 个外国人，这些人中有 808 人效忠于维多利亚女王陛下，他们控制着银行系统。

224 THE ILLUSTRATED LONDON NEWS 561 AUGUST 29, 1863

SKETCHES FROM SHANGHAI.

GROUP OF DISCIPLINED CHINESE SOLDIERS WITH EUROPEAN OFFICER.

1863 年 8 月 29 日《伦敦新闻画报》

西方人训练出的纪律严明的中国士兵

Group of disciplined Chinese soldiers with European officer.

这是一组训练有素的中国士兵和他们的欧洲长官的合影，他们就是太平军的克星——“常胜军”。在华尔、白齐文、戈登等历任欧洲指挥官的训练和领导下，清廷开始意识到，使用西方的练兵术和洋枪洋炮，中国士兵也能变成纪律严明、勇猛顽强的士兵。

THE WAR IN THE EAST: DEFENSIVE OPERATIONS AT SHANGHAI
A "TURN-OUT" OF THE BRITISH VOLUNTEER CORPS

1894年9月8日《图片报》

东方的战争：上海的防御行动，英国志愿军上街扬威

The war in the East: defensive operations at Shanghai. A "turn-out" of the British Volunteer Corps.

这个画面所描述的是中日甲午战争中的英国军队。英国号称保持中立，英国商船高升号被击沉后，日本为此做了大量的外交努力，英国并没有惩罚日本，反而因为清朝与俄国交往密切，他们在舆论上更支持日本。

1. LYING IN WAIT AT THE BOTTOM OF A DITCH TO HACK AT THE PONIES AS THEY JUMP OVER

3. THE RESULT OF A HOLE THOUGHTFULLY DUG BY A PLAYFUL NATIVE

DRAWN BY FRANK DADD, R.I.

4. A TRUCULENT PEASANT WITH A PAIL OF SEWAGE BARRING THE PASSAGE OF A BRIDGE

5. THE UNFORTUNATE

EUROPEAN RESIDENTS IN CHINA: PAPER-CHASING AT SHANGH

1894 年 10 月 20 日《图片报》

欧洲侨民在上海的撒纸追踪游戏遭到本地人的厌恶（撒纸游戏起源于英国，根据纸屑在地面上的记号追踪撒纸的人。——编者注）

European residents in China: paper-chasing at Shanghai is locally much resented.

1　躲在沟底打算偷袭欧洲人马匹的中国人
2　算总账
3　欧洲人被一个搞恶作剧的本地人挖的陷阱绊倒
4　一个刁民在拦桥泼粪
5　一个倒霉的新侨民的马跑进了村庄，落入了本地人的手中

1　Lying in wait at the bottom of a ditch to hack at the ponies as they jump over.
2　The summary revenge which was promptly inflicted.
3　The result of a hole thoughtfully dug by a playful native.
4　A truculent peasant with a pail of sewage barring the passage of a bridge.
5　The unfortunate plight of a novice whose pony has bolted into a village and fallen into the hands of the natives.

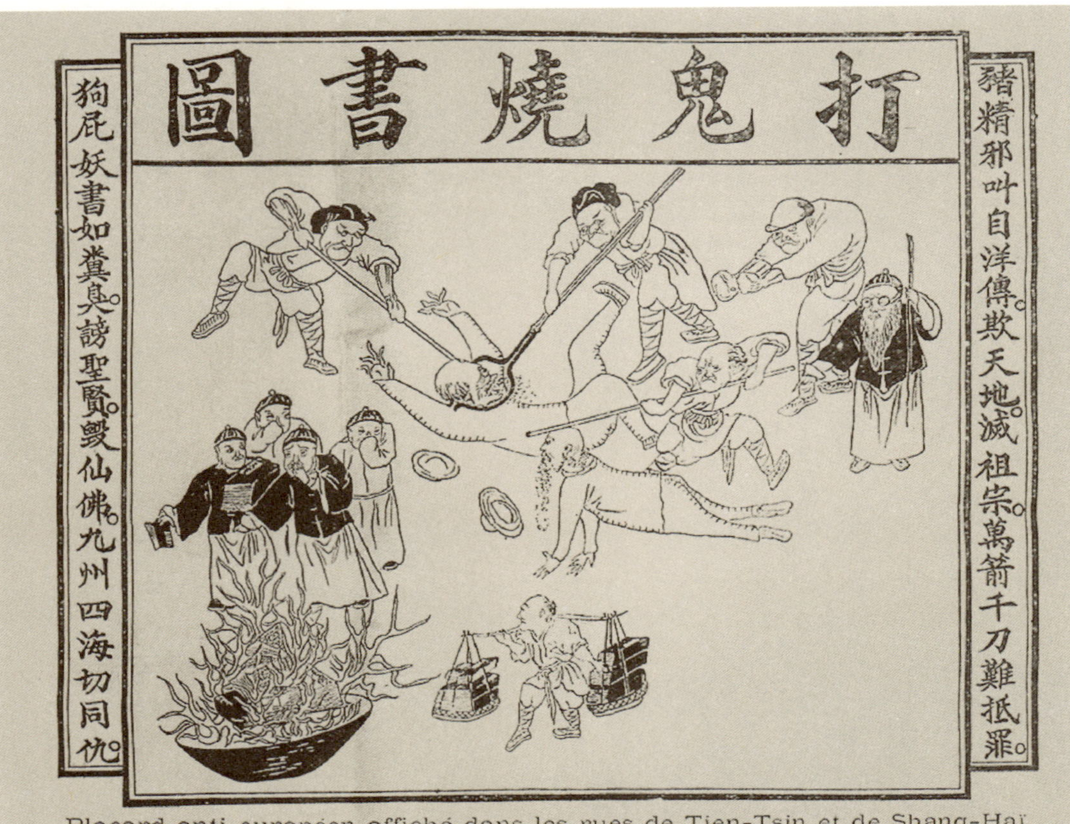

Placard anti-européen affiché dans les rues de Tien-Tsin et de Shang-Haï.

D'après une photographie communiquée par M. D. Fricot.

1891 年 12 月 5 日《插图报》

天津和上海街头的排外宣传画：打鬼烧书图

Placard anti-européen affiché dans les rues de Tien-Tsin et de Shang-Haï.

上联：猪精邪叫自洋传。欺天地。灭祖宗。万箭千刀难抵罪。

下联：狗屁妖书如粪臭。谤圣贤。毁仙佛。九州四海切同仇。

横批：打鬼烧书图。

Le Petit Journal

TOUS LES VENDREDIS
Le Supplément illustré
5 Centimes

SUPPLÉMENT ILLUSTRÉ
Huit pages : CINQ centimes

TOUS LES JOURS
Le Petit Journal
5 Centimes

Deuxième Année — SAMEDI 19 DÉCEMBRE 1891 — Numero 56

Les massacres en Chine
(SUPPLICES)

1891 年 12 月 19 日《小日报》

1　发生在中国的（对西方人的）屠杀——酷刑

Les massacres en Chine (Supplices).

8 Supplément illustré du Petit Journal

NOS GRAVURES

Les massacres en Chine

Les événements les plus graves se passent en ce moment en Chine; une révolte formidable y a éclaté qui menace non seulement les Européens et en particulier nos missionnaires, mais encore le trône de l'empereur actuel.

La chose est sérieuse comme on voit.

Il est admis, les abstracteurs de quintessence et autres philosophes à longue portée ont depuis longtemps certifié que l'Europe entière périrait par suite d'une invasion des Tartares, Mongols, Mandchous, Chinois de toute origine qui peuplent avec trop de surabondance l'empire du Milieu.

Alors que nous n'avons pas assez d'enfants, ces gens-là en ont trop, et, malgré la légende qui motive l'œuvre célèbre de rachat, les porcs n'en mangent pas assez pour empêcher que la population étouffe dans des frontières pourtant pas mal développées.

Quand les sujets du Fils du Ciel ne trouveront plus à pâturer chez eux, il faudra qu'ils cherchent ailleurs leur nourriture; l'on affirme qu'alors ils se répandront sur l'Europe comme font les sauterelles en Algérie, dévorant tout, dévastant tout.

En vain à ces vrais inventeurs de la poudre opposera-t-on les engins les plus perfectionnés ; on en tuera beaucoup, malgré quoi ils resteront encore au moins cent contre un et nous serons perdus.

En attendant cette excursion chez nous, non dirigée par les agences, ils essaient leurs crocs les uns sur les autres et se massacrent en masse.

Ils ont comme de coutume commencé par les chrétiens. Nos dessins représentent d'odieuses scènes dont ils sont les sinistres acteurs. Mais aussi ils se sont entre-déchirés de façon à diminuer notablement l'encombrement sur le sol de leur patrie.

Quel est leur mobile ?

On a peine à croire qu'il s'agisse seulement d'un mouvement politique. Les bandits monstrueux qui égorgent, saignent, brûlent et pillent ne savent probablement même point le nom de leur empereur.

C'est probablement le besoin de vivre seulement. C'est une manifestation de la bête humaine.

On a dit qu'ils voulaient se venger sur tous ceux qui ne sont pas de leur race de ce que les Américains, trop envahis par les travailleurs chinois, ne voulaient plus leur ouvrir leurs territoires.

Il est vraisemblable que cela a été imaginé par ceux qui en vue d'une action générale ne seraient point fâchés d'y intéresser les Etats-Unis dont la marine est très puissante.

Que va-t-il se passer ? L'avenir nous l'apprendra.

Il paraît difficile qu'on laisse s'accomplir, sans les réprimer, de pareils forfaits. C'est donc une nouvelle expédition lointaine qui se prépare, et l'on sait ce qu'elles coûtent.

Quoi qu'il en soit, en cette circonstance, il n'y aura peut-être point trop lieu de regretter notre argent.

Puisqu'il est convenu que nous devons être mangés un jour par les Chinois, autant retarder le moment le plus possible.

Les massacres en Chine
(INCENDIES)

2 发生在中国的（对西方人的）屠杀——火刑

Les massacres en Chine (Incendies).

这组登载在法国《小日报》上的文章和封面、封底的整版插图非常生动地为我们重现了19世纪末，西方世界在“黄祸论”的影响下，对中国的恐慌。这其中的原因众多，政治家们强调这是西方侵略者的阴谋，他们蓄意丑化中国人，造成黄种人和白种人的对立，为压迫、侵略东亚制造舆论；社会学家们会谈及奴隶制逐渐消亡后，中国苦力和华工大量涌向海外，侵占了西方人的就业机会；经济学家们往往从爆发在西方世界的、一轮接一轮的金融危机着手进行分析；而宗教界人士则倾向渲染传教团体在中国忘我的奉献以及他们所遭遇的蔑视和残暴的袭击。其实，这些观点无所谓哪个更站得住脚或哪个更重要，透过这些当年西方媒体中的图片，在这些偏激和狭隘的词句中，我们不难发现，甲午战争前同样打开国门的中国和日本对外面的世界抱着截然不同的心态，国际舆论对这两个国家的认可与同情也有着巨大的反差。与大清关系一直友善的美国在甲午战争爆发前十年通过排华法案，阻止中国移民进入；1895年，德国皇帝威廉二世甚至还亲自构思了一幅《黄祸图》……

在这篇题为《发生在中国的屠杀》的文章中，作者写道：“我们用最先进的武器对抗着这些最早发明火药的人将是徒劳的；即便我们可以杀死他们很多人，但最终，以至少100人对1人的悬殊比例，他们仍会活下去，而我们还是会输掉。不镇压他们，任由他们肆意施虐是不可能的。因此一场新远征正在筹划中，人们知道这样的远征会相当昂贵。无论如何，在这种情形下，也许没多少余地能让我们为花钱而惋惜了。既然我们某一天注定会被这些中国人吃掉，那就尽力把这一刻的到来拖得越远越好吧。”

TRAVELLING IN NORTH CHINA: AN EASY BIT OF

1883 年 9 月 15 日《伦敦新闻画报》

中国北部的商旅：谷关的一段山路

Travelling in North China: an easy bit of road in the Ku-Kwan Pass.

THE ILLUSTRATED LONDON NEWS, Aug. 11, 1894.—17[illegible]

A MONGOL COURIER CARRYING THE CHINESE MAIL ACROSS THE GOBI DESERT.

COURTYARD OF A CHINESE INN.

From Sketches by Julius M. Price.

1894年8月11日《伦敦新闻画报》

1 一个蒙古邮差穿越戈壁沙漠运送来自中国的邮件

2 一个中式驿站的庭院

1 A Mongol courier carrying the Chinese mail across the Gobi desert.

2 Courtyard of a Chinese inn.

THE RUSSIAN HEAVY MAIL ON A MOUNTAIN PASS IN NORTH CHINA.

1894年8月25日《伦敦新闻画报》

俄国的重型信件驿队翻越中国北部山区

The Russian heavy mail on a mountain pass in North China.

以上三张由《伦敦新闻画报》特派画师Price先生创作的插图描述了从俄国伊尔库茨克到北京驿道上的艰辛场景。这条驿道途经贝加尔湖南岸，穿越俄蒙边境城镇恰克图、买卖城（今蒙古国的阿勒坦布拉格）、蒙古都城乌兰巴托、戈壁沙漠，进入长城，到达张家口。驿队中的牲口在夏天拖着马车、冬天牵着冰车，很少遭遇强盗打劫，因为蒙古强盗都不愿冒犯俄国的势力。如遭遇恶劣天气，在这条驿道上行走会变得格外艰辛，这正是上面插图所希望表现的。

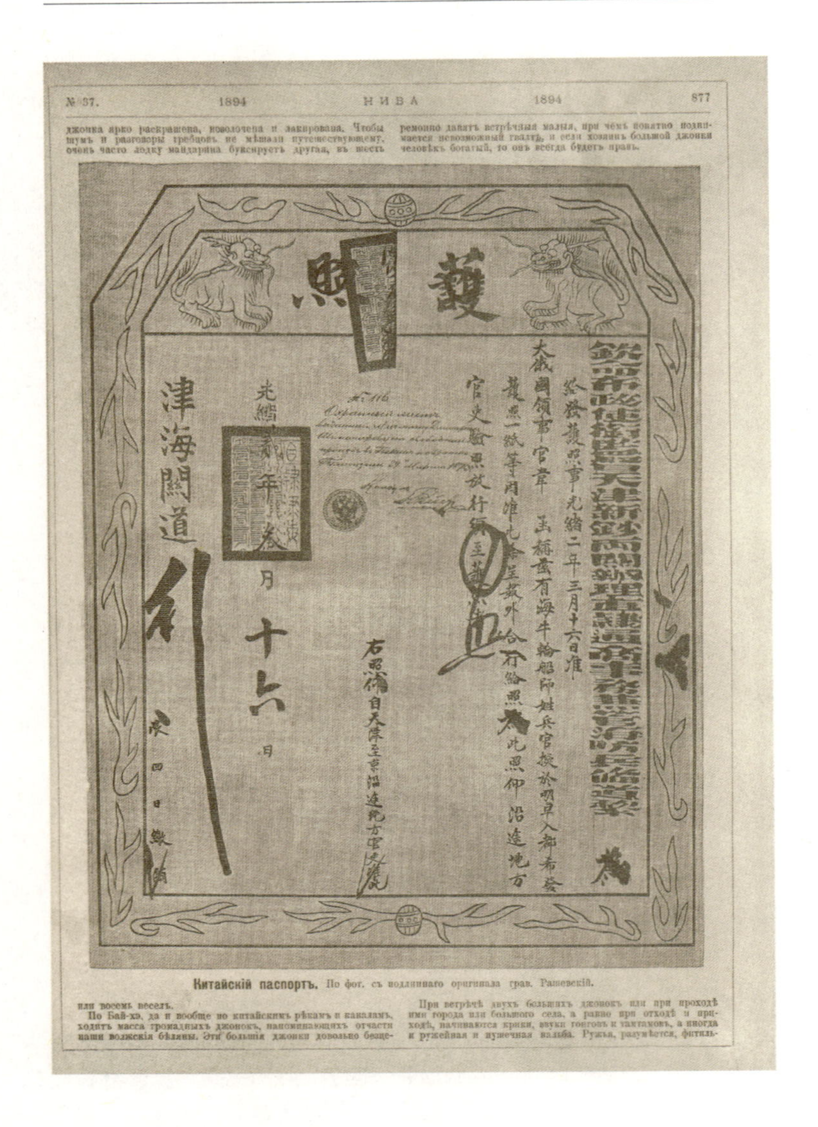

№ 37. 1894 НИВА 1894 877

джонка ярко раскрашена, позолочена и лакирована. Чтобы шумъ и разговоры гребцовъ не мѣшали путешествующему, очень часто лодку мандарина буксируетъ другая, въ шесть

ремонно давитъ встрѣчныя малыя, при чемъ понятно поднимается невозможный гвалтъ, и если хозяинъ большой джонки человѣкъ богатый, то онъ всегда будетъ правъ.

Китайскій паспортъ. По фот. съ подлиннаго оригинала грав. Рашевскій.

или восемь веселъ.

По Бай-хэ, да и вообще по китайскимъ рѣкамъ и каналамъ, ходитъ масса громадныхъ джонокъ, напоминающихъ отчасти наши волжскія бѣляны. Эти большія джонки довольно безце-

При встрѣчѣ двухъ большихъ джонокъ или при проходѣ ими города или большого села, а равно при отходѣ и приходѣ, начинаются крики, звуки гонговъ и тантамовъ, а иногда и ружейная и пушечная пальба. Ружья, разумѣется, фитиль-

1894 年《田野周刊》

中国护照（照片来自拉舍夫斯基）

Китайскій паспортъ (По фот.сь подлиннаго оригинала грав Рашевский).

俄文《田野》周刊甲午期间刊登的护照照片。这一纸护照其实相当于今天的签证，是光绪二年三月，天津新沙両关办理直隶通商事务兼管海防兵备道一名黎姓官员发给一艘俄国海牛轮船上的一位师姓兵官的，护照上说明持照人将于次日进京，请天津和北京沿途的官吏准予放行。

1893 年 1 月 7 日《伦敦新闻画报》

俄罗斯文化的渗透：一名哥萨克骑兵军官在中国东北的一个村庄

Advance of Russian civilisation: a Sotnia of Cossacks at a village in Chinese Tartary.

VIEW OF VLADIVOSTOK.

VLADIVOSTOK AND HARBOR.

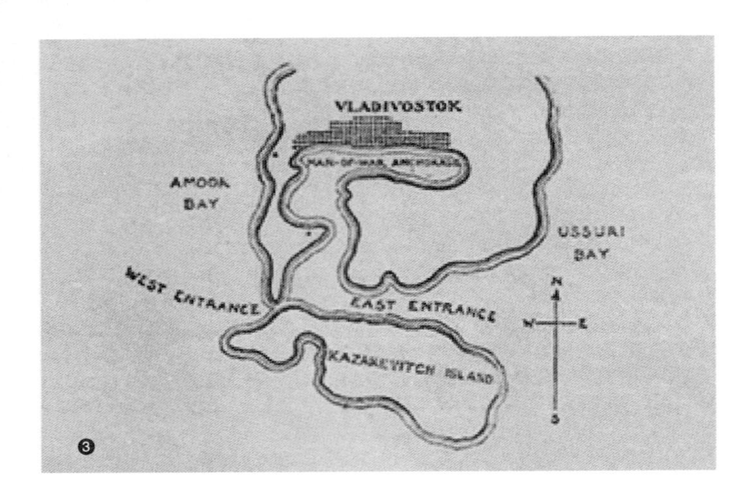

1894 年 10 月 20 日《哈珀斯周刊》发表《俄国在远东的利益》

1　鸟瞰符拉迪沃斯托克城（一）
View of Vladivostok.

2　符拉迪沃斯托克港口
Vladivostok and harbor

3　上方：符拉迪沃斯托克城	Vladivostok
阴影下方：兵舰泊位	Man-of-war anchorage
左侧上面：阿穆尔湾	Amoor Bay
左侧下面：西入口	West entrance
指北针右上方：乌苏里湾	Ussuri Bay
指北针左侧：东入口	East entrance
指北针左下方：俄罗斯岛	Kazakevitch Island

图 1 为俄国远东军港符拉迪沃斯托克。这一俄国第二大军港位于西伯利亚平原最东南角的一处港湾，处于一条长 35 英里、宽 3 英里到 10 英里的半岛的顶端。该半岛西邻阿穆尔湾，东临乌苏里湾。该港口得天独厚，极其安全，四周为陆地包围，仅通过两条较窄的水路入口才能进入其中，然而每年数月间该港口中的军舰因周围海域结冰而无法出海。俄国政府严禁外界人士刺探港口内的消息。俄国按照“军事堡垒”的建制构筑了这所军港。军港内部长期实行戒严制度。当地居民毫无民权可言，他们的生命与自由完全掌控在当地的军事头领手中。军港内部没有任何形式的贸易，进入该港的所有商船毫无例外的是为驻守军人供应补给的那些船只。这是一所由士兵与水手组成的港城；严禁所有外国领事和外国公民进入该港，除非这些人受雇于俄国政府。

图 2 展示的是港口内的布局，我们从中可以清楚地看到兵船停泊区北侧沿岸上的情形和该军港的西侧臂状突出半岛上的状况。在前面最显著的位置，是大量鱼雷和军械库。

图 3 所示，进入该军港的通道为俄罗斯岛所封堵，只有东西两个狭窄的水路入口可以通入该港。而从其中的西入口进入该港口几乎是天方夜谭。两条入口都布有水雷，而且采用后膛装填火药的陆上炮台布满了这条半岛的本土和对面的俄罗斯岛。该军港的西侧臂状突出半岛上也筑满了工事，防止有敌军从这一侧发起炮击。

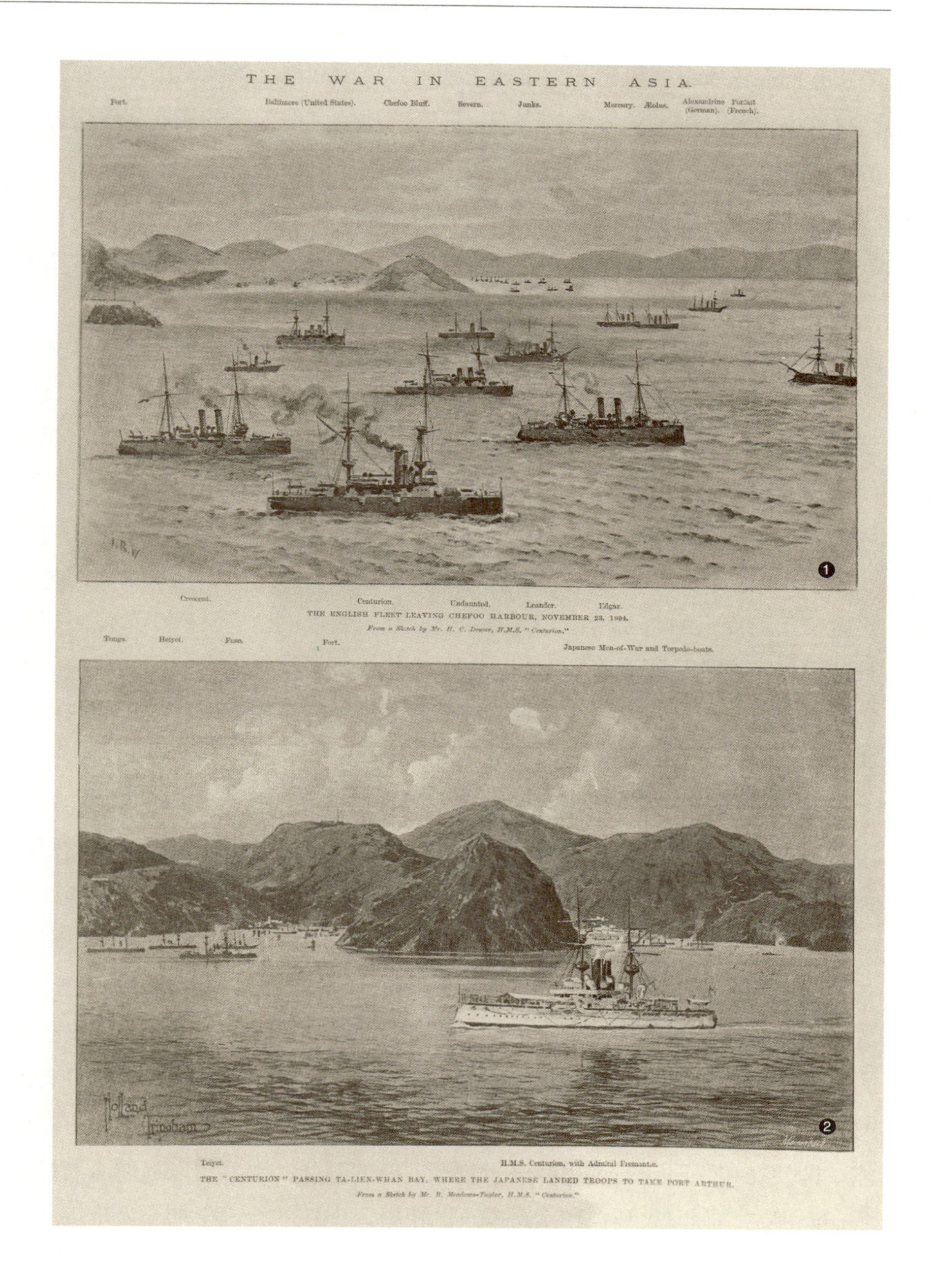

1895 年 1 月 19 日《伦敦新闻画报》

1. 1894 年 11 月 23 日，英国战舰驶离烟台港（前往旅顺）
2. “百夫长”号战列舰经过大连湾时，日本军队即将对旅顺炮台发起攻击

1. The English fleet leaving Chefoo harbour, November 23, 1894.
2. The "Centurion" passing Ta-Lien-Whan Bay, where the Japanese landed troops to take Fort Arthur.

我们在这本书中见到的大量插图都来自英国战舰上的随军画师。在当时，并不是只有中日两个国家的舰船在交战，还有观战的其他国家的战舰，他们在观战的同时把布阵图进行素描。

——编者

在我居住的上海，从我们（译者注：指美国，下同）总领事手里带走的那两名日本人，已在遭酷刑折磨后斩首处决。（此事一经传出，）我们不得不为自己的国家辩护。对身在远东的美国人来说，忠实地为我国政府的无知和犯下的错误辩护，已经成为一种常态。不过这次的情况却令人备感羞辱。我将简要复述一下这起事件，因为一旦我们在这里卷入战争，就将不可避免地面对极其严重的后果；同时，身在我国本土的人民也很有必要了解实际状况。我们曾把日本领入现代化的浪潮，也曾经主导上海庞大的商业利益。然而在这两地，我们的政府竟然很久没能组织起可称耀的海军。这种无所遮蔽、无依无靠的境地，已经让其他国家感到费解。不过现在的状况更加耻辱：我们夹在两个交战国之间，却犯下愚蠢的错误，使我们的弱势暴露得更明显。

战争（译者注：指甲午战争）爆发于 8 月，我写这篇文章的时候，已是 10 月下旬。不过到目前为止，中国水域能看到的唯一一艘美国战舰是古老的密西西比河渡船莫诺卡西号，这是一艘避难船、居住船，哪怕最大限度地发挥功能，也不过是一艘内河巡逻舰。我们知道，我国有更好的战舰安稳地停靠在平安无事的日本港口，尽管日本未来 25 年内都不会真的需要战舰，但是与纽波特港和巴尔港（译者注：美国东海岸新英格兰地区的两处养尊处优的海滨小镇）一样，那里的姑娘都魅力惊人。即使如此，我们在日本、韩国乃至整个亚洲的战舰，一共也只有巴尔的摩号、协和号和海燕号，与其他大国展现的尊严和力量相比，是一出不折不扣的滑稽剧。即使在和平时代，动用两倍于我们规模的舰队，也不足以巡航通商口岸，展示我们确保在华美国人利益和生命安全的决心。现在的状况更加令人难堪。唯有亲临此地，才能真正意识到我国的错误有多严重：我们为数不多的战舰要么留在国内，要么派往欧洲，而欧洲的外交官已经比我们自己的大学教授更能赏识我国的实力。然而在中国，在这个我们曾经统领世界贸易的地方，由于政府无法使自己的实力获得尊重，我国的力量已经化为乌有。

现在我还很安全，因为从我居住的礼查饭店望出去，就能看到俄国、法国和英国的战舰。我们美国人为两个日本人力争公平时也很安全，因为一位法国的战舰指挥官愿意帮助我们。想想看，这里是统领亚洲一半商业活动的城市，外滩上旗昌洋行（译者注：19世纪著名的美资贸易公司，1891年停业）的仓库巍然矗立，显示着我国一度在此取得的成就；然而它的倒闭也揭示出我国的影响力现在已经衰落到何等地步！

——朱利安·拉尔夫（Julian Ralph）《美国在中国的无助》

1894年10月　美国《哈珀斯周刊》

DRAWN BY J. NASH, R.I.　　U.S.S. "PETREL

A Correspondent writing from Newchwang says :—"The European and other residents, fearing disturbances from fugitives an
Governments for protection, the result being this somewhat novel position. Owing to the intense cold here (30 deg. of frost being
rapid current of the river Lian-Ho, so that ships lying in the stream have been sunk at their moorings. For this reason it was ne
these the two ships were towed with some difficulty, hundreds of coolies assisting at the hawsers. Mud fortifications have been th
and roofed, and every preparation made by which the safety of the residents can be ensured. It is probable," the writer adds, "that
cut off, owing to the disturbed state of the country preventing the usual courier service. The place is unusually full of Europeans,
large bodies of Chinese troops passing through to the front"

H.M.S. "FIREBRAND" AND THE U.S.S. "PETREL" AT NEWCHWANG FOR THE PROTECTION OF EUR

ICEBOUND IN CHINESE WATERS

1895年2月16日《图片报》

英国皇家战舰“火把”号和美国战舰“海燕”号在牛庄（牛庄，即今营口——编者注）保护西方侨民

H.M.S. "Firebrand" and the U.S.S. "Petrel" at Newchwang for the protection of European and other residents.

在中国的水域被冰封　　Icebound in Chinese waters.

H.M.S. "FIREBRAND"

ınded Chinese soldiery, petitioned their respective
common) huge blocks of ice are swept down by the
for dry docks to be dug in the Bund, and into
p round the ships, which have been dismantled
nmunication with the outside world will now be
ipally missionaries from the interior, and there are

AND OTHER RESIDENTS

一个记者从牛庄发来报道说："欧洲和其他西方国家的侨民对自己的安全忧心忡忡，他们担心逃兵和败兵为非作乱，纷纷致信各自的政府要求得到保护。这是目前这个多少有些奇怪的局面产生的原因。由于此地的严寒天气（零下三十摄氏度并非少有），巨大的冰块会被辽河湍急的水流卷下，把泊在江上的船只砸沉，因此需要在岸边挖出两个旱码头，把这两艘英美战舰拖拽进去，这不是件容易事儿，数百个中国苦力用绳索把船拉了进去，又用泥土围着战舰垒砌了一圈防水堤。这两艘船的部分设备被拆卸下来，还搭盖了防护罩，以保护侨民的安全为出发点，做了多个预案。"记者还写道："很有可能，由于局势的混乱，正常的邮政体系中断，我们这里会和外界失去联系。这片区域已经聚集了异常多的西方侨民，主要是从内陆地区聚拢过来的传教团成员，每天我们都能看到大队的中国士兵经由此地开赴前线。"

A Correspondent writing from Newchwang says: "The European and other residents, fearing disturbances from fugitives and disbanded Chinese soldiery, petitioned their respective Governments for protection, the result being this somewhat novel position. Owing to the intense cold here (30 deg. of frost being not uncommon) huge blocks of ice are swept down by the rapid current of the river Lian-Ho, so that ships lying in the stream have been sunk at their moorings. For this reason it was necessary for dry docks to be dug in the Bund, and into these the two ships were towed with some difficulty, hundreds of coolies assisting at the hawsers. Mud fortifications have been thrown up round the ships, which have been dismantled and roofed, and every preparation made by which the safety of the residents can be ensured. It is probable," the writer adds, "that our communication with the outside world will now be cut off, owing to the disturbed state of the country preventing the usual courrier service. The place is unusually full of Europeans, principally missionaries from the interior, and there are large bodies of Chinese troops passing through to the front."

1893年中国出口贸易份额（顺时针方向）：

香港	Hong Kong
英属印度	British India
新加坡	Singapore
大洋洲	Australasia
美国	United States
欧洲	Europe
俄罗斯	Russia
日本	Japan
澳门	Macao
其他	Other
英国	Great Britain

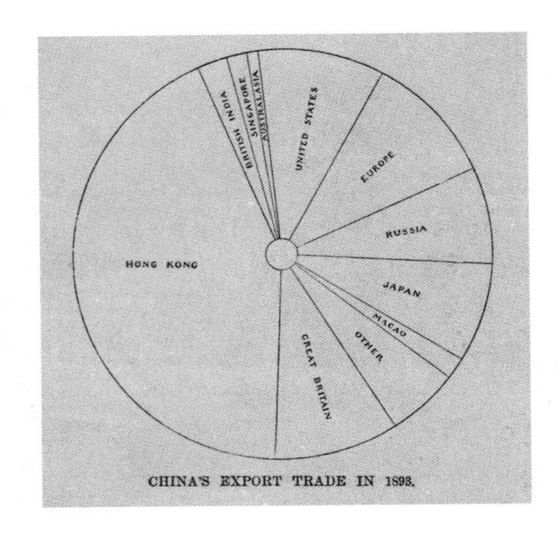

CHINA'S EXPORT TRADE IN 1893.

1893年中国进口贸易份额（顺时针方向）：

香港	Hong Kong
英属印度	British India
新加坡	Singapore
英属美洲	Br. America
美国	United States
欧洲	Europe
日本	Japan
澳门	Macao
其他	Other
英国	Great Britain

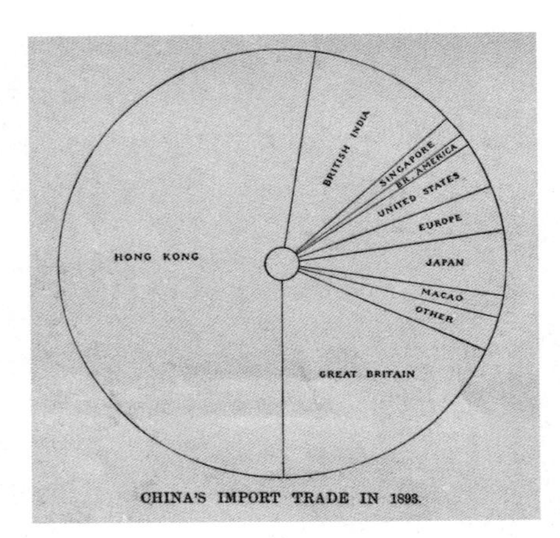

CHINA'S IMPORT TRADE IN 1893.

在美国人购买的中国商品中，丝绸和茶叶占了很大比例。它们在中国出口贸易总额中所占的份额，如下图所示：

1893年中国出口商品（逆时针）：

生丝	Raw Silk		
茶叶	Tea		
丝绸	Manufactures of silk		
原棉	Raw Cotton		
豆类和豆饼	Beans & bean cake		
草编	Straw Braid		
糖	Sugar	烟草	Tobacco
纸张	Paper	瓷器	China
羊毛	Wool	炮竹	Fire-crackers
席子	Matting	其他	All other
动物毛皮	Furs & Skins		

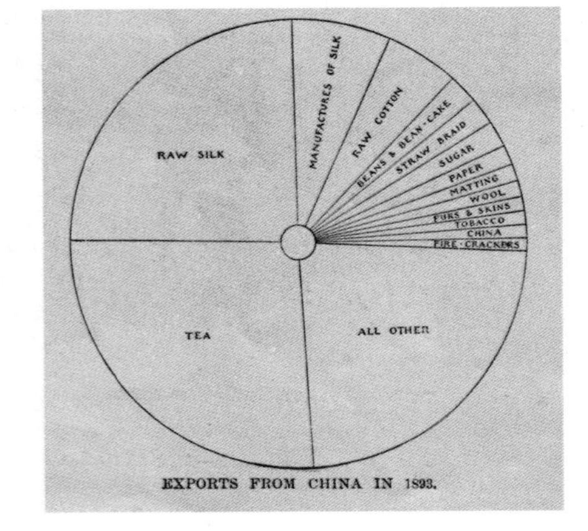

EXPORTS FROM CHINA IN 1893.

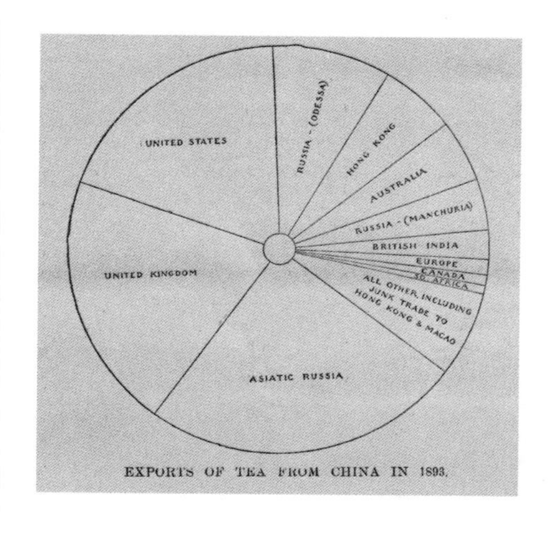

EXPORTS OF TEA FROM CHINA IN 1893.

1893 年中国茶叶出口的分布表现如左图，可以看出，俄罗斯是中国茶叶的主要客户。

1893 年中国茶叶出口贸易分布（比例从大到小）:

美国	United States	英属印度	British India
英国	United Kingdom	欧洲	Europe
俄罗斯亚洲区域	Asiatic Russia	加拿大	Canada
俄罗斯（欧洲区域）	Russia-(Odessa)	南非	So. Africa
香港	Hong Kong	其他包括到香港和澳门的帆船贸易	All other including junk trade to Hong Kong and Macao
澳大利亚	Australia		
俄罗斯（远东区域）	Russia-(Manchuria)		

1895 年 1 月 5 日《哈珀斯周刊》中国外贸的翔实数据和分析，中国进口总额远远高于出口总额。19 世纪末，中国在全球贸易份额中一度领先的丝绸和茶叶出口量都在不断地减少。

在这篇报道中，美国记者做出如下分析：因为战败，中国才被迫成为世界贸易中有序和规范的一分子。也许只有战败，中国才不得不打破排外的陈规，也许只有在四面楚歌的时候，他们才会采纳当下所憎恨的变革。在 1894 财年（1893 年 7 月 1 日—1894 年 6 月 30 日——编者注），美国对中国的出口占美国出口总额的不到 1%。美国从中国的进口约占美国进口总额的 2.5%。看上去，中国工业的觉醒都只会对美国出口贸易产生很小的影响——小到和整体出口贸易相比，可以忽略不计。相反，这样的觉醒还可能为美国带来利益，譬如，中国会为美国的纺织业提供数量更多、质量更好、价格更低廉的丝绸原材料。中国的工业觉醒会对那些在丝绸行业大量投资的国家产生竞争压力，另外，印度和日本还可能感受到茶叶上的竞争。总体而言，中国的工业化不会给我们美国带来危险，相反会让我们获益。

结　语

英国之所以对目前的冲突听之任之，甚至推动战争的爆发，有多方面的原因。首先，它并不因为把自己的盟友——中国推向窘境而内疚，相反正准备趁火打几场小劫，譬如在云南边境勘界、入侵西藏，特别是重新占据渤海湾入口处的旅顺港和朝鲜海峡上的咽喉巨文岛。其次，它也毫不掩饰牵制俄国的意图，俄国影响力在日本海和中国海的悄然壮大使得英国备感担忧。它甚至渴望看到俄国因难以容忍中、日两国瓜分朝鲜，按捺不住一时的冲动，大举全线进攻中国。

长期以来，英国在中国的策略是把俄国和法国说成天朝的敌人，而它们，不仅从中国手中夺走了整个上缅甸、缅甸掸邦和西藏南侧的山脉，更得寸进尺地威胁着四川和云南，还把自己伪装成中国皇帝真正的唯一朋友。时至今日，中国人相信英国人的这套鬼话就像相信孔老夫子的教诲一般。可是，一旦战争爆发，中国人就会立刻意识到：只有法国和俄国才是他们真正的朋友，才能干预事态的发展和保证它们领土的完整！英国奉行的是利己主义政策，只想把自己在欧洲对待土耳其的那一套搬到中国来：一面亲吻它一面攫取它的领土。

——法国国会议员弗朗索瓦·德隆克勒（François Deloncle）撰文

1894年7月30日　法国《晨报》

三　洋务与维新

终于，两派的冲突在1868年爆发了，短暂但具有决定性，流血灾难遍及日本全国。保守的帝国主义者最终胜利，但他们不敢再秉持以前的锁国主张，他们转而声称渴望改革。毫无疑问，他们遵循的政策是最明智并有利于国家发展的，即使日本当时还是有可能倒退到从前的"隐士"状态。

…………

少数开明的军事或外交官员，曾试图为中国引进欧洲的方法和机械，但是他们的建议没有得到（中国）国民的认可，这些国民的外交理念始终是驱除"洋鬼子"和他们的影响力，先驱们的好意也被误解。中国人会抵制铁路的建设，他们会用石头和泥巴砸向在河流中航行的蒸汽船。

——1895年1月5日　美国《哈珀斯周刊》

光绪皇帝屈尊学英语，是因为他和他的政治顾问们都认为，死死抱住3000年传承下来的老规矩的年代已经一去不复返了……

——1892年2月4日　美国《纽约时报》

1868年10月《哈珀斯月刊》

恭亲王

Prince Kung.

恭亲王奕訢（1833—1898），道光皇帝第六子，是中国洋务运动代表人物之一，被誉为“中国第一次近代化运动的倡导者”。第二次鸦片战争中，奕訢受命为全权钦差大臣，与英、法谈判，签订《北京条约》。1861年，咸丰死后，奕訢与两宫太后联合发动“辛酉政变”，成功地夺取了政权，被授予“议政王”之衔，负责组建总理各国事务衙门，具体办理涉外事务。1865年遭慈禧太后猜忌被革除议政王头衔，但依旧身处权力中心。1884年终于因中法战争失利被罢黜，一直到1894年中日甲午战争失败，才再度被起用，任领班军机大臣与领班总理衙门大臣。1898年逝世。

1900 年 7 月 7 日《插图报》

北京总理衙门外牌楼

Péking. – La porte du Tsoung-Li-Yamen.

匾额上的四个大字取自《史记》“遐迩一体，中外禔福”，意思是：远近中外，犹如一体，和谐统一。1861 年，总理衙门经咸丰帝批准成立，总理各国事务衙门，简称总理衙门。由奕訢、桂良、文祥三人负责，主持外交与通商事务，是洋务运动最重要的组织机构。一直运行到 1901 年。

1894 年 9 月 1 日的《插图报》对总理衙门的报道如下：

“尽管总理衙门一直遵循和秉持着帝国数百年传承下来的、被我们西方人所鄙夷的老规矩，但今天这些掌握着天朝命运的重臣们已经明白，闭关锁国的老路已不可能再走下去，中国无法继续把自己与世界割裂开来。经过很长一段时间的徘徊与探索，在完全不触及帝国政体的前提下，总理衙门的高官们跟随着恭亲王和李鸿章总督，力排众议，如履薄冰般地向一条新路走去。”

1868 年 10 月《哈珀斯月刊》

中国出访欧美使团

The Chinese Embassy.

翻译（Interpreters）、右协理海关税务司法籍职员德善（Mr. Deschamps）、海关道志刚（Chih Kang）、中国首任全权大使中外交涉事务大臣蒲安臣（Mr. Burlingame）、礼部郎中孙家谷（Sun Chia Ku）、左协理英国使馆翻译柏卓安（Mr. Brown）、翻译（Interpreters）

蒲安臣（1820—1870）是美国著名的律师、政治家和外交家，既担任过美国驻华公使，又是第一位担任中国出访西方列强的使节。1868 年到 1869 年，在恭亲王的安排下，他率领中国使团出访美国、英国、法国、普鲁士，1870 年访问俄国时，蒲安臣在圣彼得堡去世。在波士顿举行的葬礼上，马克・吐温为他写下悼词：“他对各国人民的无私帮助和仁慈胸怀，已经跨越国界，使他成为一个伟大的世界公民。”

蒲安臣使团的出访比日本岩仓具视、大久保利通、伊藤博文使团的出访早了整整两年。

L'ILLUSTRATION

Prix du numéro : 75 cent. SAMEDI 1er SEPTEMBRE 1894 *52e Année. — N° 2688*

LES ÉVÉNEMENTS DE CORÉE. — Armée impériale chinoise : canonniers tartares.

D'après une photographie de M. Vapereau fils.

S. Exc. Tchang. S. Exc. Liu. S. Exc. Shui-Tan. Le prince Tching. S. Exc. Shui. S. Exc. Souane.

ÉVÉNEMENTS DE CORÉE. — Le Tsong-li-Yamen, ou Conseil des ministres de l'Empire chinois.

D'après une photographie prise à Pékin, dans le jardin du Palais des ministres, par M. Vapereau fils.

1894 年 9 月 1 日《插图报》

1 中国炮兵

2 总理衙门前的合影（左一为张荫桓，左四为庆亲王）

1 Armée impériale chinoise: canonniers tartares.

2 Le Tsong-li-Yamen, ou Conseil des ministres de l'Empire chinois.

LITERATURE.

ASIATIC POLITICS.

Problems of the Far East: Japan, Korea, and China. By the Hon. G. N. Curzon, M.P. (Longmans, Green, and Co.)—The Hon. George N. Curzon is a scholar, a traveller, and one who has long endeavoured to form comprehensive views of the vast Continent of Asia, with its various empires, populations, and types of civilisation. If he does not entirely and minutely "survey mankind" from Britain to Japan, he labours to form a well-balanced estimate of all possible effects upon British interests resulting from apparent changes, immediate or to be expected, in the condition of the principal States from the Caspian Sea to the Pacific Ocean. This means, for the security and prosperity of our Eastern Empire and of our commerce in the farther East, the attitude of Russia, of Persia, and of China and Japan, outside the sphere of Indian political agency. So, while other writers can tell us much more of Afghanistan, Dardistan, the Pamir, Tibet, and the mountain regions, with their native tribes on the borders of Hindustan and of Burmah, we look to him for a shrewd present-day appreciation of the resources and disposition of the great Asiatic foreign powers on different sides of our Indian dominion and of our sphere of trading activity.

With a portion of these subjects, but especially, upon the occasion of the war that has recently begun in Corea, with the actual position of those two rival powers, China and Japan, in the farthest East that geography can recognise overland within the limits of the Old World—though California may also be considered to lie East, when one crosses the Pacific from Yokohama to San Francisco—Mr. Curzon's book, opportunely published by Messrs. Longmans, is fully occupied. Other books on China, other books on Japan, have told us a great deal about those countries and their inhabitants which Mr. Curzon has no need to repeat; some travellers have described Corea, which is not an inviting or particularly interesting country. But the "problem" which is just now of much practical interest—for a reason easily discerned—to English mercantile and other concerns seems to be the question whether the Chinese Empire, which is bigger and more populous than all Europe, can endure the shock of this war. Mr. Curzon's book has already been so largely quoted in our Journal that we may spare further recommendation or indication of its contents. Of the eminent Chinese statesman Li Hung Chang, much has also been said; here is his portrait once more, borrowed by permission from the volume under notice.

R. Acton.

"THE CELESTIAL."

The Kindness of the Celestial. By Barry Pain. (Henry and Co.)—Mr. Barry Pain has a quite special and sympathetic outlook on boy human nature. His stories about boys, more than anyone else's, help us to realise that these are men in miniature, swayed by the subtleties, the mixed motives, the recondite reasonings that actuate the "children of a larger growth." Boys combine these attributes with that energy and *joie de vivre* that are apt to evaporate with the first stress of life, and cause men to look back on their schooldays as the happiest in their lives. They were little men then, only unhampered by the sense of responsibility of *respect humain*, which, with grown-up people, interferes with the proper carrying out of a practical joke. An irresponsibility which, taken in conjunction with the really elegant leisure of school hours, favours the evolution of the idea of mischief. A successful deal on the Stock Exchange can hardly compare in breathless interest with the manipulation of a well-planned "booby trap." Mr. Barry Pain, however, gives due prominence to the serious side of boy nature. "If you think," he says, "that boys of seventeen and eighteen talk like children in the nursery, you have been misled by certain stories of school-life!" Mr. Pain does not attempt to mislead us. He sets down these innocently wise conversations between boy and boy, with a comprehension of the existing conditions of boy-mind of every age, in a manner that is simply masterly. "The Celestial" is a boy "with a quaint Chinese look." What more was needed to fit him with his nickname? He is "at war" with his master. "I have had a day with Liggers," he admits. "I was about two seconds late for prep. row with Liggers! Then when we got to work, I saw that fathead Smithson asleep. . . . I spilt my ink, calculating it would run across and pour over Smithson and wake him up. Liggers copped me. . . . Going in to breakfast I had a slight accident, and fell up against Liggers, and he called me a clumsy lout. . . . In the afternoon at footer, he amused himself by scragging me and hacking me, and saying I was off side when I wasn't. . . . Then in afternoon-school he sent me out of the room for blowing my nose. . . . I own it made a row . . . but I never know when it's going to make that row and when it isn't. . . ." That is the case against Liggers. The Celestial determines to "win him by kindness." The first attention paid to Liggers by the Celestial is as follows: "Liggers crumpled up a corrected prose in his hand and aimed it at the waste-paper basket. It missed. . . . The Celestial rose from his place, stepped softly across the class-room, picked up the ball of paper, carefully placed it in the very centre of the waste-paper basket, and resumed his seat." This and other kindnesses on his part have hardly the desired result. But, as he remarked later, "severity didn't do Liggers, no more did kindness, but illness made him just proper." That is the rest of the story. A rightly constituted person will positively love the Celestial. The book is a miscellany. There are several extraordinarily verisimilistic *portraits de femmes*. We have Alicia, engaged to Cuthbert and anxious to share his literary life. "Had she ever written anything?" "Oh, yes, she had done one, to see if she couldn't!" We have Elsa, the *soi-disant* man-killer, "who was quite vulgar enough to consciously avoid vulgarity"; and Mrs. Cathley, "who spent her time in efforts to imperil without losing the reputation which, as a matter of fact, she had never possessed"; and Ada, who was "simply all tact—people, as a rule, liked her (until they found her out)." To testify to the remarkable blend of humour and pathos which is Mr. Barry Pain's forte, we have the tragic story of Ellen Rider, the daughter of the people, and of Maud Drelin, "the woman of soul," that yet could never find vent in her music.

Violet Hunt.

A HIGHLAND ROMANCE.

Pharais: A Romance of the Isles. By Fiona Macleod. (Derby: Frank Murray.)—"Pharais" is the nervous and passionate story of the madness of Alastair Macleod and the doom which fell upon him, his devoted wife, and their first-born child. It had better been written in poetry: it is so much and so continuously at high pressure that it seems almost hysterical. Its success is in the way it reproduces the haunted atmosphere of the Isles. For Fiona Macleod's purpose the Isles must ever be isles of storm and stress. One never gets a glimpse of them sparkling in the sparkling water, as they must sometimes lie of a shimmering morning. For the purposes of "Pharais" they must ever reveal themselves to us in twilight or moonlight, or in the black night of storms. If there is fine weather, it makes no impress on us. The atmosphere is that of loneliness and old superstition which broods like an everlasting night upon desolate places like the Isles, and sows in the human brain the seeds of madness and melancholy. To make us feel this is the triumph of "Pharais." We would recommend the book to no one inclined to melancholy, unless, indeed, he loves his melancholy and would foster it. The gloom is the very gloom of the island-dweller, ever face to face with the wild waters that shut him away from the happy, bustling, noisy world: living in a twilight land, haunted by the ghosts himself and his fathers have created, and with the doom upon him of the sadness of the seer and the sea. Fiona Macleod writes of these things as if she had known them and lived in their shadow. The manner of the book is the manner of chanting, as of one in a vision who sees and cries aloud the things he sees. But the manner gets monotonous in a story of its length, however suitable it might be to a poem or a very short prose phantasy. The descriptions of the Isles are vivid and poetic. The genuine Gaelic poems interspersed are wild and beautiful. The book is an idyll, and one with all manner of ideals now unhappily out of fashion. There is the faith of the Gael in its pages, but, unlike the faith of the Irish Gael, it does not illuminate. On the whole, the little book, exquisitely produced, is too mournful, and pitched in too high a key. The faintest gleam of humour in it would have been its salvation, but there is neither humour nor humanity. With these things added to her Celtic passion and vision, Fiona Macleod would be a notable addition to the ranks of our writers.

Katharine Tynan.

CONVERSATIONS WITH NORTHCOTE.

Although Hazlitt's "Conversations with Northcote" has long been accessible, with other things of the critic's, in a volume of Bohn's Library, a separate reprint of it was very desirable. And that which Mr. Bentley has published, under the editorship of Mr. Gosse, is a very good reprint. It has a capital essay by the editor on "Hazlitt as an art-critic," a notice of Northcote's life, an excellent frontispiece from a portrait of him by himself, now in the possession of Lord de Tabley, and sufficient notes explaining allusions to things and persons. The only thing that may be missed is a more minute account of Northcote the artist. He has never been "taken up" by any critic or collector; and I do not remember to have seen many specimens of him in easily accessible galleries. What I have seen, I confess, has for the most part seemed to me to be distinguished by the peculiar drawing, half-theatrical, half-wooden, and by the still more peculiar furniture-polish scheme of colour which pervaded so much of British art during the end of the last century and the beginning of this. And I would that Mr. Gosse, in a few pages of "reasoned catalogue," had indicated the character and the whereabouts of such things of Northcote's as might best relieve the artist from the "unmerited obscurity" in which he has admittedly fallen.

It must, however, be confessed that though these curious conversations took place, or professed themselves to have taken place, between a painter and an art-critic, they are by no means limited in their subject to art. Indeed, without having made any very laborious sifting, but judging by more than one or two readings, I should say that the art part of the matter was actually the lesser part in bulk. The conversations (which professedly began in or about 1826) have been both at the time and since suspected of being mere vehicles for Hazlitt's own opinions on things in general, thrown into a form which was popular at the time and of which the chief example (an example, by the way, full of bitter personality against Hazlitt himself) is the "Noctes Ambrosianæ." There can be very little doubt that this is, to a certain extent, true; but that Northcote's part in the dialogue is also genuine I think there can be no doubt, even if the testimony of Patmore, which Mr. Gosse quotes, be not accepted as final. A good deal of the opinion and sentiment is neither Hazlitt's own, nor put in Hazlitt's way, and there was little in Hazlitt of the imitative and dramatic.

Whether all genuine or partly *pastiche*, however, the book is a very interesting one; and, being quite desultory in composition and very good "for thoughts," it is particularly suitable to take up at odd moments, to read on journeys, or when one takes tobacco and thinks. It has some good stories, not always very new, for Hazlitt's celebrated indifference to the hackneyedness of a quotation if he thought it appropriate distinguished him also in regard to stories. The best is, I think, the inimitable bit of coxcombry attributed to the painter Edward Edwards (who must have been a son of Smollett's Pallet) when he entered the Sistine Chapel, and, turning to his companion Romney, cried: "Egad! George, we're bit!" Good, too, is the legend of Sir Richard Phillips, not least anecdotally celebrated of booksellers, going up to Coleridge and offering him "nine guineas a sheet for his conversation." If only the offer had been accepted, and Phillips had been good for the money! I should think that Coleridge (shorthand writer's expenses paid and a decent time allowed for sleep and so forth) might have cleared about ninety guineas a day during his natural life. As for other matters, Northcote's reminiscences of the famous Reynolds-and-Johnson set are rather insignificant, and this insignificance may have counted for something in the doubts of their authenticity; but this is false logic. The portrait of Hazlitt himself is interesting, and, on the whole, favourable. Once or twice, no doubt, he breaks into his well-known fit of "quarrelling with the world," especially in a furious and undignified complaint that "Tory scribes who treat mankind as rabble and *canaille* are regarded by them as gentlemen," while he, Hazlitt, "cannot get a civil answer from a shop-boy on his own side of the question." But this is rare; and the references to Scott in particular contrast pleasantly with the rabid abuse of the "Spirit of the Age." The thing is, in short, a very agreeable pot-pourri on taste, Shakspere, the musical glasses, and a great many other things, couched in the form of a conversation between a kind of Nestor of art and, in a way, of letters, and the keenest and most original, if also the most wayward writer of his age, who was a critic pure and simple—in art, in letters, in everything. Thus that pure criticism, which, as the critic is often informed, is so detestable to a healthy palate, is tempered by some milder matter; and the milder matter is relished and zested by the criticism.—George Saintsbury.

LI HUNG CHANG, VICEROY OF TIENTSIN.
Senior Grand Secretary of State in the Chinese Empire.
From "Problems of the Far East." (Longmans, Green, and Co.)

1894年9月22日《伦敦新闻画报》

大清帝国"资深大国务卿"、"天津总督"李鸿章——照片来自《远东的问题一书》(朗文格林出版社)

Li Hung Chang, Viceroy of Tientsin.Senior Grand Secretary of State in the Chinese Empire.From *Problems of the Far East*. (Longmans, Green, and Co.)

书评版面上介绍了《东亚政治》、《天朝》两本书，并选用了李鸿章的照片。这个阶段是西方人对东亚高度关注的时刻，有关东亚的文学类和时政类作品大量出现。李鸿章传记类图书也在西方越来越多地出版，到 1901 年李鸿章去世的时候达到高潮。

1901 年 11 月 16 日的《插图报》在他去世时的报道中写道："可以说，他取代了总理衙门，负责处理与'蛮夷'间的政治、商贸关系，在最棘手的对外交涉中敏锐洞察、灵活斡旋，有些人直接说他狡黠，另一些人则赋予他一个优雅的绰号——'中国忠仆'。在远东，他的名字、作用、斡旋频繁地与重大国际事件紧密相连，在许多重要的协议书下方都可以找到他的签名。"

REGISTERED AT THE GENERAL POST OFFICE FOR TRANSMISSION ABROAD.

No. 2888.—VOL. CV. SATURDAY, AUGUST 25, 1894. THIRTY-SIX PAGES | SIXPENCE. By Post, 6½d.

GENERAL SHAN. THE LATE PRINCE CH'UN. LI HUNG CHANG.

THREE GREAT MEN OF CHINA.

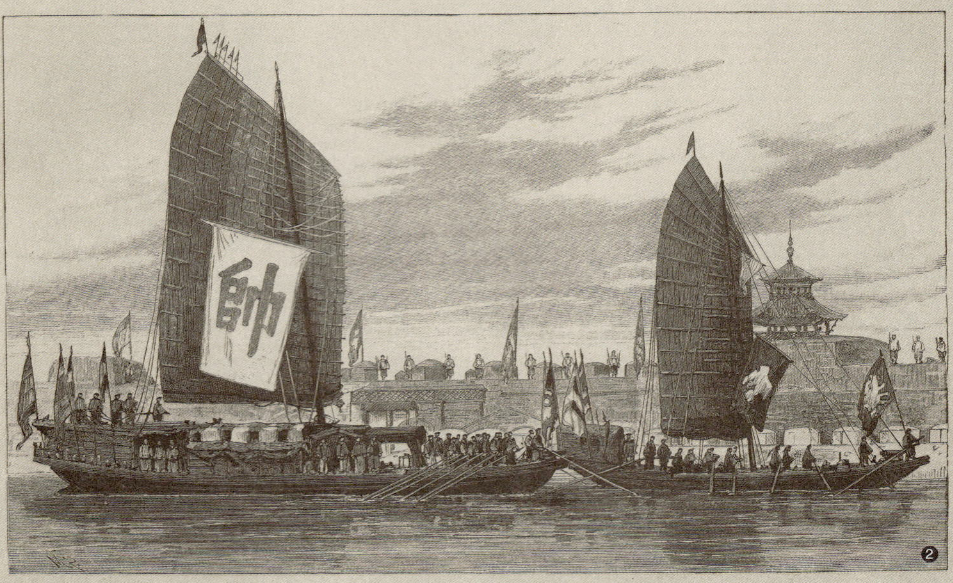

THE CHINESE PRIME MINISTER, LI HUNG CHANG, VICEROY OF CHIH-LI, GOING IN HIS STATE BARGE FROM TIENTSIN TO PAO-TING-FU.

1875 年 10 月 23 日《图片报》

1　中国士兵
2　游弋在长江上游的中国战船
3　北直隶总督李鸿章，中国军队统帅
4　金陵制造局的车间内

1　Chinese soldiers.
2　Chinese gunboat on the upper Yangtsze-Kiang River.
3　Li-Hung-Chang, Governor-General of Peichihli, Commander-in-Chief of the Chinese Army.
4　Interior of a workshop, Nanking Arsenal.

左图：

1894 年 8 月 25 日《伦敦新闻画报》

1　中国三个重要人物
善庆将军（General Shan）、醇亲王（The late Prince Ch'un）、李鸿章 (Li Hung Chang)
2　中国的"首相"，直隶总督李鸿章在他的驳船上从天津去往保定府

1　Three great men of China.
2　The Chinese Prime Minister, Li Hung Chang, Viceroy of Chih-Li, going in his state barge from Tientsin to Pao-Ting-Fu.

左边两幅图片是 1885 年海军衙门大臣醇亲王奕譞赴天津巡阅北洋水师时，为了加强宣传造声势，他们特招摄影师为其拍摄的。

HARPER'S WEEKLY

1894 年 8 月 25 日《哈珀斯周刊》

1 直隶总督李鸿章阁下（摄于 1877 年）

2 中国陆军一位名为徐润芝的参将

3 中国旧式军队官兵

4 一切为朝鲜战争准备就绪——中国现代化炮兵

1 His Excellency Li Hung Chang, Viceroy of Tchili, etc—photographed in 1877.

2 Hu Jun-Chih Tsang-Chiang. A Chinese Colonel of Infantry.

3 Chinese native soldiers with officer—old style.

4 All ready for Korea—A modern Chinese battery.

威廉·克利菲斯（William Elliot Griffis）所写的这篇报道：《中国的军力》，深入分析了中国军队的实力，两张插图照片反映出当时清军中截然不同的两支力量。

俄国《田野》周刊

朝鲜战争中的清军装束

从左至右：步兵军官、着民服的步兵、步兵（中间三人）和骑兵（最右两人）

Война въ Коpet. формы китайской арміи.

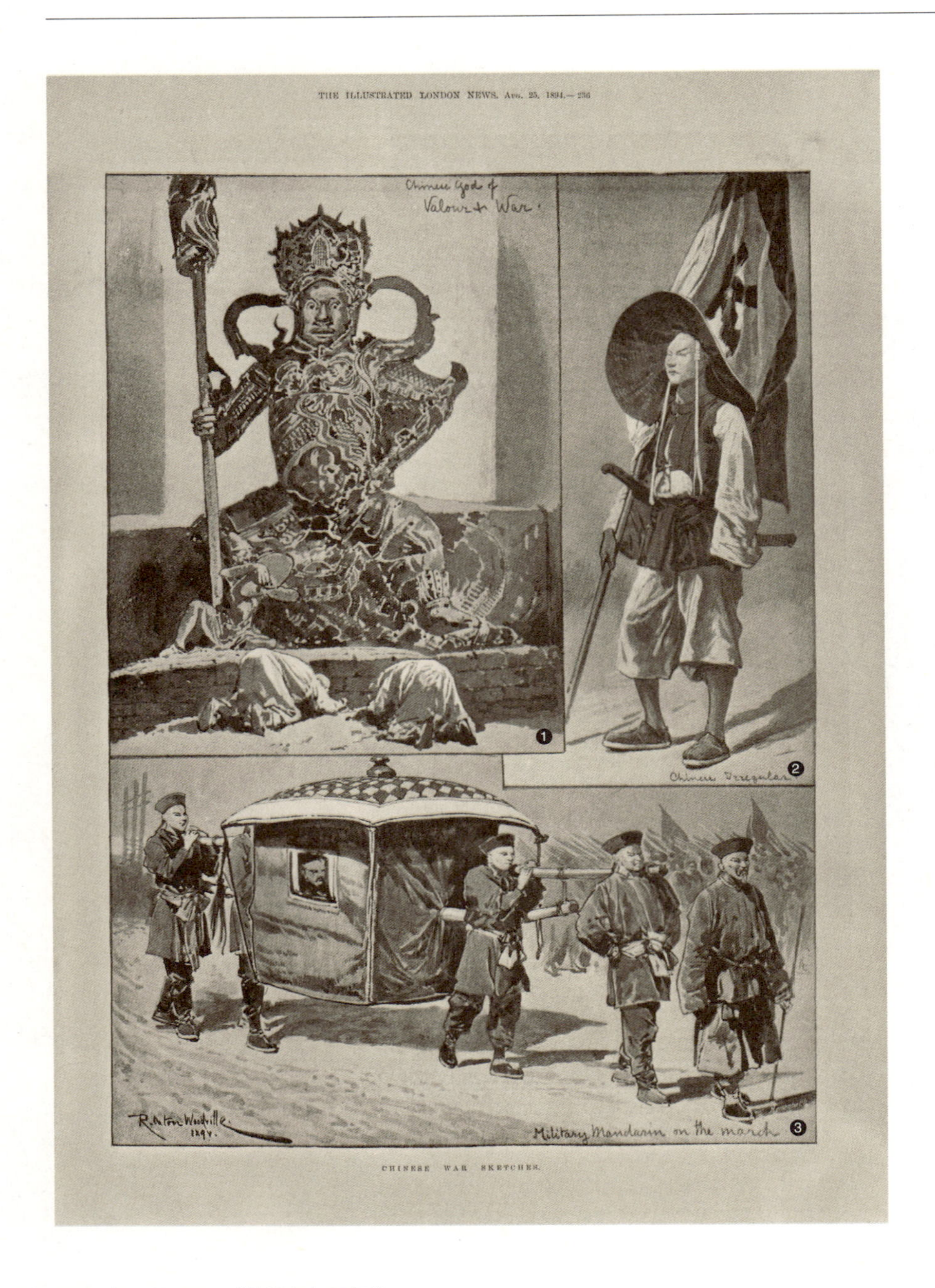
THE ILLUSTRATED LONDON NEWS, Aug. 25, 1894.—236

CHINESE WAR SKETCHES.

1894 年 8 月 25 日《伦敦新闻画报》

中国战争速写

1　中国战神

2　中国初级士兵立像

3　军官行军图

Chinese War Sketches.

1　Chinese God of Valour & War.

2　Chinese Jr. Regular.

3　Military Mandarin on the march.

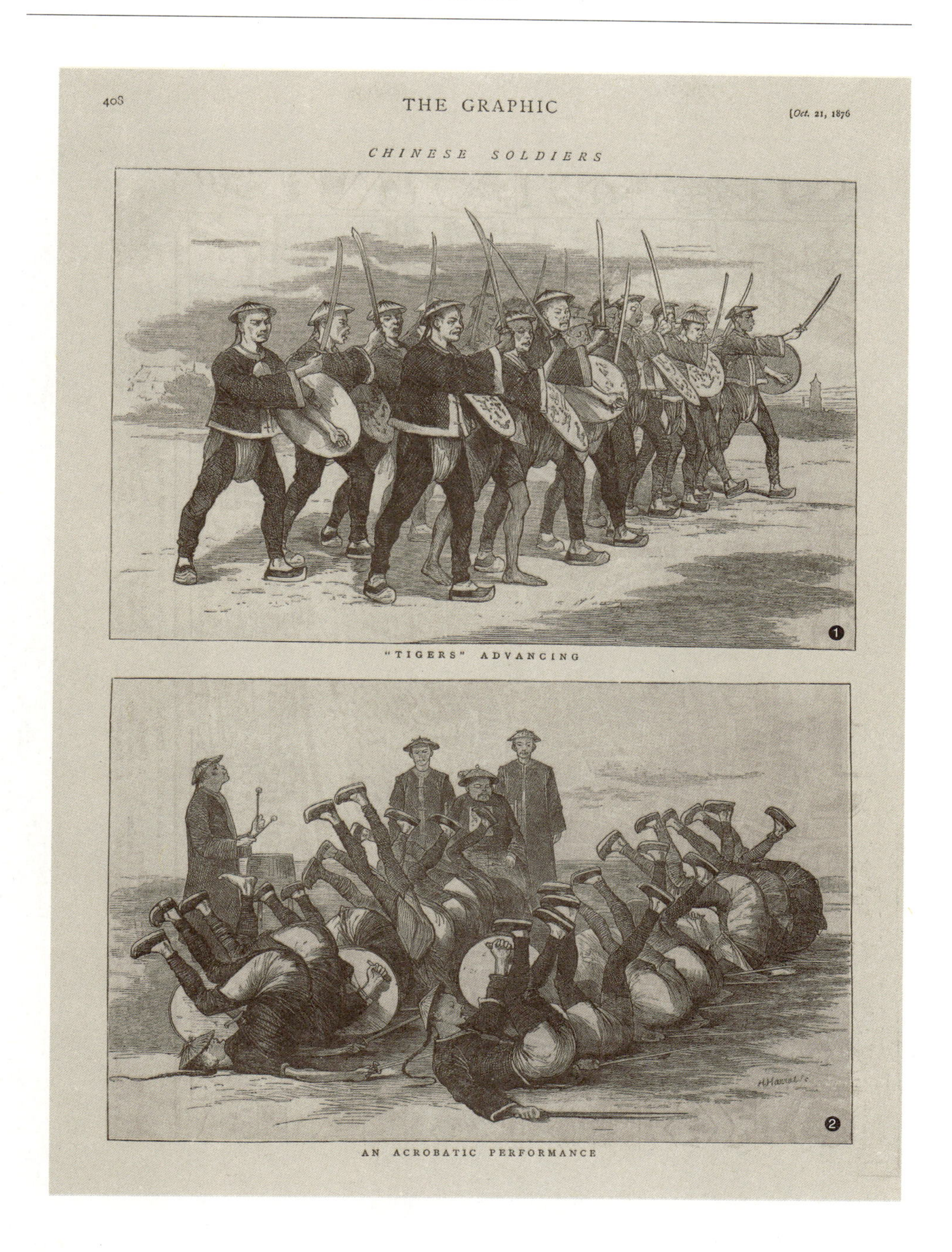
408 THE GRAPHIC [Oct. 21, 1876

CHINESE SOLDIERS

"TIGERS" ADVANCING

AN ACROBATIC PERFORMANCE

1876 年 10 月 21 日《图片报》

中国士兵（清朝八旗军旧式操练）

1 “猛虎”前进

2 杂耍表演

Chinese Soldiers.

1 “Tigers” advancing.

2 An acrobatic performance.

Chinese soldiers practising shooting by firing at a target, consisting of a metal plate about 2 feet square, suspended between two uprights. The distance vari
"any firing at a longer range, or even heard of such a thing. Neither have I seen any butts where long

CHINESE SOLDIERS PRACTISING AT TARGETS AT

FACSIMILE OF A SKETCH BY OUR SPECIAL ARTIST WITH THE CH

1895 年 4 月 13 日《图片报》

中国士兵在山海关练习打靶

Chinese soldiers practising at targets at Shan-Hai-Kwan.

中国军人练习射击，靶子是一个大概两英尺宽的铁片，挂在两根木杆上，射击距离大约在 70 码到 140 码之间。我们的画师说："我从来没见过，甚至没听说过他们在更远的距离训练射击，我根本就没见过可以训练远距离射击的靶场。"

Chinese soldiers practising shooting by firing at a target, consisting of a metal plate about 2 feet square, suspended between two uprights. The distance varies from 70 yards to perhaps double that distance. "I have not yet seen," says our artist, " any firing at a longer range, or even heard of such a thing. Neither have I seen any butts where long-range shooting could take place. "

CHINESE OFFICERS INSPECTING A MITRAILLEUSE—A SCENE IN THE NANKIN ARSENAL.

1873 年 7 月 19 日《哈珀斯周刊》

中国官员在金陵制造局视察火炮制造

Chinese officers inspecting a mitrailleuse—a scene in the Nankin Arsenal.

李鸿章创办的金陵制造局被西方誉为中国新式军工产业领头羊，图上绘制的是金陵制造局仿制的75mm德国克虏伯行营炮，甲午战争时期中日双方的陆军都曾装备过此种火炮。

1873年7月19日《哈珀斯周刊》的这篇题为《中国的火炮》的报道写道：

“南京因其在扬子江两岸优越的地理位置为它带来的秀丽风光而闻名，而今，在经历了多年的太平天国战乱后，这座城市的一大部分已经沦为废墟，昔日皇城的雄风早已不在，当年举世闻名的大琉璃塔也变成了一堆瓦砾，然而利用这废墟中的砖石，人们兴建了如今的南京兵工厂（1865年开始动工、1866年投入使用的金陵制造局——编者注），这里，中国人几年来制造出了最先进的战争武器和数千吨的弹药。

“这座兵工厂是一座砖结构建筑，四周被高墙所围，从外表看上去，像是那个曾被誉为世界奇迹的古老的琉璃塔的低调的替代品。在那座老塔的脚下，曾经是一座普通的佛教寺庙。兵工厂内，布满了先进的机器，当年寺庙的风铃声和和尚们的诵经声被蒸汽锤的敲击声和机器的隆隆声所取代。

“这张插图描绘的是几位当地官员正在检查兵工厂制造的火炮。近年来，中国人终于开始放弃对西方野蛮人的发明所持的荒唐偏见，并希望用它们来取代数千年天朝一直不舍不弃的蠢笨装置。即便在中国，一切也在变化着。”

EXTRA SUPPLEMENT TO THE ILLUSTRATED LONDON NEWS
WAR PREPARATIONS IN CHINA: WELDING A COIL FOR A GREAT

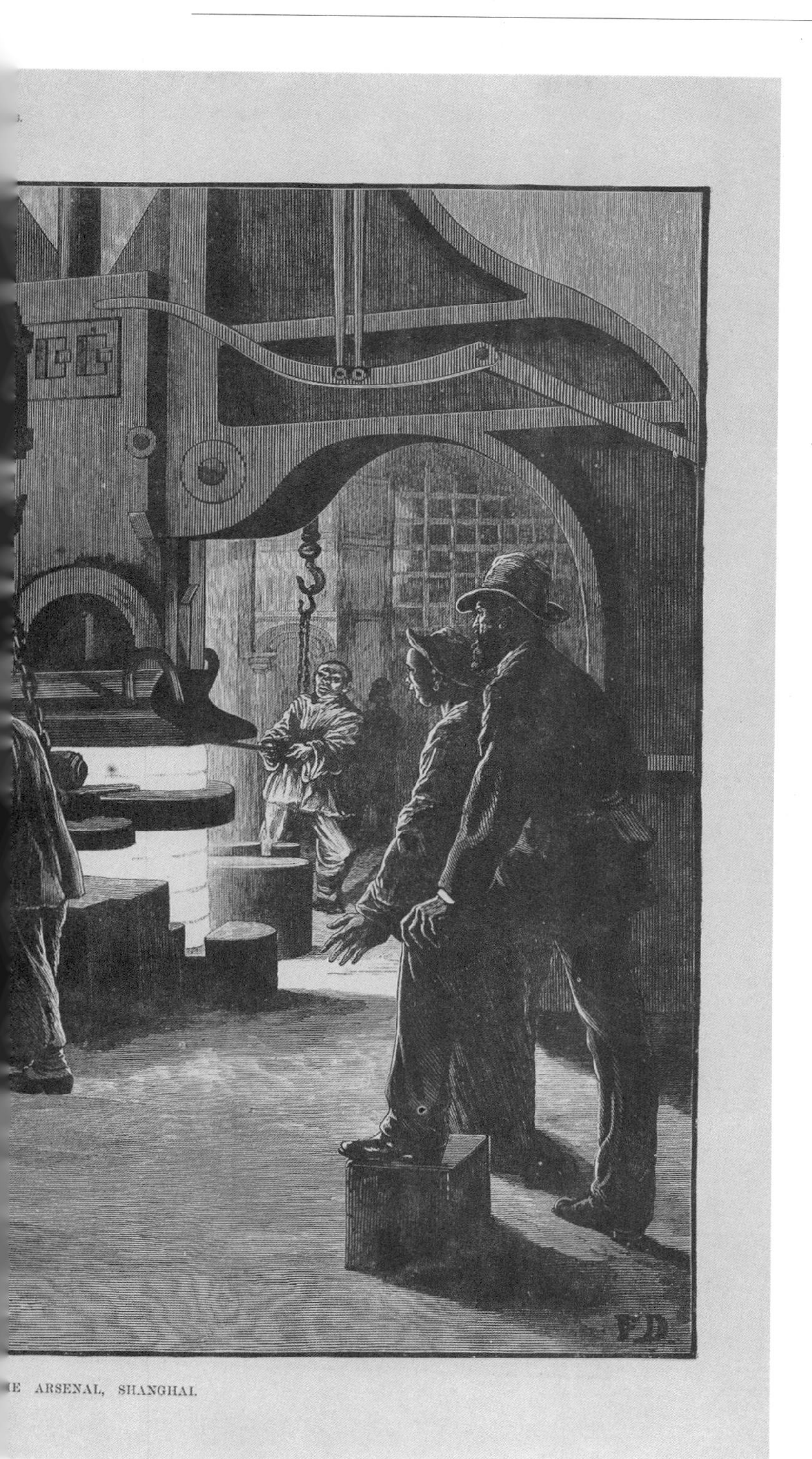

1883 年 7 月 28 日《伦敦新闻画报》

中国的战争准备：江南制造局里，工人们在焊接机枪盘管

War preparations in China: welding a coil for a great gun at the arsenal, Shanghai.

THE WAR IN THE EAST: TRAINING FOR THE CHINESE NAVY

The Cadets at drill at the entrance to the Naval College, Whampoa, under the inspection of the Viceroy's Deputy and their Excellencies Woo, Hsi, and Taontai.—From a Photograph by Mei Sang, Whampoa

A Naval and Military Training Station in China

OF the very few naval and military training stations, that at Whampoa, in Southern China, is one of the most important. It stands on Dave's Island, Whampoa, twelve miles below Canton. Just recently an iron barrier has been built across the river, near Whampoa, to prevent the upward passage of men-of-war which might attack Canton. The barrier was built in Germany and erected under the supervision of a German engineer.

On Dave's Island itself three distinct schools or colleges stand—the naval school, the military school, and the torpedo school. The two latter had, till recently, German officers amongst the instructors.

The most important school is the naval school. Cadets come from all regions of China, but mainly from districts around Foochow. They are instructed in mathematics, geography, physics, navigation, and naval engineering. Most of the instruction is given in the English language. Till recently the naval engineering was taught by an officer in the British navy, who had under his control a well-fitted and spacious workshop. The navigation was taught by an Englishman and by Chinese naval officers. The school itself is a spacious low building capable of housing at least two hundred cadets. It is divided into a number of courts which, on the ground floor, separate the large lecture rooms. The upper story is made up of the private rooms of the cadets and their Chinese instructors.

The school is directly under the control of the Viceroy of Canton, but is practically governed by two mandarins of high rank, who act as directors. In the school, for a short time, there was also a botanical department specially organised for teaching botany with reference to agriculture and forestry.

But since the departure of the able and energetic Viceroy Chang Chi Tung, and the arrival of the senile and money-grabbing elder brother of Li Hung Chang, there has been a decline in the efficiency of these colleges. The German major in the military college has returned home, the able English engineer has left, and now, under the corrupt and slack government of the staff of mainly Foochow officials, the naval college is a reflection on land of the Chinese navy on the waters. Years ago, when the Czarevitch inspected the college and the drill of the cadets, even the courteous Prince Barialinsky could not check a smile when he saw the casual and inefficient management of affairs.

A SPECIAL WAR MAP of China, Corea, and Japan, compiled from recent and authentic sources, has just been issued by Messrs. G. Philip and Son, of Fleet Street.

Kneller Hall

THE HEADQUARTERS OF MILITARY MUSIC

THERE are one or two things nowadays which are managed rather better than in the good old times, and one of them is our military music. Once upon a time—and not so very long ago—the army tradition ran that it was enough to have long hair and to speak broken English to be the bandmaster of a British regiment; and the exhibitions of our army bands were "exhibitions" in the least flattering sense of the word. But that is changed greatly now; some of our regimental bands, both at home and on colonial and Indian service, are things to be proud of; and not a little of this improvement is due to the teachings of Kneller Hall.

Kneller Hall is the school of musical education of the army, and it is a fine old place, with a splendidly harmonious front, at Twickenham. Sir Godfrey Kneller lived there, and gave his name to the building, though few traces remain of his habitation except some magnificent oaken cupboards, a series of curious casts, and the graceful chapel in the middle of the building. On Sunday mornings the little chapel holds a service the like of which can be heard nowhere else in the kingdom. The band of the Hall assembles there one hundred and fifty strong, and its resounding music is joined to that of the mustel organ and to that of a choir of forty voices. It is a volume of sound with which the tiny chapel seems to throb and tremble, and the writer, who once heard the anthem "In Thee, O Lord, I put my trust" thus rendered, will never be able to forget the overpowering effect of that magnificent thunderous harmony. There is little room for visitors in the chapel—a pretty one with, in spite of the meagre number of its years, two brass tablets recording the death of officers connected with the institution—but on a fine morning people come from many places round about and sit or stand on the lawn outside to hear the music of the service. Hardly less fine in effect is the indoor practice of the full band. In fine weather the practice is generally held out of doors; but the past capricious summer has kept it generally indoors, and, as Kneller Hall is much better suited to the needs of a gentleman's private dwelling-house than to those of a public institution, the band performs in a room which barely holds them. Inconvenience apart, the cabin'd sound is splendid, and the sight of the band thus practising is in itself very interesting. It contains many different uniforms, for it has recruits from all parts of the Empire, and one of its most accomplished performers is a black soldier of the Queen from Lagos.

There are two classes of pupils: boys who are sent from their regiments to the school between the ages of fourteen and fifteen, or (the larger number) between seventeen and nineteen, and "students," mainly young sergeants who come to qualify for bandmasterships. The boys stay from eighteen months to two years; it depends upon their capacity. The sergeants remain for longer periods. While at Kneller Hall both are, of course, under military discipline and regulations. One curious feature of the dormitories is that the lads are grouped together according to the instruments they play, and the names of the rooms bear the impress of this regulation. This room, for instance, is the "E Flat Clarionet Room;" that the "French Horn Passage." The euphoniums and the trombones lodge together. It might almost be said that the inmates of Kneller Hall eat music, drink music and sleep music. In the rooms are hung, for instance, "Scale for the Clarionet," "Theory of the French Horn;" and when the boys are not engaged in band practice they may generally be found (by the Musical Directors at any rate) in their bedrooms solemnly tootling on their appointed instruments. There are, of course, masters for each species of instrument; and the sergeant students are expected as part of their duties to assist in the teaching of the boys under the supervision of the masters. There are one hundred and twenty "pupils" and fifty "students." The latter, of course, lodge and mess apart from the boys. They have, in fact, a typical sergeants' mess; with a good library (of musical works) and opportunities for less professional recreation.

The magnificent band of the Institut ion is, however, best known to the public from the gratuitous performance, which it gives to all who care to come to listen at Whitton Park. It seldom performs away from home, and does so publicly only once a year, when it goes to St. Paul's Cathedral. But to these "At Homes," held at half-past three on the Lawn in May and September, and at four o'clock in the other summer months, people come from Richmond and Twickenham and Hounslow in flattering numbers to listen.

The band—eighty-two reed intruments, fifty-seven brass, together with percussion and spring basses—plays music which a few years ago we only expected to hear at St. James's Hall or at the Crystal Palace. Each evening it goes through a programme of eight pieces, the chief feature of which is a suite or one of the symphonies arranged for a military band by one of the students, or by one of the bandmasters of the army. Besides these it has overtures and selections, and frequently a march composed by one of its more creative "students." It is, in fine, a splendid entertainment alike to the ear and to the imagination, for the band gathered together from so many parts of the Empire contains the promise, if not the pick, of the army. The Institution, so admirably conducted and so finely productive, has lately sustained a very great loss in the death of its commandant, Colonel G. Brooke-Meares, under whose direction Kneller Hall has grown greatly both in use and estimation. The Adjutant-Quartermaster is Captain F. Mahoney, and the Director of Instruction Lieutenant S. C. Griffiths, Honorary R.A.M.

THE WAR IN THE EAST: TRAINING FOR THE CHINESE NAVY

Five of the Instructors (seated) and some of the Cadets (standing) of the Naval College, Whampoa.—From a Photograph by Mei Sang, Whampoa

1894 年 9 月 8 日《图片报》

东方的战争：中国海军的训练

The war in the East: training for the Chinese Navy.

1　在黄埔水师学堂大门前，学员和教官与前来视察的吴、谢副总督及道台大人的合影

1　The Cadets at drill at the entrance to the Naval College, Whampoa, under the inspection of the Viceroy's Deputy and their Excellencies Woo, Hsi, and Taontai.

2　黄埔水师学堂五位教官（坐者）和学员（站立者）的合影

2　Five of the instructors (seated) and some of the Cadets (standing) of the Naval College, Whampoa.

清朝当时为培养海军人才，适应海防需要，设立福州船政学堂、天津水师学堂、广东黄埔鱼雷学堂、广东水陆师学堂、烟台海军学堂、山东威海卫水师学堂、旅顺口鱼雷学堂、烟台海军学堂。致远舰管带邓世昌就是毕业于福州船政学堂的。

《图片报》的这篇报道对黄埔水师学堂进行了重点报道："水师学堂招收来自中国各地（主要是福州周边地区）的学员，并开设算术、地理、航海学以及海军工程等课程，大部分采用英语授课。目前，担任海军工程教习的是一位英国海军军官，他手下还有一间规模适中、空间宽敞的车间。航海学的教习由一位英国人和几位中国海军军官共同担任。学堂是一间宽敞又低矮的楼房，至少可容纳两百名学员。楼房被划分成几个院落，底层是分隔开的几个大讲堂，上层是学员与汉人教习的房间。学堂曾短暂开设植物学系，专门教授与农业、林业有关的植物学知识。"

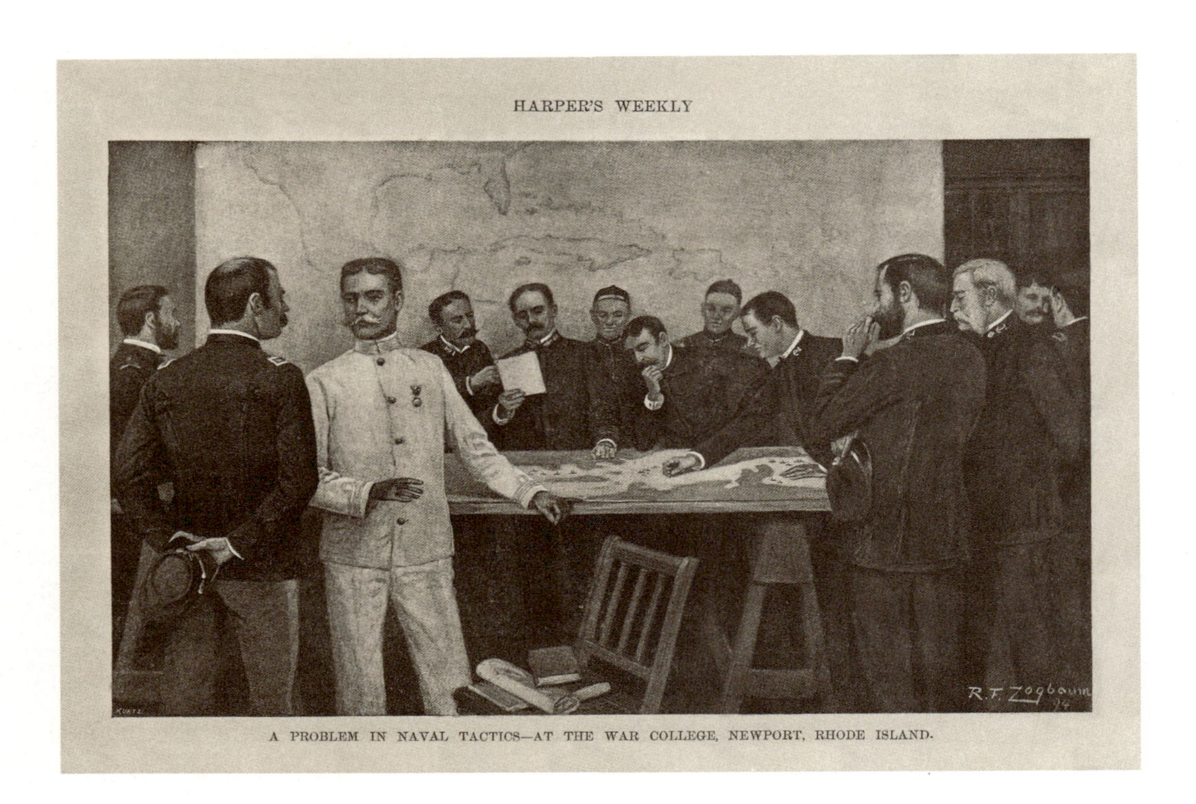

1895 年 2 月 16 日《哈珀斯周刊》

海军战术推演训练——罗德岛纽波特的美国海军战争学院

A problem in naval tactics—At the War College, Newport, Rhode Island.

1884 年 10 月，当中法两国的军舰在中国东南沿海正打得不可开交之时，美国海军战争学院在罗德岛州纽波特的一所废弃的贫民收容所中诞生了。1887 年，学院开始海军战术仿真推演训练，20 世纪美国海军所执行的几乎所有海上军事行动都在这里进行过前期模拟演练。1885 年，学院只有 4 名教员和 9 名学员，今天，这所承担着美国海洋战略与政策研究、国家安全战略决策训练和联合作战课程的学院已经培养出了总计 5 万多名毕业生，毕业后的职业主要是航空母舰和驱逐舰舰长，以及大型潜艇的艇长。近年来，该学院还组建了一个"中国海上力量研究所"。我们在这张 120 年前的版画图片上惊讶地发现了两位正在参加海军战术推演训练的中国学员的身影，他们站在一旁，正在仔细地观摩，但仿佛并没有参与到众人热烈的讨论中。这篇报道中也没有谈及该学院中的中国籍学员，但我们知道，在洋务运动的大潮中，在直隶总督李鸿章和两江总督沈葆桢的大力呼吁下，从 19 世纪 70 年代起，曾有不少中国海军留学生前往英国就读，北洋水师右翼总兵刘步蟾、左翼总兵林泰曾都在他们之列。但前往美国海军学习的记载，目前我们还没有见过。图中两位中国学员是谁？现没有考证出。

1886 年 11 月 13 日《图片报》

与中国舰队在东方—— 一位军官在日本文身

With the China squadron in the East—Tattooing an officer in Japan.

这是受雇于北洋舰队的外国军官利用在日本长崎停靠期间上岸休息时去文身。1886 年 8 月，中国北洋舰队首次访问日本长崎，北洋水兵在当地妓院寻乐并斗殴，与日本警察发生冲突。冲突直接导致北洋水兵再次上岸时遭到日本警察及市民的攻击，造成双方多人伤亡，由此引发“长崎事件”。

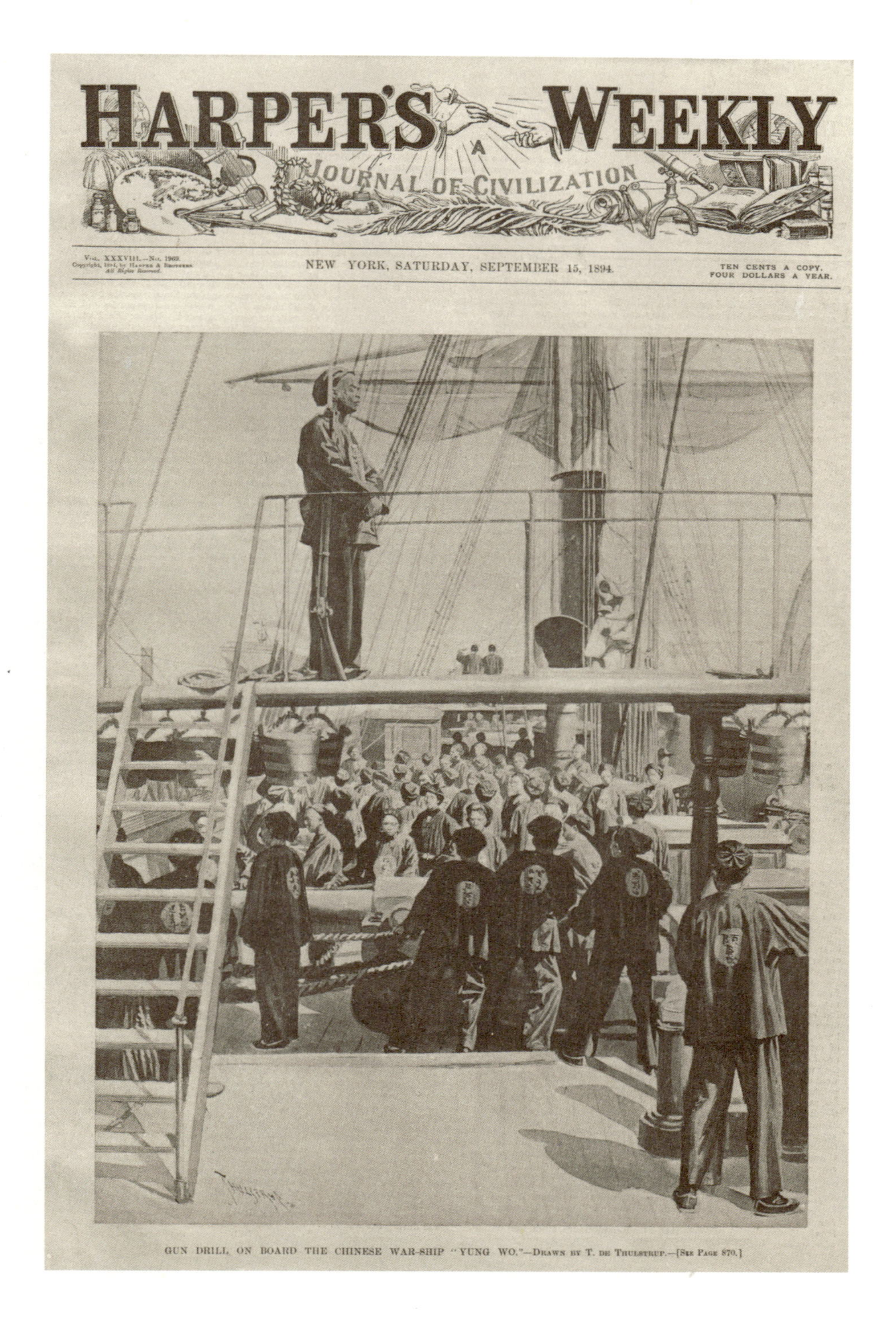
HARPER'S WEEKLY
A JOURNAL OF CIVILIZATION

Vol. XXXVIII.—No. 1969.
Copyright, 1894, by Harper & Brothers. All Rights Reserved.

NEW YORK, SATURDAY, SEPTEMBER 15, 1894.

TEN CENTS A COPY.
FOUR DOLLARS A YEAR.

GUN DRILL ON BOARD THE CHINESE WAR-SHIP "YUNG WO."—Drawn by T. de Thulstrup.—[See Page 870.]

1894 年 9 月 15 日《哈珀斯周刊》

中国扬武舰上的军事演习

Gun drill on board the Chinese war-ship "Yung Wo".

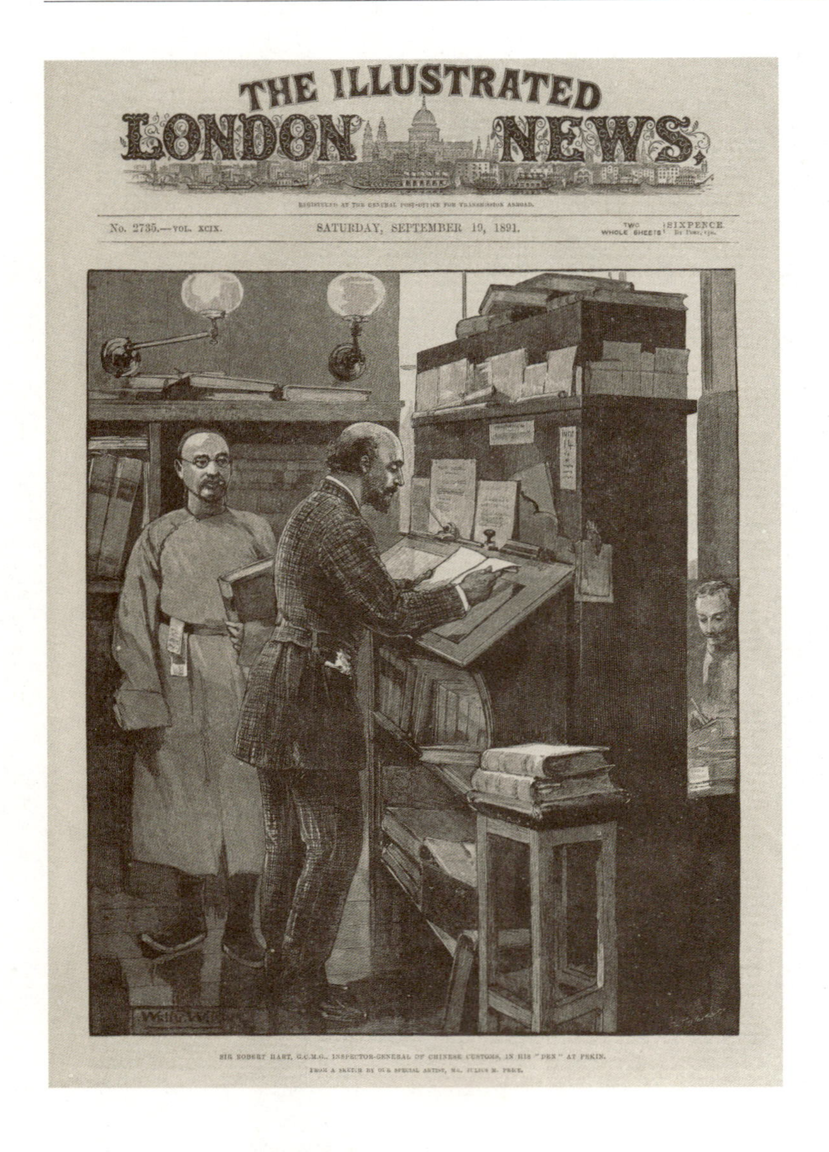

THE ILLUSTRATED LONDON NEWS

REGISTERED AT THE GENERAL POST-OFFICE FOR TRANSMISSION ABROAD.

No. 2735.—VOL. XCIX. SATURDAY, SEPTEMBER 19, 1891. TWO WHOLE SHEETS SIXPENCE.

SIR ROBERT HART, G.C.M.G., INSPECTOR-GENERAL OF CHINESE CUSTOMS, IN HIS "DEN" AT PEKIN.

FROM A SKETCH BY OUR SPECIAL ARTIST, MR. JULIUS M. PRICE.

1891 年 9 月 19 日《伦敦新闻画报》

大清总税务司罗伯特·赫德在他北京的“办公间”

Sir Robert Hart, G.C.M.G. Inspector-General of Chinese Customs, in his “den” at Pekin.

赫德（1835. 2—1911. 2），英国爱尔兰人，28 岁担任大清海关总税务司，在清朝帝国制度中创造出了唯一廉洁不贪腐的高效衙门；他主持中国海关 45 年，死后被清政府追授为“太子太保”。

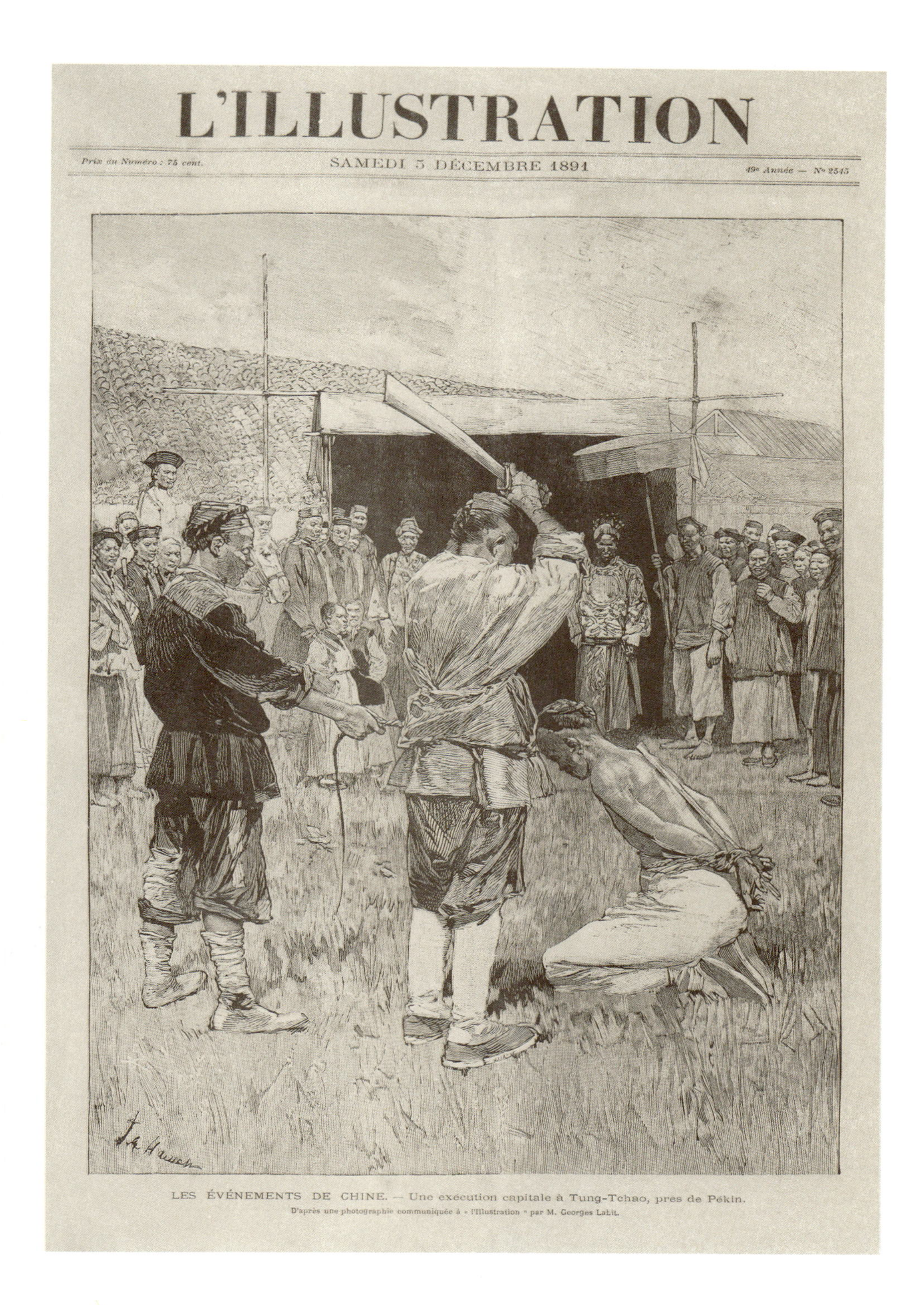

L'ILLUSTRATION

Prix du Numéro : 75 cent. SAMEDI 5 DÉCEMBRE 1891 49e Année — No 2545

LES ÉVÉNEMENTS DE CHINE. — Une exécution capitale à Tung-Tchao, pres de Pékin.

D'après une photographie communiquée à « l'Illustration » par M. Georges Labit.

1891 年 12 月 5 日《插图报》

关于中国事态的报道——一个犯人在北京附近的唐山被处极刑

Les événements de Chine.—Une exécution capitale à Tung-Tchao, près de Pékin.

LES ÉVÉNEMENTS DE CHINE. — Un tribunal chinois. — D'après des photographies communiquées par M. Georges Labit.

1891 年 12 月 5 日《插图报》

关于中国事态的报道—— 一个中国法庭

Les événements de Chine.—Un tribunal chinois.

首先是司法，看看中国官员是如何执法的吧。如果被告人在犯罪现场被抓获，或者拘禁了一段时间之后，被带上公堂。原告、证人和被告跪在地上，头挨地，依靠膝盖和肘关节爬着向前移动。在等待审判官审问及宣判的时候，一直保持着这种姿势。通常，这种审判用不了多长时间，尤其当被告是一个身无分文的可怜人的时候。在中国，其实公正是一桩无关紧要的事情，可以用钱买卖；“没钱的话，就用你的人头来偿还吧！”判决即刻执行。可怜人知道一旦落入司法部门的手中，他就没指望了。他几乎都没有抬头望一望法庭上方闪闪发光的著名哲学家——孔子的画像，也没有能瞧一眼审判桌前面的可怕的红色汉字。

前面说到，判决之后，立刻行刑。事实上，行刑的地点就在法庭门口的公共广场上。这个场景就发生在天朝的帝都附近，我们亲眼目睹了刽子手行刑。

不管可怜人是杀了一个欧洲人，还是偷了一枚价值一个生丁的铜钱，审判官都可以根据自己的喜好，判以同样的刑罚。故而说到底，谁知道这是一个十恶不赦的坏人或仅仅只是一个乞丐呢。

——《中国记事》(选译)，1891 年 12 月 5 日《插图报》

1891年12月5日《插图报》

天主教传教团在中国——天津的智障人士和痼疾患者收容所

Les missions catholiques en Chine.—Un asile d'aliénés et d'incurables à Tien-Tsin.

此处有一个奇特的细节：任何一个来中国传教的神父或修女，首先会脱掉神职人员的衣服，换上中式服装。修女们就这样穿上了短衫和蓝色裤子，把头发留起来，盘成一个中国式的大发髻；唯一的区别性标志就是她们在胸前佩戴了一枚银十字架。尽管天津的收容院属于在中国的天主教会，但它本质上是一家中国机构。然而，可以在插图中看出，除了那个站在纺车后面、身着黑色的监督者外，剩下的修女们都是欧洲人。

——《中国记事》(选译)，1891年12月5日《插图报》

SUPPLEMENT TO THE ILLUSTRATED LONDON NEWS, Nov. 24, 1894.—3

THE WAR IN THE EAST.

THE MIKADO MUTSUHITO, EMPEROR OF JAPAN,
IN THE UNIFORM OF COMMANDER-IN-CHIEF OF THE ARMY.

The Japanese Empire is of very ancient date; but in the twelfth century the hereditary Mikado was deprived of the actual ruling power; which was exercised by the Shiogoon, head of the feudal nobility. Since 1868, the Shiogoon having been overthrown, the Mikado has been the ruling Sovereign. Mutsuhito was born in 1852, and succeeded his father in 1867.

THE EMPEROR OF CHINA, TSAI-TIEN HWANG-TI.

The Manchu dynasty of Tsing was established in 1644. The present sovereign, Tsai-Tien, who reigns under the name of Kwang-Su, is ninth Emperor of the Manchu dynasty. He was born in 1871, and is nephew to the Empress Regent, mother of the last Emperor, Tung Chih. In 1887, Tsai-Tien assumed the nominal reigning authority; in 1889 took the control of government.

1894 年 11 月 24 日《伦敦新闻画报》

1 日本明治天皇——睦仁着全军统帅服

2 中国光绪皇帝——载湉

1 The Mikado Mutsuhito, Emperor of Japan,in the uniform of Commander-in-Chief of the Army.

2 The Emperor of China, Tsai-Tien Hwang-Ti.

日本帝制历史悠远，但在 12 世纪，天皇对国家的统治权力被剥夺，转由封建贵族的首领——幕府将军操控。1868 年，幕府被推翻，天皇重新成为实际的君主。睦仁 1852 年出生，1867 年继承父亲的皇位。

满族的清王朝建立于 1644 年，现任君主载湉——光绪帝是清第九位皇帝。载湉生于 1871 年，他是前任同治帝的生母——摄政皇太后的外甥。1887 年，载湉开始名义上的亲政，1889 年开始实际执政。

1895年1月5日《哈珀斯周刊》

福泽谕吉——庆应义塾大学校长铜像，大熊氏广雕刻，由热爱学校的校友捐赠

Bronze statue of Yukichi Fukuzawa, president of Keiogijiuku University, Japan.—Ujihiro Okuma, Sculptor. Presented to the School by his devoted Followers.

19 世纪后半期随着明治维新的展开，日本社会上涌现出一批主张向西方敞开大门的政治思想家，其中最著名的非福泽谕吉莫属，他著名的“脱亚入欧”理论和“争韩论”引导日本一步步地向军国主义走去。这篇对福泽谕吉的介绍题为“一位伟大的日本凡人”，日本利用西方媒体的娴熟从中可见一斑，文中写道：

“福泽谕吉从来就不是一个政治领袖，他对国家和民族后期的影响与教育主要是通过他写的著作，来教育国人。他是第一个把西方国家的社会和政治制度，连同他们的成就和先进的科学、实用的艺术展示给日本人民的人。

“据说，在日文里的一些词汇，譬如英语里面‘自由’，又譬如‘权利’和‘特权’，‘责任’和‘义务’，‘新闻’和‘演讲’等，在日本的同义词都出自福泽谕吉的创造。他把公开演讲带到了日本，这在西方国家是平常之事，但是在日本还是新鲜事物，日本人不擅长在公众面前表达。大约 20 年前，福泽先生和他的追随者在一个小房间里练习公开辩论演说术和演讲。当有一些演讲者开始可以勇敢面对观众的目光时，他在学校校园里建起了一座小礼堂，就开始了每两周一次的公开演讲。”

——《福泽谕吉——一位伟大的日本凡人》（选译）

1895 年 1 月 5 日《哈珀斯周刊》

THE ILLUSTRATED LONDON NEWS, FEB. 6, 1875.—121

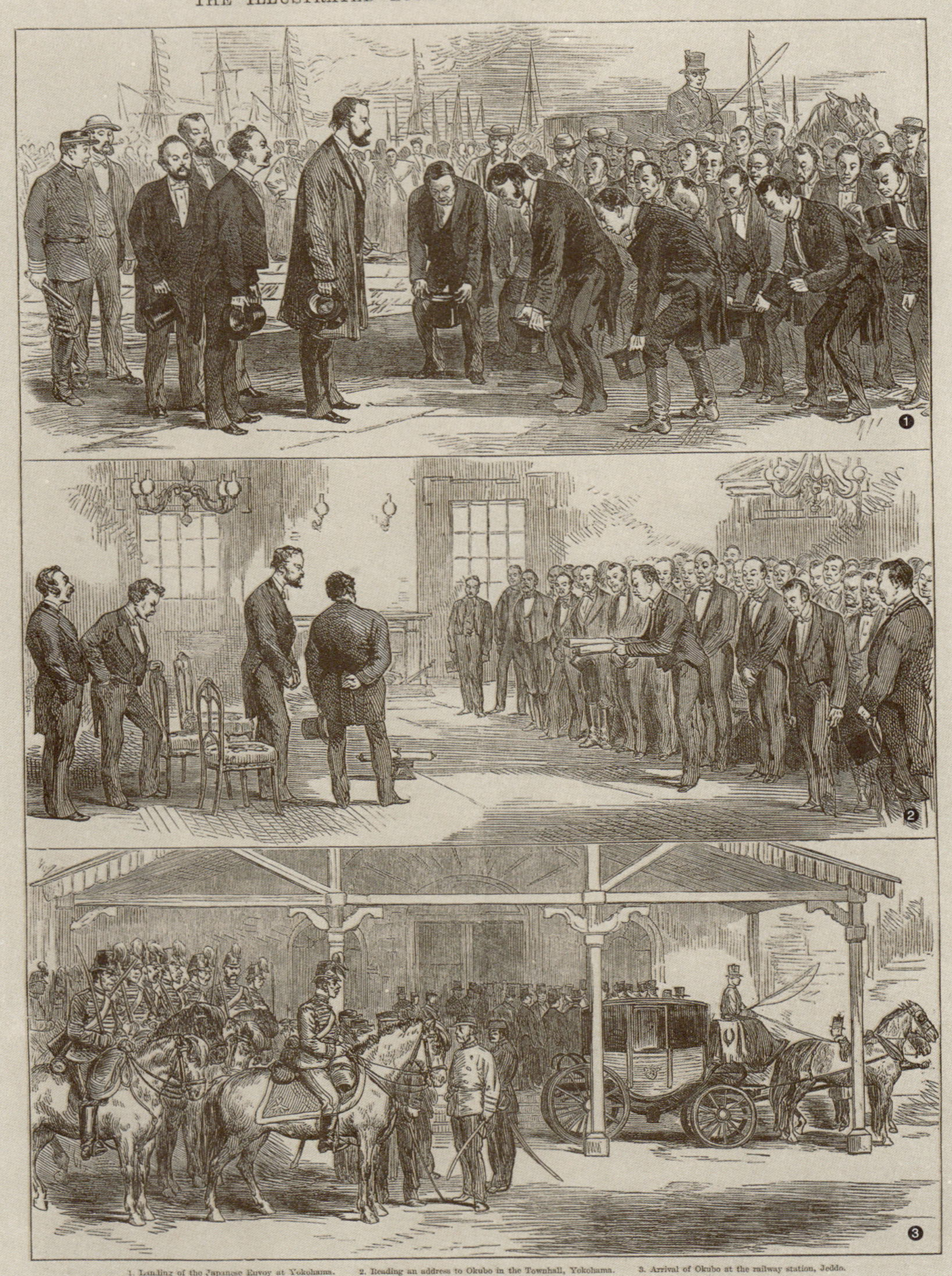

1. Landing of the Japanese Envoy at Yokohama. 2. Reading an address to Okubo in the Townhall, Yokohama. 3. Arrival of Okubo at the railway station, Jeddo.

PEACE BETWEEN CHINA AND JAPAN: SKETCHES BY OUR SPECIAL ARTIST AT YOKOHAMA.

1875 年 2 月 6 日《伦敦新闻画报》

“牡丹社事件”后，大久保利通从中国和谈归国。图为该报特派横滨画师的速写

Peace between China and Japan: sketches by our special artist at Yokohama.

1 日本和谈代表团抵达横滨
2 在横滨市政厅向大久保利通宣读欢迎辞
3 大久保利通一行到达东京火车站

1 Landing of the Japanese Envoy at Yokohama.
2 Reading an address to Okubo in the Townhall , Yokohama.
3 Arrival of Okubo at the railway station, Jeddo.

1871 年，琉球王国属民 66 人驾船遇风浪在台湾东南端登岛，54 人遭到岛上原住民杀害。1874 年 5 月，视琉球为藩属的日本以问罪为名武力登陆台湾，迫使原住民妥协，并派出内务卿大久保利通为全权办理大臣赴北京谈判。大久保利通以拒绝撤军相要挟，与清朝签订了《北京专约》，在条约中清廷变相承认了琉球与日本的藩属关系，称日本出兵台湾是“保民义举”，并承诺赔偿 50 万两白银，以换取日本于 1874 年底从台湾撤军。中国称此为“牡丹社事件”。此后清廷加强了对台湾的管理，彻底解除了对大陆人的渡台禁令，并于 1888 年在台湾设省。对日本而言，此次事件是明治政府的初次海外征讨，更是近代日本利用西方新闻媒体进行战地报道的初次体验。虽然日本政府最终只默许了一家本国媒体的记者随军赴台，但在面对英美报刊的战地报道申请时几乎有求必应，当时的《纽约先驱论坛报》甚至得到了日本官方“将极尽所能予以协助”的回应。

1894年9月29日《插图报》

1 明治天皇睦仁

2 山县有朋元帅——日本陆军司令

3 伊藤博文伯爵——内阁首相

1 S. M. Mutsu-Hito, empereur du Japon.

2 Le Maréchal Comte Yamagata—Commandant en chef de l'armée Japonaise.

3 S. Ex. le Comte Ito—Président du Conseil des ministres.

山县有朋（1836—1922），日本近代陆军之父，日本明治新军的鼻祖，甲午战争中任日军第一军司令官，因作战时独断专行被卸任。

伊藤博文（1841—1909），日本首任内阁总理大臣，明治维新的旗手。甲午战争中，伊藤博文是主战慎重派，主导清日停战，并代表日本签署了中日《马关条约》。

1894 年 10 月 27 日《哈珀斯周刊》

1　日本海军创始人——胜海舟伯爵
2　日本海军副元帅——桦山资纪
3　日本海军基地和船厂——横须贺

1　Count Katsu Awa—founder of the Japanese navy.
2　Vice-Admiral Kabayama.
3　The Japanese naval station and ship-yards at Yokoska.

胜海舟（1822—1899），日本幕府末期的开明政治家，江户幕府海军负责人，后在明治政府中任海军卿等职；明治维新后，新政府曾任命胜海舟为参议兼海军卿，但不久他便辞职退隐。

桦山资纪（1837—1922），1890 年任海军大臣，1893 年任海军军令部长；甲午战争时参与指挥；1895 年 5 月出任日本第一任台湾总督。

HARPER'S WEEKLY

A JOURNAL OF CIVILIZATION

Vol. XXXVIII.—No. 1972.
Copyright, 1894, by Harper & Brothers.
All Rights Reserved.

NEW YORK, SATURDAY, OCTOBER 6, 1894.

TEN CENTS A COPY.
FOUR DOLLARS A YEAR.

COUNT SAIGO,
Minister of the Marine.

VISCOUNT ENOMOTO,
Vice-Admiral of the Navy, and Minister of Commerce and Agriculture.

COUNT ITO,
The Prime Minister of Japan.

SHIPS OF THE JAPANESE NAVY.—Drawn by T. Morimoto.

THE JAPANESE OCCUPATION OF KOREA.—[See Page 942.]

1894 年 10 月 6 日《哈珀斯周刊》

1 西乡从道伯爵——海军大臣

2 榎本武扬子爵——海军副元帅，农业与商贸大臣

3 伊藤博文伯爵，日本首相

4 日本联合舰队

近景中的两艘为旗舰“松岛”号和“吉野”号——编者注

1 Count Saigo, Minister of the Marine.

2 Viscount Enomoto, Vice-Admiral of the Navy, and Minister of Commerce and Agriculture.

3 Count Ito, The Prime Minister of Japan.

4 Ships of the Japanese Navy.

美国著名画家沃尔斯（Theodore Wores）绘制了左图中伊藤博文画像，他为 1894 年 10 月 6 日的《哈珀斯周刊》撰写了回忆文章：“这位杰出领袖带领日本从中世纪封建社会进入 19 世纪资本主义社会，我怀着非比寻常的兴趣，开始着手在画布上呈现出他独特的气质。我在东京为伊藤爵士绘制肖像期间，多次听他愉快地提及他与李鸿章的友情，他为我展示了很多李鸿章亲笔撰写的挂在墙上的卷轴字幅，这些都是他出访北京时，李鸿章亲自赠送给他的礼物。当时是 1879 年，那时的他大概无论如何也不可能预见到，他将带领日本与中国开战。”

THE JAPANESE PARLIAMENT, OPENED BY THE MIKADO, NOV. 29, AT TOKYO.

1891 年 1 月 17 日《伦敦新闻画报》

日本国会，（1890 年）11 月 29 日于东京由天皇主持开幕

The Japanese Parliament, opened by the Mikado, Nov. 29, at Tokyo.

1891 年 1 月 24 日《图片报》

日本议会，上周二（1891 年 1 月 20 日）毁于火灾的日本新国会大楼内景（根据日本画师的画作制版）

Interior of the new Japanese Parliament House, burnt down on Tuesday last.

1889 年，《大日本帝国宪法》颁布，日本成为东亚首个拥有近代宪法的立宪君主制国家。1890 年 11 月 29 日，日本的第一届帝国议会召开，《大日本帝国宪法》于当天正式施行。这篇题为《日本的第一次议会》的报道称：国会众议院的选举过程井然有序，社会就像当时英国的选举一样平静，这并不是因为民众对政治的冷漠。恰恰相反，日本文盲率很低，从黄包车夫到富商，几乎每个人都读报、关心时政。每天清晨，投递员在公鸡打鸣前就把报纸分发到各家各户了。明治维新后没落了的武士阶层组成了自称为“社会主义”的政党，他们实际上是一群无政府主义者，在议会选举中没有取得任何席位，但据说通过恐吓和刺杀，控制了一大批议员。日本国民一直翘企帝国议会的召开，不少城市张灯结彩，欢呼雀跃。文章插图上的议会会议大厅是依照美国参议院布局设计的，议员的座席有数排，呈弧形，面朝选举出的会议主持人席，主持人后方的中心位置是天皇的宝座。然而新的议会大楼投入使用没两个月就被一场大火吞没；《图片报》的这篇报道刊发在火灾后仅四天时间，记者还不了解火灾是由电线短路引起的，所以在结尾还猜测是“社会党”人纵火。

THE HARBOR OF KOBÉ—AT THE HEAD OF THE INLAND SEA, AND THE SHIPPING-POINT FOR KIOTO AND OSAKA.

ENTRANCE TO NAGASAKI HARBOR.

NAGASAKI—THE MOST IMPORTANT PORT OF SOUTHERN JAPAN.

NAGASAKI HARBOR, SHOWING DRY DOCK.

THE INDUSTRIAL MOVEMENT IN JAPAN.—[SEE PAGE 45.]

1898 年 1 月 8 日《哈珀斯周刊》

日本的工业化进程

1 神户港——内海的尽头，大阪和京都的出海口

2 长崎港入口

3 长崎——日本南部最重要的港口

4 长崎港干船坞

The Industrial movement in Japan.

1 The harbor of Kobé—At the head of the inland sea, and the shipping-point for Kioto and Osaka.

2 Entrance to Nagasaki harbor.

3 Nagasaki—the most important port of southern Japan.

4 Nagasaki harbor, showing dry dock.

日本工业运动的发端可能在 1870 年左右。大约在此期间，日本成立了农业部门、公共工程部门。日本第一场真正意义上的改革拉开了帷幕。改革的第一桩大事就是建设通讯线路。日本的第一条铁路就是工业运动的成果，帝国政府将它修建在神户市和大阪之间，另一条架设在首都东京与横滨市之间的铁路也于同期开工。1870 年，日本铁路线总长 40 英里，时至今日，日本开行的铁路线总长达 2000 英里。

——《日本的工业化进程》(选译)，1898 年 1 月 8 日《哈珀斯周刊》

1894年9月8日《伦敦新闻画报》

三位日本军官

Japanese officers.

这张照片摄于1886年，上面的三位日本陆军军官是派到印度学习考察军事管理与设施的。中间的这位是陆军少校福岛，他的右侧是另一位日本军官，而他的左手是一位军医。在印度（英国殖民）政府的协助下，这三位日军军官由一位英军军官陪同，穿越了印度。这位英军官员就是照片后排站立的来自旁遮普第六步兵团的额穆斯顿上尉（后来在西北部边境的黑山遇害）。额穆斯顿上尉曾经评价说，他们三位“容易亲近且极为睿智”。在三个月的穿越中，他们先后考察了印度的兵工厂、兵站、军事设施，在此之后，与额穆斯顿上尉依依惜别。毋庸置疑，他们给日本带回了大量关于军队组织和训练的宝贵经验，这些经验无疑在最近日本战争部“紧张有序地征集动员了16万军队”，以及日军闪电占领朝鲜时发挥了作用。特别应该提到的是，福岛少校和他的同伴们能够流利地用英语交谈。福岛少校从印度归国后，用日文出版了《印度行纪》一书。

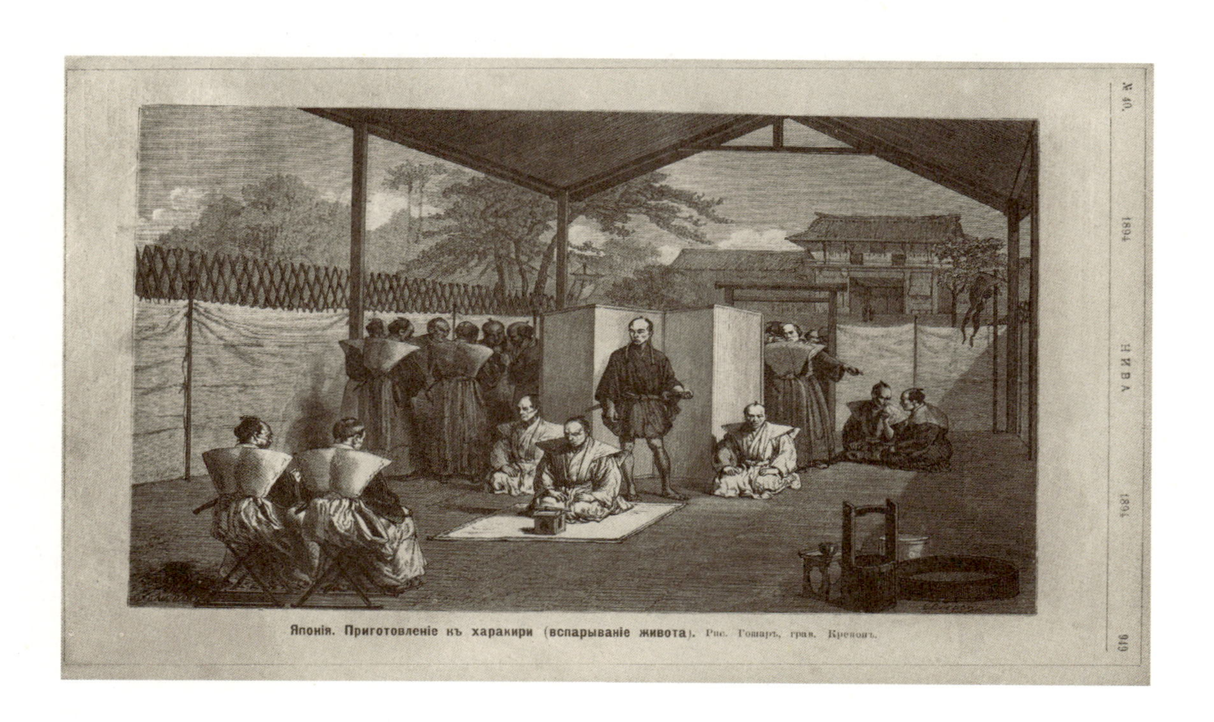

俄国《田野》周刊

日本武士准备剖腹自杀

Японія. Приготовленіе нъ харанири (вспарываніе живота).

俄国《田野》周刊

朝鲜战争中的日军装束

Война въ Корet. формы kntaйской арміи.

从左至右：近卫军官、列兵、炮兵、工兵、将军、将军的副官、近卫军官、海军军官、水兵

右图：

1894 年 10 月 20 日《伦敦新闻画报》

日本军队从 1867 年至今（1894 年）的不同发展演变阶段

Successive stages in the development of the Japanese army from 1867 to the present day.

右图整版 9 张组图展示了日本军队的发展演变，这组图片根据日本画师的水彩画制版，在西方媒体中广为流传。

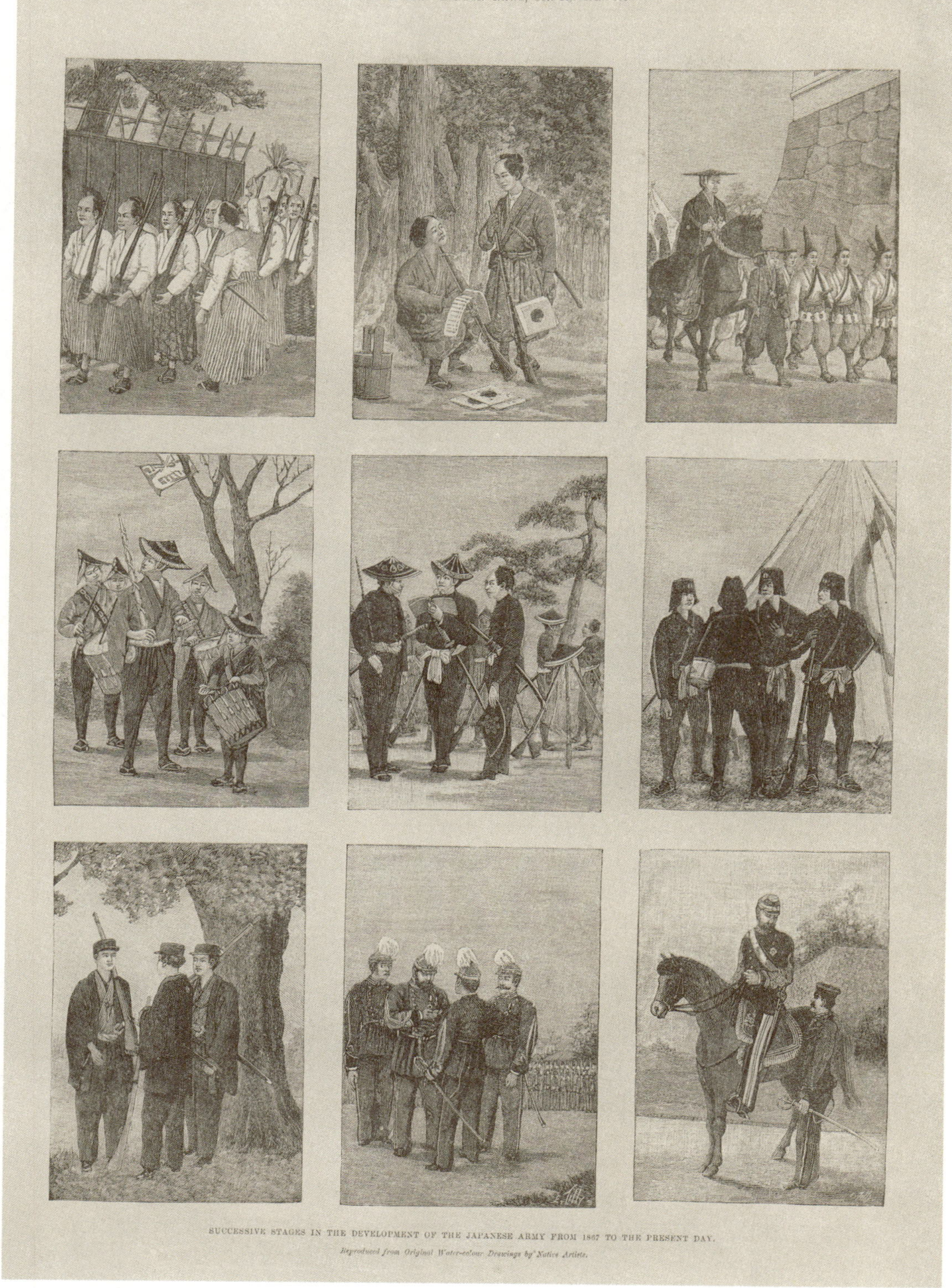

THE ILLUSTRATED LONDON NEWS, Oct. 20, 1894.—500

SUCCESSIVE STAGES IN THE DEVELOPMENT OF THE JAPANESE ARMY FROM 1867 TO THE PRESENT DAY.

Reproduced from Original Water-colour Drawings by Native Artists.

1894年9月1日《哈珀斯周刊》

1 日本天皇
2 日本皇后

1 The Emperor of Japan.
2 The Empress of Japan.

明治天皇祐宫睦仁（1852—1912），近代日本国的象征，维新改革支持者。在甲午战争期间，他作为日本陆海军最高统帅，常驻广岛大本营，督导战争。

昭宪皇后（1849—1914），本名一条美子，有“天狗娘娘”之称。她以唐太宗长孙皇后为榜样，襄助国政，开办新式女子学校，热心红十字会活动，树立坂本龙马为海军之神。

结　语

现今只有愚昧无知、顽固不化者才会臆断日本依然是个未开化的国家。事实上，日本是一个广泛推行义务教育的国家，有本土的大学、私立学校与公立学校；日本亦是一个艺术之国，日本的艺术古色古香，独具匠心，当然很可能我们的艺术留给日本人的也是这种印象。无论从道德标准还是行为规范，日本人所展现出的优雅常常令我们这些西方的基督徒们汗颜。

——本杰明・福罗文（B.O. Flower）撰文《为日本仗义执言》
1894 年 7 月　美国《竞技场月刊》

我对设宴款待我的中国官员们说，他们最大的麻烦是缺乏爱国精神、对国家的责任感以及团结一致、同仇敌忾的意愿和能力……在思考中国的这场战争和其他任何战争的时候，读者必须明白，中国并不是由一个民族构成的，而是由一群人组成的。一位美国的前外交官曾经糊涂地把中国描述为一个整体，“犹如冰川一般向敌人袭去”，实际上中国像一个百孔千疮的沙袋，一拳击去，沙子四处飞溅。

——朱利安・拉尔夫撰文《可怜的老中国》
1894 年 12 月　美国《哈珀斯周刊》

Le Petit Journal

Le Petit Journal

Le Supplément illustré

SUPPLÉMENT ILLUSTRÉ

Huit pages : CINQ centimes

ABONNEMENTS

Onzième année — DIMANCHE 8 JUILLET 1900 — Numéro 503

SY-TAY-HEOU
Impératrice douairière de Chine

1900年7月8日《小日报》

慈禧太后肖像

四　沉没的“高升”

中日战争的爆发只不过是一个以天计算的问题，甚至可能是几个小时以后的事情。日本国会对政府的不满正在与日俱增，对政府而言，与其陷入内战，一场对外的战争显然比可能陷入内战更值得期待：它可以把日本国民重新凝聚在一起；它更是一个出气阀，把日本社会和政局中近几年来的积怨排解出去。

——1894 年 6 月 29 日　上海英文报纸《字林西报》

日本国内的局势严峻，和中国开战可以缓解我们的压力，激发人民的爱国心，更重要的是，战争可以把人民和政府牢牢地绑在一起。

——战争爆发前夕，
日本驻美国公使建野乡三对美国国务卿格雷沙姆坦言

Septième année N° 43 EDITION COMPLÈTE — VINGT-CINQ CENTIMES — LITTÉRATURE ET MODE Dimanche 28 Octobre 1894

L'Illustré SOLEIL DU DIMANCHE

LA GUERRE ENTRE LA CHINE ET LE JAPON
Embarquement de recrues chinoises dans le golfe du Petchili

1894 年 10 月 28 日《星期日太阳报》

中日战争爆发，清军新募兵勇在渤海湾港口登舰赴敌

La guerre entre la Chine et le Japon. Embarquement de recrues chinoises dans le golfe du Petchili.

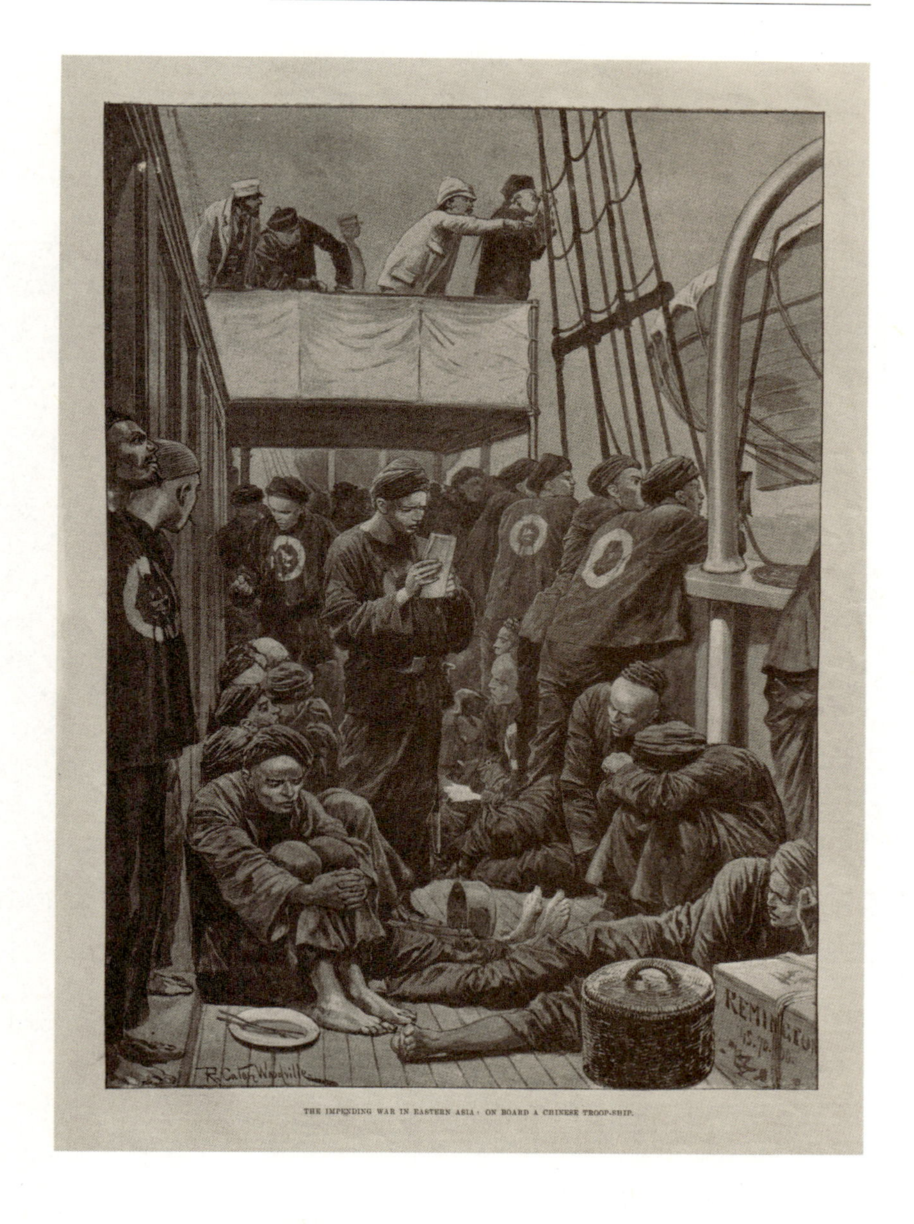

THE IMPENDING WAR IN EASTERN ASIA: ON BOARD A CHINESE TROOP-SHIP.

1894 年 8 月 4 日《伦敦新闻画报》

东亚战争一触即发：一艘中国运兵船上的情景

The impending in Eastern Asia: on board a Chinese troop-ship.

正在驶往仁川的高升号运兵船，在飞桥上向远方瞭望的有清军的两位将领、英籍船长，以及一位神秘的德国籍“私人旅客”——汉纳根（蓄络腮胡须者）。

SINKING OF THE CHINESE TROOP-SHIP "KOW-SHING" BY THE JAPANESE CRUISER "NANIWA KAN."

From an Engraving in the "Tokyo Asahi," supplied by Mr. Arthur B. Brown.

1894年10月6日《伦敦新闻画报》

中国高升号运兵船被日本浪速号巡洋舰击中后，开始沉没

Sinking of the Chinese troop-ship "Kow-Shing" by the Japanese cruiser "Naniwa Kan."

取自《东京朝日新闻》报上的版画，由亚瑟·布朗先生提供

From an engraving in the "Tokyo Asahi", supplied by Mr. Arthur B. Brown.

THE JAPANESE WAR-SHIP "NANIWA KAN."

日本“浪速”号

The Japanese war-ship “Naniwa Kan”.

日本浪速号巡洋舰，1886年6月26日交付日本海军，航速18节，马力7604，舰长东乡平八郎。

东乡平八郎（1848—1934），日本海军元帅，海军大将，侯爵，与陆军的乃木希典并称日本军国主义的“军神”。1894年7月25日，在丰岛海域发现英籍运输船高升号，担任浪速号舰长的东乡发现运输船上有中国士兵，下令发射鱼雷并开炮，1000多名中国士兵溺亡。1905年日俄战争中，他在对马海峡海战中率领日本海军击败俄国海军，成了近代史上东方黄种人打败西方白种人的先例，使他得到“东方纳尔逊”之誉。由于他和大山岩同藩，所以时人称颂“陆上大山、海上东乡”。

1894 年 9 月 22 日《图片报》

东方的战争：高升号被日军击沉。根据一名幸存者的草图绘制，左侧开炮的军舰为浪速号

The war in the East: the sinking of the transport "Kow-Shing" by the Japanese. From a sketch supplied by one of the survivors.

我看到一枚鱼雷从日本战舰发射出来，紧接着日舰的六门炮同时开火，在鱼雷命中目标时，这几门炮已经发射了两轮。鱼雷击中了我舰正中，很可能是装煤的燃料舱……我想我们就是在那个时刻从船上跳下海的。我一边游泳，一边看着我们的船开始往下沉……这个时候，日舰一直在不停地开炮……我看到一个装满士兵的小船从日舰上被放下水，我还以为他们是来救我们这些幸存者的，可悲惨的是，我完全搞错了，他们把子弹射向正在被淹没的船上的人们。

——冯·汉纳根上尉的宣誓证词，1894 年 9 月 22 日《图片报》

I saw a torpedo leaping from the Japanese man-of-war's torpedo port, and immediately afterwards all six guns opened fire. They discharged their guns twice before the torpedo arrived at its aim. It hit the ship amidships—probably exactly at her coal bunkers. ... I believe we then all jumped and swam. I , swimming, saw the ship going down. She went stern first. During this the firing continued. ...I saw a Japanese boat lowered heavily armed with men. I thought they were coming to the rescue of the remaining men, but I was sadly mistaken. They fired into the men on board the sinking ship.

—— Extract from Captain von Hanneken's sworn statement

这位高升号上的神秘旅客，就是被中国朋友们称作“韩大人”的冯·汉纳根。汉纳根出身于德国军人世家，1879 年从德国陆军退役后，经天津海关税务司德璀琳介绍，赴天津武备学堂任教官，后受到李鸿章赏识，担任其军事顾问，协助其筹办北洋水师，用德国技术和设备设计建造了旅顺金山炮台和威海卫炮台。很多历史学家和日军调查报告都相信，以“私人名义”与 1200 名清军同赴朝鲜的汉纳根，实际上受李鸿章之托去牙山协助清军修筑炮台，准备应对即将到来的战争。高升号被浪速舰击沉后，汉纳根跳水奋力地游上了丰岛。他找到一只渔船辗转到了仁川港，在那里，他说服了德国军舰伊尔达号开赴丰岛营救泅水上岸的清兵，后来一艘英国的军舰也参加了营救，200 多名被困在岛上的幸存官兵获救。李鸿章对此心怀感激，授以汉纳根花翎总兵衔，入北洋水师担任总教习兼副提督。汉纳根随即参与指挥了黄海大战，身负重伤，后离开了北洋水师。但他没有离开中国，而是为清廷策划了一整套训练新式陆军的方案，这就是后来袁世凯的新军！

1894 年 8 月 13 日《小日报》

朝鲜战局，一艘中国船被日本人击沉

Les événements de Corée. Un vaisseau Chinois coulé par les japonais.

结 语

7月26日，高升号遇难的次日，法国小炮舰雄狮号从仁川港出发，在丰岛北端，发现高升号的残骸在海面上垂直地漂浮着，两根桅杆露出水面，桅杆上攀附着40多名清兵，有的枪伤严重。雄狮号为获救人员提供了食品、淡水和衣服，并当即对伤员进行了救治，之后即迅速把所有人运送到了烟台。

日本未宣而战、击沉英国商船、见死不救，而后法、德、英三国军舰纷纷介入营救遇难官兵，给了大清的政界和舆论界巨大鼓舞。8月29日，光绪帝下旨对参与救援的三国军舰上的人员颁奖。李鸿章在电报中说“高升号系怡和船，租与我用，上挂英旗，倭敢无故击毁，英国必不答应”。然而，人道主义援助与政治立场无关，西方列强远没有像清廷期盼的那样进一步干涉日本的军事行动。西方的媒体也很快停止用激烈的言辞在中、日两国间站队，相反，他们对学术界在国际法方面的讨论表现出了浓厚兴趣。

2001年，韩国打捞公司在“高升号”沉没海域打捞出沉船遗物及部分遗骨。

——编者

中国和日本分别代表着封闭与开化两股势力，西方国家自然会更亲近日本。如果日本有最终战胜的机会，西方都应该放弃干涉的动议。然而中国的最终战败几乎是不可能想象的，因而如果西方不立即阻止这场战争，最终的结果必将是日本战败后丧失独立，继而日本也会加入中国，充满忌恨地把西方的“洋鬼佬”赶出国门。如果出于猜忌，欧洲列强不愿出兵干预，美国应该挺身而出，虽然这与美国奉行的门罗主义相违背，但事态的特殊性应该让美国考虑暂时放弃原则。为了不对全球贸易造成毁灭性的打击，冲突必须停止。

——1894年8月12日 英国《每日新闻报》

英国国际法权威、牛津大学胡兰德（T. E. Holland）教授认为：虽然敌对交火开始时双方并未宣战，但高升号被击沉本身就已经代表实际意义上的开战，无论高升号悬挂哪国国旗，日本有权利攻击一个将要对它在战争中产生巨大威胁的军事目标。日本释放了被救的中立国船员已经履行了国际法义务，它不需要道歉和赔款，胡兰德认为日本此举野蛮的主张无根据。

——1894年8月　美国《费城纪录报》

五　黄海悲歌：不沉的“致远”

感谢上天，不是在我们的家门口，而是在远东，我们见识到花费了巨款建造出来的最新一代舰艇和最新一代的引擎究竟威力如何。如果还以为亚洲人在战场上的时候依然是脊梁上涂着龙、背着弓，那就大错特错了。他们的武器配备已经和我们的一样先进了……您看到了吗？在日本，战争这么雄壮地揭开了帷幕，欧洲国家多么羡慕啊！

——1894年8月13日　法国《小日报》

1894 年 10 月 13 日《图片报》

1 日本舰千代田号军官合影

2 黄海海战中沉没的中国战船致远号军官合影

1 The war in the East: group of Japanese officers on the cruiser "Chiyoda".

2 The war in the East: group of Chinese officers on the "Chih Yuen", sunk in the Yalu River engagement.

日本千代田号装甲巡洋舰于 1891 年建成，内田正敏为舰长；其舰在甲午战争中参加了黄海海战和威海卫之战。

1887 年北洋舰队副提督英国人琅威理奉命前往英国验收致远舰、靖远舰等，随同前往接舰的管带有邓世昌，此照片是邓世昌率领致远官兵与琅威理的合影。

1894 年 9 月 29 日《伦敦新闻画报》

中国战舰镇远号上的海军军官

Officers of the Chinese war-ship “Chen-Yuen”.

由于当时摄影者标注发音问题，我们无法查找到镇远号这四位军官的真实姓名。根据音译，Hoo king Yung 可能是杨用霖（1854—1895），当时镇远大副，在 1894 年黄海海战之后，镇远舰返回威海卫时不慎触礁，管带林泰曾忧愤自杀，杨用霖升任管带，在丁汝昌和刘步蟾自杀后，拒绝代表北洋舰队向伊东祐亨投降，开枪自杀。

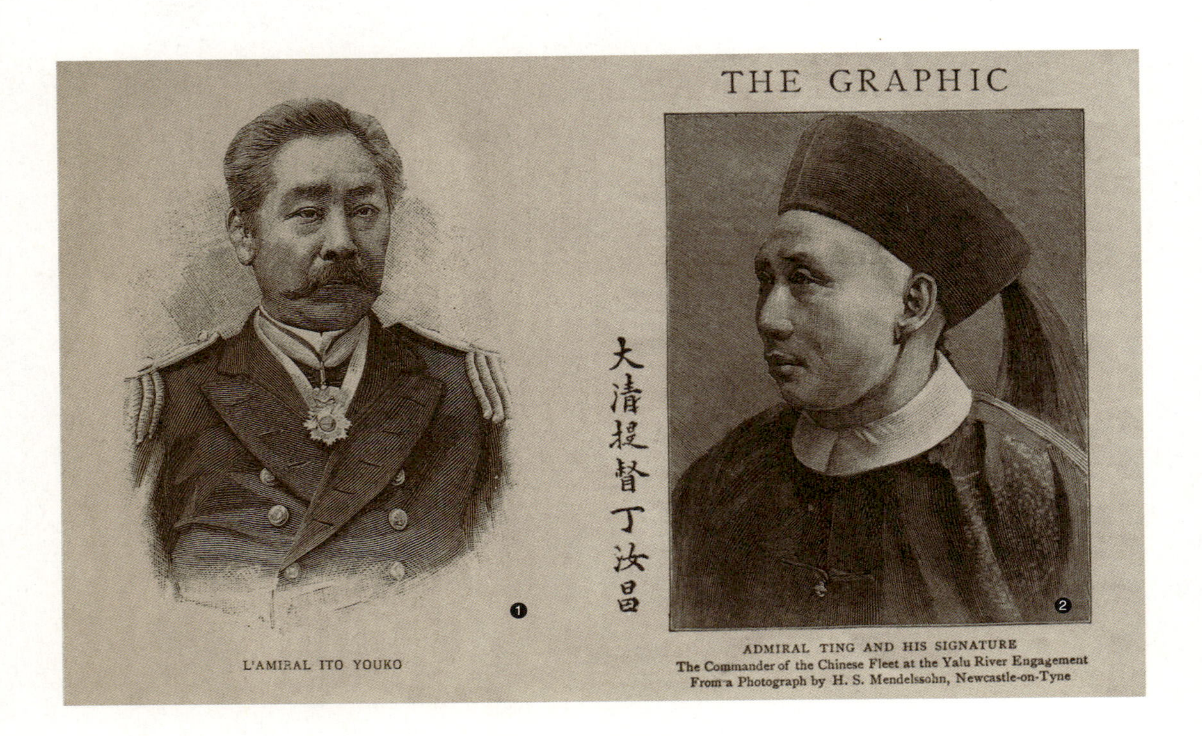

1895年2月16日《插图报》

1 参加黄海海战的日本舰队指挥官伊东祐亨元帅

1 L'Amiral Ito Youko.

1894年10月13日《图片报》

2 参加黄海海战的中国舰队指挥官、北洋水师提督丁汝昌元帅

2 Admiral Ting and his signature. The commander of the Chinese fleet at the Yalu River engagement.

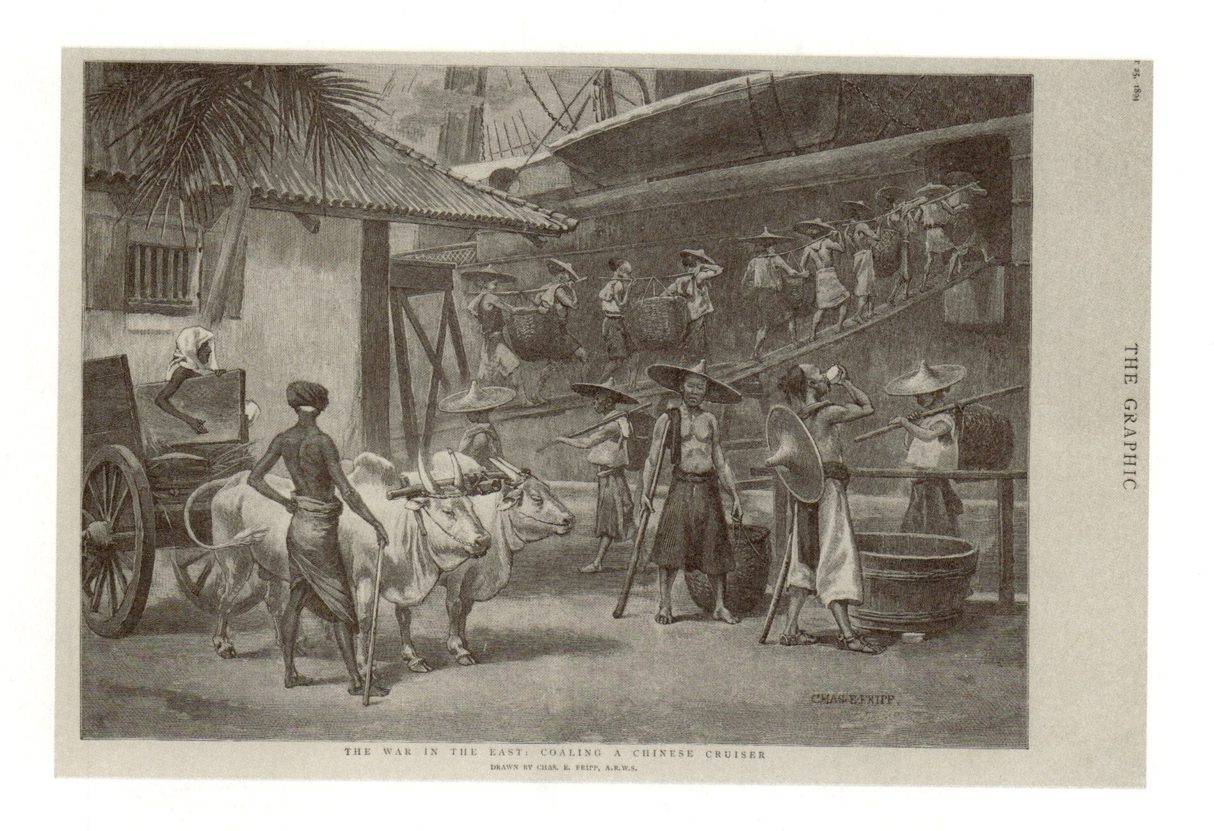

1894 年 8 月 25 日《图片报》

东方的战争：中国巡洋舰在港口添煤

The war in the East: coaling a Chinese cruiser.

北洋舰队的战舰一直采用的是唐山开平煤矿（即今开滦煤矿）提供的精选五槽煤；该煤是优质煤，燃烧力强，能提高航速；同时烟尘量小，船在行驶时，不易被敌军发现。然而在甲午战争前不久，五槽煤就被换成了散碎、劣质的八槽煤。提督丁汝昌曾致函开平煤矿负责人、醇亲王亲信张翼交涉，无果；后又向李鸿章申诉，亦无果。

SUPPLEMENT TO THE GRAPHIC, DECEMBER 1, 1894

CHINESE WARSHIPS

Illustrations and descriptions of the more important ships which took part in the battle of the Yalu and other engagements with the Japanese since the declaration of war. The details are from information received up to the present time.

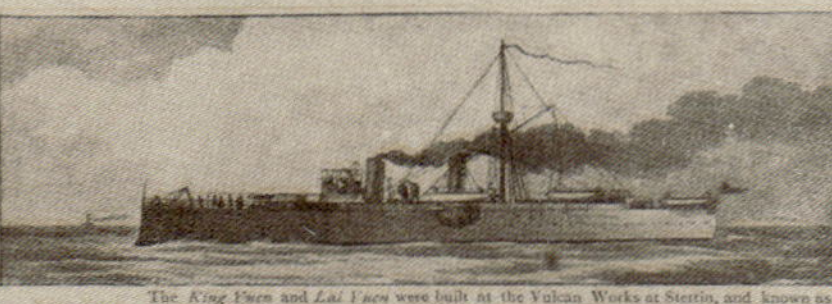

KING YUEN

The *King Yuen* and *Lai Yuen* were built at the Vulcan Works at Stettin, and known as "coast defence" ships. Their principal dimensions are:—Length, 269 feet; beam, 39 feet 4 inches; mean draught, 16 feet 8 inches; displacement, 2,900 tons. Protection is afforded by a belt of compound armour six feet wide, and from 5·1 inches to 9·5 inches thick, which extends the length of the machinery and boiler space, and is terminated by thwartship armoured bulkheads 5·1 inches thick. At the forward end of the belt a revolving turret with six-inch armour contains two 8·27-inch Krupps. The armament also comprised two 5·9-inch Krupps and seven quick-firing guns. These ships have double bottoms. Their trial speed was sixteen knots. They were both present at the battle of the Yalu River, where the *King Yuen* was cut off from her consorts and sunk by a small gunboat.

The Chinese Fleet at the battle of the Yalu was considerably overmatched in armament by that of their more energetic opponents, and suffered accordingly. Of the fourteen vessels actually engaged, in addition to the six transports and six torpedo boats, four were sunk.

CHEN YUEN

The *Ting Yuen* and *Chen Yuen* are steel battleships, built at the Vulcan Works at Stettin, and are the most powerful vessels in the Chinese Navy. They have the following dimensions:—Length, 308 feet 5 inches; beam, 59 feet; mean draught, 20 feet; displacement, 7,430 tons. Each vessel carries four 12-inch Krupp guns, echeloned in pairs within a nearly elliptical redoubt protected by 12-inch armour, two 5·9-inch Krupps, mounted right forward and right aft in machine gun-proof turrets, and eleven quick-firing guns. When new, the trial speed of these ships was 14·5 knots. There is also a belt of armour 5 feet wide on the sides and from 8 inches to 14 inches thick. These ships have double bottoms and steel protective decks 3 inches in thickness. They were the only armour-clads engaged at the battle of the Yalu River, and together fought five Japanese warships for four hours, the *Chen Yuen* having 18 killed and 42 wounded. Her fore turret was so damaged that it had to be taken out, while the upper parts, masts, funnels, ventilators, &c., were simply riddled, while scarcely a vestige of woodwork throughout the ship was left not burnt. After lying at Port Arthur undergoing repairs, she recently ran ashore while entering the harbour at Wai-Hei-Wai and is now beached and useless.

CHING YUEN

The *Ching Yuen* and *Chih Yuen* are protected cruisers, built at Elswick. Their principal dimensions are:—Length, 250 feet; beam, 38 feet; mean draught, 15 feet; and displacement, 2,300 tons. They are built of steel, and protection to the vital parts is given by a steel 4-inch deck rising amidships above the water-line, but inclined at the sides to dip below it. The engines, magazines, and steering gear are protected by this deck. Both ships have double bottoms, and are subdivided into water-tight compartments. The armament comprises three 8·27-inch Krupp guns, two mounted forward and one aft, two 6-inch Armstrongs, eight 6-pounder quick-firing guns, and six Gatlings. All the guns are protected by steel shields. At their trial trips these vessels attained an average speed of 18·5 knots. After the battle of the Yalu the *Ching Yuen* returned to Port Arthur practically uninjured.

LAI YUEN

The *Lai Yuen* and *King Yuen* were built at the Vulcan Works at Stettin, and known as "coast defence" ships. Their principal dimensions are:—Length, 269 feet; beam, 39 feet 4 inches; mean draught, 16 feet 8 inches; displacement, 2,900 tons. Protection is afforded by a belt of compound armour six feet wide, and from 5·1 inches to 9·5 inches thick, which extends the length of the machinery and boiler space, and is terminated by thwartship armoured bulkheads 5·1 inches thick. At the forward end of the belt a revolving turret with six-inch armour contains two 8·27-inch Krupps. The armament also comprised two 5·9-inch Krupps and seven quick-firing guns. These ships had double bottoms. Their trial speed was sixteen knots. After the battle of the Yalu River, the *Lai Yuen* returned to Port Arthur in a fearfully battered condition, from her mast aft burnt to a shell, and her funnels and ventilators riddled with shot.

TSI YUEN

The *Tsi Yuen* is a protected cruiser, built at the Vulcan Works at Stettin. Her dimensions are:—Length, 236 feet 3 inches; beam, 34 feet 5 inches; draught, 15 feet 9 inches; and displacement, 2,355 tons. The under-water body of the ship is covered with a 4-inch curved steel deck, which at the sides is 4 feet 9 inches below the water-line when the vessel is at her normal draught. The space between this steel deck and the one above is used as coal bunkers. The armament is composed of two 8·27-inch Krupps in a machine gun-proof turret forward, one 5·9-inch Krupp in a similar turret aft, two other 5·9-inch Krupps, and five quick-firing guns. At her trials a speed of 15 knots was realised. This vessel was present at the battle of the Yalu, but becoming separated from her consorts early in the fight, her captain removed her out of danger, and she returned to Port Arthur. It was the *Tsi Yuen* which before the battle of the Yalu is reported to have approached the *Naniwa* by a ruse and fired upon her, one shell entering the *Naniwa's* wardroom.

YANG WEI

The *Yang Wei* and *Chao Yung* were steel cruisers constructed by Messrs. Armstrong, Mitchell and Co., at their shipbuilding yard at Low Walker in the Tyne. Their dimensions were:—Length, 210 feet; beam, 32 feet; draught, 15 feet 8 inches; and displacement, 1,350 tons. They were slightly protected by thin steel decks over the engines and boilers, and originally had a speed of 16 knots. The armament in each case consisted of two 10-inch and four 4·7-inch Armstrong quick-firers, with seven lighter guns. They were both present at the battle of the Yalu, but being cut off from the main body of the Chinese fleet, were subjected to the fire of one squadron of the Japanese ships; in a burning state they were run on shore by their commanders and destroyed.

CHIH YUEN

The *Chih Yuen* and *Ching Yuen* are protected cruisers, built at Elswick. Their principal dimensions are:—Length, 250 feet; beam, 38 feet; mean draught, 15 feet; and displacement, 2,300 tons. They are built of steel, and protection to the vital parts is given by a steel 4-inch deck rising amidships above the water-line, but inclined at the sides to dip below it. The engines, magazines, and steering gear are protected by this deck. Both ships have double bottoms, and are subdivided into water-tight compartments. The armament comprises three 8·27-inch Krupp guns, two mounted forward and one aft, two 6-inch Armstrongs, eight 6-pounder quick-firing guns, and six Gatlings. All the guns are protected by steel shields. At their trial trips these vessels attained an average speed of 18·5 knots. Both were present at the battle of the Yalu, where the *Chih Yuen* was sunk after ramming another vessel.

CHAO YUNG

The *Chao Yung* and *Yang Wei* were steel cruisers constructed by Messrs. Armstrong, Mitchell and Co., at their shipbuilding yard at Low Walker in the Tyne. Their dimensions were:—Length, 210 feet; beam, 32 feet; draught, 15 feet 8 inches; and displacement, 1,350 tons. They were slightly protected by thin steel decks over the engines and boilers, and originally had a speed of 16 knots. The armament in each case consisted of two 10-inch and four 4·7-inch Armstrong quick-firers, with seven lighter guns. They were both present at the battle of the Yalu, but being cut off from the main body of the Chinese fleet, were subjected in turn to the fire of one squadron of the Japanese ships, and early in the battle the *Chao Yung* burst into flames and sank.

PING YUEN

The *Ping Yuen* is classed as a "coast defence" vessel, and was built at the Chinese dockyard at Foochow. Her dimensions are:—Length, 200 feet; beam, 40 feet; draught of water, 16 feet; and displacement, 2,850 tons. She has a complete water-line belt of 8-inch armour, a protective deck of 2 inches, and 5 inches on the turret and conning towers. She carries one 10·2-inch Krupp in her turret, two 5·9-inch Krupps on sponsons (one on each side), and eight quick-firing guns. At a trial made in 1890 she is reported to have made a speed of 10·5 knots. This vessel was in the Yalu estuary at the time of the battle, but she took no part in the engagement.

1894年12月1日《图片报》中日军舰比较：中国战舰

中国战舰 Chinese warships

经远舰 King Yuen

镇远舰 Chen Yuen	扬威舰 Yang Wei
靖远舰 Ching Yuen	致远舰 Chih Yuen
来远舰 Lai Yuen	超勇舰 Chao Yung
济远舰 Tsi Yuen	平远舰 Ping Yuen

上左文字：中国自宣战后参加黄海海战及对日作战的重要战舰，相关细节已根据最新消息更新。

Illustrations and description of the more important ships which took part in the battle of the Yalu and other engagements with the Japanese since the declaration of war. The details are from information received up to the present time.

上右文字：清朝战舰在黄海海战中遭遇劲敌，受到重创。实际参战的 14 艘战舰，除了 6 艘运兵船及 6 艘鱼雷艇外，有 4 条战舰被敌军击沉。

The Chinese fleet at the battle of the Yalu was considerably overmatched in armament by that of their more energetic opponents, and suffered accordingly. Of the fourteen vessels actually engaged, in addition to the six transports and six torpedo boats, four sunk.

JAPANESE WARSHIPS

Illustrations and descriptions of the leading ships which took part in the battle of the Yalu and other engagements with the Chinese since the beginning of the war, with details revised from information received up to the present time.

NANIWA

The *Naniwa* and *Takachiho* are sister ships and protected cruisers, built by the Armstrong firm at Low Walker. Their dimensions are:—Length, 300 feet; beam, 46 feet; and draught, 18 feet 6 inches, with a displacement of 3,650 tons. The protective deck over the vital parts, as machinery, &c., is three inches thick. The armament consists of two 10-inch Armstrongs, placed at the bow and stern, the crews of which are sheltered by a shield and the loading stations by stout steel armour; six 6-inch Armstrongs and sixteen smaller quick-firing guns. They carry about 325 officers and men each. The maximum speed of the *Naniwa* was 18·7 knots. Both these vessels were in the battle of the Yalu, though they seemingly escaped with but slight injury. It was the *Naniwa* which at the commencement of hostilities caused great excitement by sinking the transport *Kow Shing*, after herself being fired upon by the Chinese cruiser *Tsi Yuen*, an unexploded shell from the latter vessel entering the *Naniwa's* wardroom.

The Japanese at the battle on the Yalu River brought nine vessels to the attack, divided into two squadrons, with the addition of an armour-belted corvette, a gunboat, a merchant cruiser, and five torpedo boats. Of the battleships only one suffered greatly, and all could have gone into action again the next day.

ITSUKUSHIMA

The *Itsukushima* and *Matsushima* were designed as "coast-defence" vessels by M. Bertin, and built to his plans by the Société des Forges et Chantiers de la Méditerranée. Their dimensions are:—Length, 295 feet 2 inches; beam, 50 feet 6 inches; draught of water, 21 feet 2 inches; displacement, 4,200 tons. The armament consists of one 12·6-inch Canet gun, eleven 4·7 Armstrong quick-firers, six smaller quick-firers and Maxim machine guns. The trial speed was 16·5 knots. There is no hull armour, but a 1·6-inch steel deck extends fore and aft, and all hatches are covered with armoured glacis. The heavy gun is placed forward *en barbette* in a turret protected by 11·8-inch armour, and 4-inch steel shields cover the breeches of the other guns. They carry 400 officers and men each. Both these vessels were at the battle of the Yalu, and the *Matsushima* was set on fire and badly damaged. The *Itsukushima* received only a trifling amount of damage according to Japanese accounts.

YOSHINO

The *Yoshino* is a protected cruiser, built by the firm of Sir William Armstrong, Mitchell, and Company, at Elswick, from the designs of Mr. P. Watts, and the fastest vessel that has been in action. Her dimensions are:—Length, 350 feet; beam, 46 feet 6 inches; draught, 17 feet; displacement, 4,150 tons. The protective deck is 4·5 inches thick on its sloping sides, and 1·7 inch on its horizontal portion; coal is stored over the deck to increase its protection. She is armed entirely with quick-firing guns from Elswick, and carries four 6-inch, eight 4·7-inch, and twenty-two 3-pounders. At the measured mile trials, the engines developed nearly 15,000 horse-power; the mean speed, with forced draught, being 23·031 knots. The *Yoshino* accompanied the *Naniwa* on the occasion of the sinking of the transport *Kow Shing*. She was present at the battle of the Yalu, and according to a Chinese account was set on fire and badly damaged.

CHIYODA

The *Chiyoda* is a protected cruiser, built at Clydebank by Messrs. J. and G. Thomson. She has a chrome steel armoured belt, 4·5 inches thick, for about two-thirds of her length, and this is backed by coal and cellulose. A protective deck, 1 inch thick, also extends from stem to stern, covered with coal and coke. There is also a double bottom. The dimensions are:—Length, 310 feet; beam, 42 feet; draught, 14 feet; and displacement, 2,450 tons. A speed of more than 19·5 knots was attained. The armament is ten 4·7 Armstrong quick-firers and seventeen other quick-firing guns. She is said to have come out of the battle without material injury.

HI-YEI

The *Hi-Yei* was built at Milford Haven in 1878 from Sir Edward Reed's designs. She is a composite corvette, with a composite armour-belt 4·5 inches thick, extending along the ship at the water-line. Her dimensions are:—Length, 231 feet; beam, 40 feet 9 inches; draught, 17 feet 6 inches; displacement, 2,280 tons. Her armament consists of six 6-inch Krupps (three on either broadside), two 6·5-inch Krupps (one on either bow), with right-ahead fire, and 1 similar gun astern, as well as several lighter guns. Her original speed was 13 knots. The *Hi-Yei*, the *Yoshino*, and the *Naniwa* were the three warships which intercepted and sank the Chinese transport *Kow Shing*. Later the *Hi-Yei* was present at the battle of the Yalu, and set on fire and badly damaged, having to go into port for repairs.

FUSO

The *Fuso* is a central-battery battleship, designed by Sir Edward Reed, and built at Poplar in 1877. Her dimensions are:—Length, 220 feet; beam, 48 feet; draught, 18 feet 3 inches; and displacement, 3,718 tons. She was designed to carry a crew of 250 officers and men and to steam 13 knots. Her armament consisted of four 9·4-inch Krupps on the main deck and two 6·5-inch Krupps on the upper decks. The armour on the side was 9 inches, and on the athwartship bulkheads 8 inches. She was present at the battle of the Yalu, and sustained sufficient injuries to necessitate going into port for repairs.

TAKACHIHO

The *Takachiho* and *Naniwa* are sister ships and protected cruisers, built by the Armstrong firm at Low Walker. Their dimensions are:—Length, 300 feet; beam, 46 feet; and draught, 18 feet 6 inches; with a displacement of 3,650 tons. The protective deck over the vital parts, as machinery, &c., is three inches thick. The armament consists of two 10-inch Armstrongs, placed at the bow and stern, the crews of which are sheltered by a shield, and the loading stations by stout steel armour; six 6-inch Armstrongs and sixteen smaller quick-firing guns. They carry about 325 officers and men each. Both these vessels were in the battle of the Yalu, and were somewhat injured and burnt.

MATSUSHIMA

The *Matsushima* and *Itsukushima* were designed as "coast-defence" vessels by M. Bertin. Their dimensions are:—Length, 295 feet 2 inches; beam, 50 feet 6 inches; draught of water, 21 feet 2 inches; displacement, 4,200 tons. The armament consists of one 12·6-inch Canet gun, eleven 4·7 Armstrong quick-firers, six smaller quick-firers and Maxim machine guns. There is no hull armour, but a 1·6-inch steel deck extends fore and aft, and all hatches are covered with armoured glacis. The heavy gun is placed forward *en barbette* in a turret protected by 11·8-inch armour, and 4-inch steel shields cover the breeches of the other guns. They carry 400 officers and men each. Both these vessels were at the battle of the Yalu, and the *Matsushima* carried Admiral Ito's flag. The *Matsushima* fared worse than any other ship on the Japanese side. Among other injuries she was once set on fire and twice struck by shells with appalling results from the *Chen Yuen's* 37-ton gun, nevertheless, Admiral Ito kept her at the head of the principal squadron until the close of the action, when he transferred his flag to the *Hashidate*.

HASHIDATE

The *Hashidate* is similar in nearly every respect to the *Matsushima* and *Itsukushima*, but these vessels being found to labour heavily against the sea owing to the weight of the big gun forward, this 12·6-inch Canet and its turret is placed aft in the *Hashidate*. She was built at Yokosuka Dockyard in Japan. This vessel was in the battle of the Yalu River, and appears to have escaped without material damage. It was to this vessel that Admiral Ito transferred his flag when the terrible injuries received by the *Matsushima* necessitated her being sent into dock for repairs.

1894 年 12 月 1 日《图片报》中日军舰比较：日本战舰

日本战舰 Japanese warships

浪速舰 Naniwa

严岛舰 Itsukushima

千代田舰 Chiyoda

扶桑舰 Fuso

松岛舰 Matsushima

吉野舰 Yoshino

比睿舰 Hiyei

高千穗舰 Takachiho

桥立舰 Hashidate

上左文字：日军自开战就参加黄海海战和其他战役的战舰插图及说明，相关细节已根据最新消息更新。

Illustrations and description of the leading ships which took part in the battle of the Yalu and other engagements with the Chinese since the beginning of the war, with details revised from information received up to the present time.

上右文字：日军在黄海海战中投入 9 条船，分成两个战斗编队，另外，1 艘木壳装甲舰、1 艘小炮艇、1 艘商用巡洋舰及 5 艘鱼雷艇也参加了战斗。只有一艘战舰遭受重创，所有战舰均可于次日重新投入战备。

The Japanese at the battle on the Yalu River brought nine vessels to the attack, divided into two squadrons, with the addition of an armour-belted corvette a gun-boat, a merchant cruiser, and five torpedo boats. Of the battleships only one suffered greatly, and all could have gone into action again the next day.

CHIH YUEN

The *Chih Yuen* and *Ching Yuen* are protected cruisers, built at Elswick. Their principal dimensions are :—Length, 250 feet ; beam, 38 feet ; mean draught, 15 feet ; and displacement, 2,300 tons. They are built of steel, and protection to the vital parts is given by a steel 4-inch deck rising amidships above the water-line, but inclined at the sides to dip below it. The engines, magazines, and steering gear are protected by this deck. Both ships have double bottoms, and are subdivided into water-tight compartments. The armament comprises three 8·27-inch Krupp guns, two mounted forward and one aft, two 6-inch Armstrongs, eight 6-pounder quick-firing guns, and six Gatlings. All the guns are protected by steel shields. At their trial trips these vessels attained an average speed of 18·5 knots. Both were present at the battle of the Yalu, where the *Chih Yuen* was sunk after ramming another vessel.

致远号装甲巡洋舰　Chih Yuen

致远号巡洋舰由英国阿姆斯特朗公司建造，主要参数如下：船体全长250英尺，宽38英尺，吃水15英尺，排水量2300吨。整船由钢铁打造，且吃水线以上中腰部位的甲板厚4英寸，以保护船中锅炉轮机、弹药库以及操舵装置等要害部门，而首尾甲板厚度稍稍变薄。船底为双层底设计，分割为防水隔层。舰上武器装备了3门8.27英寸克虏伯主炮（两门在舰首，一门在舰尾），两门6英寸阿姆斯特朗炮，8门6磅速射炮以及6门轮转式机炮，以上武器均配备钢盾保护。致远号试航期间的平均速度达到了18.5节，并且参加了甲午海战。

The Chih Yuen and Ching Yuen are protected cruisers,built at Elswick.Their principal dimensions are:—Length,250 feet;beam,38 feet;mean draught,15 feet;and displacement,2,300 tons.They are built of steel,and protection to the vital parts is given by a steel 4-inch deck rising amidships above the water-line,but inclined at the sides to dip below it.The engines ,magazines, and steering gear are protected by this deck.Both ships have double bottoms,and are subdivided into water-tight compartments.The armament comprises three 8.27-inch Krupp guns,two mounted forward and one aft,two 6-inch Armstrongs,eight 6-pounder quick-firing guns,and six Gatlings.All the guns are protected by steel shields.At their trial trips these vessels attained an average speed of 18.5 knots.Both were present at the battle of the Yalu,where the Chih Yuen was sunk after ramming another vessel.

YOSHINO

The *Yoshino* is a protected cruiser, built by the firm of Sir William Armstrong, Mitchell, and Company, at Elswick, from the designs of Mr. P. Watts, and the fastest vessel that has been in action. Her dimensions are :—Length, 350 feet; beam, 46 feet 6 inches; draught, 17 feet; displacement, 4,150 tons. The protective deck is 4·5 inches thick on its sloping sides, and 1·7 inch on its horizontal portion; coal is stored over the deck to increase its protection. She is armed entirely with quick-firing guns from Elswick, and carries four 6-inch, eight 4·7-inch, and twenty-two 3-pounders. At the measured mile trials, the engines developed nearly 15,000 horse-power; the mean speed, with forced draught, being 23·031 knots. The *Yoshino* accompanied the *Naniwa* on the occasion of the sinking of the transport *Kow Shing*. She was present at the battle of the Yalu, and according to a Chinese account was set on fire and badly damaged.

吉野号巡洋舰　Yoshino

吉野号巡洋舰由瓦茨先生设计并由英国阿姆斯特朗公司建造，是当时世界上速度最快的水面军舰。吉野号主要参数如下：船体全长350英尺，宽46英尺，吃水17英尺，排水量4150吨。两侧面保护甲板厚4.5英寸，水平甲板厚1.7英寸。燃煤储藏在甲板上增加对船体的保护。舰上武器装备均为阿姆斯特朗公司制造的速射炮，4门6英寸速射炮，8门4.7英寸速射炮以及22门3磅速射炮。吉野号在试航中达到了15000匹马力，并通过强压通风技术使船速达到了23.031节。吉野号参与了浪速号击沉高升号运输舰事件，并参加了甲午海战。甲午海战中，吉野号船体起火并损伤严重。

The Yoshino is a protected cruiser ,built by the firm of Sir William Armstrong ,Mitchell, and Company , at Elswick, from the designs of Mr. P. Watts, and the fastest vessel that has been in action. Her dimensions are:—Length,350 feet;beam,46 feet 6 inches;draught,17 feet; displacement, 4,150 tons. The protective deck is 4.5 inches thick on its sloping sides,and 1.7 inch on its horizontal portion;coal is stored over the deck to increase its protection .She is armed entirely with quick-firing guns from Elswick,and carries four 6-inch,eight 4.7-inch,and twenty-two 3-pounders.At the measured mile trials,the engines developed nearly 15,000 horse-power; the mean speed,with forced draught,being 23.031 konts.The Yoshino accompanied the Naniwa on the occasion of the sinking of the transport Kow Shing.She was present at the battle of the Yalu, and according to a Chinese account was set on fire and badly damaged.

HARPER'S WEEKLY

CHINA.

	Displacement (Tons).	Protection.	Armament.	Speed.	Built (Year).
Chen Yuen, Ting Yuen.	7430	8 to 14 in. side, 12-in. barbette.	2 12-in.; 2 5.9-in.; 8 m.	15 knots.	1883.
King Yuen, Lai Yuen.	2900	5¼ to 9½ in.	2 8.3-in.; 2 5.9-in.; 7 m.	16 "	1888.
Ching Yuen, Chih Yuen.	2300	Protected.	3 8.3 in.; 2 6-in.; 8 6-p'd'r; 2 3-p'd'r; 8 m.	18½ "	1887.
Ping Yuen	2355	15-in. barbette.	2 8.3-in.; 1 5.9 in.; 8 m.	17½ "	1884.
Tsi Yuen	2355	Protected.	2 8.3-in.; 1 5.9-in.; 9 m.	15 "	1883.
Yang Wai, Chao Yung.	1350	Protected.	2 8-in.; 4 4.7-in. r. f.; 7 m.	16 "	1881.
Kuang Ki, Kuang Ting.	1030	Partially protected.	3 4.7-in. r. f.; 7 m.	16½ "	1891.
Two others.					
Four torpedo-boats.					

JAPAN.

	Displacement (Tons).	Protection.	Armament.	Speed.	Built (Year).
Matsushima, Ikutsushima, Hashidate.	4277	12-in. turret.	1 12.8-in.; 11 5-in. r. f.; 11 m.	17½ knots.	1890
Yoshino	4150	Protected.	4 6-in.; 8 4.7-in.; 22 3-pounders; all r. f.	23.03 "	1892
Fuso	3718	Belt, 7 in.; battery, 9 in.	4 9.45-in.; 2 6.7-in.; 5 m.	13 "	1877
Naniwa, Takachiho.	3650	Protected.	2 10-in.; 6 5.9-in.; 2 6-pounders, r. f.; 10 m.	18 "	1886
Akitsushima	3150	Protected.	1 12.6-in.; 12 4.7-in., r. f.; 6 m.	19 "	1892
Chiyoda	2450	4½ in.	10 4.72-in.; 14 1.9-in.; all r. f.; 3 m.	19 "	1889
Hiyei	2200	4½ in.	3 6.7-in.; 6 5.9-in.; 4 m.	13 "	1878
Akagi	615	Gunboat.	1 9.45-in.; 1 5.9-in.; 2 m.	13 "	1888
Saikio-Maru, a merchant vessel—chartered.					

R. F., rapid-fire guns. M., machine-guns.

TABLE SHOWING COMPARATIVE STRENGTH OF VESSELS ENGAGED IN BATTLE OF YALU.

1894 年 11 月 24 日《哈珀斯周刊·亚洲战争的故事》

作者为美国海军总出纳官尤斯塔斯·罗杰斯（ Eustace B. Rogers，U.S.N.），对中日双方舰艇性能进行了详细论证和对比：

参加黄海海战的战舰实力对比表

中国

<table>
<tr><th></th><th>排水量（吨）</th><th>防护装甲</th><th>火炮</th><th>时速（节）</th><th>制造（年）</th></tr>
<tr><td>镇远</td><td rowspan="2">7430</td><td rowspan="2">船身 8—14 吋
炮座 12 吋</td><td rowspan="2">2 门 12 吋，2 门 5.9 吋
8 门机关炮</td><td rowspan="2">15</td><td rowspan="2">1883</td></tr>
<tr><td>定远</td></tr>
<tr><td>经远</td><td rowspan="2">2900</td><td rowspan="2">5 ¼ —9 ½ 吋</td><td rowspan="2">2 门 8.3 吋，2 门 5.9 吋
7 门机关炮</td><td rowspan="2">16</td><td rowspan="2">1888</td></tr>
<tr><td>来远</td></tr>
<tr><td>靖远</td><td rowspan="2">2300</td><td rowspan="2">有装甲</td><td rowspan="2">3 门 8.3 吋，2 门 6 吋
8 门 6 吋速射，2 门 3 吋速射，8 门机关炮</td><td rowspan="2">18 ½</td><td>1887</td></tr>
<tr><td>致远</td><td>1886</td></tr>
<tr><td>平远</td><td rowspan="2">2355</td><td>炮座 15 吋</td><td>2 门 8.3 吋，1 门 5.9 吋，8 门机关炮</td><td>17 ½</td><td>1884</td></tr>
<tr><td>济远</td><td>有装甲</td><td>2 门 8.3 吋，1 门 5.9 吋，9 门机关炮</td><td>15</td><td>1883</td></tr>
<tr><td>扬威</td><td rowspan="2">1350</td><td rowspan="2">有装甲</td><td rowspan="2">2 门 8 吋，4 门 4.7 吋
有速射炮，7 门机关炮</td><td rowspan="2">16</td><td rowspan="2">1881</td></tr>
<tr><td>超勇</td></tr>
</table>

（续上表）

	排水量（吨）	防护装甲	火炮	时速（节）	制造（年）
广乙 广丙	1030	部分装甲	3门4.7吋，有速射炮，7门机关炮	16½	1891
另两艘					
四艘鱼雷艇					

日本

	排水量（吨）	防护装甲	火炮	时速（节）	制造（年）
松岛 严岛 桥立	4277	12吋 旋转炮塔	1门12.8吋 11门5吋速射炮，11门机关炮	17 ½	1890
吉野	4150	有装甲	4门6吋，8门4.7吋 22门哈乞开斯3磅机关炮，全部为速射	23.03	1892
扶桑	3718	周边7吋 炮台9吋	4门9.45吋，2门6.7吋 5门机关炮	13	1877
浪速 高千穗	3650	有装甲	2门10吋，6门5.9吋 2门哈乞开斯6磅机关速射炮，10门机关炮	18	1886
秋津洲	3150	有装甲	1门12.6吋，12门4.7吋速射炮，6门机关炮	19	1892
千代田	2450	4 ½吋	10门4.72吋，14门1.9吋 全部为速射炮，3门机关炮	19	1889

Le croiseur japonais « Naniwa-Kan ».

Le comte Saïgo, ministre de la marine.
London Stereoscopic Cy.

Un lieutenant de vaisseau.
Phot. Couturier de Béchard.

Un capitaine de vaisseau.
Phot. Pierre Petit.

Un vice-amiral.
Phot. Maruki.

Uniformes des officiers de la marine japonaise.

LA MARINE JAPONAISE. — Le croiseur garde-côtes « Matsuhsima ».

1894 年 8 月 11 日《插图报》

日本海军

1　日本巡洋舰浪速号

2　西乡从道伯爵，日本海军大臣

3　一位大副

4　一位舰长

5　一位副元帅（肖像为榎本武扬——编者注）

6　日本岸防巡洋舰松岛号（日本联合舰队旗舰）

La Marine Japonaise.

1　Le croiseur japonais “Naniwa-Kan”.

2　Le comte Saïgo, ministre de la marine.

3　Un lieutenant de vaisseau.

4　Un capitaine de vaisseau.

5　Un vice-amiral.

6　Le croiseur garde-côtes “Matsushima”.

中日两国并非蛮族，但这两个国家的文明与法兰西文明截然不同。受当前朝鲜局势的影响，中日两国开战是必然之事。两国交战，双方把所能得到的现代科技中最为强大、最为精良的武器第一次投入到战争中。

故本报认为，在此介绍一下日本海军的几种类型，以作文史记载，实为一件有趣之事。

首先是担任海军大臣的西乡从道伯爵。他是一位平民少将，虽然还很年轻，但是他在国内已经声名远播，是一位刚毅且出色的治国者。

通过观察我们为您展示的其他几位身着军装的日本军官的肖像可以看出，日本海军的等级划分与法国并不相同。日本海军在很多地方模仿了英国海军的军服，而日本陆军的军服起初在许多地方都借鉴了法国陆军的军服，但从 1870 年起，日本开始借鉴德国陆军的军服。

日本人在选择由哪些国家来建造战船这一点上，体现了兼收并蓄的特点。除了在本国设备很齐全的工厂建造船只外，他们还向英国、法国和德国订制巡洋舰、装甲舰和鱼雷艇。火炮也是通过这个办法生产出来的。

——《日本海军》（选译），1894 年 8 月 11 日《插图报》

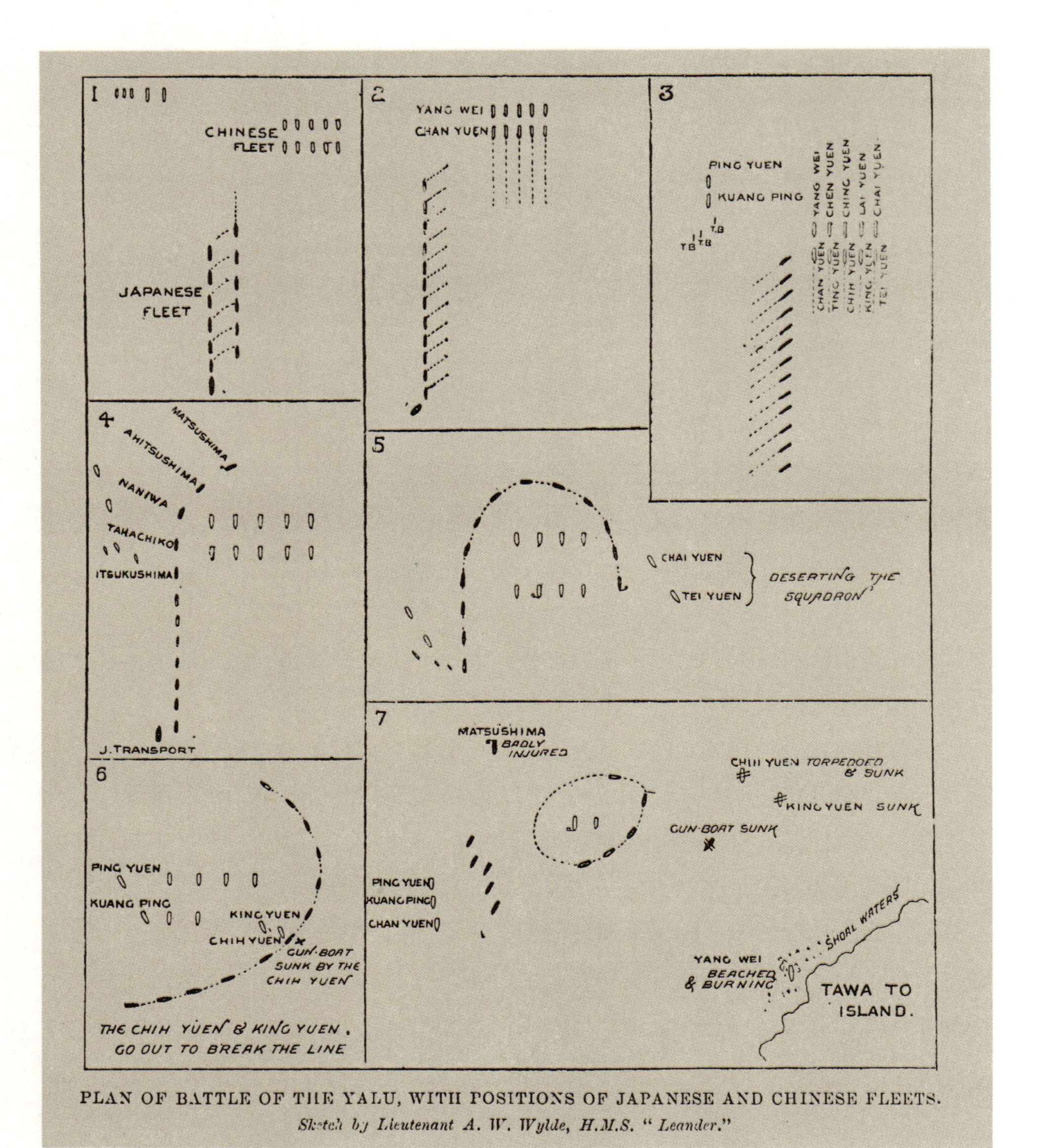

PLAN OF BATTLE OF THE YALU, WITH POSITIONS OF JAPANESE AND CHINESE FLEETS.

Sketch by Lieutenant A. W. Wylde, H.M.S. "Leander."

1894 年 11 月 24 日《伦敦新闻画报》增刊

黄海海战中日双方队形图

Plan of battle of the Yalu, with positions of Japanese and Chinese fleets.

根据英国皇家海军上尉 A.W. 魏德在利安德护卫舰上绘制的草图制版

Sketch by Lieutenant A. W. Wylde, H.M.S. "Leander".

（此图是魏德上尉根据交战双方官方发布的战况通报绘制的）

THE ILLUSTRATED LONDON NEWS

Vol. 15.—No. 380.
OFFICE: WORLD BUILDING, CITY HALL PARK.

NEW YORK, SATURDAY, AUGUST 18, 1894.

FIFTEEN CENTS A COPY,
$6 A YEAR IN ADVANCE, THE MIDSUMMER AND CHRISTMAS NUMBERS $1 A YEAR EXTRA.

THE IMPENDING WAR IN EASTERN ASIA: THE JAPANESE WAR-SHIP "YOSHINO KAN."

1894 年 8 月 4 日《伦敦新闻画报》

一触即发的东亚战争：日本战舰吉野号

The impending war in Eastern Asia: the Japanese war-ship "Yoshino Kan".

NAVAL BATTLE OF THE YALU, SEPTEMBER 17: SINKING OF THE CHINESE SHIP, "CHIH-YUEN."

FACSIMILE OF SKETCH BY LIEUTENANT A. W. WYLDE, R.M.L.I., ON BOARD H.M.S. "LEANDER."

An account of this engagement will be found on another page. The Japanese fleet is here represented circling round the Chinese. Two Chinese cruisers, t cut the Japanese line, the "King-Yuen" was set on fire by a shell, and was obliged to flood her magazine. This caused her to heel over to starboard and guns, and exposing her deck to fire. She sank in a few minutes. The "Chih-Yuen" was torpedoed, and went down bows first with screws revolving, like H.M.

1894 年 11 月 24 日《伦敦新闻画报》增刊

9 月 17 日的黄海海战，中国军舰致远号沉没

Naval battle of the Yalu, September 17: sinking of the Chinese ship, “Chih-Yuen”.

（右侧悬挂日本军旗的军舰为吉野号，左侧倾斜的军舰为致远号）

在这张插图上，日本舰队包围了中国舰队。两艘中国巡洋舰经远号和致远号试图冲破日本的包围圈，但经远号被炮弹击中起火，弹药舱进水，这使得它向右倾斜、无法操控，不仅再也无力还击，甲板也开始燃烧。数分钟后经远号沉没。致远舰被鱼雷击中，螺旋桨依然转动并露出水面，船头首先下沉，就像英国战舰维多利亚号（1893 年在地中海沉没——编者注）那样。

The Japanese fleet is here represented circling round the Chinese. Two Chinese cruisers, the “King-Yuen” and the “Chih-Yuen,” having advanced to cut the Japanese line, the “King-Yuen” was set on fire by a shell, and was obliged to flood her magazine. This caused her to heel over to starboard and rendered her unmanageable, besides preventing her working her guns, and exposing her deck to fire. She sank in a few minutes. The “Chih-Yuen” was torpedoed, and went down bows first with screws revolving, like H.M.S. “Victoria.”

DRAWN BY J. NASH, R.I.

The Chinese cruiser *Chih Yuen*, commanded by Captain Tang, early in the fight closed with one of the enemy's ships with the intention of ramming, but was herself then attacked by four Japanese ships which closed arou

THE GREAT NAVAL ENGAGEMENT OFF THE MOUT

1894 年 12 月 1 日《图片报》增刊

鸭绿江河口的大海战

The great naval engagement off the mouth of the Yalu River.

根据我刊特派随日军画师所绘草图制版

From sketches by our special artist with the Japanese forces.

由邓世昌指挥的中国巡洋舰致远号，在战斗之初先试图撞击敌舰，后被 4 艘敌舰包围，终因船底被击中沉没，船上全部将士与船同归于尽。

The Chinese cruiser Chih Yuen, commanded by Captain Tang, early in the fight closed with one of the enemy's ships with the intention of ramming, but was herself then attacked by four Japanese ships which closed around her. The Chih Yuen under this combined attack was ripped up by shots under the water and went down with all on board.

THE BATTLE OF THE YALU: FOUNDERING OF THE CHINES

From Sketches and Description by an Eye-Witness.

1894 年 11 月 10 日《伦敦新闻画报》

黄海海战——中国战船致远号沉没

The battle of the Yalu: foundering of the Chinese war-ship Chih-Yuen.

根据现场目击证人描述制版

From sketches and description by an eye-witness.

THE NAVAL BATTLE OF THE YALU.

At the head of Corea Bay, the north-eastern part of the Yellow Sea, is the estuary, very narrow at its entrance, but an inlet twenty miles long, of the Amnok or Yalu, the large river that divides China from Corea. Here, on Monday, Sept. 17, the Chinese fleet, commanded by Admiral Ting, fought the Japanese fleet, with all the weapons of European naval warfare, from noon till dusk. On both sides, as it appears from all accounts, the native officers and seamen of the two rival Eastern Asiatic empires showed as much persevering courage as any modern sea-fights have displayed. Their guns and torpedoes were skilfully handled, but the exhibition of manœuvring skill was limited by the contracted space of water. The destruction of ships, in proportion to the number engaged in conflict, was unusually great, and so was the loss of life. Three of the strongest Chinese war-ships were sunk, while another was burnt or blown up. The Chinese succeeded, having begun work at an earlier hour, in landing troops from the transports which they convoyed. But they cannot be deemed to have escaped a naval defeat, and their forces at sea are much weakened, probably beyond repair.

It was the day after the first, likely to be the last, important action of the military campaign in Corea, the capture of the only effective Chinese army at Ping-Yang, nearly a hundred miles south-east of the Yalu inlet on the road from the Chinese frontier to Seoul, the capital city. The landing of the fresh troops from China could therefore be of no use, but on the Friday before, Sept. 14, when they were embarked, Ping-Yang being deemed a strong position, there seemed good reason for sending military reinforcements. Li Hung Chang's administration is not lightly to be blamed. Nor does the conduct of Admiral Ting appear deserving of censure. He had to convoy six transports into the Yalu River inlet, not to seek a combat if it could be evaded. His fighting fleet consisted of the large and powerful ironclads, *Ting-Yuen* and *Chen-Yuen*, carrying 37-ton Krupp guns; the *King-Yuen*, *Lai-Yuen*, *Tsi-Yuen*, and *Ping-Yuen*, smaller vessels, the first two with armour-belts and strong turrets, the last unarmoured, carrying 10-ton or 12-ton Krupp guns; six unarmoured cruisers, similarly armed with guns; and four torpedo-boats; making a very respectable force. He was at the Yalu early on Monday morning.

The transports entered the river to put the troops ashore; the war-ships anchored outside. This is the Chinese account; but the Japanese say, not quite credibly, that they sighted the Chinese fleet at sea about noon, and chased it for an hour to the Yalu inlet. It would have suited Admiral Ting much better, with his superior force, to have fought on the open sea. The Japanese fighting line consisted of nine war-ships, none at all equal to the two large Chinese ironclads; they had the *Matsusima*, of 4277 tons displacement, partially armoured, carrying one large gun and a dozen smaller guns; the *Yoshino*, of which we lately gave an Illustration and description, and which is of equal size; the *Hi-yei*, a slightly armoured cruiser with three 3½-ton Krupp guns, but no first-class battle-ship. Three gun-boats and five torpedo-boats completed the Japanese force, which was commanded by Admiral Ito.

The Chinese war-ships, at the enemy's approach, formed up in single line to defend the entrance to the Yalu estuary. Nine Japanese ships attacked them, directing their fire mostly on the *Chen-Yuen* and the *Ting-Yuen*, till the *Chen-Yuen* had two of her guns disabled. After a while, two Japanese cruisers, the *Yoshino* and the *Akitsushima*, followed by three torpedo-boats, tried to break through the Chinese line at one end, to get in and destroy the transports. The *Ching-Yuen* and *Chao-Yung*, being approached by torpedo-boats, moved astern to avoid them. The two Japanese ships which had entered were driven out, very much damaged. But the two Chinese ships last named, and two or three others, encountered worse disaster. The *Chao-Yung* ran ashore, could not get off, and was set on fire by the enemy's shells; the *King-Yuen*, her decks pierced by a shell, also took fire and sank; the *Chen-Yuen's* big guns were disabled; the transport *Yang-Wei* got aground and was burnt; and the *Chih-Yuen*, after stoutly fighting three hours, was struck by a torpedo and sank with all her crew. No Japanese ship was actually destroyed, but they retired much knocked about when the fighting stopped. The remnant of the Chinese fleet next day made for Port Arthur, but seems to have become rather scattered, the transports returning to different harbours of China.

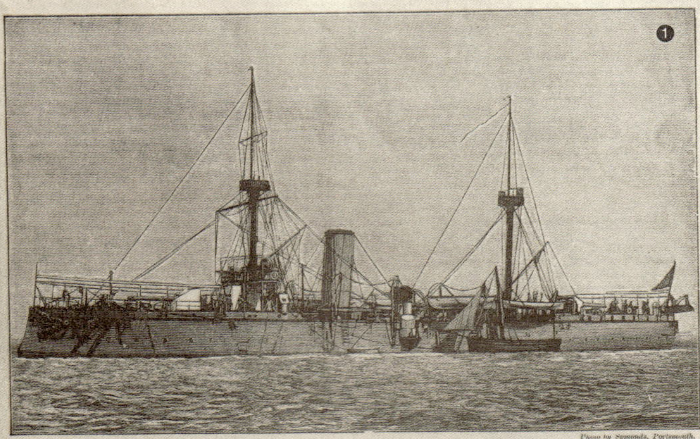

Photo by Symonds, Portsmouth.

THE CHINESE PROTECTED CRUISER "CHIH-YUEN," SUNK AT THE BATTLE OF THE YALU.

THE CHINESE UNARMOURED CRUISER "CHAO-YUNG," BURNT AT THE BATTLE OF THE YALU.

Photo by Symonds, Portsmouth.

THE CHINESE IRONCLAD BATTLE-SHIP "KING-YUEN," SUNK AT THE BATTLE OF THE YALU.

Photo by Symonds, Portsmouth.

THE CHINESE PROTECTED CRUISER "CHING-YUEN," LOST AT THE BATTLE OF THE YALU.

1894 年 9 月 29 日《伦敦新闻画报》

1 清军防护巡洋舰致远号，于黄海海战沉没

1 The Chinese protected cruiser “Chih-Yuen,” sunk at the battle of the Yalu.

2 清军非装甲巡洋舰超勇号，于黄海海战焚毁

2 The Chinese unarmoured cruiser “Chao-Yung,” burnt at the battle of the Yalu.

3 清军铁甲战舰经远号，于鸭绿江沉没

3 The Chinese ironclad battle-ship “King-Yuen,” sunk at the battle of the Yalu.

4 清军防护巡洋舰靖远号，于黄海海战损毁（实为威海卫沉没——编者注）

4 The Chinese protected cruiser “Ching-Yuen,” lost at the battle of the Yalu.

这是最早对黄海海战进行细致图文描述的西方报道，文章开头写道：“鸭绿江是中朝分界线，其入海口位于黄海东北部，西向朝鲜湾上游，入海口极窄，但入海湾绵延 20 英里长。9 月 17 日星期一，海军提督丁汝昌率中国舰队，运用欧洲海战的武器，在此处与日本舰队交火，与日军一直从中午激战到黄昏。从所有对此役的记述来看，这抗衡的两大东亚帝国参战的海军官兵所展现的英勇无畏，不亚于任何现代海战。枪炮和鱼雷的使用游刃有余，但作战指挥技巧的展现却受到了狭小水域空间的限制，参与到混战中的损毁船舰数量往往是巨大的，人员伤亡亦是十分惨重。中国战舰中最强大的三艘被击沉，而另外一艘被焚毁或者是炸毁。”

——《黄海海战》（选译），1894 年 9 月 29 日《伦敦新闻画报》

THE GRAPHIC

The Conning Tower of the *Tsi-Yuen* after being twice hit at the Battle of Yasan

Effects of a Shell at the Battle of Yasan on the Hand-steering Gear and Boat-hoisting Engine of the *Tsi-Yuen*

G

Quarter-deck of *Lai-Yuen* after the Battle of Yalu. The whole of the woodwork in the after-part of the ship is burnt while the deck beams, side plates and framing are bent and cracked

Part of the Superstructure of the *Che* where one of the heavy shot pene Mr. Hekman, gun officer

DRAWN BY J. NASH, R.I.

EFFECTS OF JAPANESE FIRE ON CHINESE

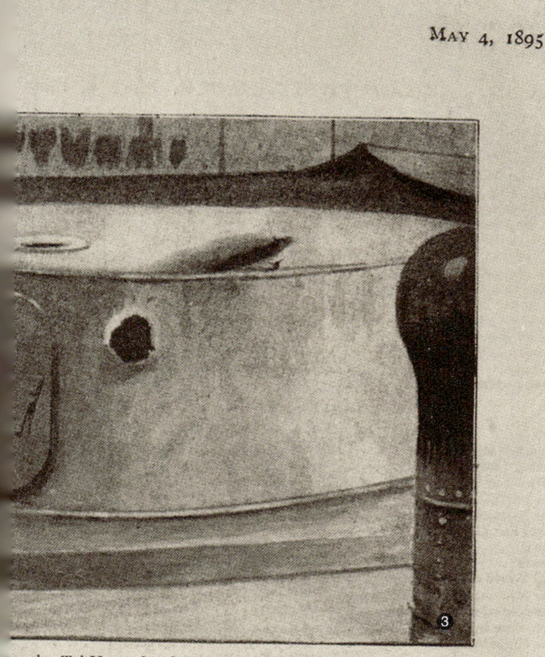

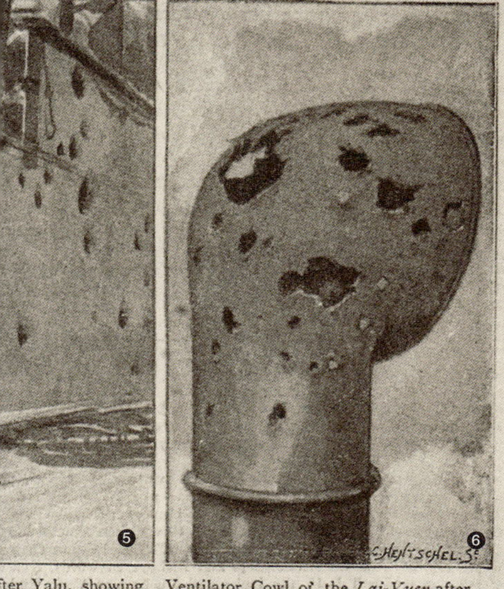

1895 年 5 月 4 日《图片报》

日本炮火对中国铁甲船的破坏

Effects of Japanese fire on Chinese ironclads.

1　济远号的指挥塔

1　The conning tower of the Tsi-Yuen after being twice hit at the Battle of Yasan.

2　济远号的舵和救生船吊轮

2　Effects of a shell at the battle of Yasan on the hand-steering gear and boat-hoisting engine of the Tsi-Yuen.

3　济远号的炮手掩体，上面的洞是一门 6 磅机关炮所致，炮弹从顶部进入、侧面钻出

3　Gun shield on the Tsi-Yuen, showing where a Six-Pound shot, at the battle of Yasan, struck the top and came out at the side.

4　来远舰的后甲板、舷侧板被火烧化或弯曲变形

4　Quarter-deck of Lai-Yuen after the battle of Yalu. The whole of the woodwork in the after-part of the ship is burnt while the deck beams, side plates and framing are bent and cracked.

5　镇远舰受伤的舰楼和它的德籍炮务官哈卜门

5　Part of the superstructure of the Chen-Yuen after Yalu, showing where one of the heavy shot penetrated. The figure is that of Mr. Hekman, gun officer.

6　来远舰的排风斗罩，一枚炮弹在其中爆炸造成了 46 个弹孔

6　Ventilator cowl of the Lai-Yuen after the battle of Yalu. A shell burst in it, making 46 holes.

1895 年 5 月 4 日《图片报》所刊的上面三张图为在丰岛海战中受伤的济远舰，下图左右两侧图片为黄海海战中受伤的来远舰，中间图片是镇远舰，照片上负伤的人为在黄海海战中负伤的镇远舰炮务官、德国人哈卜门（后授水师参将）。

THE WAR IN THE EAST—OPERATIONS OF THE JAPANESE FORCES.—FROM OFFICIAL PHOTOGRAPHS TAKEN FOR THE JAPANESE GOVERNMENT.

1. Provisions and Ammunition for the Second Army landed at Hwayuan-Kow. 2. Interior of the Hoshang Fort in Talienwan Bay, taken by the Second Japanese Army. 3. Landing-Pier constructed by Japanese in Talienwan Bay; Japanese Transports at Anchor. 4. Landing Ammunition and Provisions at Hwayuan-Kow. 5. Japanese Sailors working Machine-Gun during a Naval Battle. 6. Remains of the Chinese War-Ship *Yan-Wi*, destroyed by a Torpedo during the Battle of Yalu.

1895 年 4 月 13 日《哈珀斯周刊》

1 日本水兵在一次海战中操作机关枪

2 黄海海战中沉没的中国战舰扬威号残骸

1 Japanese sailors working maching-gun during a naval battle.

2 Remains of the Chinese warship Yan-Wi, destroyed by a torpedo during the battle of Yalu.

1894 年 11 月 17 日《伦敦新闻画报》

在旅顺整修的北洋舰队

The Chinese fleet lying in dock at Port Arthur.

四艘军舰左起：靖远号、镇远号、定远号和来远号

Ching-Yuen、Chen-Yuen、Ting-Yuen、Lai-Yuen.

英国皇家海军绘于利安德护卫舰上——A.W. 魏德绘

From a sketch by Mr. A. W. Wylde, of H.M.S. “Leander”.

1894 年 11 月 24 日《伦敦新闻画报》增刊

正在旅顺港修理的镇远舰

The Chinese ironclad battle-ship "Chen-Yuen" undergoing repairs at Port Arthur.

英国皇家海军上尉 A.W. 魏德绘于利安德护卫舰上

From a sketch by Lieutenant A. W. Wylde, on board H.M.S. "Leander".

9 月 17 日，黄海海战后镇远舰拖着满身伤痕回到旅顺港，它的舰楼和烟囱被炮弹打成了筛子，舰首的旋转炮塔被击穿，瞭望桥不见了踪影，主桅被烧毁；整修至少需要六周时间。

After the battle of the Yalu, on Sept. 17, the "Chen-Yuen" went to Port Arthur with her hull much battered, the upper works and funnels riddled by shot, the fore turret pierced, the bridge gone, and the mainmast charred by fire. The repairs would need at least six weeks.

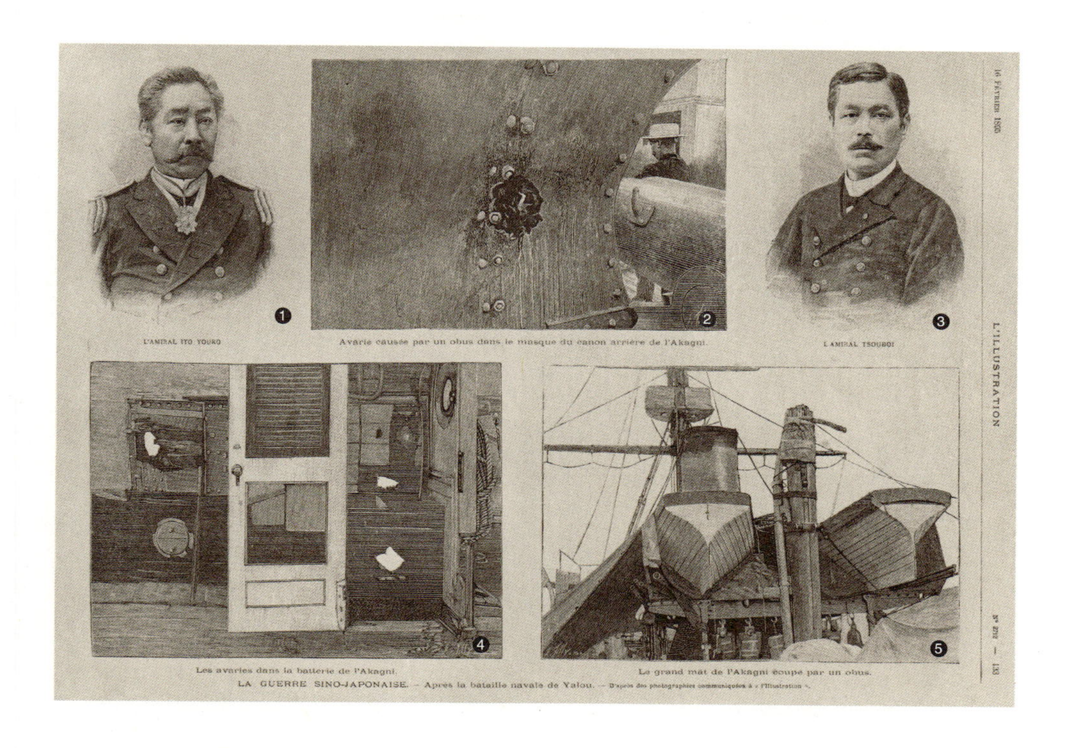

1895 年 2 月 16 日《插图报》

中日战争——黄海海战之后

1　日军联合舰队司令伊东祐亨

2　赤诚号后炮座受伤

3　第一游击队司令官坪井航三

4　赤诚号炮台受伤

5　赤诚号的主桅被炮弹炸断

La Guerre Sino-Japonaise.—Après la bataille navale de Yalou.

1　L'Amiral Ito Youko.

2　Avarie causee par un obus dans le masque du canon arrière de l'Akagni.

3　L'Amiral Tsouboi

4　Les avaries dans la batterie de l'Akagni.

5　Le grand mât de l'Akagni coupé par un obus.

坪井航三（1843—1898），甲午海军名将，第一游击队司令，以提倡单纵队驰名，早年留学美国，甲午战争时期率先在丰岛海面挑起战争，大东沟海战的时候是日本第一游击队司令，率领“吉野号”、“浪速号”、“高千穗号”、“秋津洲号”4 艘新式快速巡洋舰组成的第一游击队参加了战斗，战绩显赫，是甲午海战中的关键性人物。

1894年11月24日《伦敦新闻画报》增刊

黄海海战后，民众在长崎港参观日本军舰赤诚号和比睿号

Visiting the Japanese war-ships "Akagi" and "Hiyei" in Nagasaki harbour, after the battle of the Yalu.

根据日本的官方报道，这两艘舰艇是参加黄海海战的日军船只中受伤最重的。比睿号船尾被一门37吨位的大炮射穿，引起大火。在这两艘船停靠长崎港的3天时间里接待了6万日本民众的参观。

These two ships are stated by the Japanese to have suffered more than any others of the fleet. The "Hi-yei" was struck on the quarter by a shot from a 37-ton gun, which went straight through her and set her on fire. While in harbor these two ships were visited, in three days, by sixty thousand people.

赤诚舰，622吨，963马力，航速10.3节。甲午黄海海战中，日本自己建造的炮舰赤诚舰担任保卫西京丸的任务，舰体重伤，赤诚舰长坂元八郎太被击毙，是海战中日本唯一死亡的舰长。“二战”中，日本联合舰队将其航母命名为赤诚号。

H.M.S. "ALACRITY" VISITING THE SCENE OF THE BATTLE OF THE YALU.

The fighting-tops of the Chinese cruiser 'Chih Yuen," sunk by the Japanese fire, appear in this Sketch, furnished by Lieutenant Wylde.

1894 年 12 月 8 日《伦敦新闻画报》

英军活泼号巡洋舰在黄海海战结束后考察战场

H.M.S. “Alacrity” visiting the scene of the battle of the Yalu.

图为被日军击沉的致远号顶部的射击桅盘残骸

The fighting-tops of the Chinese cruiser “Chih Yuen” , sunk by the Japanese fire, appear in this sketch, furnished by Lieutenant Wylde.

结　语

伊东祐亨元帅的手下败将是中国的丁汝昌元帅，丁元帅是中国海军的司令官，同时也是中国军队可以依靠的极少数有才干的军官之一。丁元帅高大帅气，脸庞充满了威严，非凡的天赋使他在相当年轻的时候就官居高位。从政治角度来讲，他属于中国的改良派，赞同用欧洲的科学体系推动国家的进步。他在黄海海战中表现出的勇猛与那些贪生怕死的中国舰长形成了非常大的反差，当时丁元帅一直战斗在火力最激烈和最集中的第一线，即便脸颊和腿部受了重伤，他依然没有动摇。

——1894年10月13日　英国《图片报》

邓世昌牺牲后举国震动，光绪帝垂泪撰联“此日漫挥天下泪，有公足壮海军威”，并赐予邓世昌“壮节公”谥号，追封“太子少保”，入祀京师昭忠祠，御笔亲撰祭文、碑文各一篇。李鸿章在《奏请优恤大东沟海军阵亡各员折》中为其表功，说：“……而邓世昌、刘步蟾等之功亦不可没者也。”清廷还赐给邓母一块用1.5公斤黄金制成的“教子有方”大匾，拨给邓家白银10万两以示抚恤。邓家用此款在原籍广东番禺为邓世昌修了衣冠冢，建起邓氏宗祠。威海百姓感其忠烈，也于1899年在成山上为邓世昌塑像建祠，以志永久敬仰。1996年12月28日，中国人民解放军海军命名新式远洋综合训练舰为“世昌”舰，以示纪念。

——编者

六　中国陆军的惨败

中国的确把一支军队送上了战场…… 但我们要对比的是一支用钉耙武装起来的军队和一支拿来福枪上阵的军队，这也正是当前中国国民与日本国民之间的真实反差。

——1894年7月17日　英国《泰晤士报》

坚忍和耐力是中国种族的特点，这使得中国一直屹立在人类历史的制高点。纵使中国政府有众多弱点，面对日本，我们相信他们将从农业、工业、商业、陆海军汲取用之不竭的军事和经济资源。

——1894年8月8日　俄国《圣彼得堡日报》

英国国会议员乔治·寇松（G. H. Curzon）侯爵在他的新书《远东问题》中如是写道：从眼下与日本的这场战争来看，中国对于自己从1884—1885年的中法战争后在军事装备上取得的进步，未免“高兴得太早了”。

——1894年9月8日　英国《伦敦新闻画报》

THE ILLUSTRATED LONDON NEWS.

REGISTERED AT THE GENERAL POST OFFICE FOR TRANSMISSION ABROAD.

No. 2889.—VOL. CV. SATURDAY, SEPTEMBER 1, 1894. WITH SIXTEEN-PAGE SUPPLEMENT: ANTWERP EXHIBITION. SIXPENCE. BY POST, 6½D.

R. Caton Woodville

THE WAR IN EASTERN ASIA: CHINESE IRREGULAR TROOPS FROM THE INTERIOR ON THE MARCH.

1894 年 9 月 1 日《伦敦新闻画报》

东亚战争：清政府的团练乡勇正从内地赶赴沿海

The war in Eastern Asia: Chinese irregular troops from the interior on the march.

1894 年 11 月 24 日《伦敦新闻画报》增刊

清军强拉壮丁

Raw levies for the Chinese army.

清廷八旗军总数不到 10 万人，京津两地及各省省会的驻防兵多为八旗军。清军的辅助力量包括“营兵”和“乡兵”，有时二者亦称“绿旗兵”或“乡勇”。大清版图内全部 18 个省共可召集约 17 万名营兵或乡勇，但他们不仅毫无军事素养，而且多数人手中所持武器为弓、箭、斧、矛或火铳。在开赴前线的途中，有些壮丁肆意烧杀抢掠，百姓惧之甚于日军。

The Chinese regular army, from which the garrisons of Pekin, Tientsin, and the provincial capitals are drawn, musters considerably less than 100,000 men altogether. The only reserve force is that of the Ying-Ping, or national militia, sometimes called “the Green Flag” or “the Braves” ; of whom, possibly in the eighteen provinces, 170,000 might be called out for service, but undrilled, and mostly with hatchets, pikes, bows and arrows, and “jingals” or heavy matchlocks. Some of these raw levies have, in their march toward the seat of war, perpetrated robberies and murders and other outrages. They are more to be dreaded than the Japanese soldiers.

Ce numéro est accompagné d'un supplément musical.

L'ILLUSTRATION

Prix du numéro : 75 cent. SAMEDI 11 AOUT 1894 *52e Année. — No 2685*

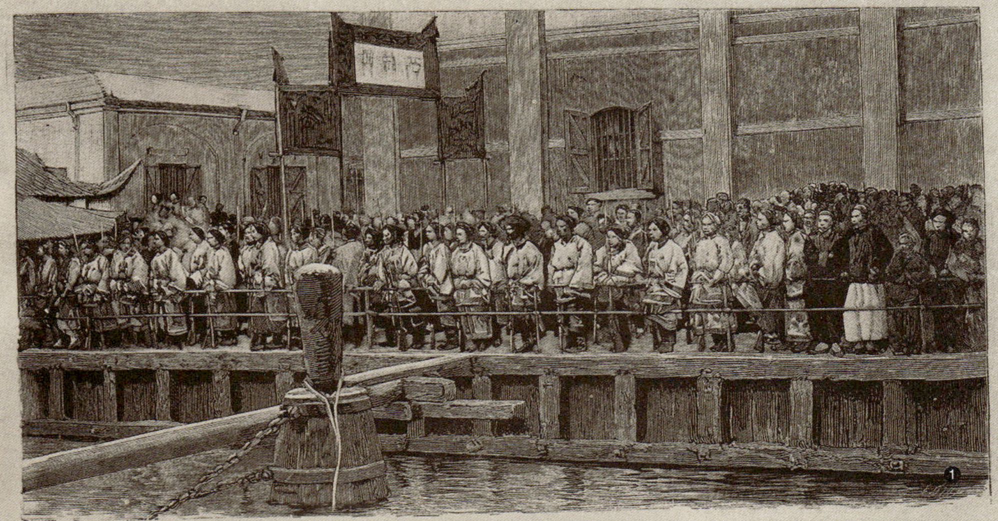

Un embarquement de troupes chinoises à Shanghaï.

LES ÉVÉNEMENTS DE CORÉE. — Réguliers de l'armée provinciale chinoise.

D'après des photographies communiquées par M. Bryois.

1894年8月11日《插图报》

1　中国军队从上海登船
2　中国省级正规军（绿营军）

1　Un embarquement de troupes chinoises à Shanghaï.
2　Réguliers de l'armée provinciale chinoise.

中国人被他们的日本邻居打败已成事实。中国军队的知名度要比日本军队小很多，故而正确审视这支中国军队是一件有趣的事情。

中国军队的麾下除了有24旗（人们称之为一个军，其下属的24旗组成了一支约有10万人的队伍）和皇家卫队之外，还有打着绿色旗帜的地方军（即绿营军）。这支由24旗组成的帝国军队分布于全国各地，它不受地方官员的统帅，而是听命于北京和总理衙门。在这些星级军队中，有一支核心部队，那就是皇家卫队。这支卫队纯粹是用来点缀排场的，它负责护送随行人员，为各种皇家仪式增光添彩。但由于装备落后，不堪一击，故而无法在日后的困境中派上用场。

其实，中国真正的军队是绿营军。虽然比较糟糕，但只有它还能勉强维护自身的荣誉。绿营军按照省份被细分成18个军。每个军有5个师，每个师又有5个营或旅。

在直隶总督李鸿章的强力推动下，中国进入了战争转型时期。此时的转型发生在天津。

皇家军事学堂是根据当时最先进的理念建立起来的，聘请了德国教员，并开始取得了可喜的成果。全国各地涌现了一批兵工厂和制造武器的作坊；克虏伯提供了火药和大型枪炮口径的零部件；雄伟的装甲舰和巡洋舰队应运而生。中国即将变成一个具有危险性的邻国。日本嗅到了这种危险，于是它加速挑起战争。这个结果是所有人预料中的。

我们在封面插图中展示的中国部队为省级军队——绿营军。

——《中国陆军》（选译），1894年8月11日《插图报》

LA GUERRE ENTRE LA CHINE ET LE JAPON. — Départ de l'infanterie de la garde japonaise

1894 年 9 月 30 日《星期日太阳报》

中日战争——日军步兵整装待发

La guerre entre la Chine et le Japon.—Départ de l'infanterie de la garde japonaise.

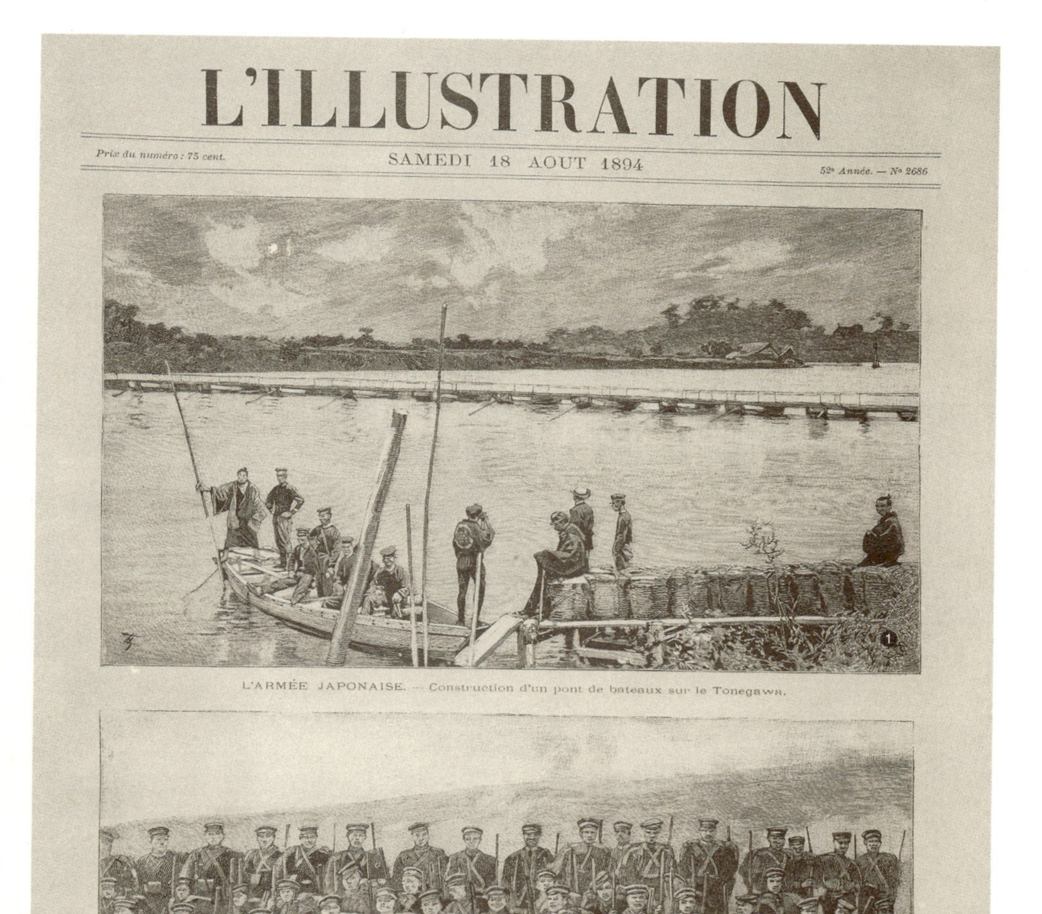

L'ILLUSTRATION

Prix du numéro : 75 cent. SAMEDI 18 AOUT 1894 52e Année. — N° 2686

L'ARMÉE JAPONAISE. — Construction d'un pont de bateaux sur le Tonegawa.

L'ARMÉE JAPONAISE. — Compagnie du génie des tschintaïs.

D'après des documents communiqués par M. le commandant Kreitmann, ancien membre de la mission militaire française au Japon.

1894年8月18日《插图报》

1 日本军队——在利根川上训练修建浮桥

2 日本军队——工兵连

1 L'Armée japonaise.—Construction d'un pont de bateaux sur le Tonegawa.

2 L'Armée japonaise.—Compagnie du génie des tschintaïs.

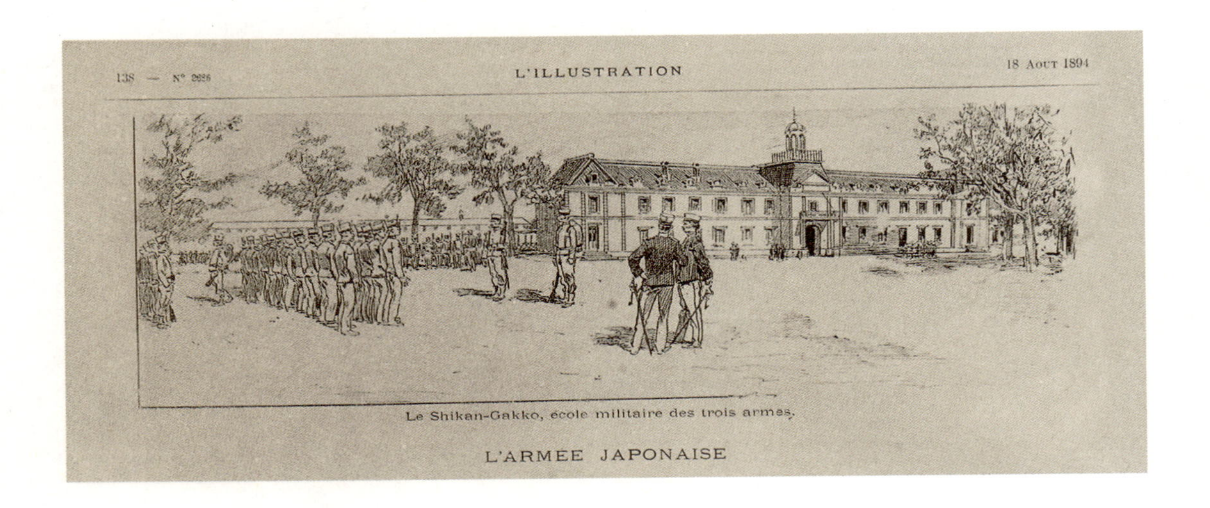

1894年8月18日《插图报》

日本陆军士官学校　　Le Shikan-Gakko, école militaire des trois armes.

近30年来，这个位于远东的独特小民族一直致力于效仿欧洲，并把所获得的成果付诸最终的实践中。即通过最先进和最科学的手段消灭邻国的数十万人，最终赢得“文明”超级强国的称号。

今天，我们呈现给读者的专题是：日本军队。这是一部日本人尽智竭力打造出的怪异机器，它的使命就是维护日本的荣耀，保持日本在亚洲的优势。

日本军队在达到目前的水平之前，经历了三个阶段，这三个阶段与日本天皇政府要求法国派遣的三批军事使团相对应。另外，还必须承认近年来第四阶段的出现，德国的影响力最终在这个阶段占了上风。受益于我们（指法国——编者注）在军队组建方面付出的巨大努力，日本人只是在我们精心培育出的成果上盖上了日耳曼军国主义的戳子而已。

——《日本的军队》（选译），1894年8月18日《插图报》

5 Janvier 1895　　L'ILLUSTRATION　　N° 2706 — 9

LA GUERRE SINO-JAPONAISE. — Depart du Mikado pour Hiroshima, quartier general japonais.

D'après un dessin japonais communiqué par M. Labit.

1895 年 1 月 5 日《插图报》

天皇（离开东京）前往日军战时的大本营——广岛，在那里他为登船赴朝的日军官兵壮行并曾一度亲自指挥作战计划

La guerre sino-japonaise.—Départ du Mikado pour Hiroshima, quaruer général japonais.

根据一幅日本画作制版

D'après un dessein japonais communiqué par M. Labit.

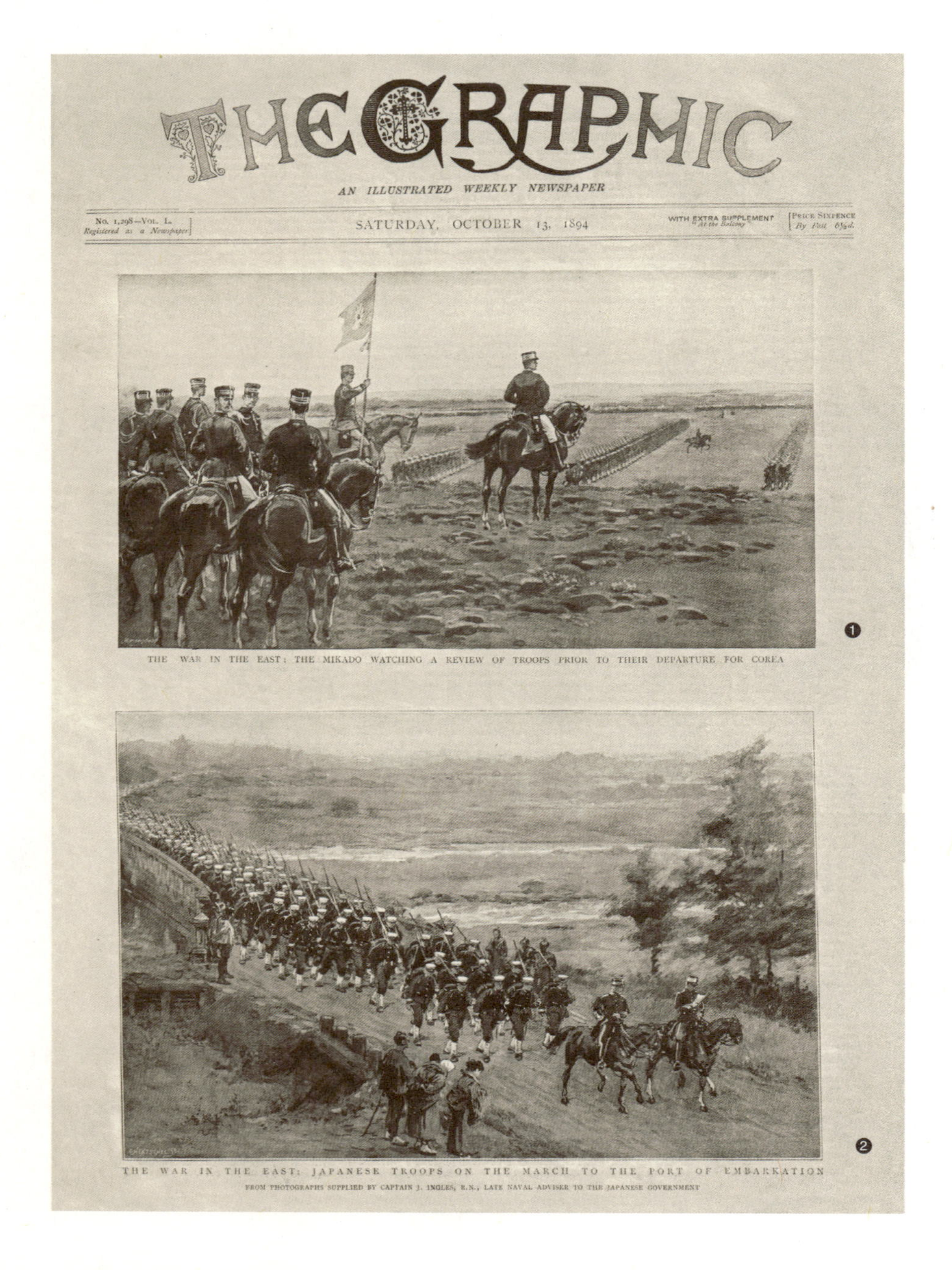

THE GRAPHIC

AN ILLUSTRATED WEEKLY NEWSPAPER

No. 1,298—Vol. L.
Registered as a Newspaper

SATURDAY, OCTOBER 13, 1894

WITH EXTRA SUPPLEMENT "At the Balcony"

PRICE SIXPENCE
By Post 6½d.

❶ THE WAR IN THE EAST: THE MIKADO WATCHING A REVIEW OF TROOPS PRIOR TO THEIR DEPARTURE FOR COREA

❷ THE WAR IN THE EAST: JAPANESE TROOPS ON THE MARCH TO THE PORT OF EMBARKATION

FROM PHOTOGRAPHS SUPPLIED BY CAPTAIN J. INGLES, R.N., LATE NAVAL ADVISER TO THE JAPANESE GOVERNMENT

1894 年 10 月 13 日《图片报》

1 东亚战争一景：日军奔赴朝鲜之前，天皇亲自检阅部队

2 东亚战争一景：日军开赴港口

原日本政府海军顾问、英国皇家海军上尉 J. 恩格斯提供照片

1 The war in the East: The Mikado watching a review of troops prior to their departure to Corea.

2 The war in the East: Japanese troops on the march to the port of embarkation.

Fromphotographs supplied by Captain J. Ingles, R.N., late naval adviser to the Japanese Government.

THE GRAPHIC

AN ILLUSTRATED WEEKLY NEWSPAPER

No. 1,299—Vol. L. Registered as a Newspaper | SATURDAY, OCTOBER 20, 1894 | THIRTY-TWO PAGES | Price Sixpence By Post 6½d.

THE WAR IN THE EAST: THE LANDING OF JAPANESE TROOPS AT CHEMULPO

FROM A SKETCH BY LIEUT. W. H. C. S. THRING, R.N., OF H.M.S. "CENTURION"

1894 年 10 月 20 日《图片报》

东方的战争：日军在朝鲜仁川登陆

The war in the East: the landing of Japanese troops at Chemulpo.

朝鲜危机发生，日军反应迅速，1894 年 6 月 5 日，日本战时大本营下达朝鲜增派混成旅团的动员令，第五师团编制下的混成旅团 8000 人奉命开赴朝鲜，归国休假中的驻朝公使大鸟圭介，带领 70 名海军陆战队员，8 日到达仁川港，488 名陆战队员实施登陆行动，10 日到达汉城日本领事馆完成应付紧急事态的集结。

1894 年 11 月 3 日《伦敦新闻画报》增刊

日军在仁川登陆

The landing of Japanese troops at Chemulpo.

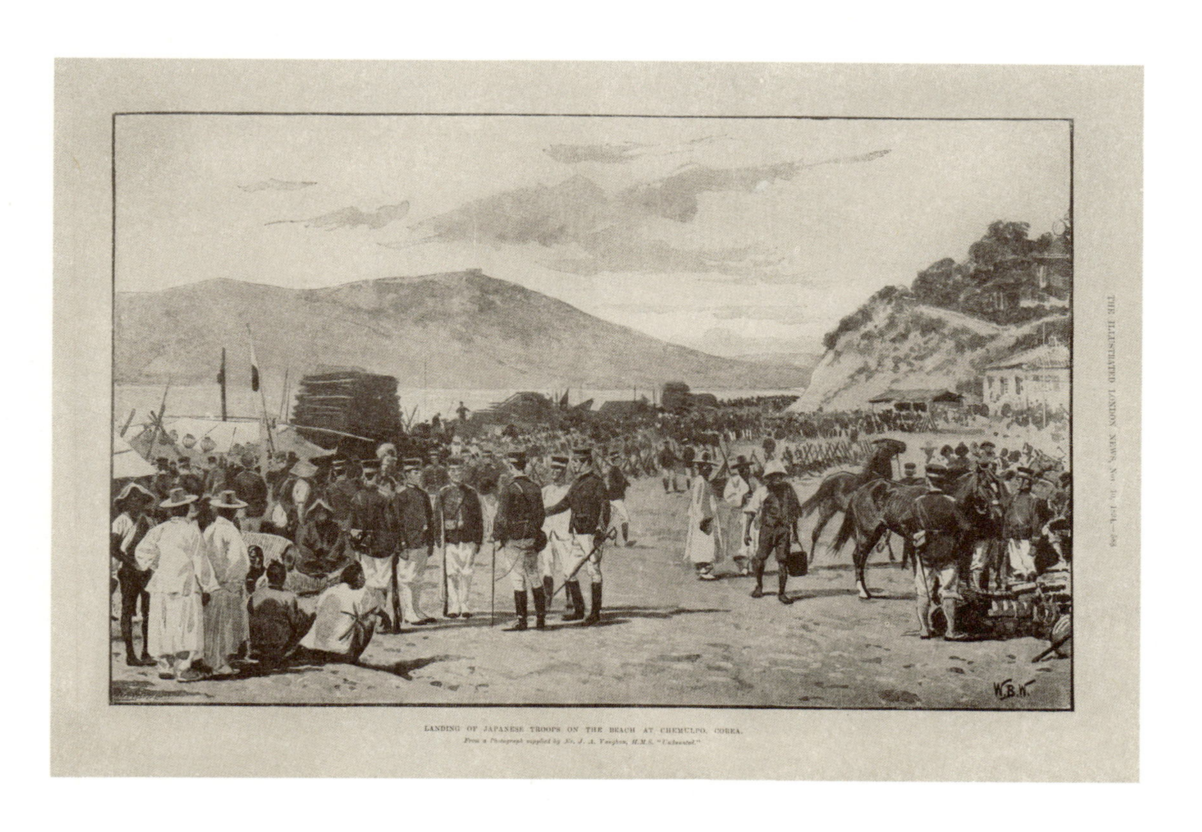

1894 年 11 月 10 日《伦敦新闻画报》

日军在朝鲜仁川登陆

The landing of Japanese troops of the beach at Chemulpo, Corea.

1895年1月5日《插图报》

中日战争——清军阵内旌旗蔽日

La guerre sino-japonaise.—Les porte-etendards de l'armée chinoise.

Throughout Corea the approach of a column of Japanese troops excites considerable interest among the usually phlegmatic natives. They sit down by the roadside and gaze on the unwonted spectacle, either in open-mouthed astonishment, or with quiet curiosity, smoking their long, queerly shaped pipes!

THE WAR IN THE EAST: JAPANESE TROOPS ON THE MARCH TO SEOUL

FACSIMILE OF A SKETCH BY OUR SPECIAL ARTIST WITH THE JAPANESE FORCES

1894 年 12 月 22 日《图片报》

东方的战争：日军开赴汉城

The war in the East: Japanese troops on the march to Seoul.

根据本刊特派随日军画师绘制的草图制版

Facsimile of a sketch by our special artist with the Japanese forces.

在朝鲜，日军无论走到哪里都会吸引一些麻木不仁的当地人前来围观。他们坐在路边呆呆地望着这些不速之客，有的表情诧异，有的则继续悠闲地抽着长长的旱烟管儿。

Throughout Corea the approach of a column of Japanese troops excites considerable interest among the usually phlegmatic natives. They sit down by the roadside and gaze on the unwonted spectacle, either in open-mouthed astonishment, or with quiet curiosity, smoking their long, queerly shaped pipes.

THE WAR BETWEEN CHINA AND JAPAN: LI HUNG CHANG'S EURO

1894年9月8日《伦敦新闻画报》

中日战争一景——李鸿章麾下由欧洲教习训练出来的一支炮兵正在向敌人开火

The war between China and Japan: Li Hung Chang's European-drilled artillery in action.

1894 年 9 月 22 日《伦敦新闻画报》

清军行营内一景

Bivouac of Chinese Soldiers.

Septième année N° 33 ÉDITION RÉDUITE — DIX CENTIMES — LITTERATURE Dimanche 30 Septembre 1894

L'Illustré SOLEIL DU DIMANCHE

LA GUERRE ENTRE LA CHINE ET LE JAPON. — Un des derniers engagements

1894 年 9 月 30 日《星期日太阳报》

中日战争——最近发生的一次交火

La guerre entre la Chine et le Japon.—Un des derniers engagements.

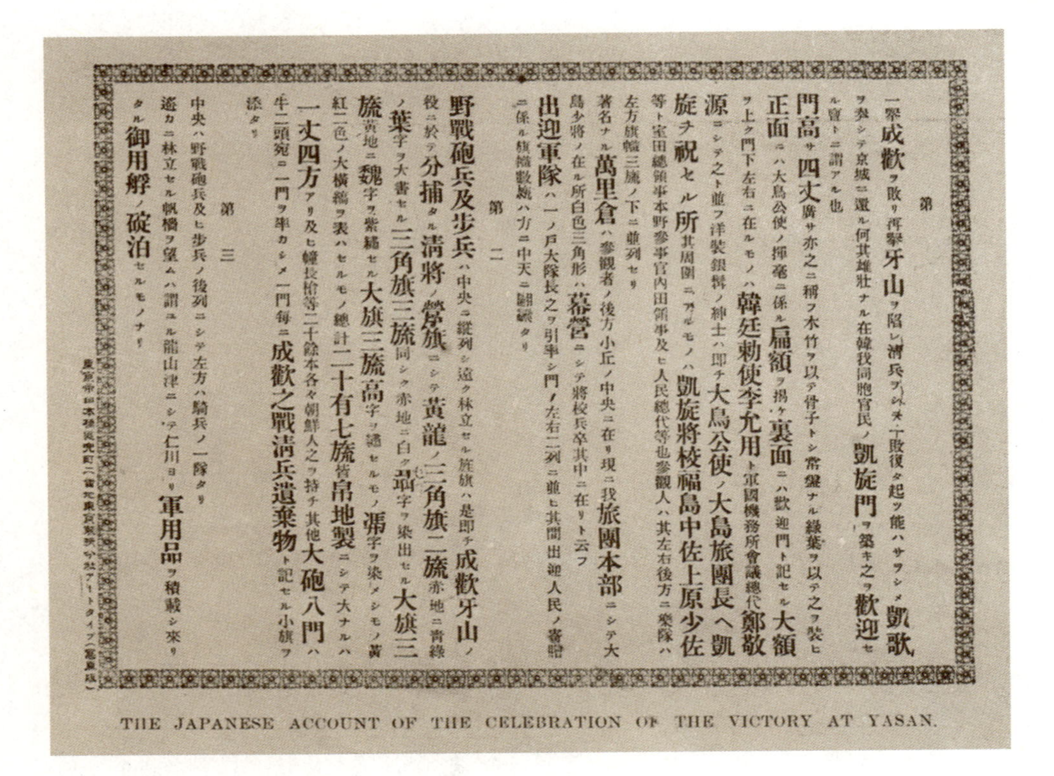

第一

一擧成歡ヲ敗リ再擧牙山ヲ陷レ清兵ヲシテ一敗復タ起ツ能ハサラシメ凱歌ヲ奏シテ京城ニ還ル何其雄壯ナル在韓我同胞官民ノ凱旋門ヲ築キ之ヲ歡迎セル實ニ謂アル也

門高サ四丈廣サ亦之ニ稱フ木竹ヲ以テ骨子トシ常盤ナル綠葉ヲ以テ之ヲ裝ヒ正面ニハ大島公使ノ揮毫ニ係ル扁額ヲ揭ケ裏面ニハ歡迎門ト記セル大額ヲ上ク門下左右ニ在ルモノハ韓廷勅使李允用ト軍國機務所會議總代鄭敬源ニシテ之ト並フ洋裝銀髯ノ紳士ハ即チ大島公使ノ大島旅團長ヘ凱旋ヲ祝セル所其周圍ニアルモノハ凱旋將校福島中佐上原少佐等ト室田總領事本野參事官內田領事及ヒ人民總代等也參觀人ハ其左右後方ニ樂隊ハ左方旗幟三旒ノ下ニ並列セリ

著名ナル萬里倉ハ參觀者ノ後方小丘ノ中央ニ在リ現ニ我旅團本部ニシテ大島少將ノ在ル所白色三角形ハ幕營ニシテ將校兵卒其中ニ在リト云フ

出迎軍隊ハ一ノ戶大隊長之ヲ引率シ門ノ左右二列ニ並ヒ其間出迎人民ノ審瞻ニ係ル旗幟數旒ハ方ニ中天ニ翩翻タリ

第二

野戰砲兵及步兵ハ中央ニ縱列シ遠ク林立セル旌旗ハ是即チ成歡牙山ノ役ニ於テ分捕タル清將ノ營旗ニシテ黃龍ノ三角旗二旒赤地ニ青綠ノ葉字ヲ大書セル三角旗三旒同シク赤地ニ白ク聶字ヲ染出セル大旗三旒黃地ニ魏字ヲ紫繡セル大旗三旒高字ヲ繡セルモノ馮字ヲ染メシモノ黃紅二色ノ大橫縞ヲ表ハセルモノ總計二十有七旒皆帛地製ニシテ大ナルハ一丈四方アリ及ヒ幢長槍等二十餘本各々朝鮮人之ヲ持チ其他大砲八門ハ牛二頭宛ニ一門ヲ牽カシメ一門每ニ成歡之戰清兵遺棄物ト記セル小旗ヲ添タリ

第三

中央ハ野戰砲兵及ヒ步兵ノ後列ニシテ左方ハ騎兵ノ一隊タリ

遙カニ林立セル帆檣ヲ望ムハ謂ユル龍山津ニシテ仁川ヨリ軍用品ヲ積載シ來リタル御用艀ノ碇泊セルモノナリ

東京市日本橋區兜町二番地東京製紙分社アートタイプ（寫眞版）

THE JAPANESE ACCOUNT OF THE CELEBRATION OF THE VICTORY AT YASAN.

1894 年 10 月 6 日《哈珀斯周刊》

日军对牙山大捷的战报

The Japanese account of the celebration of the victory at Yasan.

报道一

朝鲜成欢城首当其冲受到我军轰炸，然后我们推向牙山，痛击清军，并一鼓作气，把他们彻底赶出朝鲜的领土。我们的队伍迈着骄傲的步伐，高唱凯歌回师汉城。兴奋的日本驻朝官员和在朝日侨在汉城郊外竖起一座凯旋门，欢迎我们的勇士进入朝鲜国都。这的确是一件值得庆祝的大喜之事，因此，此举毫不过分。

这座凯旋门高、宽各 40 英尺，纯粹由竹、木搭建，外表饰以大量绿色松柏枝，寓意常青。大门正面的匾额由驻朝公使大鸟圭介亲笔题写，大门背面的匾额形制更大一些，上书“欢迎门”三个大字。大门左右两列分别站着朝鲜禁军统领李书勇、朝鲜军务统帅丁靖勇。图中那位精神抖擞、盛装打扮并与朝鲜民众站在一起的正是我们日本驻朝鲜特命全权大使大鸟圭介。他出城亲自迎接日军统帅大岛义昌少将。两人身边环列着福岛中校、上原少校、驻汉城总领事室堂、参事本野、领事牛田，以及各界民众代表。大门左侧、右侧和后方聚集了大量围观者，军乐队整齐地站在左侧彩旗下。

远处的小山上是著名的抗蒙遗址“小万里长城”，很多朝鲜民众都站在那里向这边张望。由于这座山的中央高台部分被我军据为指挥部，大岛将军麾下的官兵均驻扎在那里，即图中显示的白色旗帜构成的三角形营地内。友达连长麾下的战士在大门外分别立于左右两侧，由当地民众手执的各色彩旗高高地飘扬在两列卫兵中间的空地上。

报道二

站在中间的是炮兵和步兵；远处飘扬的两面三角形黄龙旗是从成欢和牙山战场上的清军将领手中夺来的；此外还有三面红底绿字的三角旗、三面大红旗和三面黄底镶紫边的大旗。各色旗帜，多得数不胜数，令人眼花缭乱。仅以颜色统计，旗帜的颜色总数多达 27 种。这些旗帜质地考究，均为丝绸制品，其中最大的一面达 10 平方英尺；由朝鲜人背着的日军从清军手中夺来的几十柄长矛也在其中；俘获来的 8 门大炮也被展示在这个队伍里，每一台大炮都由两头公牛拖拽前行，每门大炮的炮身上都插有一面小旗，上书：“清军在成欢战场上丢弃的战略物资”。

THE JAPANESE ARMY PASSING THE TRIUMPHAL ARCH ERECTED NEAR SEOUL

From a Photograph supplied by Mr. J. A. Vaughan, H.M.S. "Undaunted."

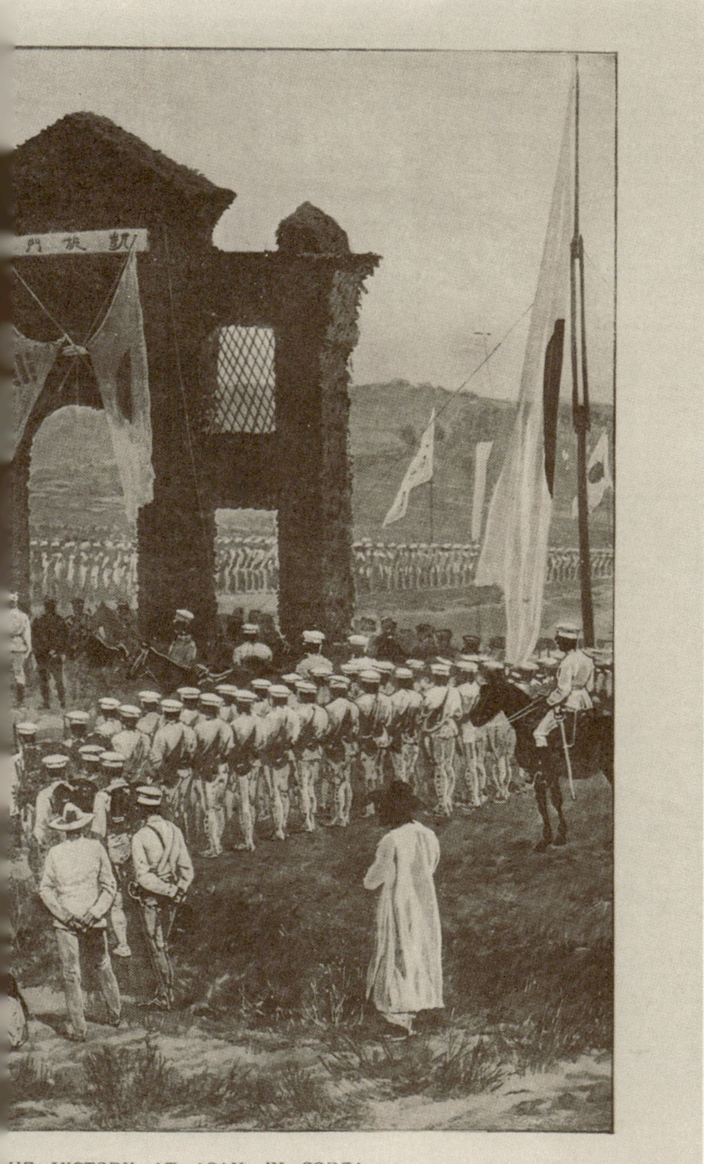

1894 年 11 月 17 日《伦敦新闻画报》

牙山大捷后，日军穿过建立在汉城附近的凯旋门

The Japanese army passing the triumphal arch erected near Seoul after the victory at Asan, in Corea.

only are the greater part of the weapons, ships, and guns used on either side supplied and manufactured by this country, but the man-o'-war's men of both nations have been taught by British officers, and educated according to British methods. To some extent, therefore, we are now watching the result of our own handiwork, and it is interesting to note how plainly can be traced the difference in the character of the two nations by the manner in which each has assimilated and profited by its instruction.

The motto of the Japanese is "thorough," and this is particularly so in the case of the naval officers who have acquired tone and character from those concerned in the early organisation and training of their sea force. Brave, intelligent, enlightened, and liberal-minded, the Japanese naval officers were bound to make a mark in the world's history if the chance was given to them. It is nearly thirty years ago now since the Mikado's Government decided to adopt the naval system of Great Britain instead of that of France, which had been tentatively tried by some of the more powerful Daimios. A number of British officers and petty officers were then engaged to act as instructors, and from that time onwards the Japanese man-of-war's men have shown in every possible way that they have profited by the suggestions and instruction of their British advisers. Their smartness and efficiency has over and over again earned the commendation of the British admirals acting as our commanders-in-chief on that station.

It must be remembered that all Japanese make good seamen, and that these islanders, with almost as much reason as ourselves, may claim a heritage in the ocean. In their civil war the gallant struggle of Admiral Enomoto is not forgotten by British naval men, nor the bold attempt of the sailors in the *Eagle* to cut out the *Stonewall Jackson* in Mayako Bay in April, 1869. Count Saigo, the present First Lord of the Japanese Admiralty, is a member of the great Satsuma clan, and a relative of his commanded the batteries which so staunchly replied to our ships in Kagoshima Bay. It is most regrettable that the inhuman and unnatural action of the captain of the *Naniwa* should have dimmed the lustre and brilliancy of the honourable achievements which have made the record of the Japanese navy one which they may well look upon with pride and satisfaction.

While the Chinese seamen are unquestionably as brave as those of Japan, they are not so lithe, active, or energetic, and this is particularly the case with the men from the south. If all the officers were up to the standard of Admiral Ting the war might have run a very different course. And if that capable officer had been allowed by the Chinese Government to carry out his intention of attacking the Japanese Fleet when it was conveying transports to Chemulpo and Fusan this would certainly have been the case. Every Englishman that has had to do with them acknowledges the splendid material for the making of soldiers or sailors which exists in China. But then while in Japan there has been continuous training on European methods for more than twenty-five years, the continuity of similar training in the Chinese sea force is not to be reckoned by so many months. It is noteworthy that the *Tsi Yuen* in the action which took place in July, and those ships which came to grief at the battle of the Yalu, were commanded by officers from the southern provinces of China. There is no question that the officers of the squadron which has been directly under the command of Admiral Ting, showed as great a superiority over their countrymen from Canton and Foochow in regard to handling their ships as the Japanese have done.

The characteristic conservatism of the Chinese nation is exhibited in regard to costume, for although the bluejackets of the Pehyang Squadron wear a uniform which is somewhat like that of our own seamen, the officers still retain a distinctly native dress. Everything we have learnt about the action of the Yalu points to the superiority of the Japanese in discipline and tactical knowledge.

VIEW OF THE DAÏ-DOKO RIVER, CROSSED BY THE JAPANESE ARMY AT THE BATTLE OF PING YANG

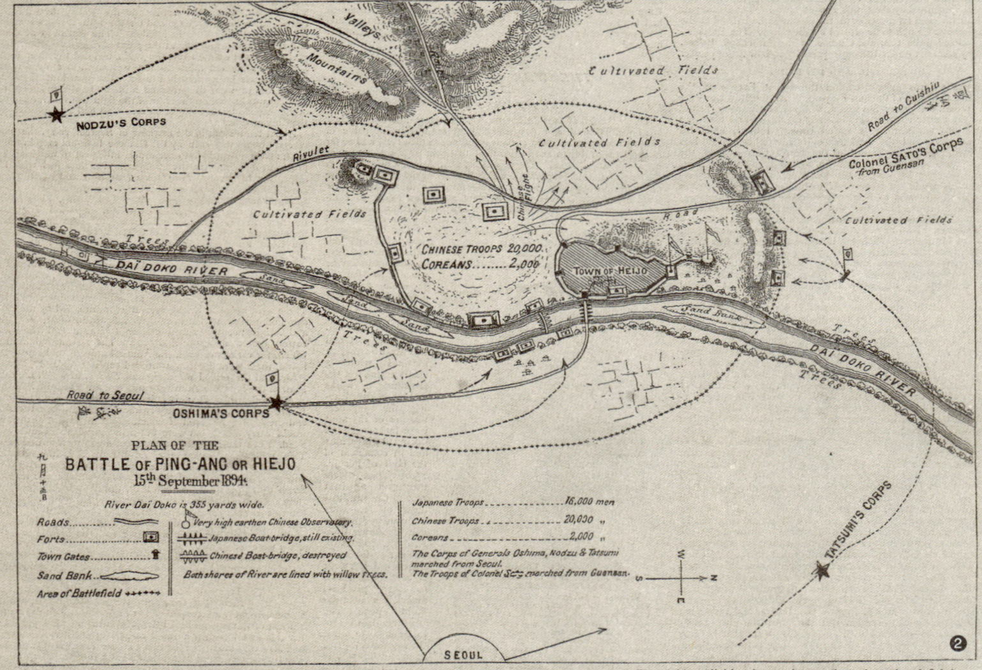

The fighting commenced at five o'clock in the morning and ended at ten o'clock in the evening of September 15. The Oshima division began the attack, and continued fighting till four o'clock, losing 136 men and about 150 wounded. The Tatsumi division came into action at six in the morning, captured the fort by the river shown on the right of the plan, and stormed the forts on the north side of the town, remaining in position till past nine in the evening. Colonel Sato commenced the attack from his side at 6 a.m., and took possession of the outer forts after a short and sharp struggle. His column had come from the port of Guensan, 90 miles distant from Ping Yang. The division under General Nodzu came into action at 10 o'clock, and surprised the Chinese from the rear, preventing them from retreating to the mountains. The following day (the 16th) the Japanese entered the town without opposition

PLAN OF THE BATTLEFIELD OF PING YANG, SHOWING THE DISTRIBUTION OF THE FORCES AND THE DIRECTION OF THE ATTACK

DRAWN BY OUR SPECIAL ARTIST WITH THE JAPANESE FORCES

1894 年 12 月 1 日《图片报》

1　平壤战役中日军渡过的大同江

2　平壤战役图，标示出军力的分配和进攻方向

1　View of the Daï-Doko River, crossed by the Japanese Army at the battle of Ping Yang.

2　Plan of the battlefield of Ping Yang, showing the distribution of the forces and the direction of the attack.

战役是 9 月 15 日清晨 5 时爆发的，一直持续到晚 10 时。大岛义昌的部队首先发起进攻，直到下午 4 点才停火，死 136 人、伤 150 人。立见尚文部队晨 6 时加入战斗，夺取了图 2 上右侧临河的堡垒并陆续攻下城北的数个堡垒，一直坚守到晚 9 时后。佐藤大佐从 6 时开始进攻，在短暂的激战中夺下了外侧的几个堡垒，他的部队是从距平壤 90 英里外的元山登陆的。野津道贯将军指挥的部队上午 10 时从后翼对清军发起突袭，切断了他们向山区撤退的后路。次日（16 日）日军在没有任何抵抗的情况下进入平壤城。

The fighting commenced at five o'clock in the morning and ended at ten o'clock in the evening of September 15. The Oshima division began the attack, and continued fighting till four o'clock, losing 136 men and about 150 wounded. The Tatsumi division came into action at six in the morning, captured the fort by the river shown on the right of the plan, and stormed the forts on the north side of the town , remaining in position till past nine in the evening. Colonel Sato commenced the attack from his side at 6 a.m., and took possession of the outer forts after a short and sharp struggle. His column had come from the port of Guensan, 90 miles distant from Ping Yang. The division under General Nodzu came into action at 10 o'clock, and surprised the Chinese from the rear, preventing them from retreating to the mountains. The following day (the 16th) the Japanese entered the town without opposition.

本刊特派随日军画师绘制

Drawn by our special artist with the Japanese Forces.

8.—SUPPLEMENT TO THE ILLUSTRATED LONDON NEWS, Nov. 24, 1894.—9

THE CAPTURE OF PING-YANG, IN COREA, BY THE JAPANESE A

FROM THE COLLECTION OF LASENBY LIBERTY, ESQ. (OF LIBERTY AND CO., LIMITED), FOR PRESENTATION TO THE JA

Ping-Yang, or Phyong-Yang, a large town of Corea, on the Tai-dong River, the chief inlet of maritime traffic from the western coast, was occupied by a Chinese army of 20,000 men, under Ge Marshal Count Yamagata, with very superior forces, marching in three separate columns by different roads to assail the Chinese earthworks, which they cannonaded on Sept. 15, and stormed next m number taken prisoners, others dispersed and put to flight. The Japanese loss was very small.

1894 年 11 月 24 日《伦敦新闻画报》增刊

日军 9 月 16 日攻陷朝鲜平壤城

The capture of Ping-Yang, in Corea, by the Japanese army, September 16.

重镇平壤，坐落在朝鲜西海岸的峡湾内，航路畅通。中国负责镇守此地的军队有两万人，由左宝贵将军率领，左将军因战败，在此役之后被处极刑（实为英勇阵亡——编者注）。日军山县有朋的军队优势突出，分三路对清军的地面工事发动进攻。这些地面工事已经在 15 日被炮火轰击过，16 日凌晨在激战后被日军夺取。中方 2300 人战死，4000—5000 人受伤，更多人被俘，其余士兵四散逃逸。日军的伤亡损失很小。

Ping-Yang, or Phyong-Yang, a large town of Corea, on the Tai-dong River, the chief inlet of maritime traffic from the western coast, was occupied by a China army of 20,000 men, under General Tso, who has since been beheaded for his defeat in this campaign. He was attacked by the Japanese Field Marshal Count Yamagata, with very superior forces, marching in three separate columns by different roads to assail the Chinese earthworks, which they cannoned on Sept. 15, and stormed next morning before daylight. Of the Chinese, 2300 were killed, four or five thousand wounded, and a still greater number taken prisoners, others dispersed and put to flight. The Japanese loss was very small.

THE WAR IN THE EAST: JAPANESE INFANTRY SCOUTS MAKING A RECONNAISSANCE NEAR PING YANG
FACSIMILE OF A SKETCH BY OUR SPECIAL ARTIST WITH THE JAPANESE FORCES

1894 年 12 月 15 日《图片报》

东方的战争：日本侦察兵在平壤勘察地形

The war in the East: Japanese infantry scouts making a reconnaissance near Ping Yang.

根据本刊特派随日军画师绘制的草图制版

Facsimile of a sketch by our special artist with the Japanese Forces.

1894 年 12 月 15 日《世界画报》

中日战争一景——平壤城外，野津道贯正在纵马巡营

La guerre Sino Japonaise — Ping-Yang—Général Nodzu passant devant le campement de ses troupes en dehors de la ville.

野津道贯（1841—1908），日本陆军元帅，甲午战争中指挥平壤战役，后接替山县有朋任第一军司令官，主持奉天南部的对清作战。

LE MONDE ILLUSTRÉ

PARC D'ARTILLERIE. — UNE BATTERIE DE MONTAGNE

FORAGE D'UN PUITS A L'USAGE DES AMBULANCES.

PING-YANG. — MUR D'ENCEINTE DÉTRUIT PENDANT LA BATAILLE.

LA GUERRE SINO-JAPONAISE. — (Dessins de M. BIGOT, notre envoyé spécial.)

1894年12月15日《世界画报》

1 炮兵阵地——一门山炮

2 为急救伤员打井取水

3 战争后，被摧毁的平壤城墙

1 Parc d'Artillerie.—Une batterie de montagne.

2 Forage d'un puits a l'usage des ambulances.

3 Ping-Yang.—Mur d'enceinte détruit pendant la bataille.

1895 年 1 月 5 日《图片报》

东方战争一景：日军在鸭绿江畔虎山战役中的一次冲锋

The war in the East: the Japanese advance at the battle of Kosan at the passage of the Yalu River.

本刊特派随日军画师绘制

Facsimile reproduction of a sketch by our special artist with the Japanese forces.

JAPANESE SOLDIERS HOLDING THE TRIUMPHAL FEAST AFTER THE VICTORY IN ASAN

THE NAVAL ENGAGEMENT OFF THE

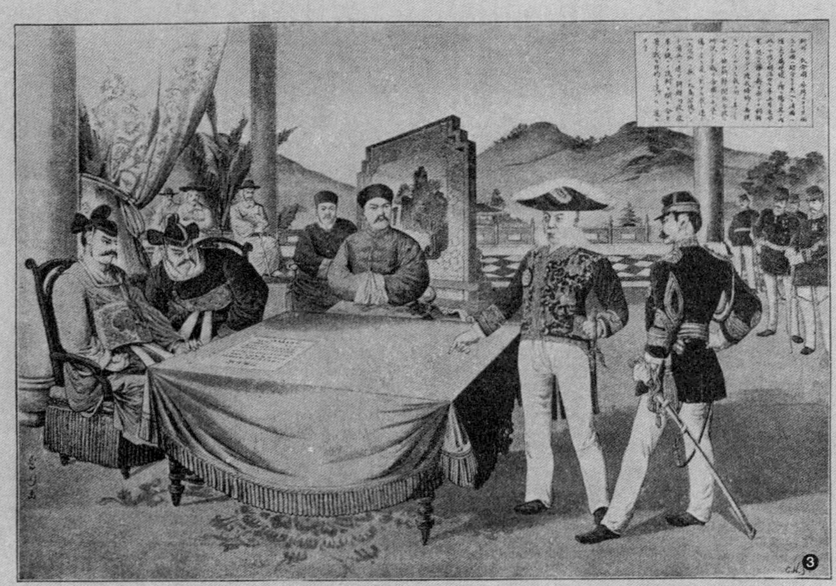

INTERVIEW BETWEEN THE JAPANESE MINISTER, MR. OTORI KEISUKE, AND COREAN OFFICIALS: MR. OTORI KEISUKE EMPHASIZING THE IMPORTANCE OF REFORMING THE CORRUPT GOVERNMENT SYSTEM OF COREA

THE GREAT VICTORY

THE WAR IN THE EAST: FACSIMILES OF SKETCHES MADE

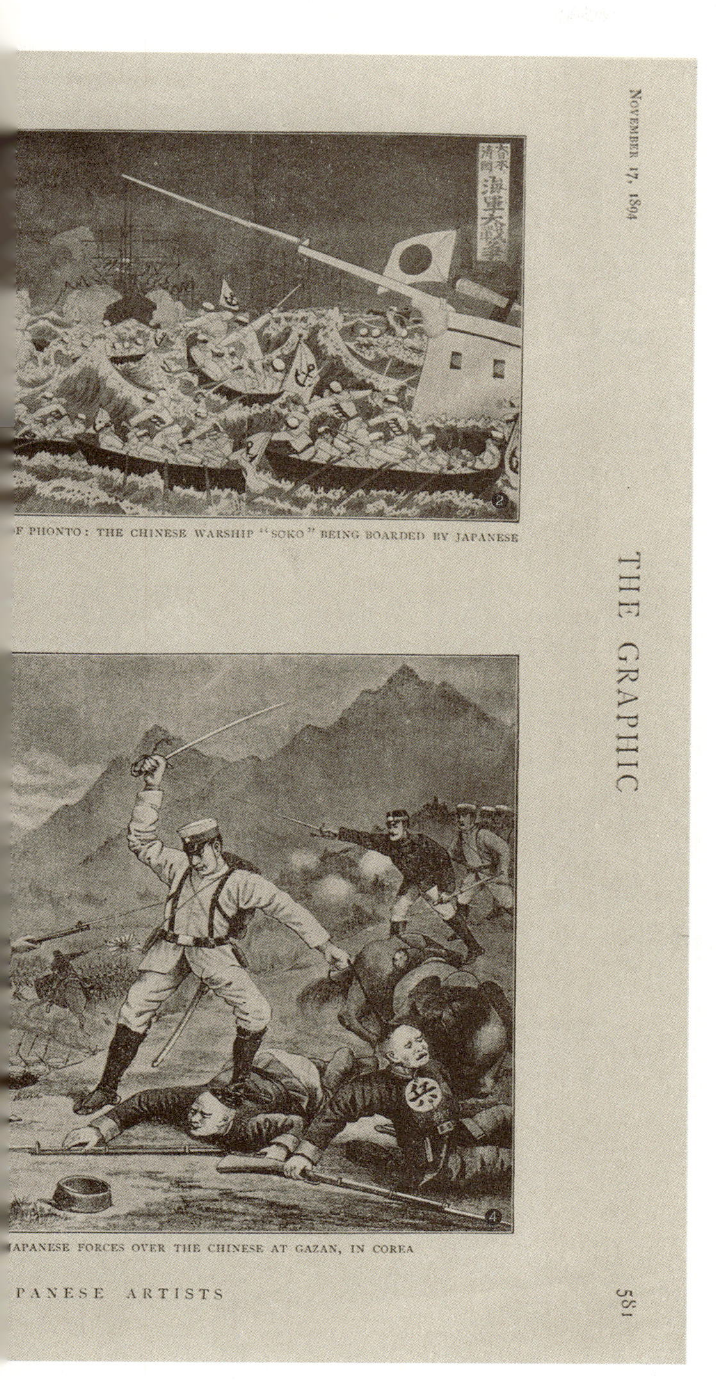
NOVEMBER 17, 1894

THE GRAPHIC

F PHONTO: THE CHINESE WARSHIP "SOKO" BEING BOARDED BY JAPANESE

APANESE FORCES OVER THE CHINESE AT GAZAN, IN COREA

PANESE ARTISTS

581

1894 年 11 月 17 日《图片报》

东方的战争：日本浮世绘画作

The war in the East: facsimiles of sketches made by Japanese artists.

1　日军在（朝鲜）牙山大捷后召开庆功宴

1　Japanese soldiers holding the triumphal feast after the victory in Asan.

2　日军与清军在朝鲜丰岛海域展开激战：日军正在抢登清军操江号运兵船

2　The naval engagement off the Island of Phonto: the Chinese warship "Soko" being boarded by Japanese.

3　日本驻朝公使大鸟圭介与朝鲜王公会谈，并强调改革腐朽朝鲜政府体制的重要性（中国清朝官员为袁世凯——编者注）

3　Interview between the Japanese Minister, Mr. Otori Keisuke, and Corean officials: Mr. Otori Keisuke emphasizing the importance of reforming the corrupt Government system of Corea.

4　日本在朝鲜虎山大败清军

4　The great victory of the Japanese forces over the Chinese at Gazan, in Corea.

THE FIRST CROSSING OF THE BOUNDARY BETWEEN COREAN AND CHINESE TERRITORY: A PONTOON BRIDG
On the 23rd October an advance force of fifteen hundred men, composed entirely of riflemen, commanded by Colonel Sato, crossed the Yalu to the northward. A Chinese earthwork had been thrown up at this point to oppose the landing, but a slight deviation enabled the detachment to c
artillerymen and infantry. They fled after the first two or three rounds had been fired, and the works were captured with a rush
JAPANESE INFANTRY, UNDER COLONEL SATO, ATTACKING A CHINESE POSITION AFTER CROSS

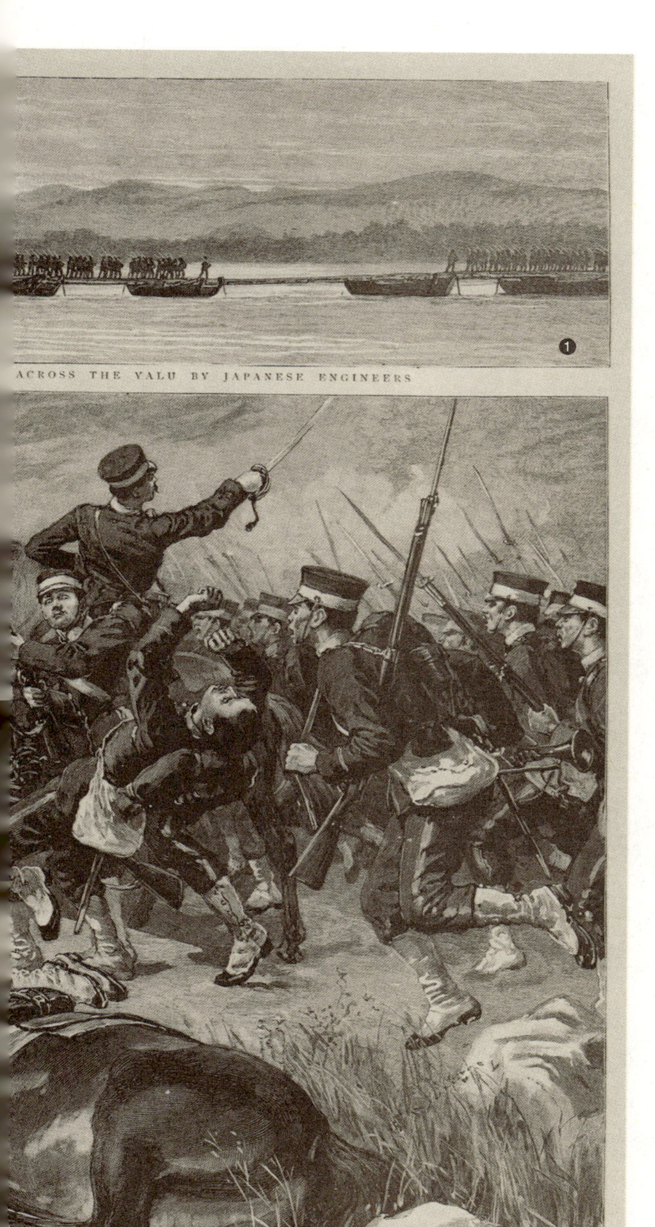

1895 年 1 月 5 日《图片报》

1　日军工兵在中朝边境第一关——鸭绿江渡口上架起一座浮桥

1　The first crossing of the boundary between Corean and Chinese territory: a pontoon bridge throws across the Yalu by Japanese engineers.

2　日军跨越鸭绿江后，佐藤大佐麾下的步兵立即向清军工事发起袭击

2　Japanese infantry, under Colonel Sato, attacking a Chinese position after crossing the Yalu.

UN DESSIN JAPONAIS — Prise d'un drapeau chinois par un officier japonais

1894年10月29日《世界画报》

一名日本军官正在夺走清军龙旗

Un dessin japonais—Prise d'un drapeau chinois par un officier japonais.

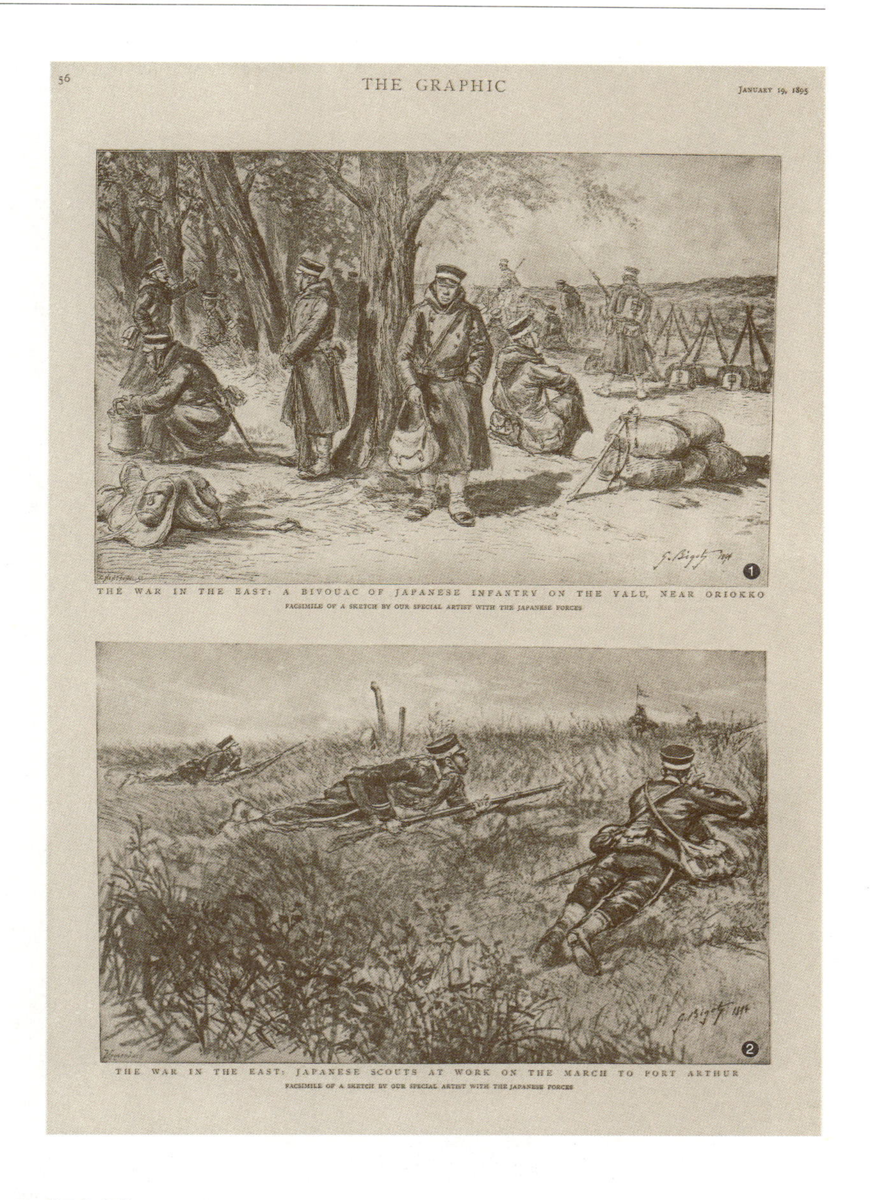
56 THE GRAPHIC JANUARY 19, 1895

THE WAR IN THE EAST: A BIVOUAC OF JAPANESE INFANTRY ON THE YALU, NEAR ORIOKKO

FACSIMILE OF A SKETCH BY OUR SPECIAL ARTIST WITH THE JAPANESE FORCES

THE WAR IN THE EAST: JAPANESE SCOUTS AT WORK ON THE MARCH TO PORT ARTHUR

FACSIMILE OF A SKETCH BY OUR SPECIAL ARTIST WITH THE JAPANESE FORCES

1895 年 1 月 19 日《图片报》

1 东方的战争——日军在鸭绿江畔安营扎寨

2 东方的战争——日军侦察兵在通往旅顺的路上勘察地形

1 The war in the East: a bivouac of Japanese infantry on the Yalu, near Oriokko.

2 The war in the East: Japanese scouts at work on the march to Port Arthur.

根据本刊特派随日军画师绘制的草图制版

Facsimile of a sketch by our special artist with the Japanese Forces.

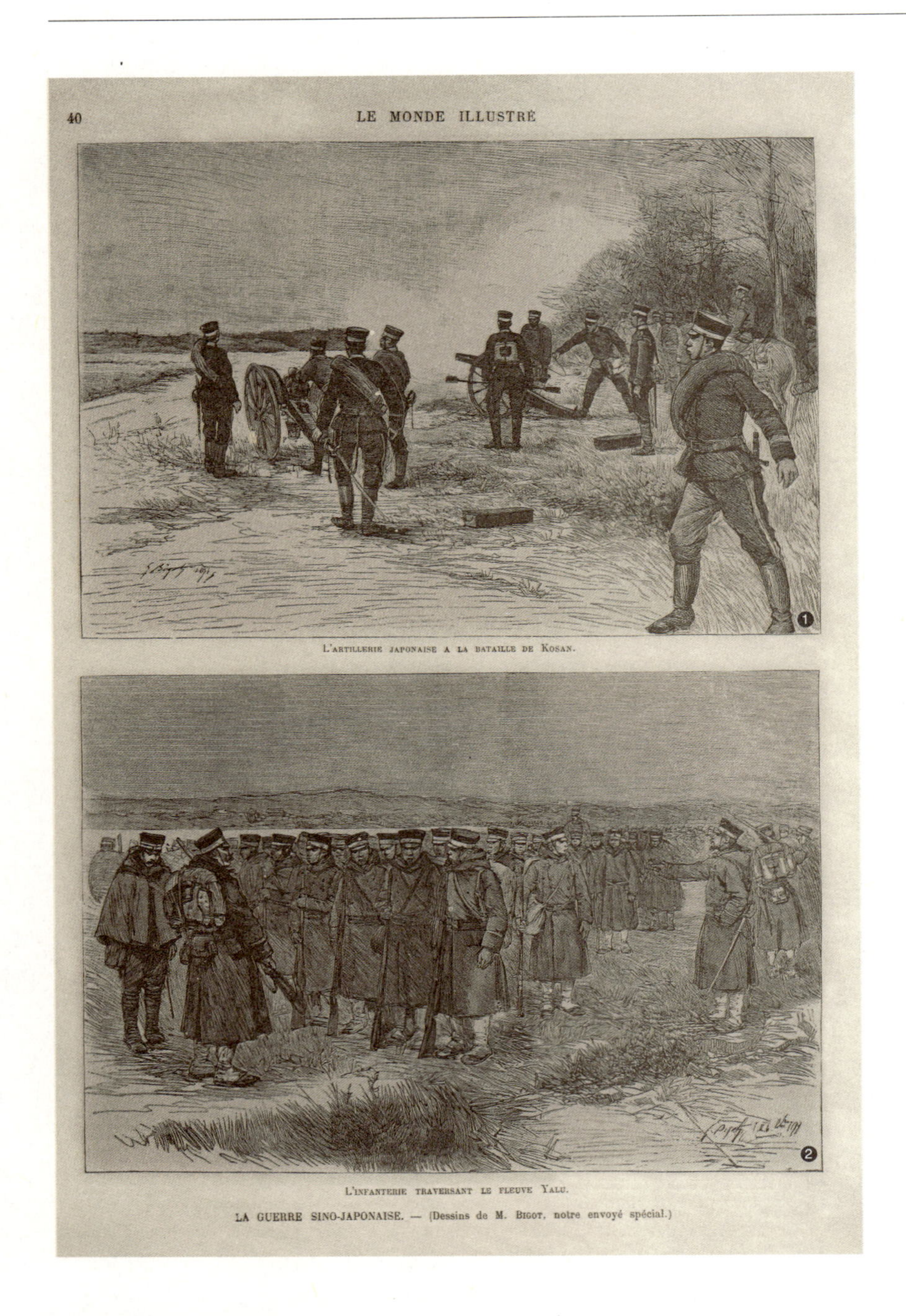
40 LE MONDE ILLUSTRÉ

L'ARTILLERIE JAPONAISE A LA BATAILLE DE KOSAN.

L'INFANTERIE TRAVERSANT LE FLEUVE YALU.

LA GUERRE SINO-JAPONAISE. — (Dessins de M. BIGOT, notre envoyé spécial.)

1895 年 1 月 19 日《世界画报》

中日战争

1　日军炮兵在鸭绿江虎山战场上

2　日军步兵越过鸭绿江

La guerre sino-japonaise.

1　L'artillerie japonaise à la bataille de Kosan.

2　L'infanterie traversant le fleuve Yalu.

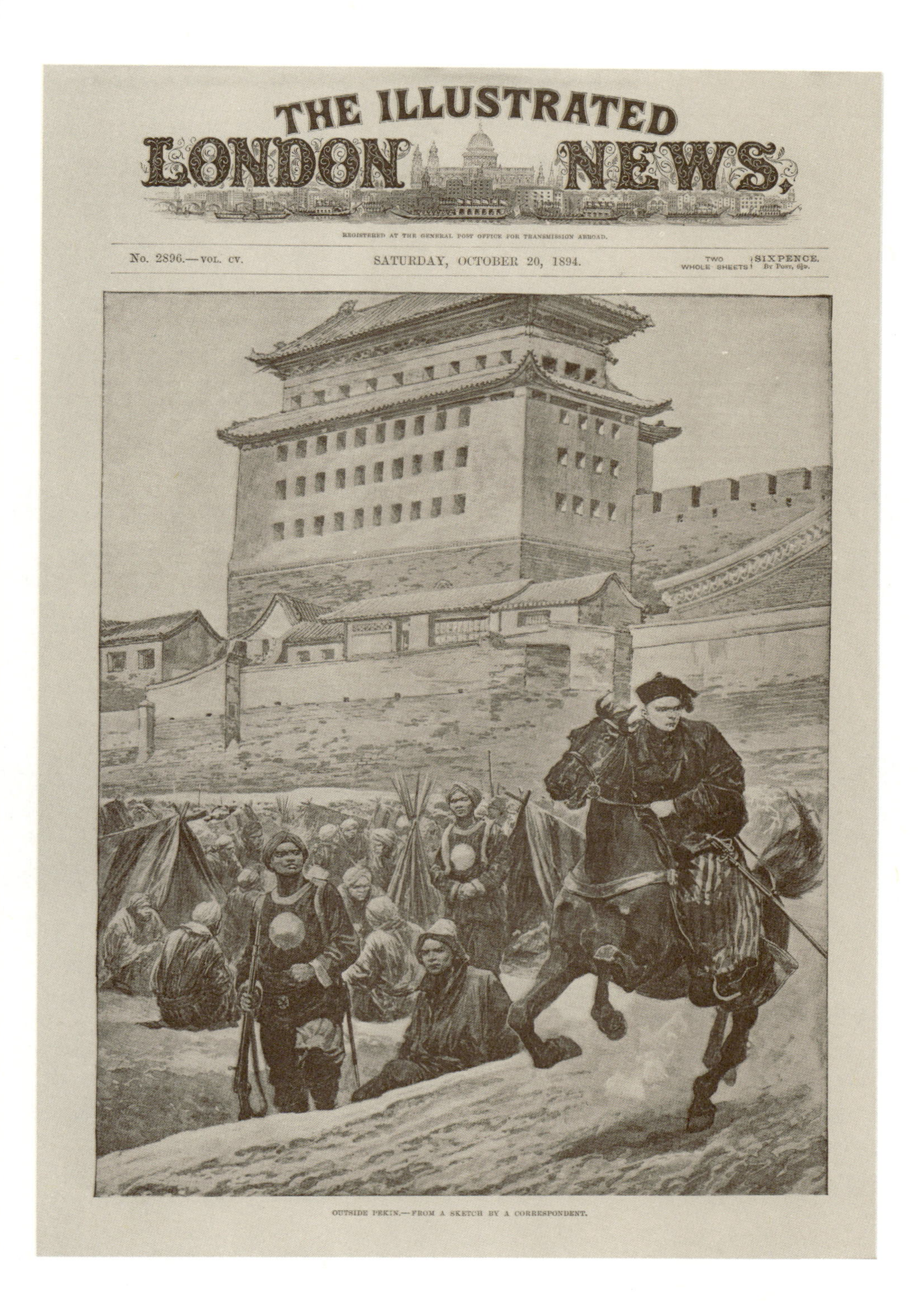

THE ILLUSTRATED LONDON NEWS,

REGISTERED AT THE GENERAL POST OFFICE FOR TRANSMISSION ABROAD.

No. 2896.—VOL. CV. SATURDAY, OCTOBER 20, 1894. TWO WHOLE SHEETS | SIXPENCE. By Post, 6½d.

OUTSIDE PEKIN.—FROM A SKETCH BY A CORRESPONDENT.

1894 年 10 月 20 日《伦敦新闻画报》

北京城外——由战地记者发回的一幅手绘场景

Outside Pekin.—from a sketch by a correspondent.

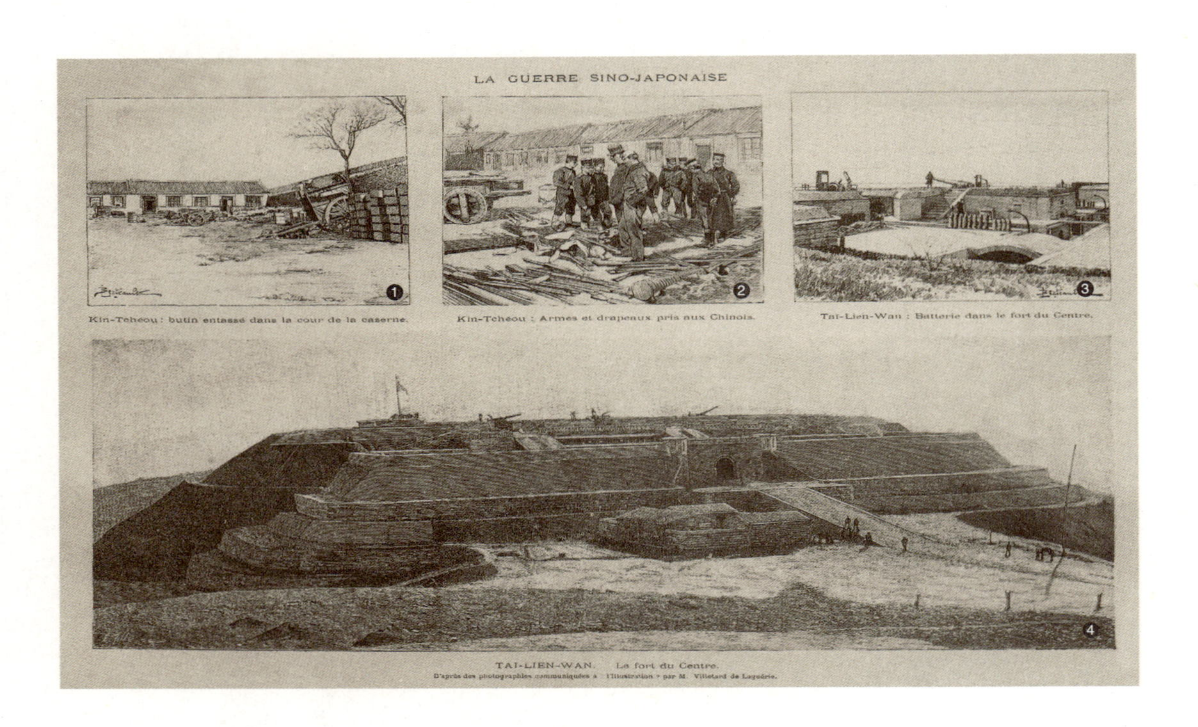

1895年2月2日《插图报》

1 1894年11月4日，金州陷落后日军的军火库中的战利品

2 金州，从中国军队缴获的武器和军旗

3 1894年11月6日，陷落的大连湾中心炮台

4 大连湾中心炮台堡垒

1 Kin-Tchéou: butin entassé dans la cour de la caserne.

2 Kin-Tchéou: Armes et drapeaux pris aux chinois.

3 Taï-Lien-Wan: Batterie dans le fort du Centre.

4 Tai-Lien-Wan.—Le fort du Centre.

伊东祐亨司令的舰队把持着大连湾，与此同时大山岩的部队兵分两路，其中一路围困了1000多名清兵把守的金州城。之后的战斗仅持续了个把小时，金州城就陷落了。中国人几乎没有抵抗就逃跑了，留下了枪炮、弹药、军旗和乐器。在我们展示的版画插图中，读者可以看到金州城的一个中国兵营，在院落内堆满了武器弹药等从天子的军队那里缴获来的战利品，甚至包括一台将官乘坐的马车！

东侧，攻打大连的战斗相对困难一些，读者看一下我们展示给大家的大连湾中心炮台和堡垒的版画插图就可以想象。在插图上有炮台的一部分炮弹，以及用来运送炮弹的隐蔽在掩体内的小道和弹药库。为了攻下这里，大山岩的第一分队在前一夜夺取金州城后与第二分队会合。在11月5日夜，日军炮兵开始炮击有3000名清兵把守的大连湾，6日上午，50多名中国士兵阵亡，坚持不住的守军开始向旅顺港撤退，日军占领大连时仅死两人、伤8人，伊东祐亨的舰队甚至没做任何事。

金州、大连两地到手以后，日军便切断了中国人和旅顺之间的所有联系。这个中国海军的基地、渤海湾的咽喉要道即将成为伊东祐亨和大山岩的盘中餐。

——《战况报道》（选译），1895年2月2日《插图报》

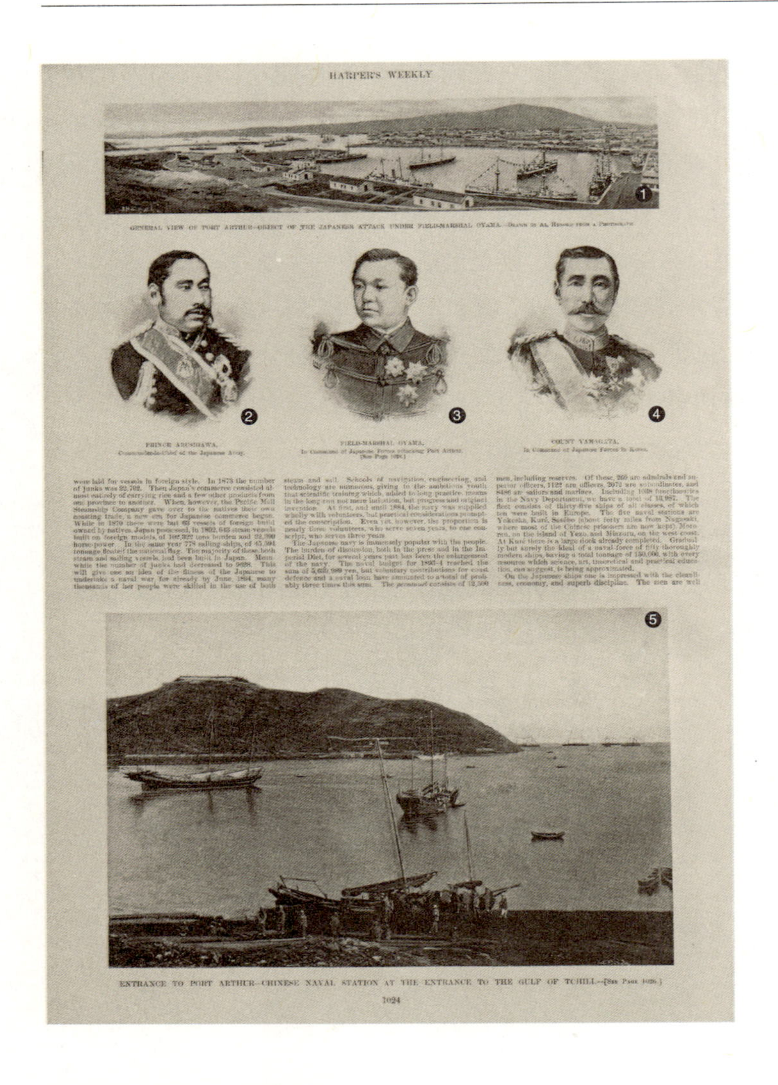

HARPER'S WEEKLY

GENERAL VIEW OF PORT ARTHUR—OBJECT OF THE JAPANESE ATTACK UNDER FIELD-MARSHAL OYAMA.—Drawn by Al. Hencke from a Photograph.

PRINCE ARUSIGAWA,
Commander-in-Chief of the Japanese Army.

FIELD-MARSHAL OYAMA,
In Command of Japanese Forces attacking Port Arthur.
[See Page 1026.]

COUNT YAMAGATA,
In Command of Japanese Forces in Korea.

were laid for vessels in foreign style. In 1873 the number of junks was 22,702. Then Japan's commerce consisted almost entirely of carrying rice and a few other products from one province to another. When, however, the Pacific Mail Steamship Company gave over to the natives their own coasting trade, a new era for Japanese commerce began. While in 1870 there were but 63 vessels of foreign build owned by natives, Japan possessed, in 1892, 642 steam-vessels built on foreign models, of [illegible] tons burden and 22,390 horse-power. In the same year 778 sailing-ships, of 45,394 tonnage floated the national flag. The majority of these, both steam and sailing vessels, had been built in Japan. Meanwhile the number of junks had decreased to 9628. This will give one an idea of the fitness of the Japanese to undertake a naval war, for already by June, 1894, many thousands of her people were skilled in the use of both steam and sail. Schools of navigation, engineering, and technology are numerous, giving to the ambitious youth that scientific training which, added to long practice, means in the long run not mere imitation, but progress and original invention. At first, and until 1884, the navy was supplied wholly with volunteers, but practical considerations prompted the conscription. Even yet, however, the proportion is nearly three volunteers, who serve seven years, to one conscript, who serves three years.

The Japanese navy is immensely popular with the people. The burden of discussion, both in the press and in the Imperial Diet, for several years past has been the enlargement of the navy. The naval budget for 1893-4 reached the sum of [illegible] yen, but voluntary contributions for coast defence and a naval loan have amounted to a total of probably three times this sum. The *personnel* consists of 12,500 men, including reserves. Of these, 260 are admirals and superior officers, 1122 are officers, 2072 are subordinates, and 8486 are sailors and marines. Including 1038 functionaries in the Navy Department, we have a total of 13,987. The fleet consists of thirty-five ships of all classes, of which ten were built in Europe. The five naval stations are Yokosuka, Kuré, Sasebo (about forty miles from Nagasaki, where most of the Chinese prisoners are now kept), Mororan, on the island of Yezo, and [illegible], on the west coast. At Kuré there is a large dock already completed. Gradually but surely the ideal of a naval force of fifty thoroughly modern ships, having a total tonnage of 150,000, with every resource which science, art, theoretical and practical education can suggest, is being approximated.

On the Japanese ships one is impressed with the cleanliness, economy, and superb discipline. The men are well

ENTRANCE TO PORT ARTHUR—CHINESE NAVAL STATION AT THE ENTRANCE TO THE GULF OF TCHILL.—[See Page 1026.]

1024

1894 年 10 月 27 日《哈珀斯周刊》

1 旅顺港一览图——陆军元帅大山岩率领日军作战的战利品

2 日军总司令有栖川宫炽仁亲王

3 日军进攻旅顺港的指挥官大山岩

4 日军在朝鲜战争的指挥官山县有朋

5 渤海湾咽喉要塞上的中国军港——旅顺港的入口处

1 General view of Port Arthur—object of the Japanese attack under Field-Marshal, Oyama.

2 Prince Arusigawa. Commander-in-chief of the Japanese Army.

3 Field-Marshal Oyama. In command of Japanese Forces attacking Port Arthur.

4 Count Yamagata. In command of Japanese Forces in Korea.

5 Entrance of Port Arthur-Chinese naval, station at the entrance to the gulf of Tchill.

376　THE GRAPHIC　MARCH 30, 1895

SKETCHES FROM THE SEAT OF WAR

THE first of our illustrations shows the head of a man who came into Newchwang just before that place was captured by the Japanese, with a tale, purporting to be from the Chinese General in command of the forces, to the effect that no goods were safe with foreigners. The man was promptly beheaded by the order of the Taotai, and his head exhibited over one of the gates of the town. Surgeon Penny, of H.M.S. *Firebrand*, stationed at Newchwang, in sending the sketch, said that although they were expecting an attack from the Japanese, the Europeans in the town had not as yet given way to panic. Since then the place has fallen into the hands of the Japanese, but the Europeans, fortunately, did not suffer either from the defeated troops or the victorious army.

Our second illustration is a facsimile reproduction of a sketch by our special artist with the Chinese, Mr. C. E. Fripp, and depicts a common scene in the camp. The man in the centre is a professional story-teller and conjurer. He gathers round him a group of soldiers, clothed in their multifolded garments, and holds them spellbound as he relates the deeds of valour of the Chinese armies and the horrible cruelty and treachery of their foes. On the opposite page is a sketch by our special artist, made at Shan-Hai-Kwan, on the Gulf of Liau-Tong, on the way to Newchwang. Shan-Hai-Kwan is the present terminus of the railway, and is a town of some importance, having 20,000 inhabitants. The Great Wall of China finds its eastern limit in the waters of the Liau-Tong Gulf some four or five miles south-east of the town. In writing of the place, Mr. Fripp says that Shan-Hai-Kwan is the depôt for stores intended for the Chinese forces in Shing King. Troops and stores were passing through the gap in the Great Wall, through which the railway runs, in an endless stream, while the work of strengthening the fortifications was being carried on night and day. The capture of Shan-Hai-Kwan would place the Japanese within striking distance of Pekin, hence the unwonted activity of the Chinese in securing the town against the expected assault of the enemy. The Great Wall of China is not in very good repair—in fact, in some places it has lost all semblance of a wall, the brick facing and platform having entirely disappeared. The action of the rain, too, has washed down the mud interior, reducing the top to a sharp ridge just broad enough for a footway. There are two gaps in the wall at Shan-Hai-Kwan, one on each side of the town, caused by the annual floods. The original builders of the wall had allowed for the floods by building arches for the water to flow through; but these proved insufficient, and the water broke through the wall, and the gaps have remained and will remain. The Great Wall will, notwithstanding all its defects, be one of the most difficult obstacles for the Japanese to overcome, but as they carried Port Arthur so easily, the capture of Shan-Hai-Kwan can only be a matter of time, and then Pekin will be at the mercy of the invaders.

THE HEAD OF A BEARER OF FALSE NEWS FIXED TO A GATEWAY
AN OBJECT-LESSON AT NEWCHWANG
From a Sketch by Surgeon H. S. Penny, R.N.

A STORY-TELLER IN THE CHINESE CAMP ON THE WAY TO NEWCHWANG
FACSIMILE OF A SKETCH BY OUR SPECIAL ARTIST WITH THE CHINESE FORCES

1894 年 11 月 10 日《伦敦新闻画报》

1　牛庄的杀一儆百
散布谣言者（称日军会杀入西方人聚居的营口——编者注）的脑袋被道台挂在了城门前。

2　开赴牛庄的清军部队，军营里讲评书的人

1　An object-lesson at Newchwang.
The head of a bearer of false news fixed to a gateway.

2　A story-teller in the Chinese camp on the way to Newchwang.

西方人在报道中所称的牛庄，以及中英《天津条约》中规定的东北唯一的开埠水陆口岸牛庄，都是指营口。它位于辽河口左岸，驻有英、美、法、瑞典等外国领事和众多西方人。营口最终在 1895 年 3 月初陷落。

THE WAR IN EASTERN ASIA: CHINESE TROOPS TRYING TO SAVE T

Drawn by R. Caton Woodville, from Photographs.

1895 年 1 月 5 日《伦敦新闻画报》

远东的战争：中国军队（在逃跑时）试图挽回他们的火炮

The war in Eastern Asia: Chinese troops trying to save their artillery.

甲午战争爆发时，中国东北大部分地区已遭受了连年涝灾，致使路况极差；清军拖拽式炮械的运输变得举步维艰，大炮一旦进入阵地就失去了进退机动性；在日军进攻的状况下，炮兵要么逃命，要么被杀，异常被动。

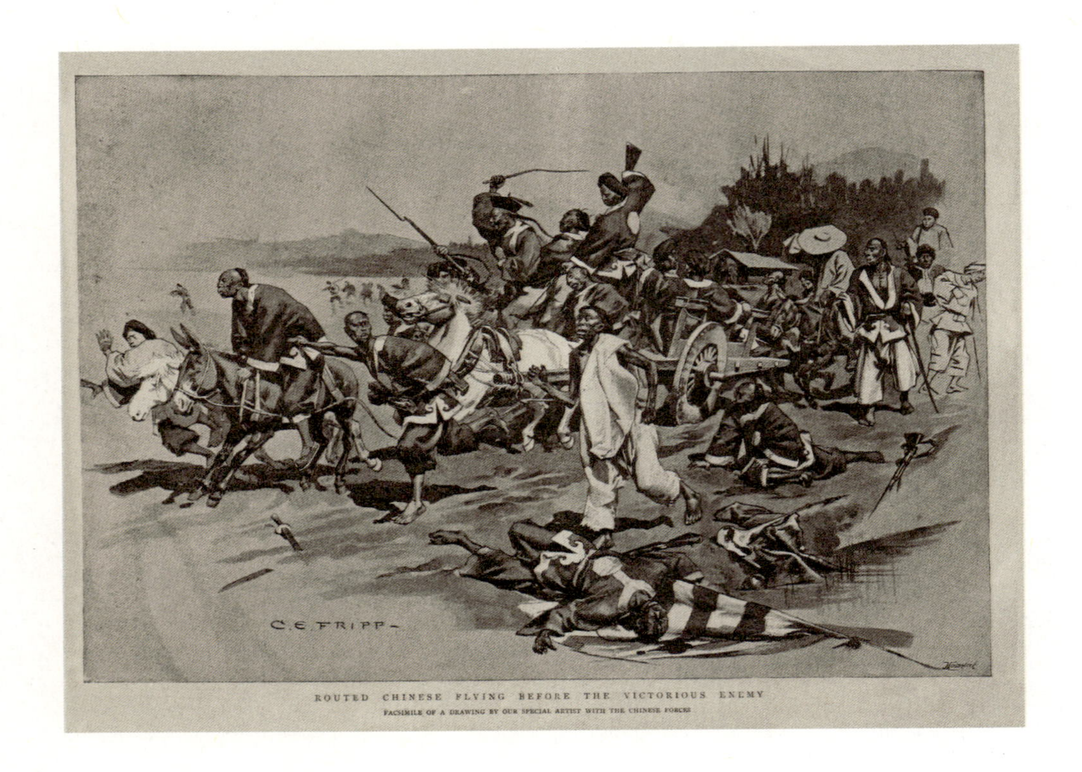

ROUTED CHINESE FLYING BEFORE THE VICTORIOUS ENEMY

FACSIMILE OF A DRAWING BY OUR SPECIAL ARTIST WITH THE CHINESE FORCES

1895 年 4 月 6 日《图片报》

中国军队在“胜利者”面前溃败而逃

Routed Chinese flying before the victorious enemy.

根据本刊特派随清军画师绘制的草图制版

Facsimile of a drawing by our special artist with the Chinese forces.

THE ILLUSTRATED LONDON NEWS, Sept. 29, 1894.—405

THE CHINESE ARMY: DISCIPLINE ON THE MARCH.

1894 年 9 月 29 日《伦敦新闻画报》

清军在行军途中惩罚一名违犯军规的士卒

The Chinese army: discipline on the march.

400 Supplément Littéraire Illustré du "Petit Parisien"

LES EVÉNEMENTS DE CHINE

SUPPLICE A PÉKIN D'UN GÉNÉRAL CHINOIS ACCUSÉ DE TRAHISON

1894 年 12 月 9 日《小巴黎人》

一位清军将领以叛国罪名在北京被处以极刑

Supplice à Pékin d'un général chinois accusé de trahison.

在战争初期，前线的中国将领发回了不少假捷报，给自己炮制了不少战功；当真相大白，纸再也不能包住火，一连串全线溃败的消息传回北京，激起了社会各界的愤慨；众多编造假捷报的将领被召回京，当即被判处死刑，并以最残酷的刑罚在集结的军队前行刑。值得思考的是，这样的极端做法是否还有意义，至少，到目前为止，日军所获取的优势已经足以确保他们将在整个战争中大获全胜，中国唯一的出路就是向日本求和或等待外国的干涉。

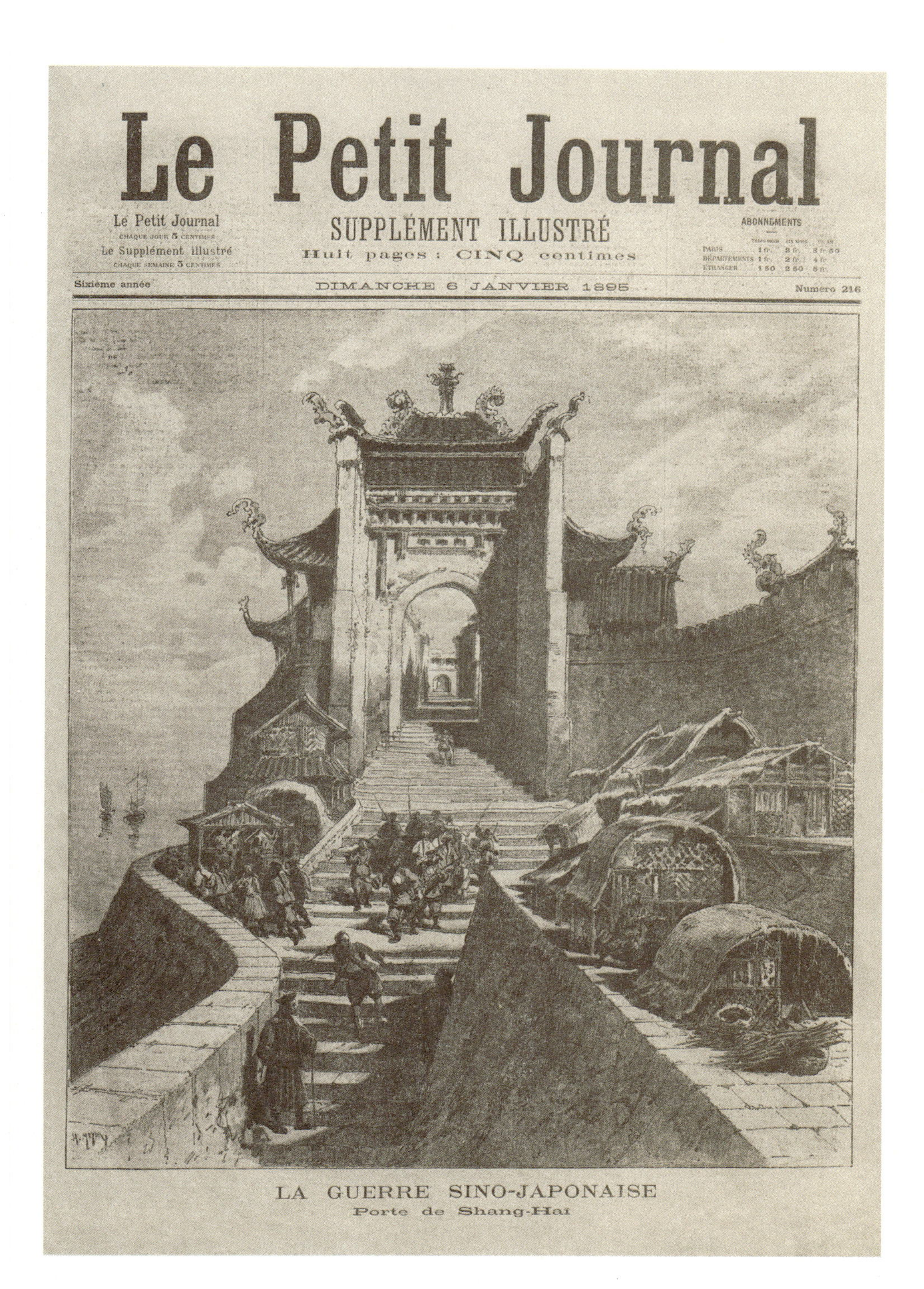

Le Petit Journal

Le Petit Journal
CHAQUE JOUR 5 CENTIMES
Le Supplément illustré
CHAQUE SEMAINE 5 CENTIMES

SUPPLÉMENT ILLUSTRÉ
Huit pages : CINQ centimes

ABONNEMENTS

	TROIS MOIS	SIX MOIS	UN AN
PARIS	1 fr.	2 fr.	3 fr 50
DÉPARTEMENTS	1 fr.	2 fr.	4 fr
ÉTRANGER	1 50	2 50	5 fr.

Sixième année — DIMANCHE 6 JANVIER 1895 — Numéro 216

LA GUERRE SINO-JAPONAISE
Porte de Shang-Haï

1895 年 1 月 6 日《小日报》

中日战争一景：清军在山海关加强设防

La guerre sino-japonaise: Porte de Shang-Haï.

结　语

与士兵的军事素养相比，士兵的数量已经显得微不足道，特别是在技术、冷静和胆识决定一支军事力量优劣的今天，这个道理就更加显而易见。30年前，一个士兵的功能还仅仅是把子弹推入枪膛然后胡乱横扫一气。那个年代，也许人数上的优势还会把对手在勇气和军事训练上的一部分优势抵消掉，但即便是在那时，区区5000名英国士兵已经足以攻入北京城。

——1894年8月　美国《匹兹堡快讯》

到目前为止，中国几乎将所有的钱和精力都花在了海军上，而陆军总体上看是被忽视了。路过中国的任一兵工厂、堡垒和固定防御时，我们都禁不住要问中国人到底有没有陆军？现代观点认为，一个国家如果除了最原始的手推车和平底船之外，没有铁路，没有交通工具，也没有南北水运线，怎么可能调遣或补给军队？若海军强大这也许是可能的。对中国来讲，幸运的是，战争目前还在边界。因而它的首要任务是把日军抵挡在外，并一如既往地在相邻的朝鲜半岛作战。

毫不过分地讲，除直隶省之外，清朝没有现代意义上的军队 。只有在李鸿章管辖的省份，才有一支拥有现代化装备、经过现代化训练和武装的军队。李鸿章代表着新大清的思想和理念。大清能为突如其来的战争做出准备，应该归功于李鸿章不折不挠的毅力和强大的决心。

——1894年8月25日　美国《哈珀斯周刊》

七　旅顺屠杀真相

在屠城发生的第三个夜晚，大山岩陆军司令的国际法顾问——有贺长雄[①] 先生来旅顺衙门拜会（我们这些）随军记者，我们正在屋子中央的火盆边抽烟。有贺先生入座后，就问我："维利耶先生，请毫无顾忌地告诉我，你会不会把过去三天的状况称作'屠杀'？"这真是一个令人惊讶的问题，而且它发自一个日军军官。我环顾了一下我的同行们，克里曼（Creelman）[②] 、克温（Cowen）[③] 和哈特（Hart）[④] 先生，他们也同样被这个问题惊住了。我回答："有贺先生，您的那个用词放在这个事件上并不贴切。"我对他说，第一天日军遇到的挑衅（指日军屡次遭遇的清军虐俘的事件，见本章 1894 年 12 月 15 日《世界画报》插图——编者注）也许可以算作日军行为的借口，但后两天的工作应该用另外一个词来形容。然而有贺先生并没有追问我那个词是什么，但我思考了一下，还是说出了："那是冷血的屠宰。"那就是一场冷血的屠宰。

——弗里德里克·维利耶《旅顺港的真相》
1895 年 3 月《北美评论》第 160 卷

---

① 日本国际法专家、教授。有贺长雄曾留学于德、奥，曾任教于日本陆军大学校、海军大学校、东京帝国大学、庆应义塾大学、早稻田大学，1894 年 10 月受伊藤博文之托奔赴陆军前线，协助大山岩处理战争中的国际法问题，成为日本陆军第二军司令部的随军国际法顾问。1896 年用法文出版《日清战以国际法论》，为日本摆脱战争和虐杀责任雄辩，其中记录了大量屠杀场面。在中国清末留学日本热潮中，他是很多中国青年的老师。1913 年 3 月起，他出任中华民国政府法律顾问，经历袁世凯、黎元洪、冯国璋、徐世昌四任大总统任期，1919 年辞职。

② 美国《纽约世界报》记者。

③ 英国《泰晤士报》记者。

④ 英国《路透社电信》记者。

LE MONDE ILLUSTRÉ 39

NOS GRAVURES

Benjamin Godard. — Un musicien qui n'avait pas encore donné son œuvre définitive, un artiste délicat et charmant que de nombreuses compositions pour orchestre, pour piano et pour chant, toutes empreintes d'originalité et de distinction, auraient suffi à rendre célèbre, à défaut d'œuvres de plus haute envergure, telles que *Jocelyn* et *Dante*, dont de très belles pages resteront, Benjamin Godard vient de mourir en pleine jeunesse, à la veille peut-être du succès complet qu'il était digne de remporter au théâtre. On sait qu'il venait de mettre la dernière main à *la Vivandière*, que l'on va représenter à l'Opéra-Comique.

Les débuts du jeune maître regretté furent des plus heureux. On applaudit d'abord le virtuose qu'il était comme violoniste. Ce ne fut qu'ensuite qu'il s'adonna à la composition.

Nulle facilité n'égala la sienne, et il prodigua les mélodies exquises en un flot de lieds d'une délicieuse

BENJAMIN GODARD.

(Photographie REUTLINGER.)

finesse et que tous les chanteurs ont rendus populaires.

Qui ne se souvient de la *Chanson de Florian*, de la *Chanson arabe*, des *Bois d'Andilly*, de *Te souviens-tu de ta promesse?* de *Viens, une flûte invisible*.... et de tant de pages émues et sincères?

Les pianistes ont abusé de ses compositions, qui ont le rare mérite d'être admirablement écrites pour l'instrument, et qui toutes sont de la plus piquante originalité. Est-il besoin de rappeler les *Mazurkas*, les *Pages d'Album*, la *Saxonne*, les *Hirondelles*, les *Études* dont l'une des plus typiques : le *Cavalier fantastique*, est tout un poème?

Et parmi les œuvres d'orchestre : la pittoresque *Kermesse*, un des tableaux de genre les plus poussés et les plus réussis ; les *Scènes de ballet*, la *Symphonie légendaire*, avec la page incomparable des Elfes ; toutes choses qui ont fait fortune dans les grands concerts symphoniques où l'on se souvient encore du succès du *Tasse*, une cantate dramatique couronnée à l'un des premiers concours organisés par la Ville de Paris.

On le voit, bien qu'il meure au seuil de la maturité, à l'heure où l'artiste est en possession de toute la plénitude de ses moyens, de toute la vigueur de son inspiration, Benjamin Godard laisse une œuvre assez complète, pour que son nom ne soit pas oublié et pour qu'il honore grandement notre école musicale française dont le brillant compositeur restera l'un des représentants les plus personnels et les mieux inspirés.

La guerre sino-japonaise. — Les Japonais continuent à remporter des victoires consécutives et à avancer vers Pékin, malgré les troupes chinoises de plus en plus nombreuses qu'ils rencontrent toujours devant eux.

1

GÉNÉRAL OSHIMA.

On raconte que les Célestes en sont encore aux moyens d'antan pour effrayer les envahisseurs.

N'auraient-ils pas fait déguiser en soldats les femmes d'une ville assiégée, afin de faire croire aux Japonais qu'elle était défendue par une garnison d'importance?

Ces derniers, qui jadis croyaient aussi aux dragons peints et aux casques aux figures de monstres, pour terrifier l'ennemi, ont, malheureusement pour leurs adversaires, fait bien des progrès dans l'art de la guerre, et ils ne se prennent plus à d'aussi pauvres ruses.

Comment en douter en voyant l'allure de ces troupes martiales, et la tenue de cette artillerie japonaise à la bataille de Kosan, reproduite dans nos gravures? Cette bataille de Kosan qui remonte au 25 octobre, aura été l'un des principaux faits d'armes de cette campagne.

La veille, pendant la nuit, l'armée japonaise jeta

3

AMIRAL ITO.

un pont militaire sur le Yalu, et le lendemain de bonne heure, le gros de l'armée commandée par le

4

GÉNÉRAL OSEKO.

maréchal Yamagata et le général de division Nodza, traversa le fleuve et attaqua vigoureusement Kosan, la position défendue par les Chinois.

Le combat fut très chaleureux et les Chinois perdirent trois cents hommes. Les Japonais restèrent maîtres de la place et le 26, lorsqu'ils commencèrent à attaquer la ville de Kiurenjo, l'ennemi s'était déjà retiré.

Pauvres Chinois!... Pauvres personnages de potiches, si cruellement réveillés de leur paisible rêve de faïence, et mis en miettes par ces intrépides petits Japonais qui, eux aussi, furent bien longtemps des héros d'écrans et d'éventails!

Comme ils ont changé depuis ce temps... depuis même que, dans ses livres, M. Loti peignait les Japonais comme de petits fantoches assez ridicules! Il y a lieu d'en revenir.

Quelques portraits des principaux chefs de l'armée de l'Empereur du Japon, ne manqueront pas d'intéresser nos lecteurs. Ce sont ceux de l'amiral Ito et des généraux Oshima, Oseko, Yamadji.

2

GÉNÉRAL YAMADJI.

Beaux-Arts : *Le pain quotidien*, tableau de Mlle Rœderstein. — « *Panem nostrum quotidianum da nobis hodie*... » C'est la propre parole de la quotidienne prière que le Christ lui-même nous a enseignée, qui a inspiré au peintre cette toile d'un caractère très simple et très charmant à la fois. Le groupe est heureux, de ces jeunes enfants et de cette sœur aînée, grave et douce comme une jeune mère, qui leur prépare la « becquée », et dans la sobriété du décor, la variété des attitudes et la diversité des expressions ressort avec une intensité très personnelle.

Anvers : *Le procès de Mme Joniaux*. — Les échos de cette affaire, dont le retentissement est considérable en Belgique, nous parviennent jusqu'en France, où la physionomie de l'accusée et son attitude devant le tribunal intriguent fort tous ceux qui suivent le compte rendu des débats.

Ce qu'il y a de réellement admirable chez Mme Joniaux, c'est l'énergie avec laquelle elle résiste aux coups répétés que l'interrogatoire lui porte. Sa présence d'esprit, ses brusques ripostes émerveillent ceux-là mêmes qui dans l'auditoire ne mettent pas un instant en doute sa culpabilité. Ses réponses trahissent bien quelquefois un certain embarras, mais si léger, si vite « réparé » ! Plusieurs fois aussi, il lui est arrivé un jour d'essuyer quelques larmes. Mais ces larmes, est-ce à l'énervement qu'il faut les attribuer ou au sentiment que sa situation s'aggrave?

Après avoir mis à la charge de Mme Joniaux cinq ou six crimes, peut-être davantage, l'instruction ne retient plus contre elle que trois empoisonnements ce qui est encore assez coquet :

1° L'empoisonnement de sa sœur, Mlle Léonie Ablay, morte subitement chez elle le 14 janvier 1892 ;

2° L'empoisonnement de son oncle maternel, M. Jacques Van den Kerckhove, ancien sénateur du royaume de Belgique, mort subitement chez elle, au mois de mars 1893 ;

3° L'empoisonnement de son frère, M. Alfred Ablay, mort subitement chez elle, au mois de février 1894.

Tous ces crimes auraient eu le même but ; permettre

1895 年 1 月 19 日《世界画报》

1 大岛义昌将军	1 Général Oshima.
2 山地元治将军（旅顺大屠杀的命令由他发出）	2 Général Yamapji.
3 伊东祐亨元帅	3 Amiral Ito.
4 大迫尚敏将军	4 Général Oseko.

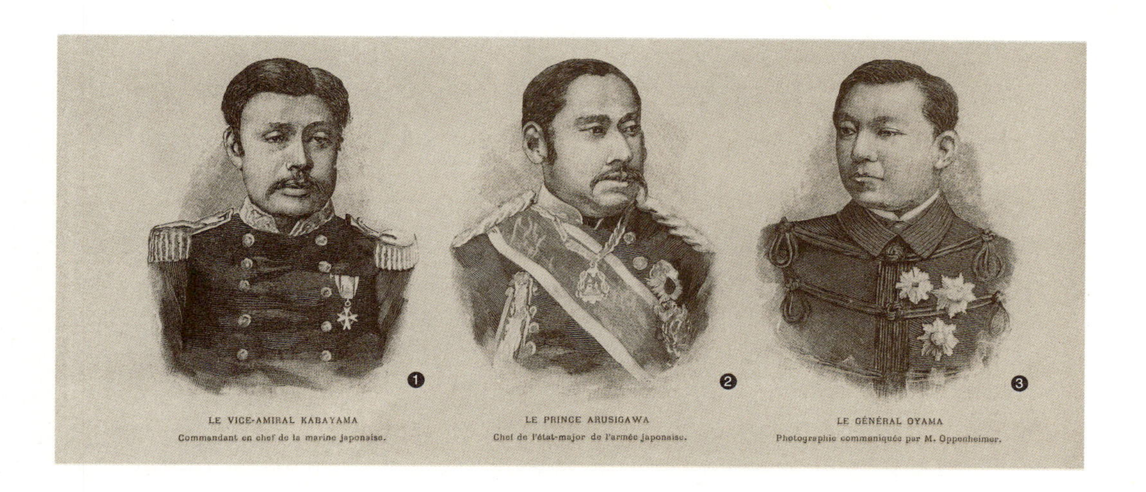

1894 年 12 月 8 日《插图报》

1　桦山资纪副元帅，日本海军司令部总长

2　有栖川宫炽仁亲王，日军总参谋长

3　大山岩将军

1　Le Vice-Amiral Kabayama. Commandant en chef de la marine Japonaise.

2　Le Prince Arusigawa Chef de l'état-major de l'armée Japonaise.

3　Le Général Oyama.

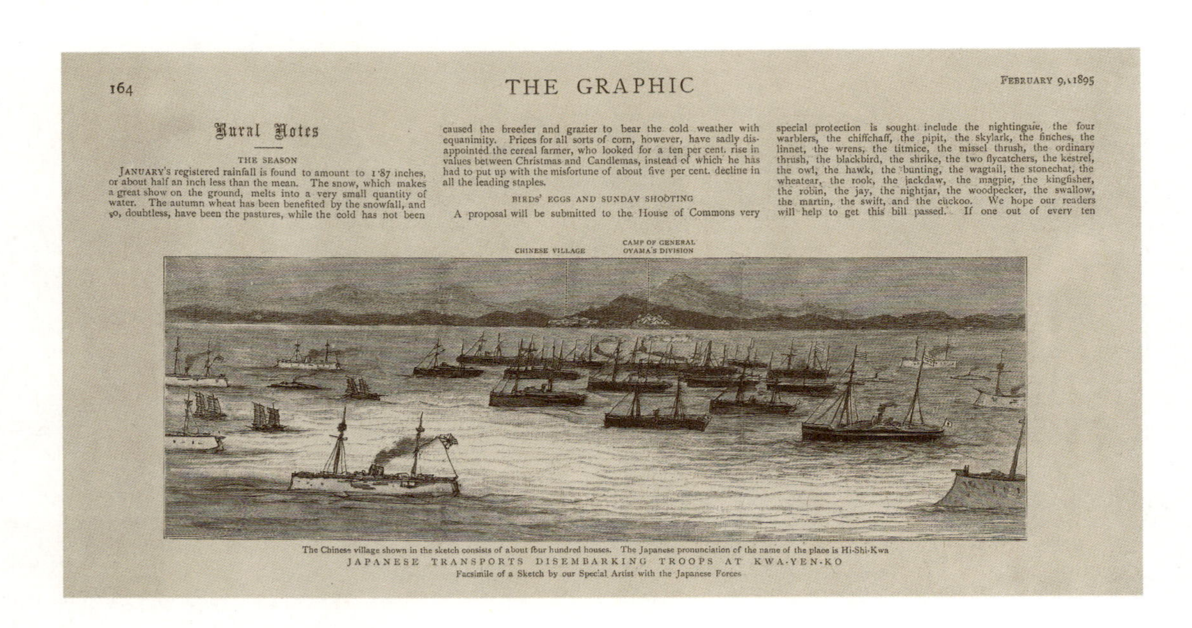

164 THE GRAPHIC FEBRUARY 9, 1895

Rural Notes

THE SEASON

JANUARY'S registered rainfall is found to amount to 1·87 inches, or about half an inch less than the mean. The snow, which makes a great show on the ground, melts into a very small quantity of water. The autumn wheat has been benefited by the snowfall, and so, doubtless, have been the pastures, while the cold has not been caused the breeder and grazier to bear the cold weather with equanimity. Prices for all sorts of corn, however, have sadly disappointed the cereal farmer, who looked for a ten per cent. rise in values between Christmas and Candlemas, instead of which he has had to put up with the misfortune of about five per cent. decline in all the leading staples.

BIRDS' EGGS AND SUNDAY SHOOTING

A proposal will be submitted to the House of Commons very special protection is sought include the nightingale, the four warblers, the chiffchaff, the pipit, the skylark, the finches, the linnet, the wrens, the titmice, the missel thrush, the ordinary thrush, the blackbird, the shrike, the two flycatchers, the kestrel, the owl, the hawk, the bunting, the wagtail, the stonechat, the wheatear, the rook, the jackdaw, the magpie, the kingfisher, the robin, the jay, the nightjar, the woodpecker, the swallow, the martin, the swift, and the cuckoo. We hope our readers will help to get this bill passed. If one out of every ten

The Chinese village shown in the sketch consists of about four hundred houses. The Japanese pronunciation of the name of the place is Hi-Shi-Kwa

JAPANESE TRANSPORTS DISEMBARKING TROOPS AT KWA-YEN-KO

Facsimile of a Sketch by our Special Artist with the Japanese Forces

1895 年 2 月 9 日《图片报》

日本军队乘运输船在花园口登陆

Japanese transports disembarking troops at Kwa-Yen-Ko.

插图背景上标示出中国村镇大约有 400 户人家，日文的发音大致为“西石花”

The Chinese village shown in the sketch consists of about four hundred houses.

The Japanese pronunciation of the name of the place is Hi-Shi-Kwa.

THE ILLUSTRATED LONDON NEWS, JAN. 19, 1895.—77

THE WAR IN EASTERN ASIA.

Fort. Fort. Docks. Fort.

The march of the Japanese army was between the two forts on the left. INSIDE PORT ARTHUR HARBOUR. Torpedo-boats.

From a Sketch by Mr. B. Meadows-Taylor, H.M.S. "Centurion."

Japanese Fleet in the distance. Two Cruisers and Torpedo-boats.

Storming of the Forts by Japanese advance guard. Field Battery.

THE STORMING OF PORT ARTHUR BY THE JAPANESE.

From a Sketch by Mr. B. Meadows-Taylor, H.M.S. "Centurion."

1895 年 1 月 19 日《伦敦新闻画报》

1　旅顺港内　　1　Inside Port Arthur Harbour.

图片左侧：日军的攻势是由此图片左手边两座山头上的碉堡的中间地带发起的

The march of the Japanese army was between the two forts on the left.

图片右侧：在旅顺湾待命的日军鱼雷艇　　Torpedo-boats.

2　日军对清军碉堡发起猛攻　　2　Storming of the forts by Japanese .

图片左上：远处海面待命的日本舰队，两艘巡洋舰和数艘鱼雷艇

Japanese Fleet in the distance. Two cruisers and torpedo-boats.

图片左侧：陆军突击队向碉堡发起猛攻

Storming of the forts by Japanese advance guard.

图片中间：战地炮兵　　Field battery.

英舰“百夫长”号，米铎泰勒绘　From a sketch by Mr. B. Meadows-Taylor, H. M. S. “Centurion” .

1895 年 1 月 12 日《图片报》

旅顺港陷落：在获胜的日军面前中国士兵四散逃跑

After the fall of Port Arthur: Chinese soldiers flying before the victorious Japanese.

根据一位英国军官提供的草图绘制

From sketches by a British officer.

在占据有利地形后，日军顺着山坡向下冲，穿过山谷浅滩，然后又冲向对面山坡上的清军工事。后来，在这些工事背后发现了成百上千的空弹壳，这表明日军通过山谷时曾遭遇过猛烈的炮火阻击。尽管如此，日军还是成功地将清军逐出了工事，赶上了山顶。这座山上到处都是清军逃跑时遗弃的大衣、弹药袋。

After capturing one important position the Japanese advanced down the hill side, across the shallow inlet, and up against the earthworks on the opposite side. Behind these works were afterwards found thousands of empty cartridge cases, showing what a heavy fire the Japs must have been exposed to while crossing the creek. In spite of this fire they carried the works and drove the Chinese up the hill side. This hill was strewn with thick coats, pouches containing cartridges, and all kinds of things the Chinese threw away in their flight.

LE MONDE ILLUSTRÉ 381

PING-YANG. — CADAVRES DE SOLDATS JAPONAIS MUTILÉS PAR LES CHINOIS.

1894 年 12 月 15 日《世界画报》

在平壤，日军士兵被中国军人分尸

Ping-Yang.—Cadavres de soldats japonais mutilés par les chinois.

在今天为大家展示的版画中，一个令人发指的情景描绘出中国人的残忍。他们把所有落入手中的（日本）士兵的脑袋全部割下，之后在他们的耳朵上打孔，用一根绳子穿过后挂在木桩上。日军在平壤战役后发现了多具缺少头颅的日本兵尸体，在进城的途中，他们就这样发现散落一路的、被撤走的中国人毁容的日本兵头颅。

Parmi les épisodes que nous reproduisons aujourd'hui, se trouve une scène assez tragique qui donne une idée de la férocité des Chinois. Ils coupent la tête de tous les soldats qui leur tombent sous la main; puis après avoir percé les oreilles, ils les traversent d'une corde et la suspendent ensuite à un poteau. C'est ainsi que les Japonais, après la bataille de Ping-Yang, ont retrouvé les corps de leurs soldats décapités, en poursuivant leur route, ils ont fini par découvrir, abandonnées çà et là, les têtes à moitié défigurées, que les Chinois avaient laissées, en abandonnant leurs positions.

NOVEMBER 500,353 CIRCULATION.

Nearly 140,000 People who wanted "Help" have asked for workers in The World during 1894. It is an unfailing resource for situation-seekers—the Greatest Labor Exchange in existence.

The World.

"Circulation Books Open to All."

Nearly 145,000 Houses, Rooms and Apartments have been advertised in The World during 1894. The tenants found for them would make a population for a mighty city.

SUNDAY'S 351,842 CIRCULATION.

VOL. XXXV. NO. 12,175. PRICE TWO CENTS. NEW YORK, THURSDAY, DECEMBER 20, 1894. PRICE TWO CENTS. 14 PAGES.

THE FIRST PHOTOGRAPH OF AN ACTUAL BATTLE.

REAR OF THE JAPANESE BATTERIES FIRING ON KINCHOW.

(REPRODUCED FROM A PHOTOGRAPH FORWARDED FROM CHINA BY THE WORLD'S WAR CORRESPONDENT.)

THE MASSACRE AT PORT ARTHUR.

At Least Two Thousand Helpless People Butchered by Japanese Soldiers.

THREE DAYS OF SLAUGHTER.

Gen. Oyama and His Officers Make No Attempt to Stop the Atrocities.

THE TOWN SACKED FROM END TO END

Streets Choked with Mutilated Bodies of Men, Women and Children While the Soldiers Laughed.

FIELD MARSHAL OYAMA.

CHINESE RETREATING TO PORT ARTHUR.

WAR CORRESPONDENTS COOKING THEIR DINNER.

1894 年 12 月 20 日《纽约世界报》

这篇报道来自美国《纽约世界报》的记者克里曼（1859—1915）之手。

甲午战争期间，克里曼随日军第二军战地采访。旅顺屠杀事件发生后第四天，即 11 月 24 日，克里曼在西方媒体中率先发回通讯："我亲眼看见旅顺难民并未抗击犯军”；“我见一人跪在兵前，叩头求命。兵一手以枪尾刀插入其头于地，一手以剑斩断其首。”

为防止报道大屠杀的原稿遭到日军没收，克里曼将报道原稿分两路寄出，于12月19日到达纽约编辑部。第二天，由《纽约世界报》的社长普利策亲自编排，在“旅顺大屠杀”标题下，克里曼写道：“日本为了朝鲜的解放，采取突如其来的介入进而变成野蛮的战争。事情的性质已经不是文明与野蛮间的纠葛，日本终于揭开自身的假面具，在最后四日里，征服军的足下彻底蹂躏了文明。”

克里曼及《泰晤士报》记者克曼和英国《旗帜》、《黑与白》两报的记者威力·阿斯顿都发回了令世界震惊的旅顺屠杀事件的报道，面对世界舆论，日本政府积极拉拢和利用国际媒体，为自己辩护。同时在几个西方报刊上发表所谓真相报道，并对克里曼等人进行攻击和污蔑。

在这个关键时刻，清政府及驻欧美各国大使，对旅顺屠城事件竟然采取沉默态度。致使欧美社会对新闻的真实性产生动摇，并随后产生质疑。日本政府最终走出困境。

假如没有克里曼、普利策等正义媒体人的报道，旅顺虐杀事件也许就此湮没于历史中。

约瑟夫·乔·普利策（1847—1911），美国大众报刊的标志性人物。普利策奖和哥伦比亚大学新闻学院就是据他的遗嘱创办的。

1895年1月26日《伦敦新闻画报》

日本人攻入旅顺	The Japanese at Port Arthur.
根据本刊特派随日军画师的草图绘制	From a sketch by an artist with the Japanese forces.

日军在夺取内陆要塞后，进入旅顺的主要大街。街道两旁的房屋均遭洗劫，从头到尾残骸遍布。路面上，可以看见散开的箱子、破损的椅子、器皿、雨伞、扇子、锄头、油灯、死猫死狗—— --片凄惨景象。

The Japanese advanced through the main street of the town, after taking the inland forts. Houses on both sides were looted, and the street was strewn from end to end with debris. In the roadway were chests burst open, broken chairs and crockery, umbrellas, fans, hoes, oil lamps, dead dogs and cats—a melancholy spectacle of wreckage.

DRAWN BY C. W. WYLLIE　　FROM SKETCHES BY LIEUT. W. H. THRING, R.N.

TRANSPORTS ENTERING THE INNER HARBOUR IMMEDIATELY AFTER THE HOISTING OF THE JAPANESE FLAG

1895 年 1 月 12 日《图片报》

旅顺港刚刚升起日本军旗，（日本）运兵船就驶入了内港

Transports entering the inner harbour immediately after the hoisting of the Japanese flag.

C.W. 威利根据皇家海军中尉 W.H. 苏凌的速写绘制

Drawn by C.W.Wyllie from sketches by Lieut.W.H.Thring, R.N..

1895 年 1 月 12 日《图片报》

东方的战争：旅顺陷落后的场景

The war in the East: Scenes after the fall of Port Arthur.

旅顺港陷落后发生令人发指的杀戮——男人、女人和孩子被屠戮，尸横遍街、数以百计，胜利者因兴奋而疯狂、因发现自己的数名战友被肢解并被悬挂在寺庙中而暴怒。图为日本军夫从港口边的浅滩上搬运中国人的尸体。

At the fall of Port Arthur the slaughter of Chinese was fearful—men, women, and children were massacred, and their bodies strewed the streets in hundreds; the victors being madly excited and infuriated by the discovery of the bodies of several of their countrymen horribly mutilated and hung up in a Joss House. Japanese coolies removing Chinese dead in the basin of the harbour.

英国皇家陆军画师 C.J. 斯丹尼兰根据皇家海军军官 D.J. 麦克纳博的速写绘制

Drawn by C.J. Staniland, R.I. from sketches by D.J. Mcnabb, R.N..

rades mutilated, was being continued in cold blood now. Thursday, Friday, Saturday, and Sunday were spent by the soldiery in murder and pillage from dawn to dark, in mutilation, in every conceivable kind of nameless atrocity, until the town became a ghastly Inferno to be remembered with a fearsome shudder until one's dying day. I saw corpses of women and children, three or four in the streets, more in the water; I stooped to pick some of them out to make sure that there could be no possibility of mis-

JAPANESE SOLDIERS MUTILATING BODIES.

take. Bodies of men strewed the streets in hundreds, perhaps thousands, for we could not count—some with not a limb unsevered, some with heads hacked, cross-cut, and split lengthwise, some ripped open, not by chance but with careful precision, down and across, disemboweled and dismembered, with occasionally a dagger or bayonet thrust in private parts. I saw groups of prisoners tied together in a bunch with their hands behind their backs, riddled with bullets for five minutes, and then hewn in pieces. I saw

英文图书《日清战争》中的插图，1895 年出版

日军士兵正在肢解中国人尸体

Japanese soldiers mutilating bodies.

1895 年 2 月 2 日《图片报》

以上图片，即便令人毛骨悚然，但足以佐证近来媒体刊出的有关日军占领旅顺港后施行暴行的报道

The above illustration, despite its somewhat gruesome character, warrants publication
in view of the recent discussion with regard to the occupation of Port Arthur by the Japanese.

得胜的日军进入失守的旅顺港

The fall of Port Arthur: The entry of the victorious army.

照片为本报随日军记者拍摄

From a photograph sent by our special artist with the Japanese forces.

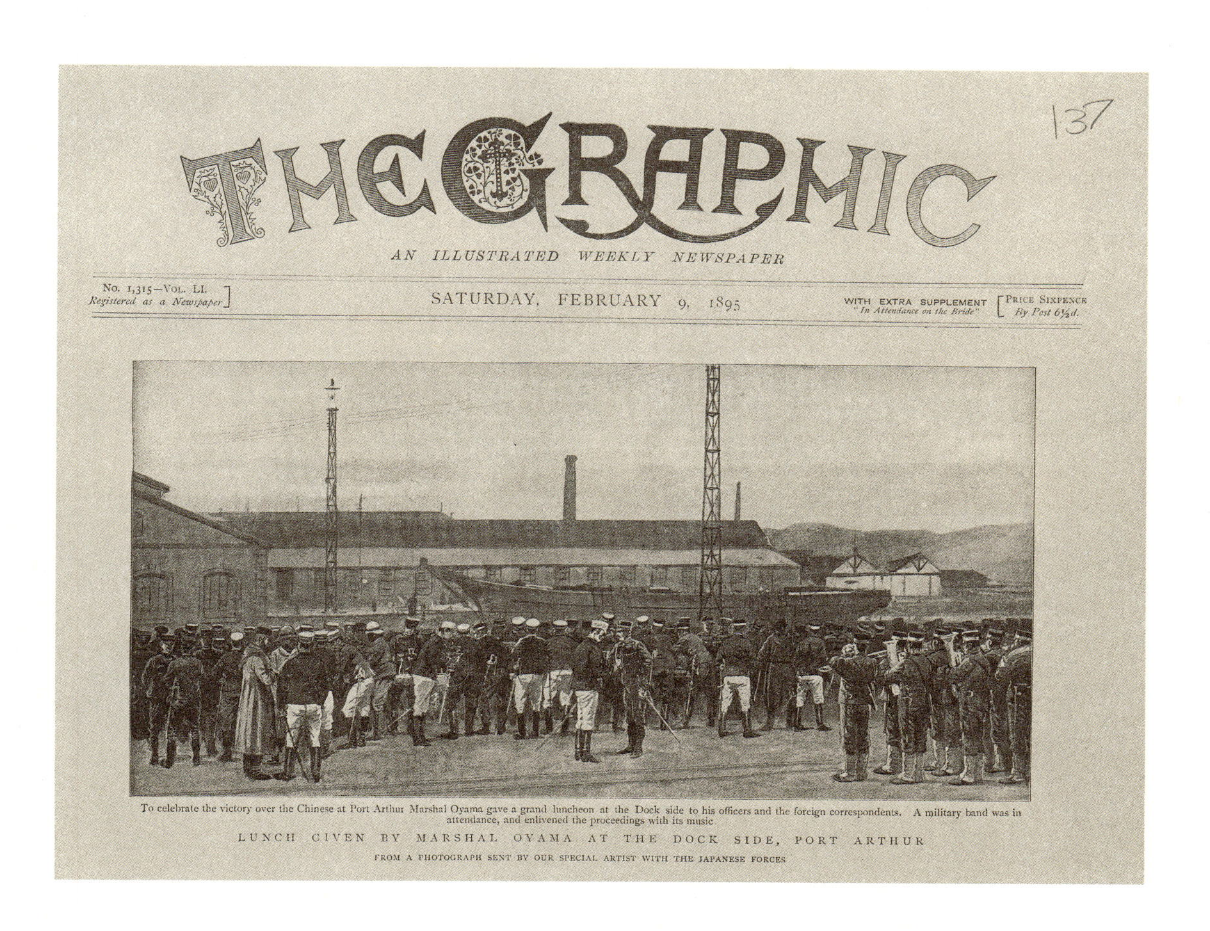
137

THE GRAPHIC

AN ILLUSTRATED WEEKLY NEWSPAPER

No. 1,315—Vol. LI. Registered as a Newspaper

SATURDAY, FEBRUARY 9, 1895

WITH EXTRA SUPPLEMENT "In Attendance on the Bride"

PRICE SIXPENCE By Post 6½d.

To celebrate the victory over the Chinese at Port Arthur Marshal Oyama gave a grand luncheon at the Dock side to his officers and the foreign correspondents. A military band was in attendance, and enlivened the proceedings with its music

LUNCH GIVEN BY MARSHAL OYAMA AT THE DOCK SIDE, PORT ARTHUR

FROM A PHOTOGRAPH SENT BY OUR SPECIAL ARTIST WITH THE JAPANESE FORCES

1895 年 2 月 9 日《图片报》

旅顺港码头，大山岩元帅的午宴

Lunch given by Marshal Oyama at the dock side, Port Arthur.

为庆祝胜利，大山岩元帅在旅顺港码头举行盛大的午餐会，参加者有军官、外国记者；
为烘托气氛，军乐队现场演奏

To celebrate the victory over the Chinese at Port Arthur Marshal Oyama gave a grand luncheon at the Dock side to his officers and the foreign correspondent. A military band was in attendance, and enlivened the proceedings with its music.

结　语

（11月）21日，旅顺市街的巷战仍在进行，炮声枪声如雷贯耳，尸横遍地，惨如地狱。突然从新街的集仙茶楼剧场传出悠扬的戏剧演唱和锣鼓声，当荷枪实弹的（日本）士兵冲入剧场，惊愕地发现：在血流成河的城市一角，居然有一个剧团还在演出！剧场内没有一名观众，士兵们面对的似乎是一群没有灵魂的木偶！

——1894年12月　日本《邮便报知新闻》

剧场内10岁至15岁的少年演员约有百十余人，包括这里的成人在内，剧团大约200人，都是旅顺道台从北京、天津请来的戏班子，也有说是北洋舰队提督丁汝昌带来的。巷战中，剧团的17名成人被枪弹毙命，其余180人在接受（日本）第二军司令部审查后，被命令从25日起，每日昼夜各演出一场，为日本官兵庆贺大捷、迎接新年助兴……

—— 1894年12月　日本《国民新闻》

八　威海卫的陷落

曾担任中国海军总教官的英国海军军官琅威理认为，防卫严密的威海卫是不可能被攻陷的。然而，刚刚卸任日本海军大学顾问的英格尔上尉则认为，枪炮是由人驾驭的，如果威海卫的堡垒不能被守军正确地防卫，坚船利炮也无济于事。日本海军的鱼雷艇已经三次成功进犯威海卫城下而没能让守军变得更聪明的事实，足以激发起“英勇的岛民”动摇威海卫的更大决心。

——1894 年 8 月　美国《纽约先驱报》

"The Tartar cavalrymen, with their rough little white horses, mingled with the crowd. They were warmly clad in sheepskin coats, each of a pattern to suit individual liking, worn under the cotton uniform ; some wore large fur caps, whilst the infantry had dark blue cotton turbans wrapped in various patterns round their heads, the pigtail being worn underneath"

TARTAR CAVALRY AT TIENTSIN ON THEIR WAY TO THE FRONT

FACSIMILE OF A SKETCH BY OUR SPECIAL ARTIST WITH THE CHINESE FORCES

1895年2月16日《图片报》

清军八旗骑兵前往前线途经天津

Tartar cavalry at Tientsin on their way to the front.

八旗骑兵和他们勇猛的小白马混在一起熙熙攘攘地前行。他们用羊皮袄把自己捂得严严实实，每个人的皮袄都各不相同，外面还罩着军大衣。有的人戴着巨大的皮帽，而步兵则用长围巾把自己的脑袋裹成五花八门式，里面藏着他们的猪尾巴长辫。

The Tartar cavalrymen, with their rough little white horses, mingled with the crowd. They were warmly clad in sheepskin coats, each of a pattern to suit individual liking, worn under the cotton uniform; some wore large fur caps, whilst the infantry had dark blue cotton turbans wrapped in various patterns round their heads, the pigtail being worn underneath.

CHINESE TROOPS NEAR LAICHOW ON THE WAY TO CHEFOO

FACSIMILE OF A SKETCH BY OUR SPECIAL ARTIST WITH THE CHINESE FORCES

1895 年 3 月 2 日《图片报》

中国增援军队在莱州附近，向烟台芝罘湾进发途中

Chinese troops near Laichow on the way to Chefoo.

Lord Randolph Churchill*

THE words with which Lord Macaulay concludes his essay on Lord Byron might, with a few necessary changes, be applied to Lord Randolph Churchill. A few more years will destroy whatever yet remains of the magical potency which once belonged to the name of Randolph Churchill. To us he is still a man, young, noble, and meteoric. To our children he will be merely a statesman; and their impartial judgment will appoint his place among statesmen, without regard to his rank or his personal fascination. For the present we can scarcely judge him impartially, but, as Mr. Escott points out in his well-reasoned monograph, without him the Conservative party would never have come into office in 1886. It is true that Mr. Escott puts the matter rather too strongly in the following passage, but with due deductions there is the keynote of the political history of the past few years in his remarks. He is dealing with what might have happened had Lord Randolph taken serious offence at the lectures to which he was subjected at the hands of the older Conservatives, and had he gone over to the Gladstonians and boldly bidden for the succession to their leader: —

In that hypothetical ambition he might or might not have succeeded. One thing is certain. In the event of such a secession, the Conservative defeat at the winter election of 1885, instead of decisive, would have been overwhelming; Dissentient Liberalism (*sic*) would to-day be an unknown product, Mr. Gladstone's Home Rule Bill of 1886 would have become law, and before now, from the Giant's Causeway to Cape Clear, from John o' Groat's to Beachy Head, Conservatism would not have had an inch of ground for its foothold.

In view of Lord Randolph's subsequent career, and the illness that not long afterwards began to show itself, it may safely be said that his great service to the State was done in the years from 1883 to 1886, and that his personality did shape the course of events in those years in no small degree, owing to the new life which he breathed into the Conservative party.

Mr. Escott's monograph is not a life, but a study of the life of Lord Randolph, written with the purpose of setting forth the real purport of his public career in English political life and the causes which made his successful action possible. As a boy the characteristics which made him a leader of men showed themselves a school. Even as a little lad he defied his disciplinarians, and was inclined to domineer over his contemporaries.

If he could not often, or always, excel, he generally contrived to be notorious, the first to be involved in a scrape, the first to extricate his comrades from it. He often shirked a lesson; he never feared the birch; he never shrank from interposing himself between a playfellow and the official chastisement of their associated delinquencies. The one condition he insisted upon from his equals was loyalty to his lead. Provided that was forthcoming, he was himself staunchness and championship incarnate to his followers. As for the public opinion of the place, the criticism of boys not in his set, he cared as little for that as he did for the censure of the Orbilius of the hour.

These qualities he afterwards showed as the leader of the Fourth Party in the House. But the secret of his power in the country lay in the fact that he knew better than any one else the political temper of the masses he addressed and the language in which he could most effectively convey his meaning to them. Actuality was the keynote of his addresses, and he employed telling phrases—often fortuitous combinations of simple words taken accidentally from a newspaper paragraph—as a refrain to fix the anticipatons of his audience, or at periodic intervals more closely to arrest their attention.

Sudden as had been his rise to power, his fall was even more sudden, and we now have Mr. Escott's testimony to the truth of his reasons for so suddenly resigning the Chancellorship of the Exchequer. Lord Randolph had told the Prime Minister and the Secretary for War in the previous October that unless some effort was made to reduce the expenditure he could not remain Chancellor of the Exchequer, and as nothing led him to suppose that the Conservative chiefs did not consider him as indispensable as he thought himself, he seems to have calculated that he would gain his point. But he reckoned without Lord Salisbury's strength of character and without Mr. Goschen's willingness to join the Government. Had the Cabinet surrendered to him he would have been their master, but his bold stroke miscarried. As he himself said, it was with a sensation of dismay, resembling a cold water douche to his back, that he learned one day at luncheon that Mr. Goschen was to be Chancellor of the Exchequer and that he was not the indispensable man he had imagined himself to be. That day in December really ended Lord Randolph's career, though few people realised it, and the rest of his life is too recent to need comment.

* "Randolph Spencer-Churchill, as a Product of His Age." By T. H. S. Escott. (Hutchinson and Co.)

CHINESE TROOPS ON THE MARCH FOR WEI-HAI-WEI

DRAWN BY OUR SPECIAL ARTIST WITH THE CHINESE FORCES

A Russian Composer*

NOTHING is more remarkable in the history of modern Russian music than the curious dualism of its chief representatives. Hardly any of them were musicians pure and simple. César Cui has risen to the rank of General, and is a Professor of Fortification at the School of Military Engineering at St. Petersburg; Rimsky-Korsakoff began life as a naval officer, and for some time combined composition and theoretical studies with his duties on shipboard; Moussorgsky was an officer in the army, and Borodin, the subject of this very interesting memoir by M. Alfred Habets, excellently translated by Mrs. Newmarch, was a man of science who held the Professorship of Chemistry at the Academy of Medicine in St. Petersburg to the day of his death. The disadvantages of this divided allegiance are strikingly exhibited in the volume before us, for Borodin was an extremely conscientious man who never allowed his devotion to music to stand in the way of his professional duties. His leisure was so extremely circumscribed that for a great part of the year he would only snatch odd moments for the indulgence of his creative instinct. The situation was almost tragic. It was not, as he says, that he could not find a couple of hours a day, but he had not the leisure of mind to withdraw himself from occupations and preoccupations which had nothing to do with music. "One needs time," he writes to one of his friends, "to concentrate one's self to get into the right key, otherwise the creation of a sustained work is impossible. For this I have only a part of summer at my disposal. In the winter I can only compose when I am ill and have to give up my lectures and laboratory. So, my friends, reversing the usual custom, never say to me, 'I hope you are well,' but 'I hope you are ill.' At Christmas I had influenza and could not go to the laboratory. So I stayed at home and wrote the Thanksgiving Chorus in the last act of *Prince Igor*." Hampered by these untoward circumstances, Borodin gave little to the world, but much of it was of permanent value. His two symphonies have already met with enthusiastic recognition in Germany and Belgium, while his wonderfully picturesque symphonic sketch "In the Steppes of Central Asia," introduced in England by Sir Charless Hallé, is as brilliant and realistic as one of the canvases of Veretschagin. Though Borodin was little over fifty at his death, though he was no conductor and unversed in the arts of self-advertisement, his unquestioned genius had met with cordial appreciation from some of the greatest musicians of the day, notably Liszt, of whom Borodin's letters give a most vivid and sympathetic picture. For the rest he seems to have been a man of remarkable personal worth and considerable literary as well as scientific attainments. The long letter to his wife, who survived him only a few months, given at the close of the volume, is one of the most charming and touching evidences of romantic conjugal attachment that we have ever read. It only remains to be said that this attractive book throws a flood of light on the growth of the modern Russian school, of which Borodin was one of the most conspicuous ornaments.

* "Borodin and Liszt." By Alfred Habets. Translated by Rosa Newmarch. (London: Digby, Long and Co.)

1895年6月15日《图片报》

向威海卫进发的中国军队

Chinese troops on the march for Wei-Hai-Wei.

THE ILLUSTRATED LONDON NEWS, Nov. 3, 1894.—560

THE CHINESE FLEET LYING UNDER SHELTER OF FORTS AT WEI-HAI-WEI, SEPTEMBER 12.

From a Sketch by Mr. A. W. Wylde, H.M.S. "Leander."

1894 年 11 月 3 日《伦敦新闻画报》

9 月 12 日，北洋舰队躲避在威海卫港口中

The Chinese fleet lying under shelter of forts at Wei-Hai-Wei, September 12.

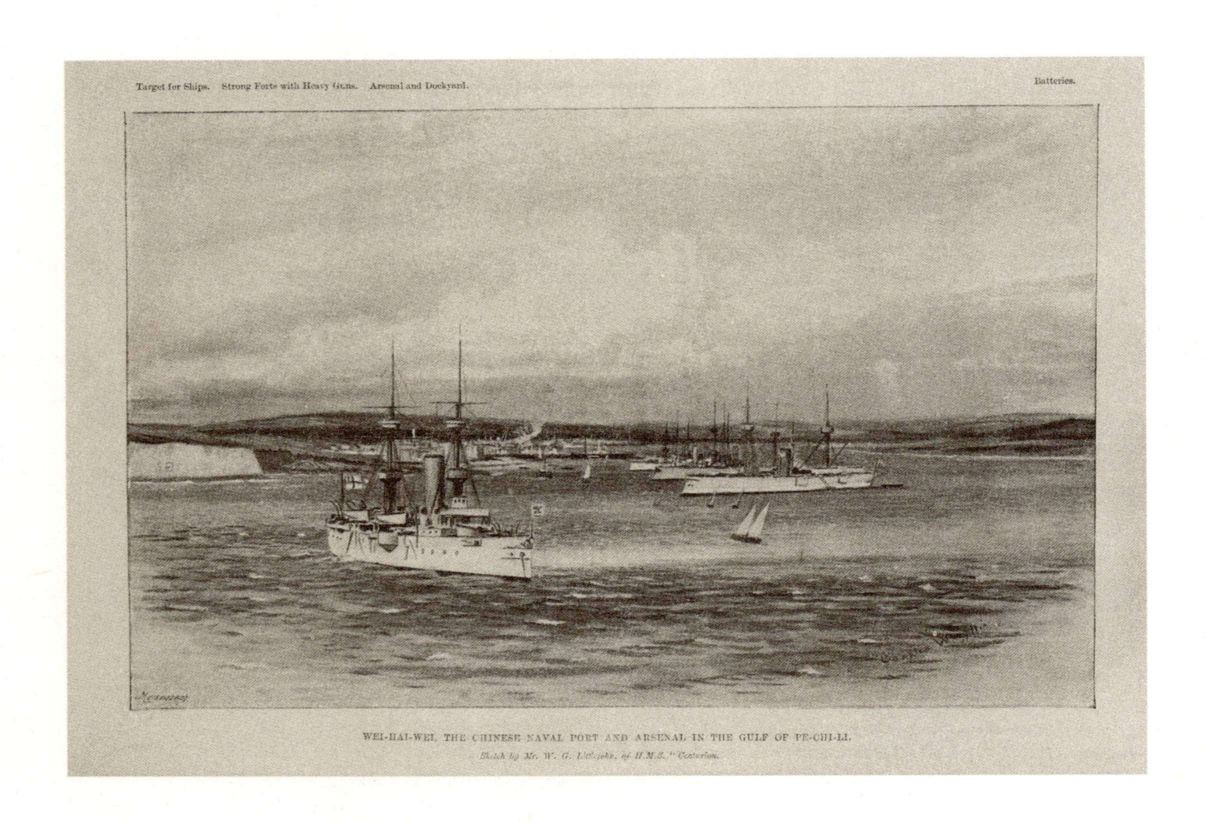

1894 年 10 月 20 日《伦敦新闻画报》

威海卫——渤海湾的中国海军港口和军械库

Wei-Hai-Wei, the Chinese naval port and arsenal in the Gulf of Pe-Chi-Li.

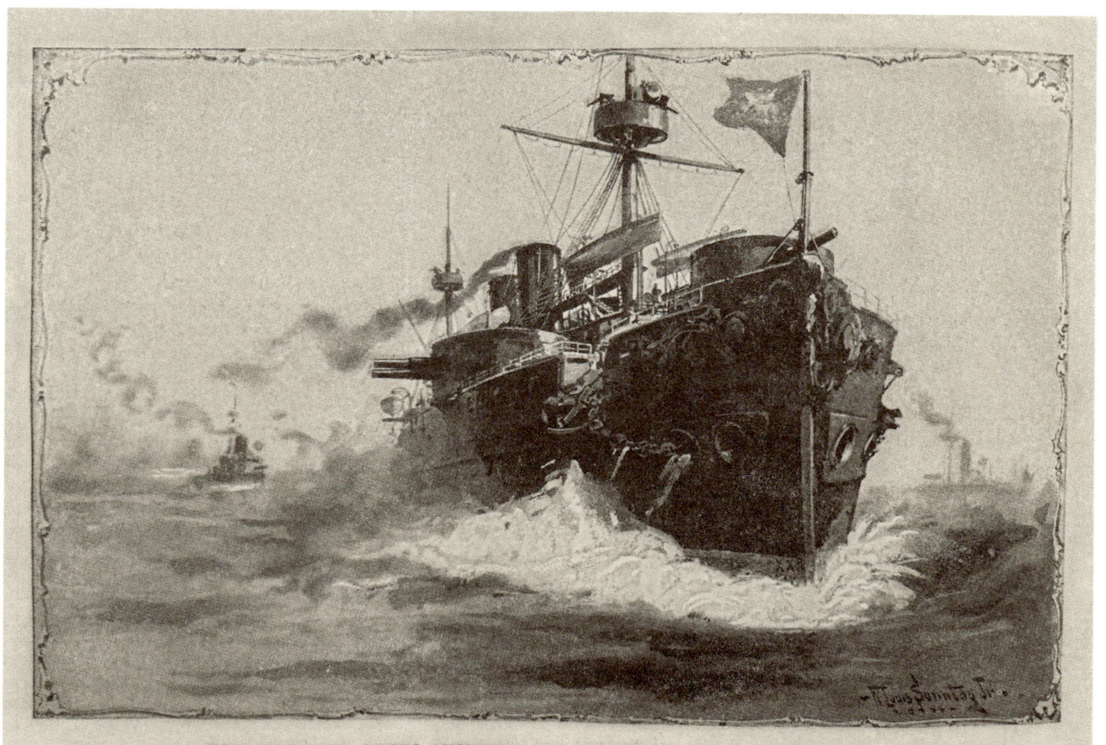

THE CHINESE STEEL-ARMORED BARBETTE CRUISER "CHEN-YUEN,"
Sister Ship to the *Ting-yuen*, both of which were sunk by the Japanese during the Engagement in the Harbor of Wei-Hai-Wei, February 7, 1895.
Displacement, 7430 Tons; Length, 308.5 Feet; Beam, 59 Feet; Draught, 20 Feet; Twin Propellers, 6200 Horse-Power; Speed, 14.5 Knots.

1895 年 2 月 16 日《哈珀斯周刊》

中国铁甲炮舰镇远号

The Chinese steel-armored barbette cruiser "Chen-Yuen."

定远号的姊妹舰，于 1895 年 2 月 7 日在威海卫被日军双双击沉（其实镇远舰并没有在威海卫被击沉，而是被日军虏获，战后以战列舰的身份编入日本海军，并参加了后来的日俄海战——编者注）

Sister Ship to the Ting-Yuen, both of which were sunk by the Japanese during the Engagement in the Harbor of Wei-Hai-Wei, February 7, 1895.

镇远号铁甲舰是中国清朝海军从德国的伏尔铿造船厂订购的炮塔铁甲舰，清末北洋水师主力舰之一，属定远级铁甲舰，当时有东洋第一坚舰之称。1880 年（光绪六年）订购于德国伏尔铿船厂，排水量 7335 吨，马力 6000 匹，航速 14.5 节，造价为 110.3 万两白银。1885 年由刘步蟾等人带回国。1888 年北洋舰队正式成军，被授为左翼总兵的林泰曾兼管带，定员 331 人。

286 THE GRAPHIC March 9, 1895

FROM A SKETCH BY C. E. LLOYD-THOMAS, R.N., H.M.S. "EDGAR"

The British warships which are cruising in Chinese waters to look after the safety of British subjects in the Treaty ports and other towns, witnessed the landing of the Japanese troops from their cruisers in Yung Chin Bay, preparatory to the attack on Wei-hai-wei. The weather was fine and clear, but very cold, the ground being mostly covered with snow, the hill tops, curiously enough, standing out bleak and bare. There were fifty-two Japanese ships at anchor, including the battleships and armoured vessels. In the meantime, closer to Wei-hai-wei, some Japanese gunboats were clearing the way for the troops by shelling some villages on the beach

THE JAPANESE LANDING TROOPS IN YUNG CHIN BAY FOR THE ATTACK ON WEI-HAI-WEI

1895 年 3 月 9 日《图片报》

攻打威海卫的日军在荣城湾登陆

The Japanese landing troops in Yung Chin Bay for the attack on Wei-Hai-Wei.

为了保护条约港，通商口岸的侨民在中国水域巡视的英国军舰目睹了准备攻打威海卫的日军在荣城登陆的过程。当时天气晴朗，大地被白雪覆盖，远山却光秃秃的，有一种怪异的伤感。52 艘日本军舰在这里抛锚，包括几艘装甲战舰。日军一步步地迫近威海卫了，为了给步兵开道，炮舰开始对海岸边的一些村庄进行轰炸。

The British warships which are cruising in Chinese waters to look after the safety of British subjects in the Treaty ports and other towns, witnessed the landing of the Japanese troops from their cruisers in Yung Chin Bay, preparatory to the attack on Wei-Hai-Wei. The weather was fine and clear, but very cold, the ground being mostly covered with snow, the hill tops, curiously enough, standing out bleak and bare. There were fifty-two Japanese ships at anchor, including the battleships and armoured vessels. In the meantime, closer to Wei-Hai-Wei, some Japanese gunboats were clearing the way for the troops by shelling some villages on the beach.

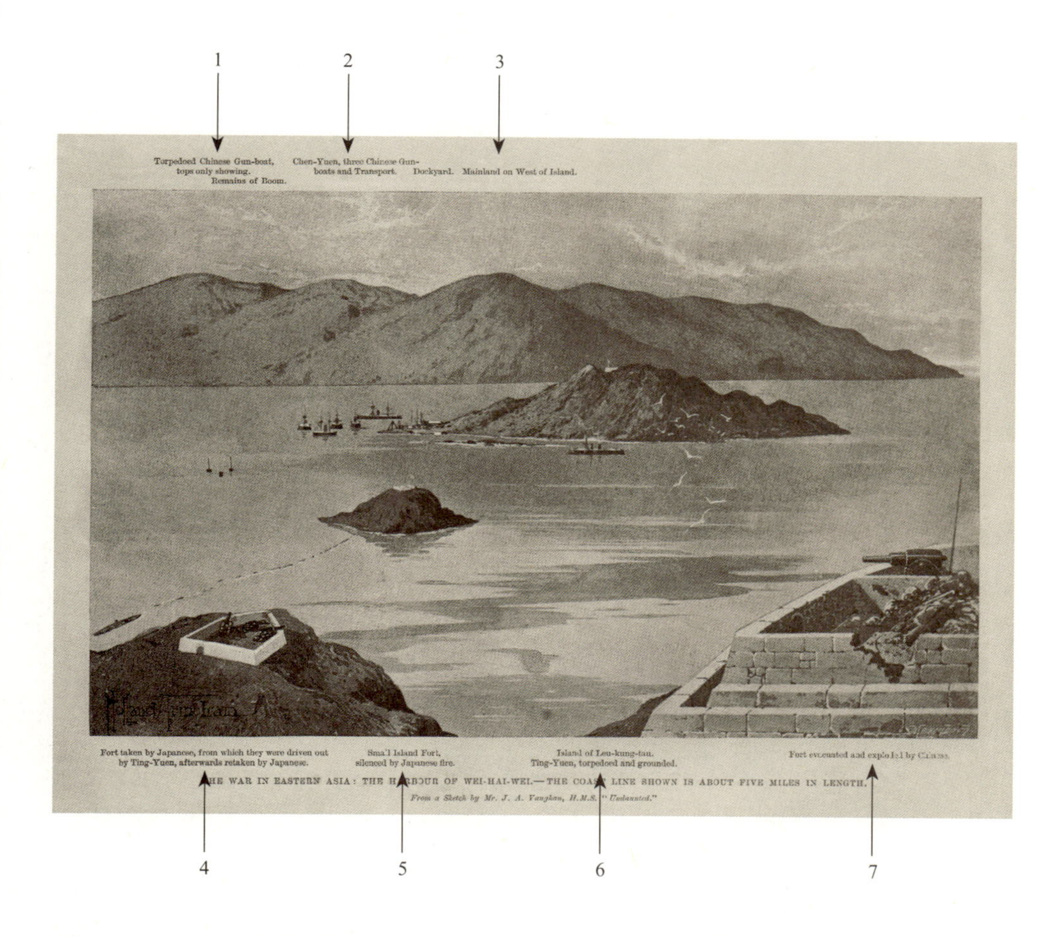

1895 年 4 月 13 日《伦敦新闻画报》

东亚的战事：威海卫港和它 5 英里长的海岸线

The war in Eastern Asia: the Harbour of Wei-Hai-Wei—the coast line shown is about five miles in length.

1　被击沉的中国战舰，下桁的残骸	1　Torpedoed Chinese gun-boats, tops only showing. Remains of boom.
2　镇远舰，三艘炮舰和运兵船	2　Zhen-Yuen, three Chinese gun-boats and transport.
3　船坞，海岛西侧的大陆	3　Dockyard. Mainland on west of island.
4　日军夺取此炮台后被定远舰驱走，后又重新占领	4　Fort taken by Japanese, from which they were driven out by Ting-Yuen, afterwards retaken by Japanese.
5　小岛上被日军摧毁的炮台	5　Small island fort, silenced by Japanese fire.
6　刘公岛，定远舰中鱼雷后沉没	6　Island of Leu-kung-tau. Ting Yuen, torpedoed and grounded.
7　清军撤离前毁掉的炮台	7　Fort evacuated and exploded by Chinese.

328.—THE ILLUSTRATED LONDON NEWS, MARCH 16, 1895.—329

THE WAR IN EASTERN ASIA: LANDING OF JAPANESE TROOPS AT SH

From a Sketch by Mr. F. C. Hoste, R.N.

The British fleet was at Chefoo when word was brought that the Japanese Third Army Corps had re-embarked, and was about to effect a landing at some other port on the coast. Accordingly,
Japanese were landing at Shan Tung Promontory, having the intention of attacking Wei-hai-Wei in the rear by land. There were about twenty-three battle-ships, gun-boats, and torpedo-boats cr

1895 年 3 月 16 日《伦敦新闻画报》

东亚之战：日军登陆山东半岛

The war in Eastern Asia: landing of Japanese troops at Shan Tung Promontory.

收到日军第三军团再次登船并在（中国）海岸其他一个港口实施登陆的消息时，英国舰队正在烟台。于是，英国舰队转道前往仁川港；后来，埃俄罗斯号带来的消息说，三万日军正在登陆山东半岛，意图从陆路后方抢攻威海卫。共有 23 艘日军战舰、炮艇及鱼雷艇在附近巡航。随后传到英国的消息，是这张图片所呈现事件的续篇。

The British fleet was at Chefoo when word was brought that the Japanese Third Army Corps had re-embarked, and was about to effect a landing at some other port on the coast. Accordingly the British ships proceeded to Chemulpo; the "Eolus" next came with the tidings that about thirty thousand Japanese were landing at Shan Tung Promontory, having the intention of attacking Wei-Hai-Wei in the rear by land. There were about twenty-three battle-ships, gun-boats, and torpedo-boats cruising about. The subsequent news which has reached this country is an interesting sequel to this picture.

THE ILLUSTRATED LONDON NEWS

REGISTERED AT THE GENERAL POST OFFICE FOR TRANSMISSION ABROAD.

No. 2894.—VOL. CV. SATURDAY, OCTOBER 6, 1894. TWO WHOLE SHEETS | SIXPENCE. BY POST, 6½D.

THE JAPANESE WAR-SHIP "YOSHINO."

THE WAR IN EASTERN ASIA: NAVAL ATTACK ON THE FORTS AT WEI-HAI-WEI.

From a Sketch by Mr. E. J. Rosevere, on board H.M.S. "Mercury."

1894 年 10 月 6 日《伦敦新闻画报》

东亚的战争：日本战舰吉野号进攻威海卫要塞

The war in Eastern Asia: naval attack on the forts at Wei-Hai-Wei.

日本吉野舰

The Japanese war-ship “Yoshino”.

吉野舰，英国制造，1894 年 3 月 6 日交付日本海军，是当时最快速的巡洋舰。吉野舰在黄海海战中，击沉北洋舰队致远舰。吉野舰原为中国建造，由于中国经费短缺，转由日本购买。本期画报以此舰为封面，认为此舰是中日海战胜负关键之一，该报内页还对吉野舰的性能做了详细介绍：“吉野”的速度尤其惊人，每小时超过 23 节，马力高达 15000 匹，排水 4200 吨。这艘船以及“浪速”和“高千穗”都由阿姆斯特朗—米彻尔公司制造。“吉野”还是世界上最强大的巡洋舰，长达 350 英尺，宽为 $46\frac{1}{2}$ 英尺，双层底，吃水 17 英尺，双螺旋桨推进，最大载煤量 1000 吨。它的装备包括 4 个 6 英寸的大炮，可发射 100-1b 的射弹，其位置摆放使得三门大炮可以同时向正前方发射，其中的两门可以借助第三门大炮，向船正后方开火；有 22 个能够发射 3 磅重炮弹的机关炮，大多分布在桅盘和舷窗，还有 5 个鱼雷发射管；钢质保护甲板大于两英寸厚。

SEPT. 29, 1894 THE ILLUSTRATED LONDON NEWS 395

OUR ILLUSTRATIONS.

THE WAR IN EASTERN ASIA.

There has been no sensational event in the Chino-Japanese War since the great naval battle at the mouth of the Yalu. An engagement, however, is anticipated between the Chinese forces, consisting mostly of Hunanese "braves," badly armed, with no discipline in particular, and probably wanting supplies, and the victorious Japanese army in Corea. Accounts differ as to the numbers of the Hunanese soldiers whom the transports succeeded in landing in face of the Japanese fleet. One account fixes them at 7000, another at 38,000. The Japanese movements in the north of Corea are variously interpreted. They may mean an advance on Manchuria, or China proper, with reference to an ultimate march to Pekin, or they may have for their object the cutting off of the raw levies huddled together in an improvised camp on the Yalu. Meanwhile, the military machine in Japan is being managed with the utmost zeal and ability. Eighty thousand new troops are going to the front immediately, a special war session of the Japanese Parliament has been ordered, and the utmost enthusiasm prevails in Tokio and throughout the country. On the other hand, we hear of nothing but confusion and disorganisation in China. The Empress is said to be making fresh contributions to the war fund, but the destruction of China's first fighting line at the battle of Ping-Yang has compelled her to fall back on raw recruits, who are not armed or disciplined on European methods. Li Hung Chang, the great Viceroy of Pe-chi-li, is being made to bear the brunt of the follies of the Tsung-li-Yamen, and has suffered further disgrace in the loss of his Peacock's Feather. These childish details contrast strongly with the essentially modern and business-like method in which Japan is conducting the war. Of the fleets engaged in the battle of the Yalu nothing certain is known. The probability is that the Chinese have lost command of the sea, and that Admiral Ting will not again meet the Japanese war-ships in the open. If this is so, China may be said to be defeated already beyond the hope of recovery. If the command of the sea at both horns of the Gulf of Pe-chi-li has gone over to Japan, China has little hope of winning back her lost ground in Corea. The all-disturbing rumour of the week from the Japanese point of view is the story of the sending of Russian troops to the north of Corea with a view of keeping Chinese border ruffians in order. The news comes from various quarters—Russian, Japanese, German—but it is very vague and contradictory in terms. Of course, if Russia interferes, all calculations as to the issue of the war will be upset.

SALE OF SLAVE GIRLS IN EGYPT.

The abolition of the slave trade has been one of the chief objects of the English intervention in the affairs of Egypt, and the recrudescence of the evil under the patronage of members of the governing class has excited strong feeling throughout the civilised world. Ali Pasha Cherif, a notable of great wealth, was President of the Legislative Council, and in that capacity lately protested against the maintenance of the "Slave Bureau," or office charged with the Suppression of Slavery, as a needless expense, since slavery was practically extinct in Egypt. Shortly afterwards the very same personage, Ali Pasha Cherif, and several other Pashas were convicted of purchasing negresses. They have been tried by court martial. In order to escape, Ali Pasha Cherif claimed Italian protection, but this claim was disallowed by the Italian Government. Should the Khedive attempt to exercise his prerogative of mercy in favour of these high personages, he will produce a most unfavourable impression on the Western Powers. Our Illustration represents the negresses, natives of Siwah, an oasis on the frontier of Tripoli, who were illegally bought by the Pashas.

MR. STODDART'S CRICKET TEAM.

We are learning day by day of the progress of Lord Hawke's cricket team in America, and soon the news will be varied by records of the excellent players who have just left Tilbury under the captaincy of Mr. A. E. Stoddart, to uphold the honour of Great Britain in Australian cricket-fields. Mr. Stoddart is evidently not affected by superstition, for the team numbers thirteen men. The names of those who boarded the *Ophir* on Sept. 21 were Mr. Stoddart and Mr. F. G. J. Ford, both of whom do valiant service on behalf of Middlesex; Mr. L. H. Gay, who plays for Somerset; Mr. A. C. MacLaren, Albert Ward, and Briggs, whom Lancashire claims; Peel and Brown, the Yorkshire professionals; Humphreys, a solitary though very useful representative of Sussex; and Brockwell, Richardson, and Lockwood, whose exploits will be watched with keen interest by their Surrey admirers. Mr. H. Philipson, of Oxford University, joined the *Ophir* at Naples. The cricketers were very warmly greeted as they went on board, and in the smoking-room of the steam-ship ardent followers of the game, including the veteran Hon. Ivo Bligh, Lord Darnley, Mr. V. T. Hill, and Mr. C. E. Green, bade them farewell with many wishes for their success in Greater Britain.

THE CITY OF BATH.

Of the many cities in England few are so "beautiful for situation" as Bath. Its history is no less unique. It has furnished novelists like Fielding and Dickens with the groundwork of some of their cleverest pictures of social life—that "light of other days" which is not dimmed but only changed. The story of Bath stretches far into the past; as a Roman city it contains many traces of the art and usages which found a home therein in the days of Vespasian. The mineral springs which have made it a medical Mecca for centuries still supply an increasing flow of water to those who visit the Grand Pump-Room, where stands a statue of Beau Nash, the Master of the Ceremonies, who may safely be called the founder of modern Bath. The city has been for eight centuries the seat of a bishopric, and its beautiful abbey is often designated a cathedral, although it is in reality only a parish church. Mr. Freeman, who for long lived in the neighbourhood of Bath, has carefully traced the vicissitudes which befell the abbey. It was finally restored by Sir Gilbert Scott at a cost of £30,000. Certain statuary in it is by Flaxman and Chantrey. In the abbey is the grave of Malthus the economist. The Guildhall contains portraits of William Pitt, who represented Bath in Parliament for a time, Marshal Wade, of road-constructing fame, and others of whom Bath is proud. Surrounding the city are many charming spots of interest. The Prince of Monaco, it may be mentioned, is just now "taking the waters" at Bath, as a cure for the rheumatism contracted on his recent African cruise.

Photo by [illegible]

ADMIRAL TING, OF THE CHINESE NAVY.
COMMANDER IN THE RECENT BATTLE AT THE MOUTH OF THE YALU RIVER, COREA.

THE DOGE'S PALACE AT VENICE.

In Mr. Ruskin's opinion, the rebuilding, in the fifteenth century, by Doge Foscari, of the older Palazzo Ducale reared by Doge Ziani in the twelfth century, and subsequently enlarged, on the site of the original edifice of the Byzantine period, was "the knell of the architecture of Venice" for Mr. Ruskin does not approve of the Renaissance style. The building actually constructed under Foscari's rule, part of the old buildings having been burnt, was decreed in 1422 by Doge Mocenigo. In 1574, another great fire destroyed much of the interior. The architects employed in its repair and completion were Giovanni Rusconi, and three members of a family named Bueno; the latter designed the two principal colonnades supporting the outer walls of the palace. The capitals of the massive corner pillars, at three angles of the building, the third being out of sight adjacent to St. Mark's Cathedral, are boldly decorated with colossal groups of sculpture. These angles are distinguished also, in two instances, by the character of the decorative foliage. There is the "Fig-tree Angle," at which the subject represented is that of Adam and Eve, or the Fall of Man; and there is the "Vine Angle," which exhibits the Drunkenness of Noah. The figures of Solomon and the two women disputing the motherhood of the child, with the little boy, and the executioner ready to cut the child asunder, are conspicuous at the "Judgment Angle." The capital belongs to the later or Renaissance period, and though it has great beauty, hardly possesses the symbolic power and subtlety of the work of some of the earlier craftsmen, whose exquisite designs Mr. Ruskin has minutely described. Other features, external and interior, of the Venetian Ducal Palace have often been detailed. Most visitors are chiefly interested by its historical and romantic associations, and by the pictures of Tintoretto and other great painters.

HOLBEIN'S PORTRAIT OF ERASMUS.

The publication of Mr. Froude's "Life and Letters of Erasmus" (Longmans) at a moment when the great historian is lying dangerously ill, has a pathos all its own. Mr. Froude is "game" to the last. In these lectures, which are probably the most fascinating that were ever delivered by a Regius Professor, he treats us once again to all the eccentricities of judgment to which he has devoted so many volumes in the past. Here, once more, Henry VIII. is the model king, and members of ecclesiastics who cross the path alike of Henry and Erasmus are rogues and scoundrels of the most pronounced type. Yet, when all is said, Mr. Froude's picture of Erasmus will be acceptable to the English reader for many a year to come. We see the great scholar despoiled of his inheritance by treacherous guardians; we see him as a student of the most omnivorous kind, but assuming, like all the students of his century, that it was the province of the rich to patronise learning, and writing begging-letters of the most astounding character to people of rank. In middle life Erasmus becomes the most striking figure of his age. We have the Kings of France and England, the Pope, and the Emperor alike begging that he will accept their bounty and will reside at their Courts. Pure learning was surely never placed upon such a pedestal, and one rejoices that it should be so of one of whom Mr. Froude eloquently says that he was "never false to intellectual truth." Our Engraving is from the well-known portrait by Holbein.

SPORT IN THE "ROCKIES."

The Rocky Mountains, so termed in North American geography, form but a part of the more or less parallel series of mountain ranges occupying a breadth of several hundred miles between the plains or prairies in the middle of that Continent and the slopes towards the Pacific coast. Their highest summits are in the extreme north, Mount Logan, in British territory, and Mount St. Elias, in Alaska, considerably exceeding 20,000 ft. Some of the grandest scenery, and perhaps the best region now available for the sportsman in pursuit of big game, will be found near the frontier, on both sides, between the south of British Columbia and the adjacent States of Washington, Idaho, and Montana. From the north, by the valleys of the Kootenay and the Columbia Rivers, after leaving the Canadian Pacific railway route, or by the United States lines through Dakota and Wyoming, this region can be approached. The Selkirks, a secondary range in British Columbia westward of the Rockies, were noticed in our last. The intervening space, a secluded land of many streams and lakes, is inhabited by the Flathead and other Indian tribes. Mr. W. Baillie-Grohman, author of "Camps in the Rockies," who fifteen years ago visited the Kootenay Lake, riding by way of Bonner's Ferry when the Northern American lines of railroad were not in existence, has good hunting adventures to relate. Besides the animal called a mountain goat, which is really a species of antelope, styled by naturalists *Haplocerus montanus*, there is the wapiti, as our sketches bear witness, in the forests of that region. For the bison, miscalled buffalo, one may now search the plains to the south in vain; only a few hundred survive in the highland valleys of Idaho and thereabouts. Civilisation is a good thing, but unfavourable to big game.

1894年9月29日《伦敦新闻画报》

近期朝鲜鸭绿江口之战的清朝海军指挥官：舰队司令丁汝昌

Admiral Ting, of the Chinese Navy.

Commander in recent battle at the mouth of the Yalu River, Corea.

丁汝昌（1836. 11—1895. 2），清朝北洋水师提督，参与创建北洋水师，清日战争黄海海战失利，威海卫之役失败后，拒不投降，引咎自尽。伊东祐亨派船护送其灵柩回京。

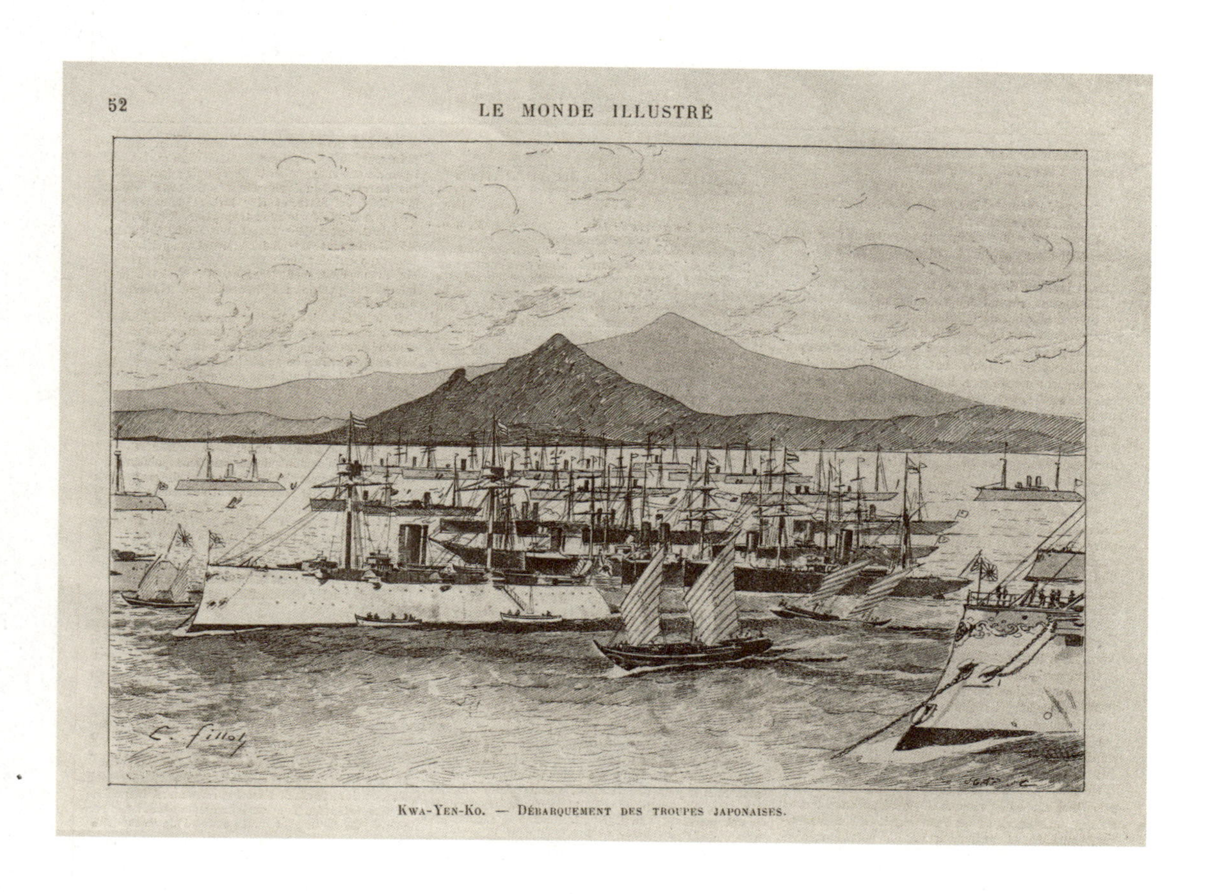
52　LE MONDE ILLUSTRÉ

KWA-YEN-KO. — DÉBARQUEMENT DES TROUPES JAPONAISES.

1895 年 1 月 26 日《世界画报》

日军在花园口登陆

Kwa-Yen-Ko.—Débarquement des troupes japonaises.

THE NAVAL BATTLE AT WEI-HAI-WEI.—Drawn by R. F. Zo

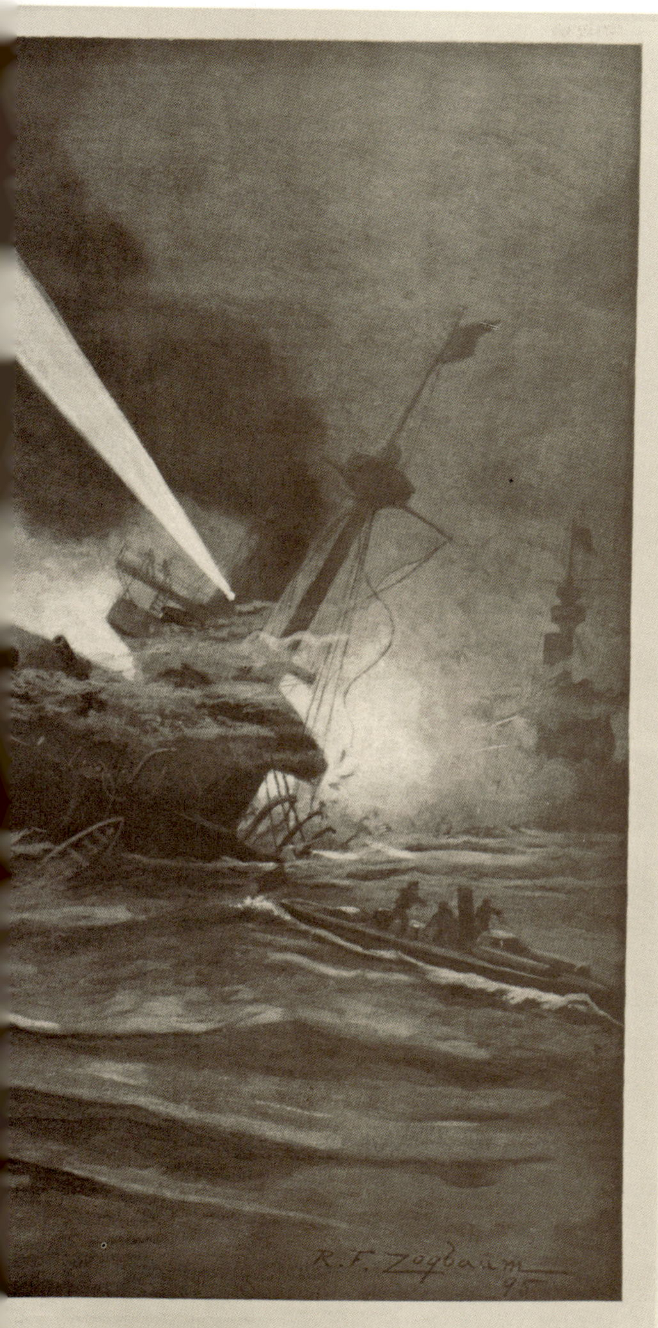

AGE 472.]

"The Japanese waited until the moon had gone down, when fifteen boats slipped away from the fleet towards the east entrance of the harbor. The boats gradually crept towards the Chinese ironclads. These were all under cover of the island forts. One of the Japanese torpedo-boats, approaching the 'Ting-yuen,' fired two torpedoes. Both took effect, and the vessel sunk at once. Instantly all was in commotion in the harbor, but by this time all the other torpedo-boats were close up. The ironclads and forts opened a wild fire, and the torpedo-boat which sank the 'Ting-yuen' was destroyed by a hail of shot, eight of her crew being drowned. Only one Japanese boat escaped entirely uninjured."—LONDON MAIL.

1895 年 5 月 18 日《哈珀斯周刊》

威海卫海战

The naval battle at Wei-Hai-Wei.

日本人一直等到月亮完全被遮住，15 艘舰艇离开了舰队朝港口驶去。他们蹑手蹑脚地向中国铁甲舰围拢过去，他们非常清楚自己已经完全进入到中国舰队和炮台的火力范围之内，其中一艘鱼雷艇靠近定远舰，射出两颗鱼雷，皆命中目标，定远舰即刻开始下沉。瞬时，军港乱成一团，清军开始醒悟过来，但已经晚了，所有的日本鱼雷艇已经形成了包围圈。清军的铁甲舰和炮台枪炮怒射，击沉定远舰的那艘鱼雷艇在一串冰雹般的轰炸中解体，8 名船员被淹死。只有一艘日舰毫发无损地逃出了清军的炮火。

——摘自《伦敦邮报》

"The Japanese waited until the moon had gone down, when fifteen boats slipped away from the fleet towards the east entrance of the harbor. The boats gradually crept towards the Chinese ironclads. These were all under cover of the island forts. One of the Japanese torpedo-boats, approaching the 'Ting-yuen,' fired two torpedoes. Both took effect, and the vessel sunk at once. Instantly all was in commotion in the harbor, but by this time all the other torpedo-boats were close up. The ironclads and forts opened a wild fire, and the torpedo-boat which sank the 'Ting-yuen' was destroyed by a hail of shot, eight of her crew being drowned. Only one Japanese boat escaped entirely uninjured."

—London Mail

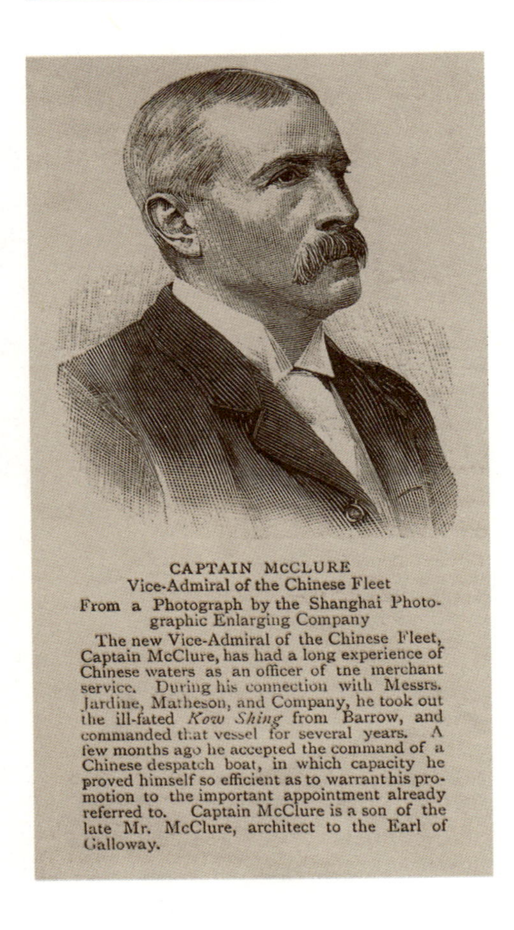
CAPTAIN McCLURE
Vice-Admiral of the Chinese Fleet
From a Photograph by the Shanghai Photographic Enlarging Company
The new Vice-Admiral of the Chinese Fleet, Captain McClure, has had a long experience of Chinese waters as an officer of the merchant service. During his connection with Messrs. Jardine, Matheson, and Company, he took out the ill-fated *Kow Shing* from Barrow, and commanded that vessel for several years. A few months ago he accepted the command of a Chinese despatch boat, in which capacity he proved himself so efficient as to warrant his promotion to the important appointment already referred to. Captain McClure is a son of the late Mr. McClure, architect to the Earl of Galloway.

1894年12月1日《图片报》

马格禄船长　Captain McClure.

中国海军副司令 Vice-Admiral of the Chinese Fleet.

在马格禄船长被任命为中国海军副司令（帮办北洋海军提督）之前，曾在商业航运领域工作多年，还担任过怡和洋行的高升号商船（后被日军击沉）船长，熟悉中国水域。数月前，他接受了在一艘中国的通信船上任船长的职位，表现出色，被提升为中国海军副司令。马格禄的父亲是苏格兰加洛韦伯爵的建筑设计师。

The new Vice-Admiral of the Chinese Fleet, Captain McClure, has had a long experience of Chinese waters as an officer of the merchant service. During his connection with Messrs. Jardine, Matheson, and Company, he took out the ill-fated Kow Shing from Barrow, and commanded that vessel for several years. A few months ago he accepted the command of a Chinese despatch boat , in which capacity he proved himself so efficient as to warrant his promotion to the important appointment already referred to. Captain McClure is a son of the late Mr. McClure, architect to the Earl of Galloway.

这篇短文没有提及的是在马格禄荣获提升的原因中，可能有两个比他在通信船上的出色表现更为突出的事，即汉纳根的离职和琅威理的婉拒。

黄海海战后，在丰岛海战后刚刚被提升为北洋水师副提督和总教习的汉纳根向清廷陈述，认为黄海海战由于“中国海军近八年中未曾添一新船，所有近来外洋新式船炮，一概乌有，而倭之船炮，皆系簇新，是以未能制胜”。建议清政府向智利、德国、英国购买快船，聘请外国将弁水手同船来华，新旧合成一大军，并委婉要求清廷委任自己为全军水师提督。这些逆耳忠言虽被清政府倾听却未能付诸实施，汉纳根遂离开北洋海军。清政府又拟邀北洋首任副提督、总教习琅威理回华助战，那时琅威理已成为英国皇家海军后备队38艘军舰的统帅，他婉拒清廷邀请的公开理由是英国宣布中立，他不能以现役军人身份前往中国，又不愿辞去现任的海军职务。只有在战后当英国政府许可时才可能前往；但他私下却提出了中国政府难以接受的苛刻条件，如必须由皇帝以玺书形式颁给他海军最高职衔，等等。

天津海关税务司德璀琳为李鸿章推荐了英国人马格禄为帮办北洋海军提督。通过丁汝昌传谕各管驾以下员弁，谨受指挥。马格禄并无海军背景。根据北洋海军定远号洋员戴乐尔在他的回忆录中评价："彼已过中年，且以沉湎于酒著名。"1895年2月11日在威海卫失守后，马格禄率领另外两位北洋舰队中的洋员美国人浩威、德国人瑞乃尔以及中国官员数人商定了向日军投降的事宜，以北洋海军提督名义向日本侵略者乞降。日本正式占领威海卫后，马格禄及其他洋员被遣送至烟台。

262 THE ILLUSTRATED LONDON NEWS MARCH 2, 1895

SCIENCE JOTTINGS.

BY DR. ANDREW WILSON.

Mr. Eadweard Muybridge, whose researches in the difficult and complex subject of animal locomotion are so well known, and who himself may be regarded as the foremost exponent of the scientific study of animal movements, has favoured me with a letter in which he refers to the subject of the kinetoscope and its applications to the reproduction of animal movements. It will be remembered that I made some inquiry regarding an exhibition of similar nature to the kinetoscope, which was seen by a friend of mine at Blackpool. Mr. Muybridge thinks that the exhibition referred to may have been his demonstration of the science of animal locomotion, illustrated by aid of his zoopraxiscope. In this exhibition, photographs of animals and birds were projected on a screen, and exhibited "in apparent motion as in life." The occasion in question was that of a lecture given about six years ago by Mr. Muybridge, at Blackpool, on the invitation of the Home Reading Union.

Mr. Muybridge informs me that in 1887 or thereabouts an article appeared in the *Nation*, of New York (from the pen of the editor, Mr. W. P. Garrison), suggesting the possibility of combining the phonograph with the zoopraxiscope so as to reproduce not merely the peculiar characteristics of, say, an orator delivering a speech, but also, at the same time, the words as they fell from his lips. It was about this period that Mr. Muybridge, then on a visit to Mr. Garrison, delivered a lecture at Orange, New Jersey, where Mr. Edison's laboratory is situated. He was consulted by Mr. Edison regarding his (Mr. Muybridge's) investigations on animal locomotion and on the construction and method of working the zoopraxiscope. "As is my custom," says Mr. Muybridge, "I gave him a full description of my experience and of the instruments." Turning now to the zoopraxiscope itself, we find this ingenious instrument described by Mr. Muybridge himself, who tells us that, "in the presentation of a Lecture on Zoopraxography, the course usually adopted is to project, much larger than the size of life, upon a screen, a series of the most important phases of some act of animal

COLONEL THEODOR SCHNELL,
Instructor to the Chinese Artillery Service.

motion (the stride of a horse while galloping, for example) which are analytically described. These successive phases are then combined on the zoopraxiscope, which is set in motion, and a reproduction of the original movements of life is distinctly visible to the audience."

So far, then, it seems to me Mr. Muybridge has answered my original query concerning the application of the kinetoscope principle to scientific investigation. In respect that his zoopraxiscope shows a whole series of movements under discussion to an audience, it must be claimed for it, I should say, that it is superior to the kinetoscope, into which (as I saw it) only one spectator can gaze at a time. Doubtless the principle of the two machines is the same, but at least it is satisfactory to know that in Mr. Muybridge's hands the demonstration to an audience of animal movements (photographed, I must add, by a most complex apparatus) is *un fait accompli*. His little treatise on Zoopraxography was published in 1893 by the University of Pennsylvania, at which seat of learning Mr. Muybridge's researches were carried out. It is no light thing in the progress of science to find that the graphic method of appealing to our senses and of demonstrating the problems of animal locomotion has proved in this scientist's hands so completely successful. We may rest content, also, that the kinetoscope principle has not been lost sight of, and, presumably, has been thus anticipated by the zoopraxiscope in scientific research.

A few weeks ago I referred to certain investigations on the development of centres in the brain, and anticipated in my remarks that, sooner or later, we would have definite accounts given us of these investigations. The desire for further information has been so far gratified in that we are now told something definite regarding these curious and important advances in our knowledge of brain-ways. The researches are those of Professor Flechsig, of the University of Leipsic, a well-known physiologist. In the course of his University rectorial address, the professor gave an account of his studies in the innermost centres of brain-action. He has been tracing the development of the nerve fibres which link together the nerve-cells of those regions of the brain devoted to the governance of our conscious life, which fibres constitute the means of communication between body and brain, and *vice versâ*. It seems that in the very young infant, while its lower brain-centres, or those governing the essential actions through which life is maintained, are well developed, the nerve fibres of the cerebrum (or great brain) are imperfectly evolved. This is as though the telegraphic apparatus which is to serve the conscious messages of its future life had not been perfected. There are thus few nerve-pathways in the brain of the infant. Those which are developed discharge the duty of connecting together the body's exterior, certain sense organs, and the brain; so that, in its own feeble, but vitally necessary, fashion, some definite relation may be maintained between the infant-body and its surroundings.

Then development proceeds. It is described that new nerve-tracks begin to be formed leading from the exterior to the brain, slowly growing in its sensitiveness and in the display of conscious life. The smell-tracks come first in order, it is said, because for the selection of food (regarded from a purely animal standpoint) this sense is all-important. Hearing, it is alleged, comes last in order of development; perhaps naturally so, as our most complex possession of all in the way of a sensory apparatus. Later on these developing nerve-paths shoot out not only towards the higher centres of the brain, but towards the lower centres which obey the behests of the superior brain parts, and which command our muscles and other organs. The apparatus of the sense of touch, with its multitude of resulting connections, is thuswise evolved. We are told this sense has connected with it about two hundred and fifty thousand separate pathways leading to and from the skin surface. Still later on, pathways develop from the brain-centres of the senses to the higher mental centres, and thus is laid the foundation of the conscious life.

THE WAR IN EASTERN ASIA.

An interesting sidelight on the War is cast by the accompanying Illustrations, which we owe to a German correspondent. It appears that the only European instructor to the Chinese forces present at Wei-hai-Wei was Colonel Theodor Schnell, whose portrait we give herewith. The

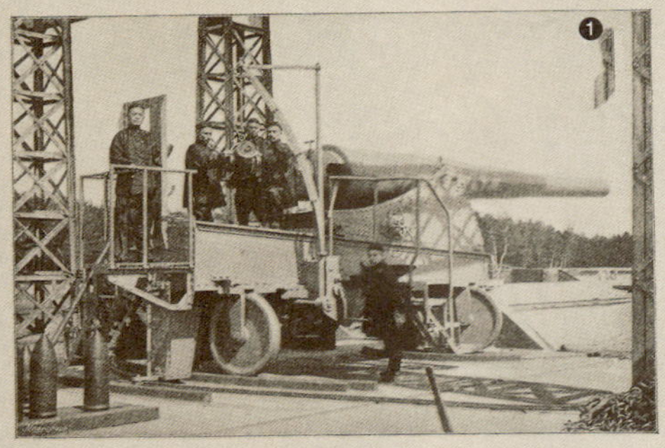

CHINESE ARTILLERY OFFICERS UNDER COLONEL SCHNELL'S COMMAND.

Colonel, who is a German by birth, has been in the Chinese service for a quarter of a century. He has been engaged in instructing the artillery during this time. He was one of the three Europeans who were reported as having been killed or captured at Wei-hai-Wei, but later reports certify that, at all events, he has not suffered death. The Japanese have taken possession of the arsenal, forts, and war-ships at Wei-hai-Wei with the order and method which have distinguished them on previous occasions. The *Chen-Yuen*, having been repaired sufficiently to be seaworthy, has sailed for Japan. Marshal Oyama and his staff are living in the buildings till lately occupied by the Chinese Government, and a careful inventory of the contents of the torpedo-station is being taken. The Japanese Government is asking its Parliament to sanction a fresh vote of credit amounting to 100,000,000 yen. Already 150,000,000 yen has been spent on this war. There is, it is stated, no intention on the part of the Japanese to occupy Chefoo. The bird's-eye view of that important place which we give on another page shows it to be thickly populated. While public interest centres on the war, rather than upon the *fons et origo mali*, there is a propensity to lose sight of the Corean difficulty itself. Corea has been the subject of much consideration by the Japanese Government, and the reforms which Count Inouye is preparing are so sweeping, and, in certain respects, so novel, that the careful observer of politics in the Far East may well pause before he commits himself to an opinion upon them.

CHINESE ARTILLERY AT DRILL.

1895年3月2日《伦敦新闻画报》

1 瑞乃尔指挥下的中国炮兵	1 Chinese artillery officers under Colonel Schnell's command.
2 中国炮兵教习，西奥多·瑞乃尔上校	2 Colonel Theodor Schnell instructor to the Chinese artillery service.
3 训练中的中国炮兵	3 Chinese artillery at drill.

这篇报道中写道："这几张关于瑞乃尔的照片是德国记者发给本刊的。据我们所知，曾在威海卫中国军队工作的唯一一位西方教官是德国出生的西奥多·瑞乃尔上校。他服务于中国军队，教授和训练炮兵已经长达25年。在日军攻打威海卫的初期报道中，他是三位被传伤亡的西方人之一，后又有报道称他并没有死。"

这篇报道没写错，瑞乃尔没有死也没有在威海卫战役中受伤，而是被占领了刘公岛的日军在2月18日遣送到了烟台。在这之前数日，他一直鼓动、逼迫丁汝昌投降日军，未果。又在丁汝昌自杀后积极促成了降约的签订。1870年，德国克虏伯炮厂委派瑞乃尔来到中国，旋被李鸿章聘为陆军教官。后经天津海关税务司德璀琳推荐，瑞乃尔被聘为旅顺炮台教习。甲午中日战争爆发后，瑞乃尔由天津调往威海。1907年卒。

——《远东的战事》(选译)，1895年3月2日《伦敦新闻画报》

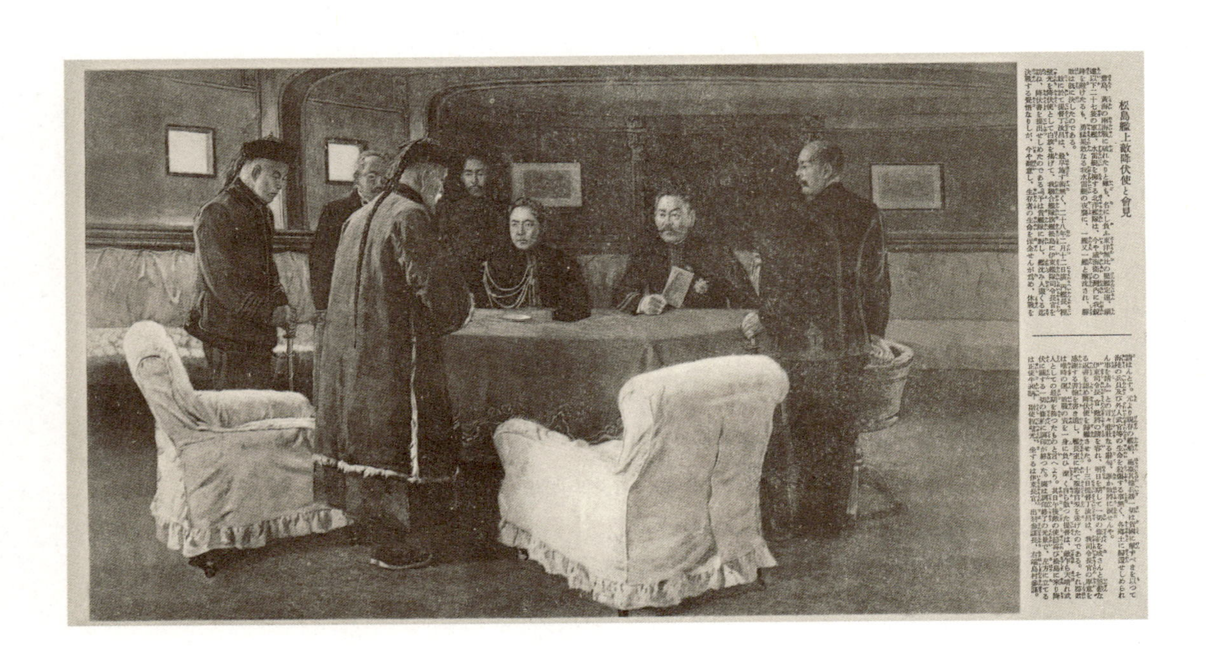

日本《御国之誉》(浮世绘)

松岛舰上会见降敌使节

虽然北洋舰队在丰岛、黄海两次海战中战败，但毕竟在亚洲久负盛名。拥有坚船“定远”、“镇远”等27艘军舰和水雷艇的北洋舰队，尽管躲在威海卫的港湾里躲避我军的锋芒，但被勇猛果敢的我军水雷艇，在夜袭中一艘一艘击沉，胜负结果已经可以确定了。

鉴于此状，北洋舰队提督丁汝昌，已是无计可施，明治二十八年二月十二日他派广丙舰长程璧光担任投降使节，船挂白旗，来我联合舰队松岛舰拜见舰队司令长官伊东，呈交投降书。“面对贵军舰队，我们本有战斗到船没人亡的决心，但现在已经改变看法，为了保全生存者的性命，向贵军请求休战。目前现存的舰船、炮台等一切武器都会献给贵国，请不要伤害我方海陆军士兵和外国武官，让他们各自返乡。”使节说着这样悲壮的话语，流下败军之泪。

伊东司令长官同意了敌将的请求，写了一封积极的回信，约定以明日为期，签订一系列条约，放回了投降使节。二月十三日，北洋舰队提督丁汝昌，遗留下了感谢我军司令长官好意的书函，在舰长室服毒自尽。胜败自有天定，像他这样把败军之责一身独揽，为保名节而自行了断的提督，纵使是我们的敌人，也得说他是以值得敬佩的军人方式完结了人生。那一天下午，敌军使节再次来到松岛舰，签署了与投降有关的一切条约。图中所示就是条约签订完毕时的情景。站在左边的是敌方正使牛昶昞、副使程璧光，坐着的是伊东长官、出羽参谋长，右边的是岛村参谋。

——日本《御国之誉》

结 语

尽管清军实际情况潦倒没落至此，但在中日战争爆发伊始，这篇文章的德国撰稿人曾做出如下判断：战争初期日军定会占到上风，但如果中日之战相持日久，最后挨打的还是日本人。作者说，在我离开中国之时，旅顺港沦陷于日军之手的消息尚未传到国外，当时所有欧洲军事专家和海军专家的预断与前述判断完全不谋而合。大家都一致认为如果日军打算获得最终胜利，它需要挥师直捣北京，否则后期清军定会反败为胜。因为，整个漫长的冬季休战期不经意间给清军提供了一个喘息休养的机会，使其有充分的时间培养或挑选富有经验和阅历的军事统领；知耻而后勇的清政府定会拼尽所有，以排山倒海之势把数以百万计的兵力和军饷砸向战场，直至日军筋疲力尽、招架不住。

发生在东方的海战给我们带来什么？我们现在必须面对一个新的东方强国！最近的胜利可能会使它更加好斗，从中国虏获的四五艘战舰将使它的舰队更加雄伟……显然，我们是所有列强中受到震荡最大的一个，因为我们的商业利益和殖民地遍布地球的每一个角落。

——1895年2月2日　英国《帕尔摩报》

九　战争中的生与死

自一场不寻常的革命后，依照天皇的命令，日本决心摈弃自己的文明，去拥抱欧洲文明。人们首先能够想到的是：这场意料之外的运动最多不过使这个奇特国家的男人们戴上大礼帽，女人们则穿上胸衣。然而，他们如今正在对庞大的邻国发起的战争向我们证明了，这次变革出人意料地深刻！在配备了统一的西式军服和武器的同时，日本军官们还掌握了军事理论和传统。的确，为了生存而战斗的需求意识必定主宰着这次变革。而我们刚刚收到一些来自东京的照片让我们看到，他们证明：日本的复兴甚至更加彻底，并且深入到了人道机构领域，这些机构依照最先进的医学理论组建起来，救治了大量伤残战俘。这场复兴已经使这个远东一隅跻身于欧洲文明强国之列。

——1894 年 12 月 29 日　法国《插图报》

SURRENDER OF CHINESE GENERA

From a Sketch by an Eye-Witness.

1895 年 1 月 26 日《伦敦新闻画报》

投降的中国官兵

Surrender of Chinese generals and staff.

THE GRAPHIC

AN ILLUSTRATED WEEKLY NEWSPAPER

No. 1,310—Vol. LI.
Registered as a Newspaper

SATURDAY, JANUARY 5, 1895

WITH EXTRA SUPPLEMENTS

PRICE SIXPENCE
By Post 6½d.

AFTER THE BATTLE OF PING YANG: JAPANESE OFFICERS INTERROGATING CHINESE PRISONERS

FACSIMILE REPRODUCTION OF A SKETCH BY OUR SPECIAL ARTIST WITH THE JAPANESE FORCES

1895 年 1 月 5 日《图片报》

平壤战役后，日本军官审问中国俘虏

After the battle of Ping Yang: Japanese officers interrogating Chinese prisoners.

甲午战争中，清朝在册战俘 1790 人，日军在高升号事件、朝鲜战役及旅顺口虐杀事件中都暴露出其残忍的一面；但为了争取国际媒体舆论，日本对部分俘虏也采取怀柔手段，设立收容所、战俘救护员，并为死亡俘虏设立墓碑；借此向国际媒体展示自己是文明国家，故意向西方展示自己是所谓的文明之师，然而本性难改，在后续的战争中其残暴性更是有目共睹。

1894 年 12 月 29 日《插图报》

中日战争——平壤战役结束后的中国战俘

La guerre Sino-Japonaise.—Après la bataille de Pyeng-Yang: prisoniers chinois.

1895年3月9日《图片报》

日本军队押送中国俘虏

Japanese troops convoying Chinese prisoners.

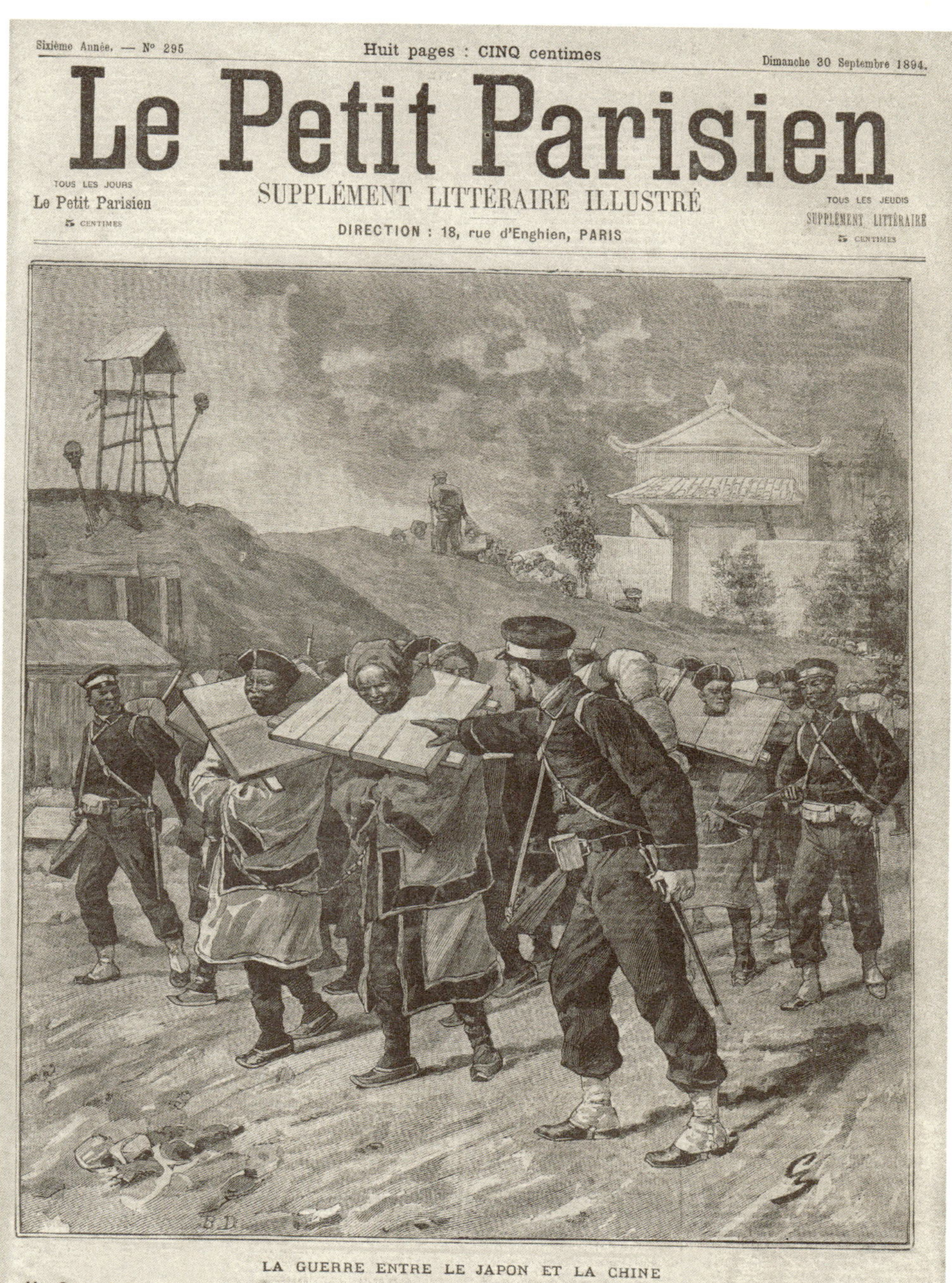

Sixième Année. — N° 295

Huit pages : CINQ centimes

Dimanche 30 Septembre 1894.

Le Petit Parisien

TOUS LES JOURS
Le Petit Parisien
5 CENTIMES

SUPPLÉMENT LITTÉRAIRE ILLUSTRÉ

DIRECTION : 18, rue d'Enghien, PARIS

TOUS LES JEUDIS
SUPPLÉMENT LITTÉRAIRE
5 CENTIMES

LA GUERRE ENTRE LE JAPON ET LA CHINE

Un Convoi de Prisonniers Chinois conduit par les Soldats Japonais après la bataille de Ping-Yank

1894 年 9 月 30 日《小巴黎人》

日中战争：平壤战以后，日本士兵押送一队中国俘虏的场景

La guerre entre le Japon et la Chine. Un convoi de prisonniers chinois conduit par les soldats japonais après la bataille de Ping-Yank.

1895 年 4 月 27 日《图片报》

中国俘虏被押赴东京途中

Chinese prisoners on the way to Tokio.

当 34 名中国俘虏抵达日本新桥，天不亮就在此等候看俘虏热闹的日本民众，用高声嘲笑、投掷石块的方式来迎接，对着他们起哄、咒骂、投石子。警察虽然事先准备好了几辆公车，但是在押送俘虏们换乘汽车时，警察费了九牛二虎之力才阻挡住狂躁的暴民，押解俘虏的车辆随后驶往火车站。中国俘虏就这样被火车运送到了东京附近的樱花镇佐仓。

When a convoy of thirty-four Chinese prisoners arrived at Shimbashi the crowd, which had been waiting to see them since daybreak, received them with yells of derision, and some stones were thrown. The police, who had taken the precaution to engage several omnibuses, had great difficulty in keeping back the excited mob while the prisoners were put into these vehicles, which were to take them to the railway station. The prisoners were conveyed thence by train to Sakura, a town near Tokio.

根据本刊特派随日军画师的草图绘制

From a sketch by our special artist with the Japanese forces.

1895 年 4 月 20 日《图片报》

东京的中国俘虏：每天例行的放风散步

Chinese prisoners in Tokio: The daily promenade.

东京的中国俘虏获准每天下午在门迹大寺（即日本皇子、皇族、摄政家的子弟出家的寺院 ——编者注）的庭院中进行一个半小时的身体锻炼。每次总有一大群好奇的日本人围观他们。

Every day the Chinese prisoners in Tokio are allowed to exercise themselves in the court of the great Temple of Monseki for an hour and a half in the afternoon. There is always a crowd of wondering Japanese to stare at them.

fatigue. Horses and ponies are rare in Corea, and the Japanese contend that the coolies are far more satisfactory in every way for transport than horses, as they cost less, carry more, and are far more to be relied upon. The Corean policeman is a very important personage, though there is not much ordinary police work to be done, as the Coreans are a stolid, sad-faced people, and quiet in their manners except when a faction fight breaks out. In that case they fight for days with great fury, but as they always do it at a season set apart for such diversions the police do not trouble to interfere with them. The police are dressed in the ordinary costume of the Coreans, and wear the huge glazed hat and the full wadded trousers common to all but the very poor. Their chief employment is punishing people for the strange offences which are considered blameworthy in the Corea, matters which in England would be settled by a fine at the police court, but which in Corea are punished by severe floggings or even by death. If it were not so easy to commit a Corean crime the police would have an easier time of it than they now have, as the dull and apathetic people would not as a general rule give much employment to an English policeman. One of the sketches by Mr. Fripp, in this particular instance drawn from descriptions furnished by eye-witnesses, shows the manner in which the titular lords of Corea treated their dependents before the advancing Japanese astonished them by driving them out of the country. The Chinese mode of action with the unfortunate natives was very high-handed; and they treated the Coreans as if they were the inhabitants of a conquered country, and robbed and plundered them right and left in the early days of the war. The Commissariat Department in the Chinese army is very primitive in its organisation, and the soldiers helped themselves to what they wanted, and if the owners objected shot or otherwise maltreated them with all a Chinaman's indifference to suffering. Another illustration represents a Chinese soldier dressed in a manner to defy the bitter weather and shows a characteristic mode of carrying provisions. Another observer has remarked that Chinese soldiers when near an encampment always seem to be carrying cabbages. The soldiers are well accustomed to do with little, and with their bread and cabbages and a little rice, can manage to get through a good deal of work. In many cases the Chinese who were taken prisoners were better off than their comrades who had to beat a retreat in the face of the pursuing Japanese through the snow-bound Corea into Manchuria, for the retreating army naturally suffered great privations, while the prisoners were treated by the Japanese in a fashion which astonished them, accustomed as they were to the Oriental plan of putting prisoners to death to avoid the trouble and expense of keeping them. The result of the campaign has shown how the Japanese have profited by European instruction, and their imitation of European ways, while the Chinese, in spite of their purchases of arms and ammunition and their borrowing of officers from Europe, have remained much in their old Celestial habits, and have but little improved since the days of bows and arrows and match-lock guns. Their soldiers are merely an armed rabble, brave enough when it comes to a hand-to-hand fight from which they cannot escape, but utterly uninterested in the war, and without a particle of trust or belief in their leaders. Their hatred and loathing of the Japanese is intense, but their method of expressing it in warfare is as primitive as it was in the days when they first occupied Corea and had their first battles with the Japanese over that debatable land.

"There are military duties to be done, to be done."

CHINESE SOLDIER LADEN WITH PROVISIONS

CHINESE SOLDIERS PLUNDERING COREANS

FACSIMILES OF SKETCHES BY OUR SPECIAL ARTIST WITH THE CHINESE

1895 年 3 月 9 日《图片报》

1 （中国士兵边走边唱）“军务在身，军务在身”
  中国士兵肩挑生活补给

2 中国士兵抢掠朝鲜人

1 “There are military duties to be done, to be done.”
  Chinese soldiers laden with provisions.

2 Chinese soldiers plundering Coreans.

根据本报特派随清军画师的速写制版

Facsimiles of sketches by our special artist with the Chinese.

One of the first duties to be performed on the arrival of Japanese troops in a Corean village is the sinking of wells so that the men, especialy those in hospital, may have a supply of good water, a matter about which the Coreans themselves seem to trouble very little. In many cases this is very difficult to find, and has been the cause of a great deal of sickness in the Japanese army

THE WAR IN THE EAST: JAPANESE SOLDIERS SINKING A WELL

FACSIMILE OF A SKETCH BY OUR SPECIAL ARTIST WITH THE JAPANESE FORCES

1894 年 12 月 22 日《图片报》

东方的战争：日本士兵挖井图

The war in the East: Japanese soldiers sinking a well.

日本军队到达朝鲜村庄的首要任务之一，就是挖井，以保证军队，尤其是医院的伤病员能喝到干净水。然而，饮用水源对于朝鲜人而言似乎并无大碍。但是，日本军队往往很难挖掘出井水，这导致大量日本士兵患病。

One of the first duties to be performed on the arrival of Japanese troops in a Corean village is the sinking of wells so that the men, especially those in hospital, may have a supply of good water, a matter about which the Coreans themselves seem to trouble very little. In many cases this is very difficult to find, and has been the cause of a great deal of sickness in the Japanese army.

4—SUPPLEMENT TO THE GRAPHIC, OCTOBER 27,

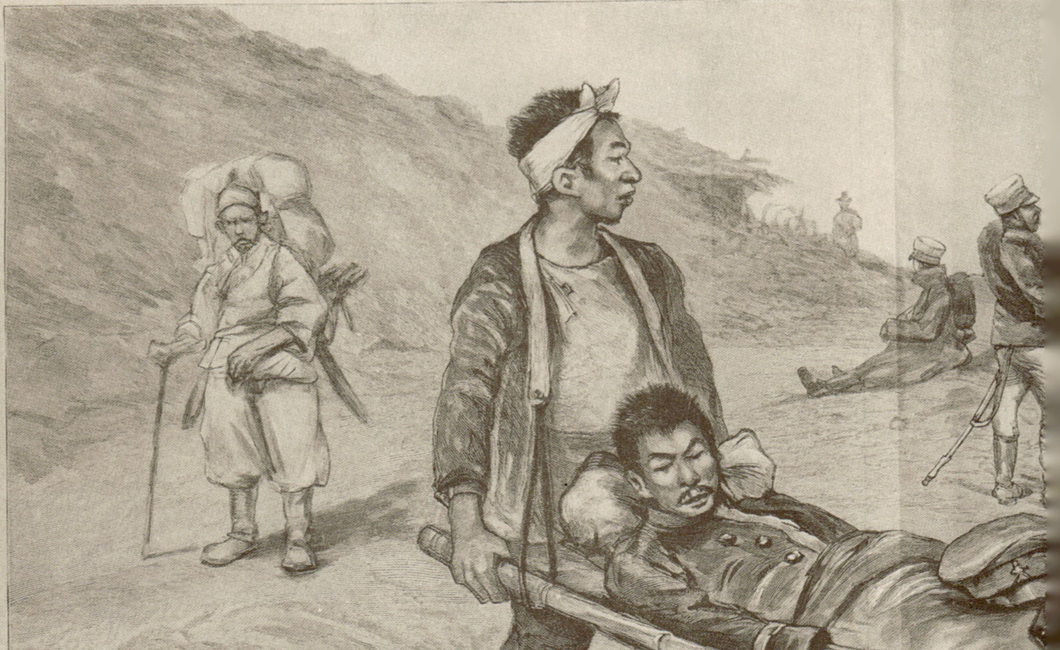

"The soldiers were very clever in constructing temporary litters for the conveyance of the wounded where the regular ambulance corps of the Japanese army had not yet arrived.

THE WAR IN THE EAST; BRINGING IN THE WOUNDED FROM THE FRON

DRAWN FROM LIFE BY OUR SPECIAL ARTIST WITH THE JAPAN

1894年10月27日《图片报》

东方的战争：一次交火战后，日军侦察兵负伤被撤离前线

The war in the East: Bringing in the wounded from the front after a skirmish during a reconnaissance.

在小规模战役中，从前线撤下的伤兵，被人用一副竹子制成的临时担架抬着走。这是在正规救护联队到达前，把伤员运到营地的一种很便捷的方式。

THE WAR IN THE EAST : THE AMBULANCE CORPS OF THE JAPANESE ARMY AT WORK

1894 年 10 月 13 日《图片报》

东方的战争：工作中的日本救护部队

The war in the East: The ambulance corps of the Japanese army at work.

CONVALESCENT SOLDIERS ON THEIR RETURN TO JAPAN, WAITING TO EMBARK AT FUSAN

DRAWN BY OUR SPECIAL ARTIST WITH THE JAPANESE FORCES

1894 年 10 月 27 日《图片报》

康复期的伤兵即将返回日本，在釜山港等待登船

Convalescent soldiers on their return to Japan, waiting to embark at Fusan.

本报特派随日军特约画师绘制

Drawn by our special artist with the Japanese forces.

HARPER'S WEEKLY

SCENES AFTER A BATTLE.

SOME of the grewsome features attendant upon modern warfare are illustrated this week by the sketches which come from HARPER'S WEEKLY'S special artist accompanying the Japanese forces in Manchooria. It is after the excitement of battle is over that these scenes are enacted. Long lines of dejected-looking prisoners, with their hands tied in front of them, are marched back from the front, accompanied by a guard of Japanese cavalry and infantry, to be turned over to the prison-guard farther in the rear, and to be eventually sent in ships to Japan. When first captured the Chinese soldiers have always displayed great fear and alarm over their coming fate at the hands of the invaders, for they themselves invariably murder and mutilate their prisoners. But after a few weeks of captivity with the Japanese they become reassured and encouraged by the kind and civilized treatment they receive, and many of them volunteer to return to the front to act as guides and scouts for their captors. Almost all assert that their treatment in captivity is more humane than that which they have received at the hands of their own officers.

The prisoners and the wounded being disposed of, squads of Japanese soldiers are detailed to collect the dead and to identify them. The bodies are brought from all parts of the battle-field and laid in a row, faces up, and then the adjutants of the several regiments that were engaged in the fight make out the correct list of the dead and missing. This work being completed, the funeral service is read, and the dead are then buried. In the early part of the war, before the Chinese offered enough resistance to cause many deaths, each soldier was buried in a separate grave, and, so far as possible, a stake with his name was placed at the head But lately there have been so many deaths, both of Japanese soldiers and of coolies, through disease, that the officers of the Mikado's army have found it necessary to bury many men in one pit, and in some cases to burn the dead, so as to prevent an epidemic. The bodies are placed in pine boxes and lowered into a pit, at the bottom of which have been placed several cords of wood. The coffins are then covered with bundles of straw, soaked with petroleum, and set on fire. This operation is performed at some lonely spot at a distance from the camp, but the columns of fire rise high over the flat country, and give a weird and ghostly aspect to the dark and deserted battle-field.

CREMATING THE BODIES OF SOLDIERS AND COOLIES WHO HAVE DIED OF DISEASE.

AFTER THE BATTLE—JAPANESE OFFICERS IDENTIFYING THE DEAD.

A WINTER'S NIGHT.

COME, close the curtains, and make fast the door,
Pile high the logs, and let the happy room
Red as the rose on wall and ceiling bloom,
And bring your golden flagons forth and pour
Full drinking of some ancient summer's store
Of spice and sweetness, while to ruddy gloom
The fire falls. And lest any sound of doom
Be heard, let music on her wide wings soar

Yet shall you never make the door so fast
That no moan echo on the song, no shape
Dull the wine's fragrance and the blaze obscure,
And breathe the dark chill of the outer blast,
Till you shall turn and shudder to escape
The awful phantom of the hungry poor!

HARRIET PRESCOTT SPOFFORD.

1895年1月19日《哈珀斯周刊》

1 （日军）火葬士兵及病亡的日军军夫苦力

2 战后——日本军官在辨认死者身份

1 Cremating the bodies of soldiers and coolies who have died of disease.

2 After the battle—Japanese officers identifying the dead.

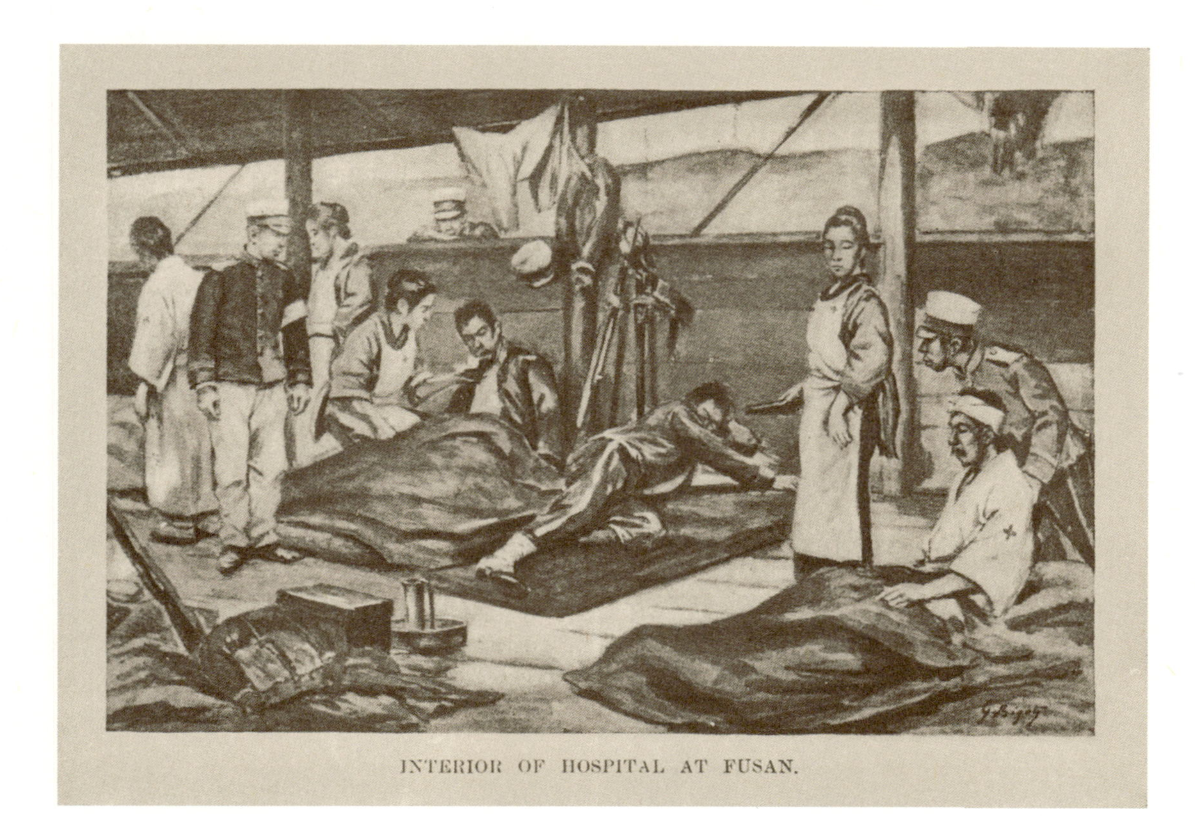
INTERIOR OF HOSPITAL AT FUSAN.

1894 年 11 月 10 日《哈珀斯周刊》

釜山，医院内部图

Interior of hospital at Fusan.

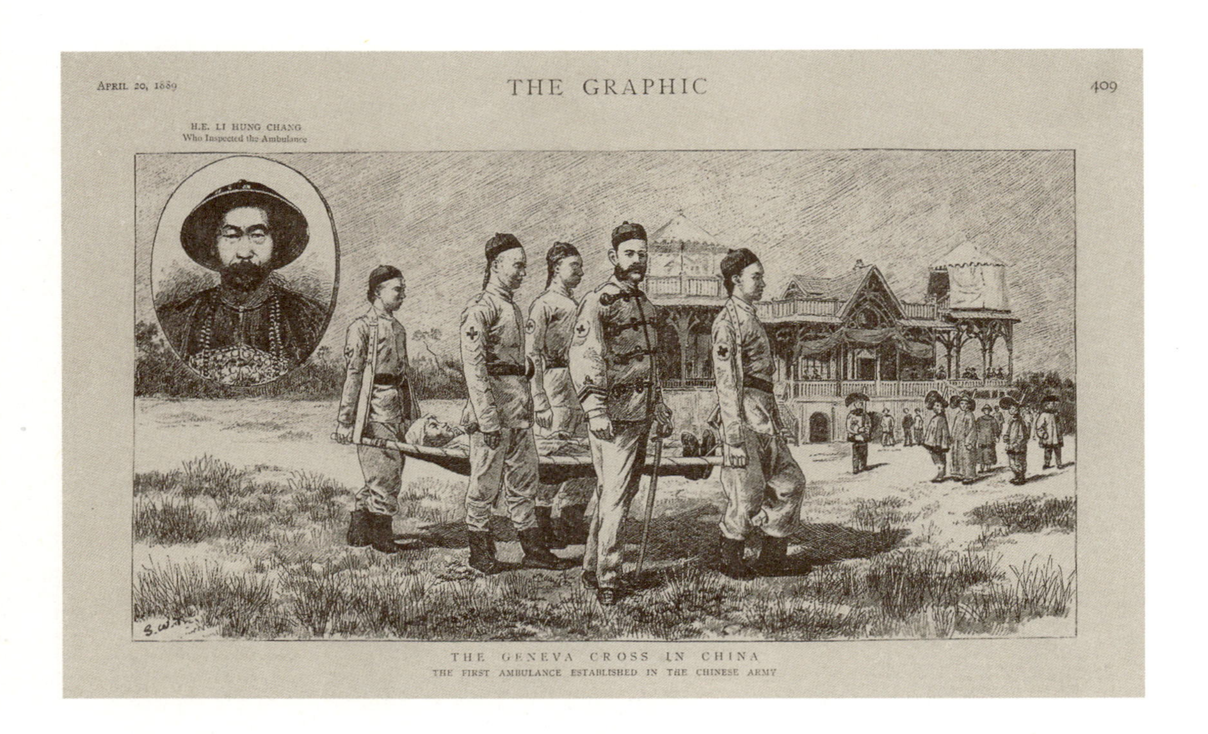

1889 年 4 月 20 日《图片报》

日内瓦的红十字在中国——中国军队中的第一支急救队建立

The Geneva Cross in China. The first ambulance established in the Chinese Army.

左上：李鸿章视察急救队

H.E. Li Hung Chang. Who inspected the ambulance.

甲午战争开战的 5 年前，红十字会已经在中国创建了第一支战地急救队，但显然，在这次战争中清军仍然没有随军的医疗编制，伤患者无法得到及时救助。战争开始后，在中国的西方传教团体迅速创办了多家红十字慈善医院，对伤兵和难民展开了无偿救助。这些医院分布在营口、烟台、天津等地，其中天津的红十字医院得到了李鸿章的支持，规模较大。

JAPANESE TROOPS MAKING THEIR CHINESE PRISONERS CARRY OFF THE DEAD AND WOUNDED
AFTER THE FIGHT AT PING YANG: A CORNER OF THE FIELD OF BATTLE
DRAWN FROM LIFE BY OUR SPECIAL ARTIST WITH THE JAPANESE FORCES

1894 年 12 月 1 日《图片报》

平壤之战后：战场一角

After the fight at Ping Yang: A corner of the field of battle.

日本军队让中国俘虏搬运死伤人员

Japanese troops making their Chinese prisoners carry off the dead and wounded.

1894年12月8日《图片报》

日军的战地公墓

A Japanese cemetery on the field of battle.

第六工兵营在开赴前线途中，稍作停留，特意为阵亡官兵致哀。军号已经吹响，图中的士兵正在举枪致敬。

The sixth battalion of engineers on their way to the front halt to render military honours to comrades killed in battle. The bugle has just sounded, and the men are shown presenting arms.

结　语

甲午战争中，中日两国军队在对待阵亡将士的做法上截然不同，清军死亡推计25000人，日军死亡13488人（其中病亡12000多人），军夫阵亡7000—8000人，凡有战斗过的地方都有日军临时墓地安葬阵亡的将士，从朝鲜到中国《马关条约》签订后，日本政府决定将安葬在海外日军遗骨火化后运回国内安葬，并规划出专门的军人墓地。在中国，只有皇帝认可的死难将士才能得到隆重安葬。丁汝昌自杀之后，棺材被漆成黑色，不能下葬，因为他是败军之将。

——编者

中国士兵仿佛没有思考过人生，他们不知道自己为什么而生，为什么而死。在中国百姓眼中，中国的军队贪婪劫掠、凶残懦弱，他们是敌手的笑柄，也是国民的灾难。他们缺乏训练、军饷微薄、武器落后，甚至饿着肚子奔赴杀场，他们没有基本的防护，也很少有训练有素的军官指挥。一旦受伤，他们往往被战友们遗弃在战场，他们冷漠麻木，除了对自己生命的怜悯。他们为捍卫什么而战呢？什么都没有？他们会丢掉什么？什么都没有？那么，他们为什么去拼命呢？中国的国防似乎被托付给一支这样的军队，日本正在消灭着他们。而日本士兵充满战斗的激情……随意挑选出他们中的任何一个，他们有好的待遇、好的训练，更有好的指挥官的带领。

——1895年2月13日　英国《帕尔摩报》

SURRENDER OF CHINESE GENERALS AND STAFF.

From a Sketch by an Eye-Witness.

十 《马关条约》：中国之辱

1895年3月21日，一条从海底传来的电文称："日本已拿下渔翁岛。"三天后，澎湖岛也被占领了。日本第四军团经过在广岛数月特训后，目前已经成功占据台湾一隅。在中日和平谈判中，有一项特别明确的条款是：割让台湾。

——1895年5月4日　美国《哈珀斯周刊》

这是一场充满展示效应的战争。短短几个月的时间，东方两个巨人彻底交换了位置。中国，一直以来被视为东方世界的霸主，却被发现是头披着狼皮的绵羊；而日本，仿佛从来没被我们仔细地注意过，却一跃成为我们这些列强中的一员，无论我们是否愿意看到它的加入。如果日本已经在我们西方世界的不知不觉中获得了令人敬佩的地位，清政府及其官员的腐败也正在我们的熟视无睹下葬送着中国。

——1894年12月28日　中国英文报纸《字林西报》

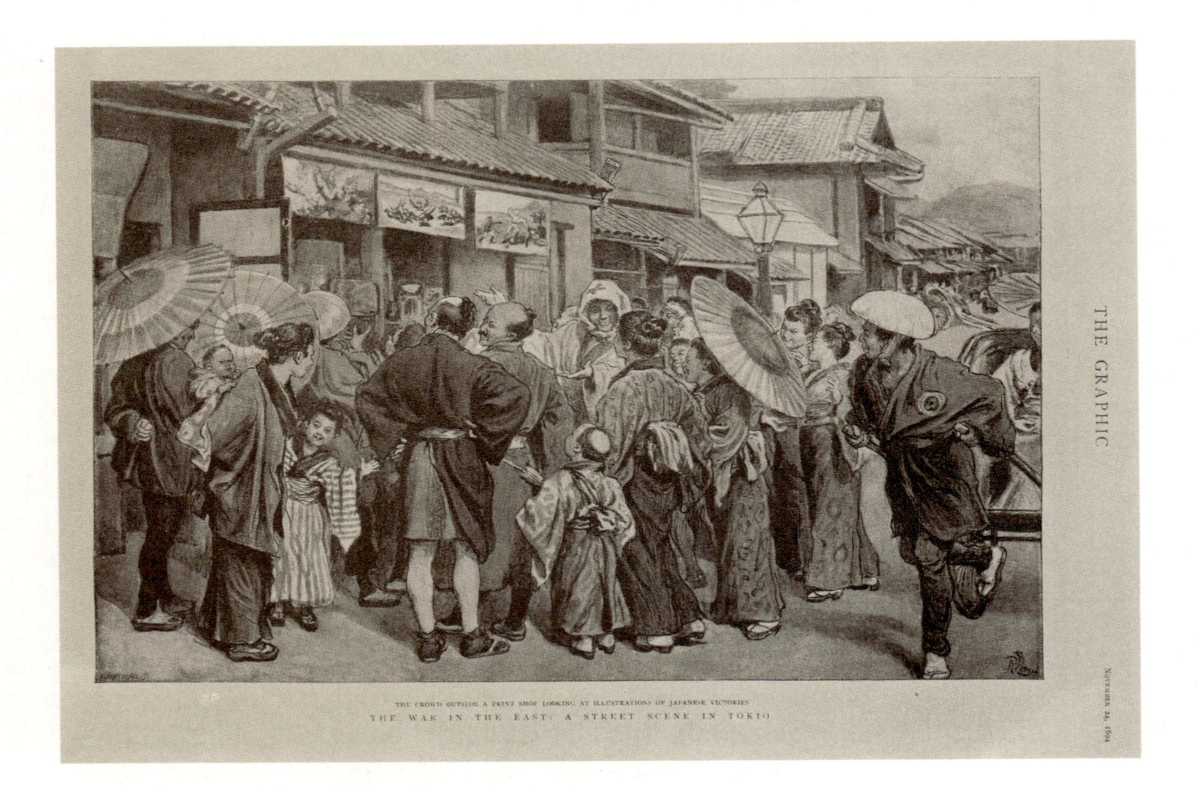

1894 年 11 月 24 日《图片报》

东方的战争：东京街景，在书店外观看日本胜利海报的人群

The war in the East: A street scene in Tokio.

The crowd outside a print shop looking at illustrations of Japanese victories.

甲午战争在日本民众各阶层中表现出不同态度，战争狂热首先在知识界蔓延，福泽谕吉著文称：日清战争是文明与野蛮的战争，不单纯是人与人、国与国之战，而是新旧两种文明的冲突，为了人类文明的进步，无须讨论任何纠缠不清的战争理由。

战争前夜，日本国内处于经济萧条的恐慌之中，民众最关心的仍旧是自己的生计；战争的胜利使国内矛盾得到缓和，国家和民众从战争中获得意想不到的利益，国民生活水平大幅提高，明治维新后国家出现了前所未有的繁荣。

1895 年 3 月 9 日《伦敦新闻画报》

张荫桓率领的中国赴日求和使团在“中国捷运”号英国皇家邮轮上。

Chang Yen Hoon, Chinese peace envoy, on board the “Empress of China”.

图上右起第三位洋人模样者可能是美国前国务卿、中国使团顾问福斯特。

福斯特（1836—1917），为本杰明·哈里森总统的国务卿。1894 年中日甲午战争结束后，他受清政府总理各国事务衙门邀请，一同与日本进行谈判。

The War in the East

CELESTIAL red tape delays the peace negotiations with Japan to the great detriment of the Chinese cause. Valuable time has been lost at Pekin over the preliminary *pourparlers*, preparing elaborate credentials, and so forth, while Li Hung Chang must stop again at

Chang Yen Hoon went to Japan as the Chinese Emperor's Ambassador Plenipotentiary to negotiate terms of peace between the two countries, The Japanese, however, refused to deal with him as it was found that he had not full powers. Chang Yen Hoou has been Minister to the United States, to Spain, and to Peru. His age is 59, his native place being Canton. He is Minister of Foreign Affairs at Pekin. His secretary and interpreter, Laing Shung, accompanied him to Japan

HIS EXCELLENCY CHANG YEN HOON

The first Envoy sent by China to Japan to negotiate terms of peace before the despatch of Li Hung Chang

Photographed on board the R.M.S. *Empress of China* by G. D. Bowles, R.N.R.

1895 年 3 月 9 日《伦敦新闻画报》

张荫桓阁下：在派出李鸿章之前，清朝派往日本谈判和平条款的首位全权公使

His Excellency Chang Yen Hoon.

The first Envoy sent by China to Japan to negotiate terms of peace before the dispatch of Li Hung Chang.

张荫桓作为中国皇帝的特命全权大使被派往日本与日方就和平条件谈判，因日方发现其权力有限，拒绝与其谈判。张荫桓 59 岁，广东省人，曾任驻美、西班牙、秘鲁大使。现任外交部长，他的秘书与翻译陪同前往。

Chang Yen Hoon went to Japan as the Chinese Emperor's Ambassador Plenipotentiary to negotiate terms of peace between the two countries, the Japanese, however, refused to deal with him as it was found that he had not full powers. Chang Yen Hoon has been Minister to the United States, to Spain, and to Peru. His age is 59, his native place being Canton. He is Minister of Foreign Affairs at Pekin. His secretary and interpreter, Laing Shung, accompanied him to Japan.

根据在“中国捷运”号英国皇家邮轮上赴日本乞和途中拍摄的照片制版

Photographed on board the R.M.S. Express of China.

1895 年 3 月 31 日《小巴黎人》

中日战争——总督李鸿章离开中国赴日求和

La guerre entre la Chine et le Japon.—Le Vice-Roi Li-Hung-Chang quittant Pékin.

日本浮世绘

1895 年 4 月 17 日，中日在日本下关签订《马关条约》，出席签订仪式的有：从火炭盆右侧起，依次为：李鸿章、罗丰禄和伍廷芳；火炭盆左侧的两位依次为：李经芳和马建忠；坐在李鸿章谈判桌对面的从右至左依次为：伊藤博文、陆奥宗光、内阁书记官伊东已代治、外相秘书田中敬依。

Hôtel où a été ratifié le traité de paix entre la Chine et le Japon.

1895 年 7 月 6 日《插图报》

烟台，《马关条约》签署之后，中日两国交换条约的旅馆

Hotel où a été ratifié le traité de paix entre la Chine et le Japon.

1895 年 5 月 8 日，中日两国在烟台芝罘交换两国皇帝的批准书，条约正式生效。

L'ILLUSTRATION

LAO YU

1898 年 10 月 8 日《插图报》

老于（刘永福的别名——编者注）

Lao Yu.

在中国当前动荡不安的背景下，应该预料到刘永福这个人物随时都会再次成为焦点。他在远东地区声名远扬，被称为老于。

1897 年 5 月 25 日，刘永福带领 3500 名随从抵达广州，在城外靠近北城门的地方安营扎寨。后来他从中越边境又吸收了一支 2000 人的小部队，从边境到广州他们一路抢掠，而且只要刘永福的军队一出现，各城的驻军就像人间蒸发一般。

这位黑旗军首领的使命是什么呢？

根据一些人的观点，由于对清政府的软弱心生不满，两广真正的大佬黄振山（音译）与中部省份的几个官员结成联盟，决心阻止政府向西方列强割让领土。因此，黄与两广总督谭钟麟达成一致，向刘永福以及他所率领的黑旗军求助。

据另一些人的看法——毋庸赘言，这是英国人的说法——正是法国把刘永福这个曾经的敌人武装起来，其目的是阻止英国势力对广州的渗透。

最后，据说刘永福傲慢地向两广总督暗示，自己之所以率部驻守广州，是直接服从于天朝的调遣。

不管怎样，这位在广州附近扎营的黑旗军首领正在等待大事的降临。是什么样的大事呢？他打算扮演怎样的角色呢？这一点很难知晓，但可以肯定的是，在当前的情况下，没人比他更有能力在中国策动一场全国性的叛乱，并取得胜利。

60 岁左右的刘永福个子高大，身材并不彪悍，但长得十分健壮。眼小，颧高，耳长。面色倒不是真的发黄，而是呈灰白色，就像蒙古人的肤色一样。他的胡子差不多只有 12 根毛，又黑又硬，分布在嘴角的周围。

——《黑旗军头领——刘永福》（选译），1898 年 10 月 8 日《插图报》

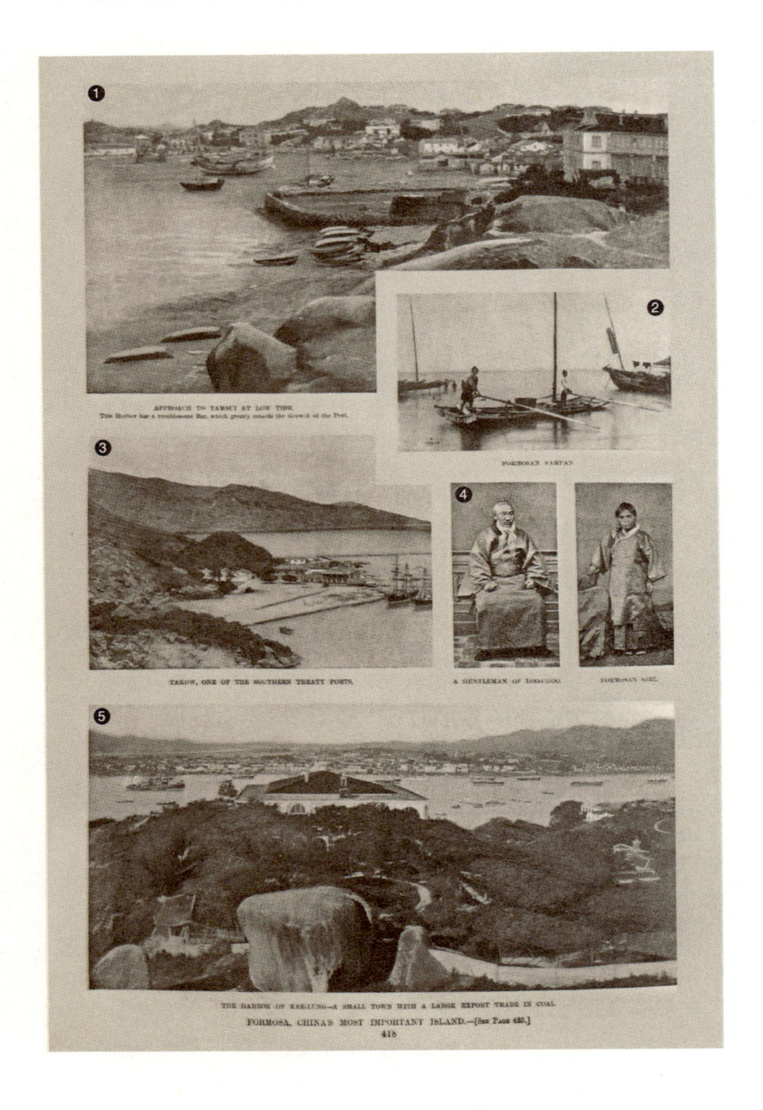

1895 年 5 月 4 日《哈珀斯周刊》

台湾，中国最重要的岛屿

1 淡水退潮

这个港口受一个泥沙坝的阻碍，发展受到了制约

2 台湾的舢舨

3 打狗（高雄），南部的条约港口

4 琉球的一位老人和一个台湾女孩

5 基隆港—— 一个重要的煤矿出口小镇

Formosa, China’s most important island.

1 Approach to Tamsui at low tide.

This harbor has a troublesome bar, which greatly retards the growth of the port.

2 Formosan Sampan.

3 Takow, one of the southern treaty ports.

4 A gentleman of Loo-Choo. Formosan girl.

5 The harbor of Kee-Lung—a small town with a large export trade in coal.

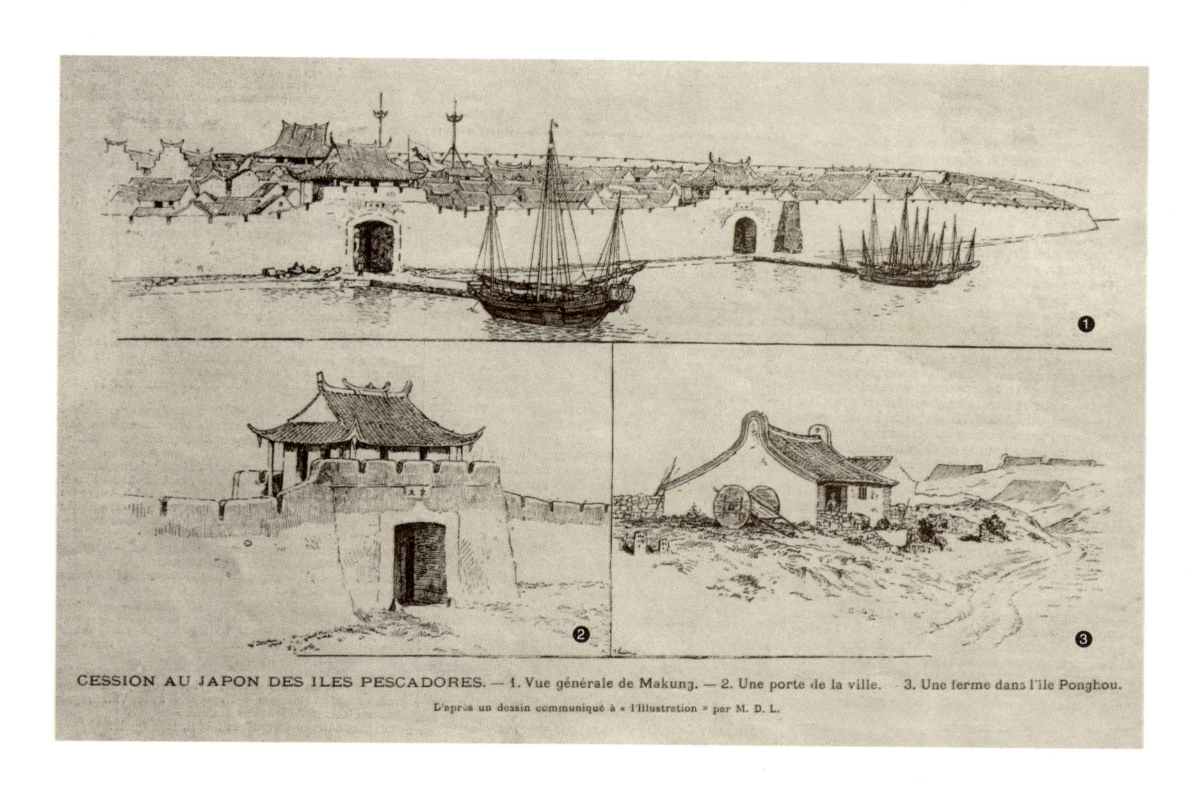
CESSION AU JAPON DES ILES PESCADORES. — 1. Vue générale de Makung. — 2. Une porte de la ville. 3. Une ferme dans l'île Ponghou.

D'après un dessin communiqué à « l'Illustration » par M. D. L.

1895 年 5 月 11 日《插图报》

澎湖列岛被割让给日本

1 马公城鸟瞰图

2 马公城的一个城门

3 一个普通农舍

Cession au Japon des Iles Pescadores.

1 Vue générale de Makung.

2 Une porte de la ville.

3 Une ferme dans l'île Ponghou.

结　语

从大不列颠动用武力推倒中国闭关锁国者的壁垒，直至大约12个月以前，我们英国在远东几乎一直把持着无人挑战的支配权，长达50年之久。我们在新加坡和香港所占有的战略位置，我们在当地那支被细心呵护的威严海军，我们压倒一切竞争对手的海运优势，我们巨大的区域商业利益——每年500万英镑的进口额和1200万英镑的出口额，所有这些只是我们在远东所享有的一部分特权而已；如果再加上我们在中、日所控制的富可敌国的条约港和正在成为远东通用语言的英文，英国在这一区域至高无上的话语权是毋庸置疑的，而且这一影响力不仅被远东的（中、日）两大强国公开接受，也被其他（欧美）列强所默认。

然而在过去的12个月中，局势完全改变了！无法阻止的中日战争把英国东亚政策的基础假设条件彻底颠覆了，我们再也不能把中国当作一个可以被唤醒且极具潜能的合作对象，相反日本已经向世界证明它已跻身于世界强国之列。

虽然在战争开始后，英国政府的调停政策让日本感到我们意欲剥夺他们的胜利果实，在一定程度上伤害了日本人对我们的情感，并迫使日本向其他列强靠拢，但战后英国政府明智地拒绝了俄、法、德的三国联盟，没有参与它们对日本——依照中日《马关条约》的规定——占领中国辽东半岛的干涉。由此，一条通往彼此谅解与赏识的道路被打通了，英日双方必将结成联结大英帝国与东方的利益共同体。

——1895年9月24日　英国《泰晤士报》

十一　故国有所思

由于我们的通讯记者并没有看到近期几个独立历史事件之间的联系，所以他们的电报显得有些耸人听闻了。虽然目前的态势没有他们所说的那么严重，但中国在这最后四五周的发展状况，却无疑将为欧洲各国明年的国际政策指明方向。

这种局面的产生有三个缘由：其一，中国和日本的战争，在这场战争中中国之孱弱暴露无遗；其二，俄罗斯大刀阔斧地修建跨西伯利亚铁路，以此连通其在亚洲的小麦和煤矿产地，进而控制北太平洋地区；其三，英国和德国在非洲的矛盾激化，英国企图控制非洲大陆的所有内部地区，丝毫没有顾及德国也要成为殖民大国的野心。

——《关于中国的纷争》，1898 年 1 月 8 日　美国《哈珀斯周刊》

1895 年 1 月 19 日《图片报》

中国皇帝在北海坐冰车，冰车为奥地利皇帝所赠

The Emperor of China sledging on the lake in the Palace Gardens, Pekin.

北京紫禁城皇家花园里的太液池，夏天荷花盛开，冬天冰封三尺。冬天，宫里的人会到结冰的湖面上滑冰橇；第一位享受这项娱乐的往往是皇帝陛下，他刚刚收到奥地利赠送的一辆新冰车。

The lake Fai-yi-chi in the Palace Gardens of the Forbidden City, Pekin, is, in the summer, covered with lotus, but in the winter, when frozen over, it is used by the inmates of the Palace for sledging, and among the first to avail himself of this opportunity for a little amusement is his Imperial Majesty, who has just had a new sledge sent out to him from Austria.

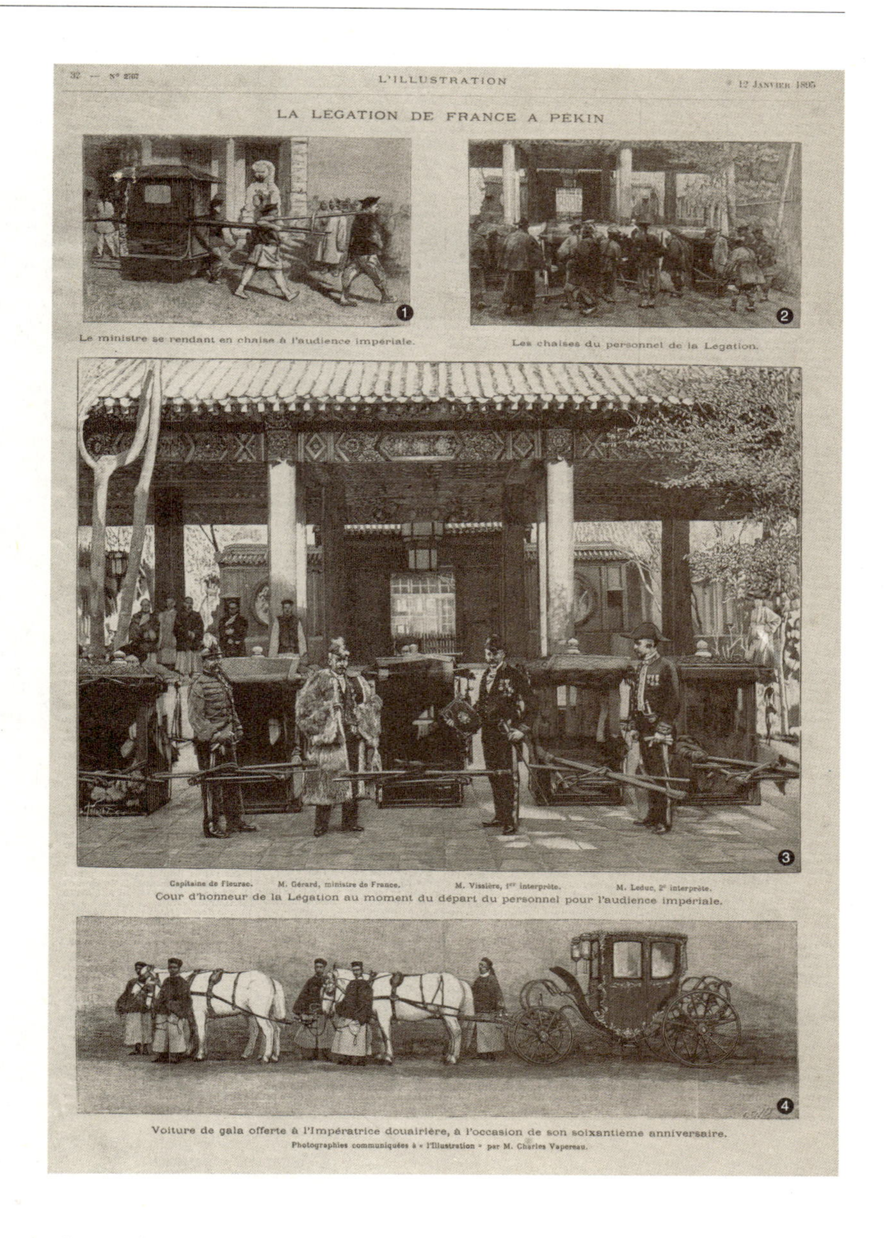
32 — N° 2707　　L'ILLUSTRATION　　12 JANVIER 1895

LA LEGATION DE FRANCE A PÉKIN

1 Le ministre se rendant en chaise à l'audience impériale.

2 Les chaises du personnel de la Légation.

3 Capitaine de Fleurac.　M. Gérard, ministre de France.　M. Vissière, 1er interprète.　M. Leduc, 2e interprète.

Cour d'honneur de la Légation au moment du départ du personnel pour l'audience impériale.

4 Voiture de gala offerte à l'Impératrice douairière, à l'occasion de son soixantième anniversaire.

Photographies communiquées à « l'Illustration » par M. Charles Vapereau.

1895 年 1 月 12 日《插图报》

1　（法国）公使乘轿觐见（光绪）皇帝

2　公使馆其他人员的轿子

3　法国公使和随员在领事馆院内整装待发准备进宫觐见皇帝时的合影

4　法国赠送给慈禧太后 60 岁寿辰的礼物—— 一架马车

1　Le ministre se rendant en chaise à l'audience impériale.

2　Les chaises du personel de la Légation.

3　Cour d'honneur de la Légation au moment du départ du personel pour l'audience impériale.

4　Voiture de gala oferte à l'Impératrice douairière, à l'occasion de son soixantième anniverssaire.

DRAWN BY W. SMALL

In connection with the celebration of the birthday of the Dowager Empress, an Imperial Audience was held, at which all the Foreign Ministers and Legations were present. This was an important event, being another step towards breakin
This is the first time that Foreign Ministers have been accorded this privilege, and permitted to desecrate the particularly Imperial soil wi

AN IMPERIAL AUDIENCE AT PEKIN WITHIN THE PRECIN

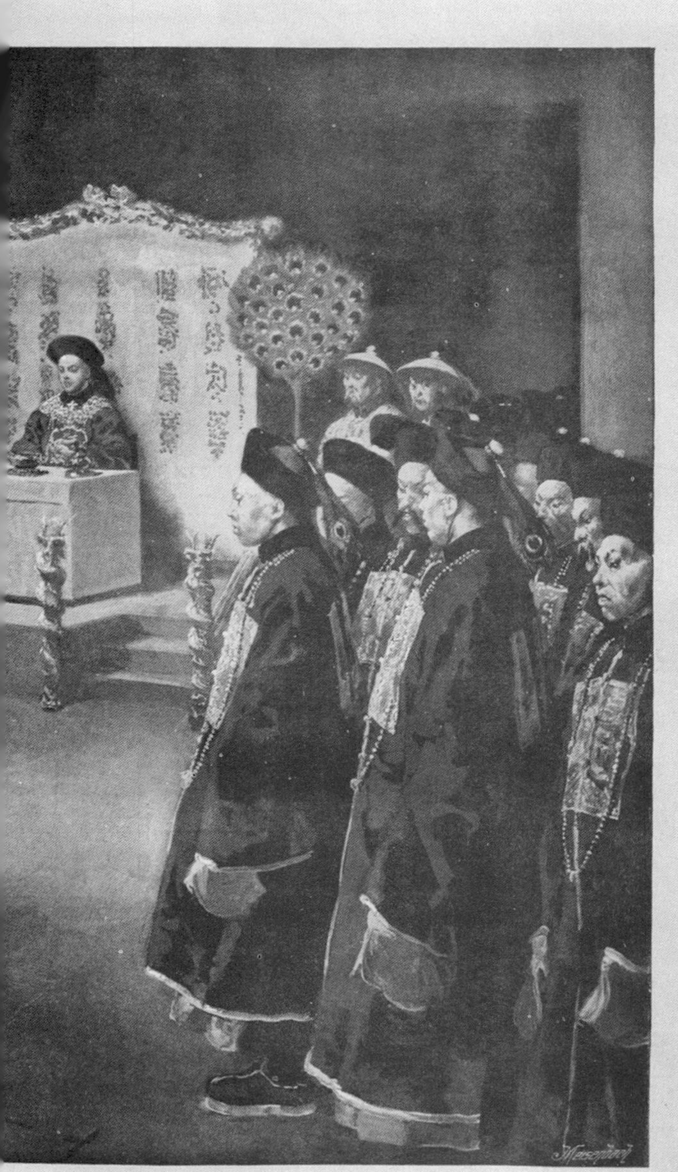

1895 年 2 月 16 日《图片报》

为庆祝慈禧太后生日，皇帝首次在紫禁城内接见外国使臣

An Imperial audience at Pekin within the precincts of the "Forbidden Town".

借为慈禧太后庆贺寿辰之机，皇帝接见了所有国家驻华公使和使团。这是一个关键时刻，这是打破皇帝周边禁区的另一次进步，因为接见仪式是在"禁城"内举行的。这是外国驻华公使们有史以来第一次获此殊荣，被允许用他们野蛮人的皮靴玷污黄瓦高墙内的神圣土地。

In connection with the celebration of the birthday of the Dowager Empress, an Imperial audience was held, at which all the Foreign Ministers and Legations were present. This was an important event, being another step towards breaking down the barriers of the seclusion surrounding the Emperor, for the reason that the audience was held within the precincts of the "Forbidden Town". This is the first time that Foreign Ministers have been accorded this privilege, and permitted to desecrate the particularly Imperial soil within the yellow-tiled wall with their barbarian boots.

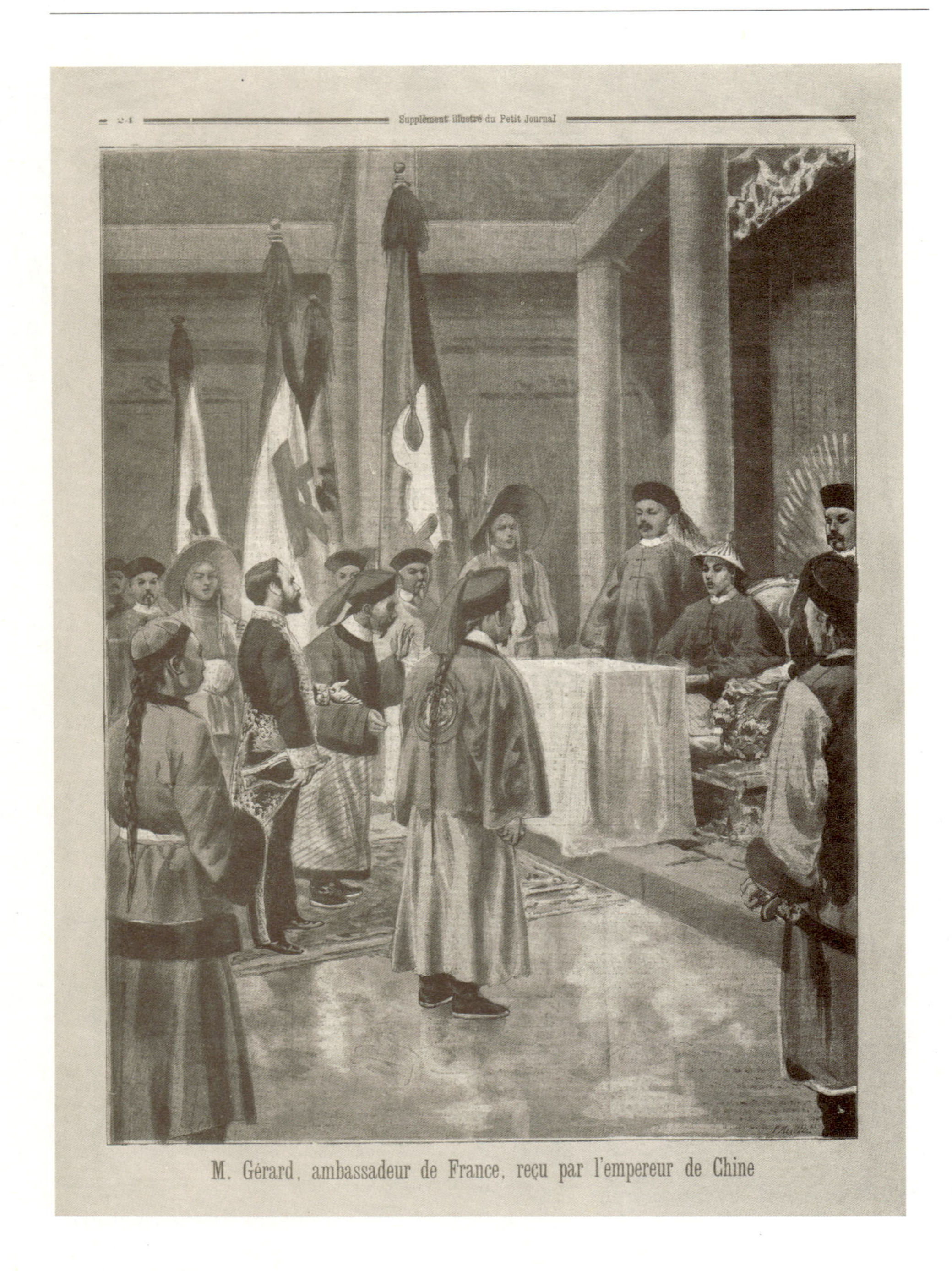

1895年1月20日《小巴黎人》

中国皇帝（光绪）接见法国大使杰拉德

M. Gérard, ambassadeur de France, reçu par l’empereur de Chine.

Ce numéro est accompagné d'un supplément musical.

L'ILLUSTRATION

Prix du numéro : 75 cent. SAMEDI 27 JUILLET 1895 53e Année. — No 2735

LA GARDE DES LÉGATIONS EN CHINE PAR LES MARINS EUROPÉENS

Dans la rue des Légations, à Pékin : les marins français allant rendre visite à leurs camarades du poste de Peï-Lang.

Les marins français à Pékin : la leçon de tir à l'arc.

D'après les photographies de M. le Dr J. Matignon.

1895 年 7 月 27 日《插图报》

1 在北京外国使馆区的街上，法国海军去拜会他们在北堂哨所的同事

2 在北京的法国水兵向清军学射箭

1 Dans la rue des Légations, à Pékin: les marins français allant rendre visite à leurs camarades du poste de Peï-Lang.

2 Les marins français à Pékin: la leçon de tir a l'arc.

LA GARDE DES LÉGATIONS EN CHINE

On se souvient des inquiétudes qui se firent jour à Pékin même, parmi la colonie européenne, au cours de la guerre malheureuse engagée contre le Japon. On avait tout à redouter, en effet, d'une foule alarmée et surexcitée par les revers.

Il n'en fut rien heureusement, mais cette situation n'en autorisait pas moins les gouvernements européens à prendre toutes les précautions de nature à sauvegarder les intérêts et la vie de leurs nationaux. Déjà le gouvernement chinois avait pris les devants et placé une garde devant chaque légation; nous avons ici même indiqué (dans notre numéro du 2 mars), en montrant les éléments dont elle était formée, combien pouvait être précaire, à un moment donné, une pareille protection. C'est donc sans étonnement que l'on vit, vers la fin de février, des détachements de marins français, russes, espagnols, anglais et italiens monter à Pékin et s'installer devant leurs Légations respectives.

Quand nos matelots du *Bayard* arrivèrent sous les murs de la ville, il faisait un froid très vif et un vent glacial soufflait de Mongolie; nos hommes, sous la conduite des aspirants de Grancey et Quesnel, n'en avaient pas moins fait vaillamment, tantôt à pied, tantôt en charrette, le voyage de Tien-Tsin à Pékin.

Le détachement, fort de cinquante hommes, avait été partagé en deux compagnies : l'une resta à la Légation et l'autre fut dirigée sur le Peï-Lang, la plus importante des quatre missions catholiques de Pékin et la résidence de l'évêque.

Le service n'eut rien, du reste, d'extraordinairement dur, et nos mathurins eurent plus d'une bonne aubaine. Les membres de la Légation, en effet, et les quelques Français habitant la ville, pensaient souvent à eux et leur envoyaient volontiers des suppléments de nourriture, de tabac, de vins et de liqueurs. De temps à autre, les marins restés à la Légation partaient à ânes pour aller rendre visite à leurs camarades de Peï-Lang, aussi bien partagés qu'eux-mêmes, car les missionnaires étaient aux petits soins pour eux.

Des fêtes aussi étaient organisées pour distraire les hommes et leur laisser un bon souvenir de leur séjour dans la capitale du Céleste Empire; puis des jeux de toutes sortes : jeux de quilles, jeux de boules, tirs au pistolet et à la carabine, avec des prix. On n'avait même pas oublié le tir à l'arc, cher aux Chinois, et l'une de nos photographies montre un soldat tartare donnant une leçon pratique à nos marins.

Les détachements de marins qui vinrent s'installer à Pékin se composaient de 50 Français, 50 Russes, 50 Anglais, 20 Espagnols et 10 Italiens. Les Américains et les Allemands ne débarquèrent pas et restèrent à Tien-Tsin, prêts à toute éventualité. Le détachement du *Bayard* était commandé par MM. de Grancey et Quesnel, secondés par M. le Dr Matignon, aide-major de l'armée, médecin de la Légation et des détachements français, espagnol et italien.

La garde de la Légation de France.

LA GARDE DES LÉGATIONS EN CHINE. — Arrivée des marins du « Bayard » sous les murs de Pékin.

D'après des photographies de M. le Dr J. Matignon.

3　法国公使馆的护卫

4　从巴雅号（法国远东舰队的铁甲巡洋舰）来到北京（增援）的法国海军士兵

3　La garde de la Légation de France.

4　La garde des Légations en Chine.—Arrivée des marins du “Bayard” sous les murs de Pékin.

住在北京的西方外交使团、传教士和其他侨民一直担忧中日之间的战争可能会殃及到他们的人身安全，于是列强派出海军士兵在天津登陆，进驻各国在北京的公使馆：法国 50 人，俄国 50 人，英国 50 人，西班牙 20 人，意大利 10 人，美国和德国的水兵留守天津，以防不测。法国的 50 名海军官兵是从巴雅号（曾是中法战争时法国舰队旗舰）上调遣来京的，他们到达北京后兵分两路，一部分驻扎在公使馆，一部分保卫北堂（即西什库教堂）。这组报道中的图 1 是驻守公使馆的水兵学着骑驴去西什库教堂看望那里的战友；图 2 是公使馆为水兵们组织了多项有奖娱乐活动，实弹打靶、向清军学习射箭都成了娱乐项目。

1896 年 7 月 19 日《小巴黎人》

在爱丽舍宫，李鸿章受到法兰西共和国总统接见

Li-Hung Chang reçu par le Président de la République à l'Élysée.

据《小巴黎人》报道，李鸿章已经在欧洲停留了两个多月，他并不着急，在中国一败涂地地输给了日本之后，看上去他是希望为他的国家找到雪耻的办法。一路上，他思索、比较、评判，从出席新沙皇亚历山大二世的加冕礼始，他接连访问了俄国、德国、比利时。现在，他已经到法国数日了。所到之处，他仔细学习西方国家的军队组织，研究最先进的武器。他在爱丽舍宫晋见了法国总统富尔，并作为嘉宾观看了法国 7 月 14 日国庆节的阅兵式。

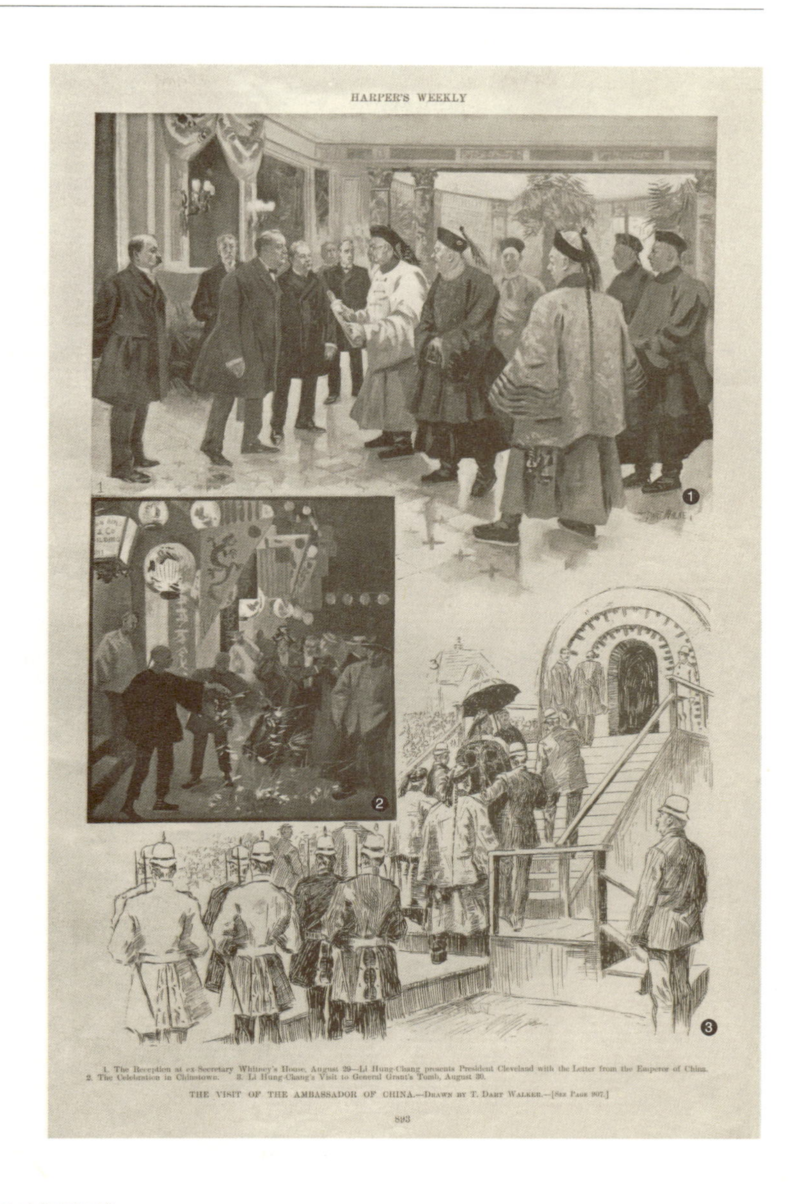

1896 年 8 月 29 日《哈珀斯周刊》

李鸿章访美

1　8 月 29 日，在前国务卿惠特尼的宅邸，李鸿章向克利夫兰总统递交中国皇帝的国书

2　唐人街的庆祝

3　8 月 30 日，李鸿章瞻仰格兰特将军墓

The visit of the Ambassador of China.

1　The Reception at ex-Secretary Whitney's House, August 29—Li Hung-Chang presents President Cleveland with the Letter from the Emperor of China.

2　The Celebration in Chinatown.

3　Li Hung-Chang's visit to General Grant's Tomb, August 30.

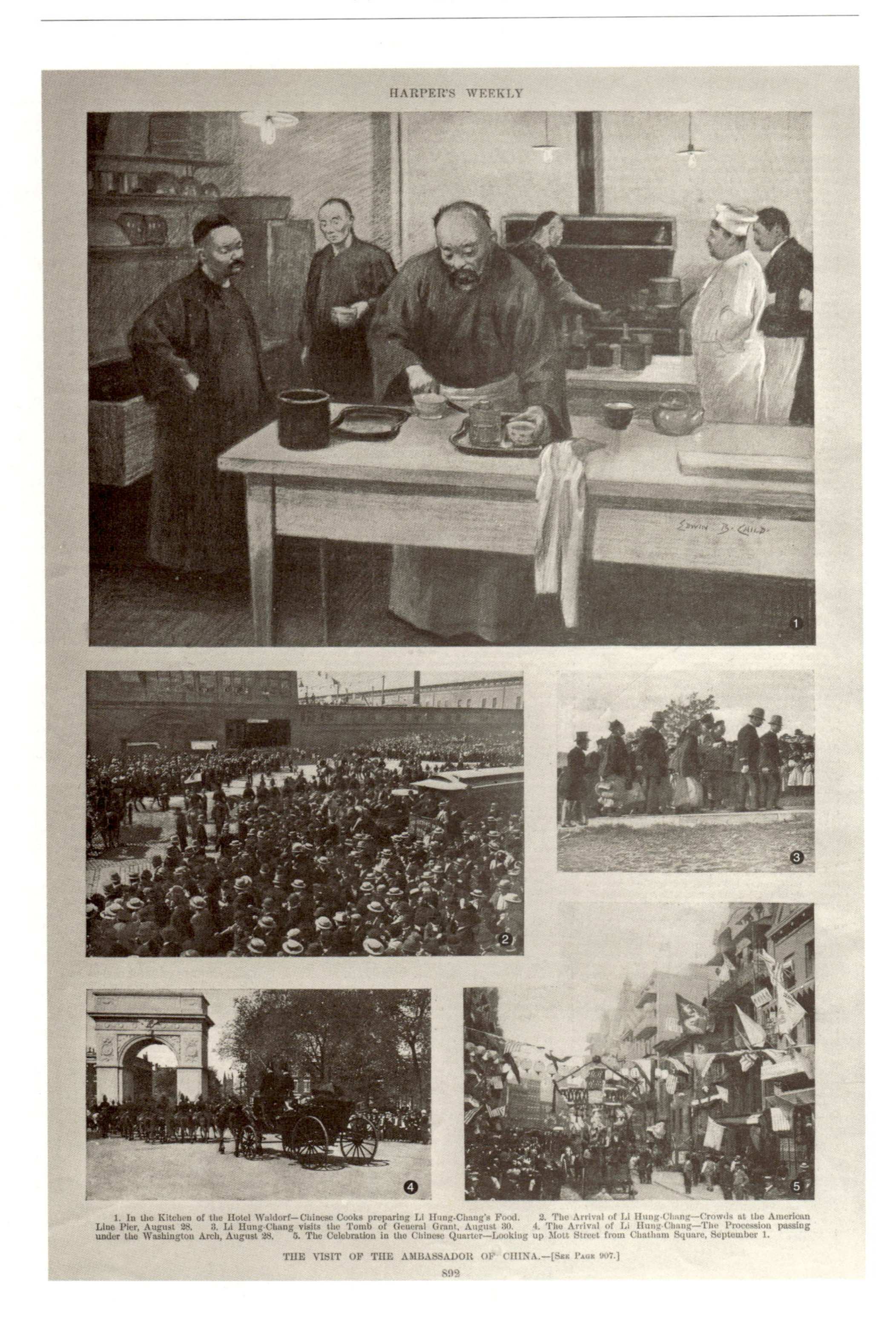

HARPER'S WEEKLY

1. In the Kitchen of the Hotel Waldorf—Chinese Cooks preparing Li Hung-Chang's Food. 2. The Arrival of Li Hung-Chang—Crowds at the American Line Pier, August 28. 3. Li Hung-Chang visits the Tomb of General Grant, August 30. 4. The Arrival of Li Hung-Chang—The Procession passing under the Washington Arch, August 28. 5. The Celebration in the Chinese Quarter—Looking up Mott Street from Chatham Square, September 1.

THE VISIT OF THE AMBASSADOR OF CHINA.—[See Page 907.]

892

1896年9月12日《哈珀斯周刊》

李鸿章访美

1　李鸿章访美时下榻纽约第五大道上的华尔道夫酒店，他自带的厨师正在酒店的厨房为他的中国胃烹制中式饭菜

2　8月28日，纽约码头欢迎李鸿章的人群

3　8月30日，李鸿章瞻仰格兰特将军墓

4　8月28日，李鸿章的马车仪仗队经过华盛顿凯旋门

5　9月1日，为迎接李鸿章的访美，纽约唐人街上张灯结彩

The visit of the Ambassador of China.

1　In the Kitchen of the Hotel Waldorf—Chinese cooks preparing Li Hung-Chang's food.

2　The arrival of Li Hung-Chang—crowds at the American Line Pier, August 28.

3　Li Hung-Chang visits the Tomb of General Grant, August 30.

4　The arrival of Li Hung-Chang—the Procession passing under the Washington Arch, August 28.

5　The Celebration in the Chinese Quarter—looking up Mott Street from Chatham Square, September 1.

自从法国的拉法耶特侯爵1824年访问美国之后，这个国家就再没有迎接过像李鸿章这样尊贵的客人了，即便是把威尔士亲王的那次访美算在内，这样说也毫不过分，毕竟威尔士亲王仅仅是因为出身而得显贵，而且他访美的时候还非常年轻，不过是一个友好的使者。相比之下，李鸿章大人则因为自身所取得的非凡成就而尊贵。他已年过古稀，此次作为一名特殊的使者访美，他带着世界上最年长的国家对最年轻的国家的问候。李鸿章还是我们这个国家第一次用“元老前辈”来称呼的一位贵客。出于中国人对于亡者的尊重，李鸿章对于已故的（美国前总统）格兰特将军极为崇敬，这使得他的这次访问多了一分感伤力，也毋庸置疑使得美国人心中产生了一丝慰藉。这也多少解释了为什么美国人民用热烈的欢呼、万人空巷的奇迹和热情洋溢的问候来迎接这位享有大清一品“伯爵”、太子太傅、直隶总督等各种称号的长者。

李鸿章在纽约的最后一天去了布鲁克林，然后还接受了美国记者的正式采访，之后和斯特朗市长进行了官方的会谈。在布鲁克林，他对联合俱乐部很感兴趣，特别是俱乐部门前刚刚竖立的格兰特将军像。在采访中，他适机表达了对排华法案中不公之处的看法，他说从经济角度考虑，这个法案实在是不明之举，从政治角度考虑，这似乎又与这个口口声声宣称自由的国家不相符。他的言辞虽温和，但也确确实实是指责。第二天一早，他就动身去了费城，结束了纽约之旅。

在纽约的这些时日里，成千上万的人都目睹了李鸿章的尊容，一开始人们还对

他身穿黄马褂和帽子上的孔雀羽毛感到好笑和好奇。之后的几天里，人们越来越发现这位长者的伟大之处，自然也愈发尊敬他。人们都普遍相信李鸿章的美国之旅在某种程度上对于中国具有划时代意义，是中国古老文化的一个转折点。人们也确信，如果李鸿章再年轻25岁，中国必定会获得重生。但从这样的观点中，我们也不难看出此次访问的悲剧因素，毫无疑问，此次访问也见证了中国文明的终结。为了保全国家，中国必须牺牲它古老的（政治）体系。李鸿章看清了这个问题，因为在谈及中国的未来时，他难道没有说“我们必须保护国家主权，不允许任何人危及我们的神圣权力”吗？

这一次，李鸿章又扮演了和俾斯麦一样的角色，因为祖国的统一始终都是俾斯麦心之所系。同样，中国的主权和传承也是李鸿章的心之所系。

——《李鸿章访美》（选译），1896年9月12日《哈珀斯周刊》

李鸿章的心情不会太好，尤其是在最近中国和日本的战争中，他的皇帝在奖励了他一件象征着信任与荣誉的黄马褂之后，又把它剥夺了。这次李鸿章是穿着黄马褂来访的，可是我们无从猜测他回国后是否还能继续穿这件衣裳。德国人一手为李鸿章组织了盛大的节目，一手紧攥着订货单，随时准备着把德国的军火、弹药和教官兜售给他。李鸿章对接待很是满意，却在下单的时候冷冰冰……在我国，他通过翻译与总统以及朝野的不少政治家进行了交流，每个与他交谈过的人都对他赞佩不已，却没有从中找到任何重要的话题。这位衣服上系着水晶扣子的大人却不愿解开扣子敞开心扉……法国对所有的贵宾都会用心款待，但愿李鸿章回到中国后还能记得起我们的盛情，这事儿值得期盼，但不必去指望。

——《李鸿章》（选译），1896年7月26日《小日报》

Le Petit Journal

Le Petit Journal
CHAQUE JOUR 5 CENTIMES
Le Supplément illustré
CHAQUE SEMAINE 5 CENTIMES

SUPPLÉMENT ILLUSTRÉ
Huit pages : CINQ centimes

ABONNEMENTS

	SIX MOIS	UN AN
SEINE ET SEINE-ET-OISE	2 fr.	3 fr. 50
DÉPARTEMENTS	2 fr.	4 fr.
ÉTRANGER	2 50	5 fr.

Septième année　DIMANCHE 26 JUILLET 1896　Numéro 297

LES HOTES DE LA FRANCE
Le vice-roi Li-Hung-Chang, ambassadeur extraordinaire de Chine

1896 年 7 月 26 日《小日报》

法兰西的贵宾李鸿章总督，中国的特别使者

Les hotes de la France. Le vice-roi Li-Hung-Chang, ambassadeur extraordinaire de Chine.

THE INTERNATIONAL INSTITUTE OF CHINA.

UNUSUAL attention has lately been directed to affairs in the Far East. The greatest diplomats of Europe, Asia, and America have suddenly been brought face to face with a strange medley of unexpected complications, concentrated in the ancient empire of China. The people of that country, hitherto intensely conservative, have been compelled by the force of circumstances to move with the great movements of the world and the time. Conditions have changed, and with the change have arisen new opportunities along lines of progress, enlightenment, and reform. Whoever would seek to use time, money, and energy with the least possible waste must note the new conditions and meet the new opportunities. What may have been best a few years ago may not be best to-day.

REV. GILBERT REID, Peking.

Recognizing the significance of the present time in the affairs of the Far East, a company of men, resident in China, have combined in the effort to establish in the city of Peking the International Institute of China. Already men connected with the nationalities of Great Britain, France, Germany, Holland, and the United States are on the committees to further the interests of the proposed institute. Men of other nationalities have shown their endorsement of the work by contributing to it. Men who are sincere in their wish to promote the welfare of the Chinese people and to strengthen the Chinese government have come forward to show their good-will toward this new enterprise.

This International Institute, to be started in the capital of China, is a combination of various features distinct in other lands. First, there will be a library and reading-room, to bring together books and periodicals in the Chinese language, to which will be added such from other countries as will be deemed advisable in the future. This will be the first library of the kind to be erected in China, and it is purposed to make it a model for public-spirited Chinese to follow in other sections of the country. Second, there will be a museum, or permanent exposition building, to display the arts and inventions of different nations and to impress the Chinese with the best features of our Christian civilization. Third, there will also be reception-rooms, to bring together the leading men of China and those from other countries who may desire to meet them in a social and friendly way. Fourth, there will be an auditorium for public lectures on all questions of importance, and to be used as a meeting-ground for both foreigners and Chinese who congregate in the large city of Peking. Fifth, there will be class-rooms for giving information and instruction to the grown-up men in official life, or who have literary degrees—a plan modelled somewhat after the University Extension course in this country.

The peculiarity of this work is the definite purpose to reach those who possess the largest influence in China, and through them to affect for good the whole population of that country. As one largely responsible for carrying out this proposed plan, I may say that I deem the undertaking to be feasible because of what has already been accomplished without the aid of any such institutional work. Personally, during the few years that I have lived in China I have found it possible, in a social way, without any introduction from other foreigners and without any political pressure brought to bear upon them, to make the acquaintance of as many as four hundred of the Chinese mandarins. This, of course, has been secured only through concentration of effort, and by a willingness to conform to many of the Chinese usages and to recognize the good points which many of them possess. Within this circle of friends are included all but one of the Emperor's cabinet, every one of the eleven members of the Imperial Board of Foreign Affairs, many censors of rank, men of highest literary distinction, and upwards of one hundred officials now holding office in the different provinces. An associate in the work is the Rev. Dr. Martin, author of *A Cycle of Cathay*, who has also had large acquaintance with distinguished men in the government, owing to his position, held for over thirty years, as president of the Imperial College and adviser to the Foreign Office. If such a number of influential men, many of whom are intensely conservative, can thus be reached with no attractions, how reasonable is it for us to expect that, with such attractions as this institute will afford, still greater influence can be exerted on these same men, and also an influence over others not yet reached, so that together they will be inclined to adopt measures, approve plans, and assist all efforts for the uplifting of their own people, and for the strengthening of their own government.

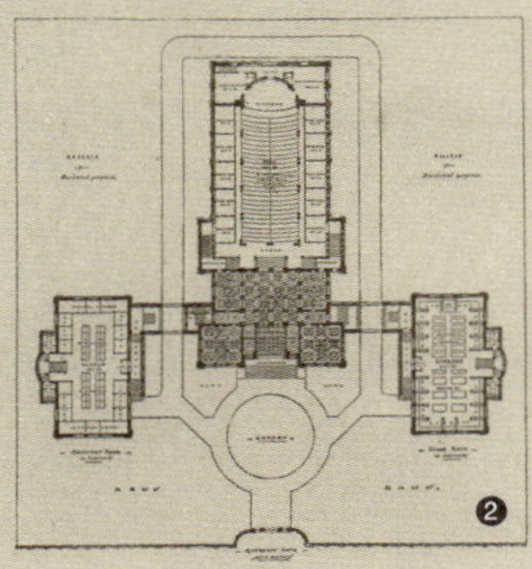

PLAN OF BUILDINGS AND GROUNDS.

The Grand Secretary, Li Hung-Chang, in a letter which he presented to me April 12, 1897, to be used for publication in this country, made the following statement:

"You have set about solving this problem in a way that should commend itself to every friend of humanity. Unquestionably, if you can give to the blind leaders of our people light and learning enjoyed in the West, they in turn will lead our people out of their darkness."

Then, referring especially to his friends in the United States, he closed with these words:

"If it would interest them to know that I regard you highly, and will give you a helping hand in your future efforts to bring more light into the world and encourage higher aims for aspirations, you may use for that purpose this letter," etc.

The Imperial Board of Foreign Affairs, as representing the government, has, for the first time in its history, been willing to formally sanction under its seal such a plan for an international institute. Promises have been made by men of that body to bestow still greater honor by memorializing the Emperor for Imperial recognition so soon as the plan may be carried out. There is already abundant proof that the execution of this plan will not long be delayed. Already in China I have been able to secure contributions to the amount of $15,000. Most of this came from individual Chinese. Governor Hu, Director-General of Railroads in North China, the Metropolitan Viceroy Wang Wen-Shao, of Tien-tsin, and Viceroy Chang Chih-Tung, in Central China, were among the number to indicate their good-will by rendering financial aid. The work at present is carried on in a humble Chinese house rented for not more than $7 per month, and though new and grander buildings are planned for the future, it is still intended to bring Western ideas to the Chinese by methods of conciliation and adaptation.

GOVERNOR HU, Director-General of Railroads.

This plan, so largely endorsed in China, is now brought to the attention of people in this country and Europe. Already commercial bodies and educational institutions have indicated their willingness to co-operate. As soon as the money can be secured for the erection of the buildings, a larger appreciation on the part of the Chinese themselves will at once be manifested. The door for progress will be open as never before. Two buildings will cost each $13,000.

The main central building will consist of two parts—the front part will cost $14,000, and the auditorium, or larger part, will cost $35,000. Altogether, the estimated cost is only $75,000. Three competent English architects stipulate to erect these buildings, according to drawings already made, within this amount. This plan, presented to public-spirited men in the United States, offers an unusual opportunity to help in a large and generous way this new endeavor to open up China more widely and peaceably to the whole world—to commerce, to education, to civilization, and to all the varied forms of Christian missions.

Should pamphlets or other information be desired, inquiries may be made of the Fleming H. Revell Company, 158 Fifth Avenue, New York city, or of the bankers Brown Brothers, 59 Wall Street.

GILBERT REID.

PROPOSED BUILDINGS FOR THE INTERNATIONAL INSTITUTE OF CHINA, AT PEKING.

METROPOLITAN VICEROY WANG WEN-SHAO, OF TIEN-TSIN.

VICEROY CHANG CHIH-TUNG.

1898 年 4 月 9 日《哈珀斯周刊》

1　牧师李佳白，北京
1　Rev. Gilbert Reid, Peking.

2　建筑及平面设计图
2　Plan of buildings and grounds.

3　主管铁路的胡总督
3　Governor Hu, Director-General of Railroads.

4　中国国际学会的拟建建筑，北京
4　Proposed buildings for the International Institute of China, at Peking.

5　直隶总督王文韶，天津
5　Metropolitan viceroy Wang Wen-Shao, of Tien-Tsin.

6　总督张之洞
6　Viceroy Chang Chih-Tung.

一批在中国居住的有识之士认识到了目前远东事务的重要性，同心合力，计划在北京组建中国国际学会。英、法、德、美及荷兰的人士已经成立了委员会，以促进拟建的学会的利益。其他国家的人士都对本学会作出了贡献，表示了对我们工作的支持。那些真诚希望为中国百姓谋取利益、巩固中国政府的人士，也主动表示了他们对这项新事业的善意。

李鸿章大学士于 1897 年 4 月 12 日写给我一封信，已在本国发表。他在信中做了以下声明："你致力于解决问题的方式，当受到各方友人的赞叹。倘若你能为盲目治理百姓的官员带来西方的光明和学识，他们即可带领百姓走出黑暗。"

然后，他在结束时特别提到了他的美国朋友："如果他们感兴趣，知道我甚是赏识你，并会在将来助你为世界带来更多光明、鼓励人们确立更远大的目标，你可将此信作为引荐之信。"等等。

——《国际学院计划》（选译），1898 年 4 月 9 日《哈珀斯周刊》

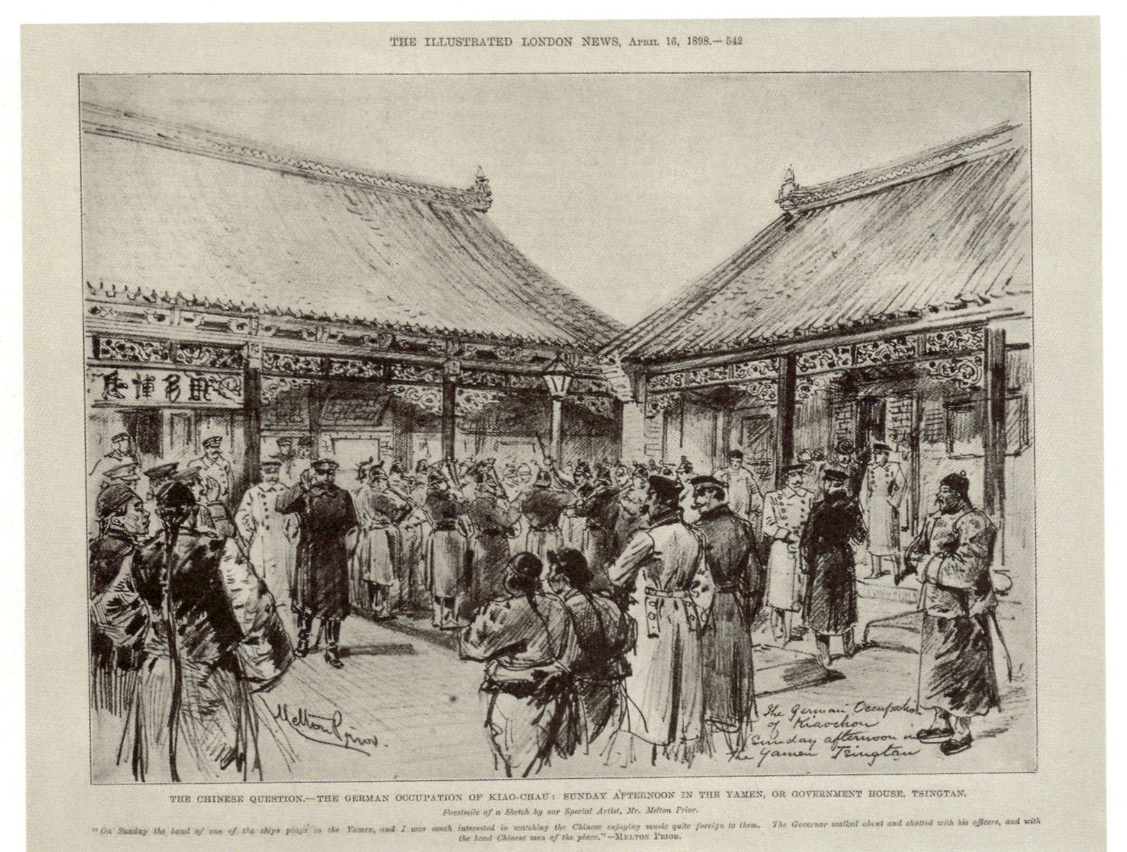

THE ILLUSTRATED LONDON NEWS, APRIL 16, 1898.—542

THE CHINESE QUESTION.—THE GERMAN OCCUPATION OF KIAO-CHAU: SUNDAY AFTERNOON IN THE YAMEN, OR GOVERNMENT HOUSE, TSINGTAN.

Facsimile of a Sketch by our Special Artist, Mr. Melton Prior.

"On Sunday the band of one of the ships plays in the Yamen, and I was much interested in watching the Chinese enjoying music quite foreign to them. The Governor walked about and chatted with his officers, and with the head Chinese men of the place."—MELTON PRIOR.

1898 年 4 月 16 日《伦敦新闻画报》

中国问题——德国占领胶州。德国军官在青岛衙门举行音乐会

The Chinese Question.—The German occupation of Kiao-Chau: Sunday afternoon in the Yamen, or Government House, Tsingtan.

周日，一艘战舰上的军乐队来到衙门里演奏，我好奇地观察那些中国人，他们听着对他们而言完全陌生的音乐，却显得饶有兴趣。总督与他的属员，以及在场的中国最高官员聊着天。

——梅尔顿 · 普莱尔（本报特派画师）

On Sunday the band of one of the ships plays in the Yamen, and I was much interested in watching the Chinese enjoying music quite foreign to them. The Governor walked about and chatted with his officers, and with the head Chinese men of the place.

—Melton Prior

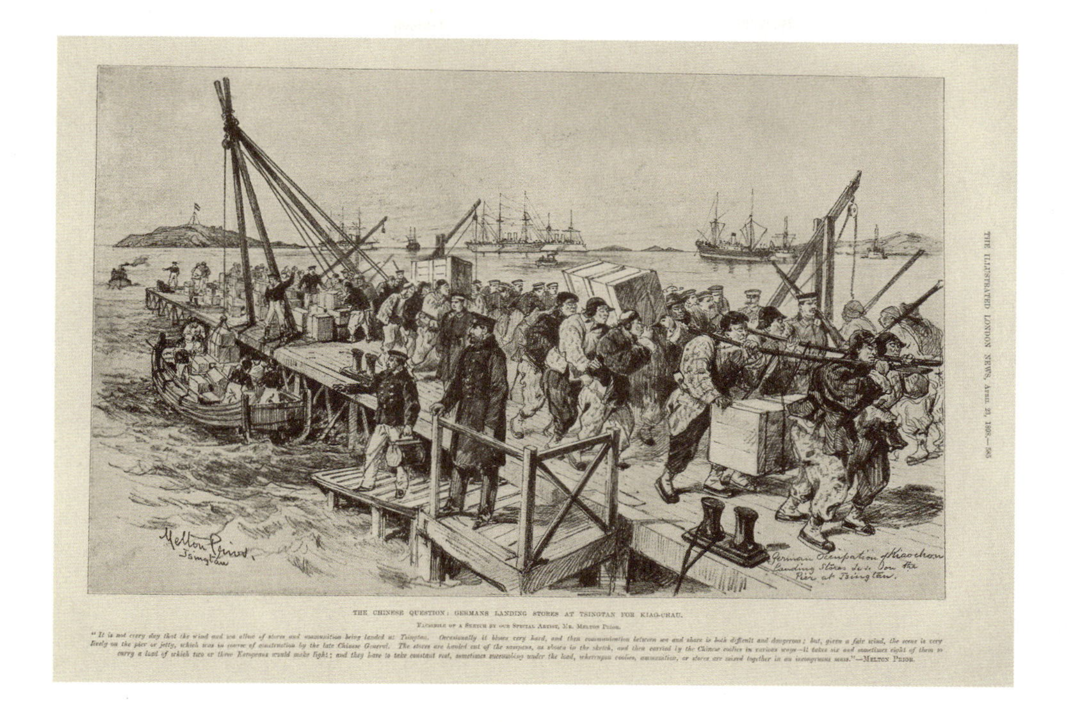

1898 年 4 月 23 日《伦敦新闻画报》

中国问题——德国军舰在青岛胶州卸下物资

The Chinese Question: Germans landing stores at Tsingtan for Kiao-Chau.

青岛并不是每一天都风平浪静，能让人们随时卸载物资和弹药。狂风大作时，海上和岸上的通讯既艰难又危险。但只要风速正常，码头和防波堤上就会熙熙攘攘，青岛的最后一个中国将军还没来得及结束他启动的防波堤修建工程，工程就中止了。物资先从小船上被卸下来，就像插图上的样子，然后中国苦力们用五花八门的方法搬走它们。搬运两三个欧洲工人轻松抬走的货物往往需要六个甚至八个中国苦力，而且他们还需要边走边歇脚，有时还因不堪重负而倒下。苦力、货物、弹药，构成了一团乱糟糟的场面。

——梅尔顿·普莱尔（本报特派画师）

It is not every day that the wind and sea allow of stores and ammunition being landed at Tsingtan. Occasionally it blows very hard, and then communication between sea and shore is both difficult and dangerous; but, given a fair wind, the scene is very lively on the pier or jetty, which was in course of construction by the late Chinese General. The stores are hauled out of the sampans as shown in the sketch, and then carried by the Chinese coolies in various ways—it takes six and sometimes eight of them to carry a load of which two or three Europeans would make light; and they have to take constant rest, sometimes succumbing under the load, whereupon coolies, ammunition, or stores are mixed together in an incongruous mass.

— Melton Prior

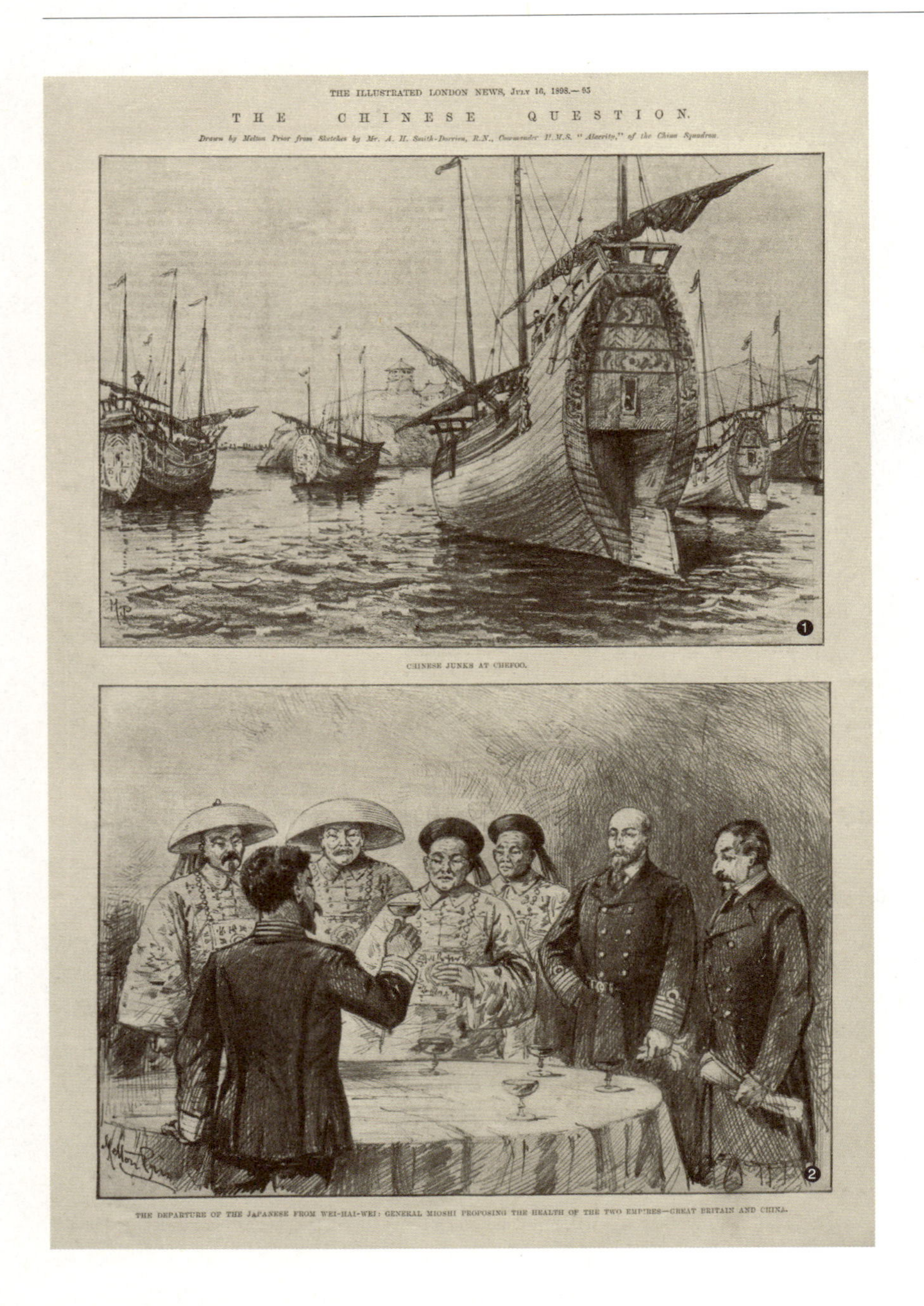

THE ILLUSTRATED LONDON NEWS, JULY 16, 1898.—65

THE CHINESE QUESTION.

Drawn by Melton Prior from Sketches by Mr. A. H. Smith-Dorrien, R.N., Commander H.M.S. "Alacrity," of the China Squadron.

CHINESE JUNKS AT CHEFOO.

THE DEPARTURE OF THE JAPANESE FROM WEI-HAI-WEI: GENERAL MIOSHI PROPOSING THE HEALTH OF THE TWO EMPIRES—GREAT BRITAIN AND CHINA.

1898年7月16日《伦敦新闻画报》

1 烟台的中国帆船

2 日本撤离威海卫，三园子将军为大英帝国和大清帝国举杯（日本人撤离威海卫后仅一天，英国海军就向清朝强行租借——编者注）

1 Chinese junks at Chefoo.

2 The departure of the Japanese from Wei-Hai-Wei: General Mioshi proposing the health of the two Empires—Great Britain and China.

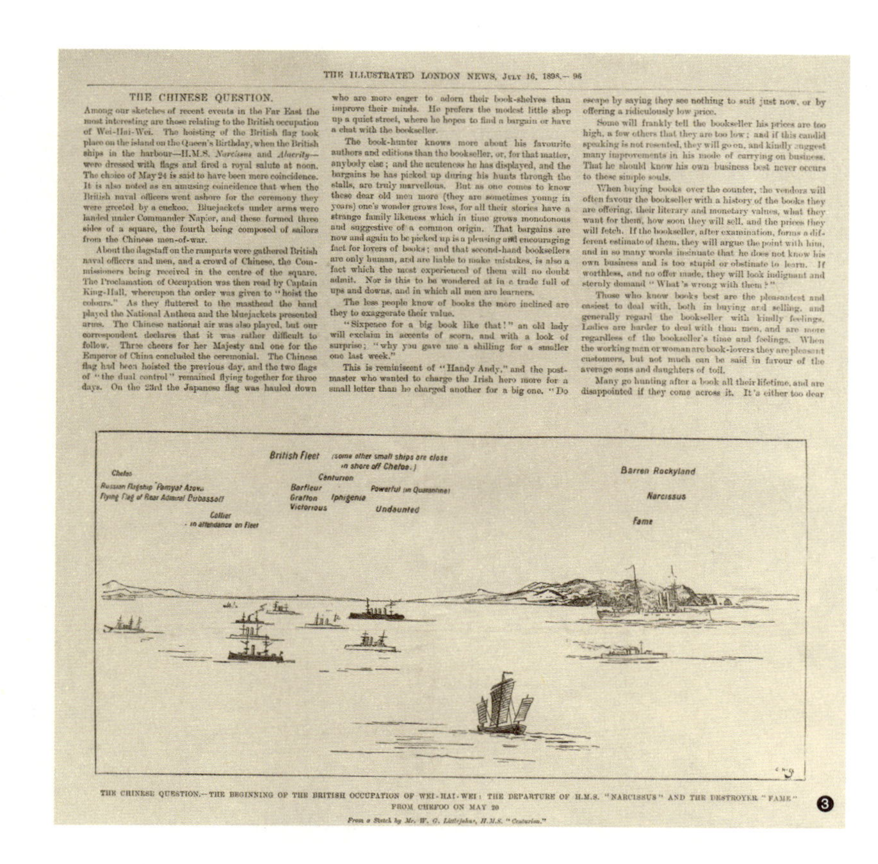

THE ILLUSTRATED LONDON NEWS, JULY 16, 1898.— 96

THE CHINESE QUESTION.

Among our sketches of recent events in the Far East the most interesting are those relating to the British occupation of Wei-Hai-Wei. The hoisting of the British flag took place on the island on the Queen's Birthday, when the British ships in the harbour—H.M.S. *Narcissus* and *Alacrity*—were dressed with flags and fired a royal salute at noon. The choice of May 24 is said to have been mere coincidence. It is also noted as an amusing coincidence that when the British naval officers went ashore for the ceremony they were greeted by a cuckoo. Bluejackets under arms were landed under Commander Napier, and these formed three sides of a square, the fourth being composed of sailors from the Chinese men-of-war.

About the flagstaff on the ramparts were gathered British naval officers and men, and a crowd of Chinese, the Commissioners being received in the centre of the square. The Proclamation of Occupation was then read by Captain King-Hall, whereupon the order was given to "hoist the colours." As they fluttered to the masthead the band played the National Anthem and the bluejackets presented arms. The Chinese national air was also played, but our correspondent declares that it was rather difficult to follow. Three cheers for her Majesty and one for the Emperor of China concluded the ceremonial. The Chinese flag had been hoisted the previous day, and the two flags of "the dual control" remained flying together for three days. On the 23rd the Japanese flag was hauled down

who are more eager to adorn their book-shelves than improve their minds. He prefers the modest little shop up a quiet street, where he hopes to find a bargain or have a chat with the bookseller.

The book-hunter knows more about his favourite authors and editions than the bookseller, or, for that matter, anybody else; and the acuteness he has displayed, and the bargains he has picked up during his hunts through the stalls, are truly marvellous. But as one comes to know these dear old men more (they are sometimes young in years) one's wonder grows less, for all their stories have a strange family likeness which in time grows monotonous and suggestive of a common origin. That bargains are now and again to be picked up is a pleasing and encouraging fact for lovers of books; and that second-hand booksellers are only human, and are liable to make mistakes, is also a fact which the most experienced of them will no doubt admit. Nor is this to be wondered at in a trade full of ups and downs, and in which all men are learners.

The less people know of books the more inclined are they to exaggerate their value.

"Sixpence for a big book like that!" an old lady will exclaim in accents of scorn, and with a look of surprise; "why you gave me a shilling for a smaller one last week."

This is reminiscent of "Handy Andy," and the postmaster who wanted to charge the Irish hero more for a small letter than he charged another for a big one. "Do

escape by saying they see nothing to suit just now, or by offering a ridiculously low price.

Some will frankly tell the bookseller his prices are too high, a few others that they are too low; and if this candid speaking is not resented, they will go on, and kindly suggest many improvements in his mode of carrying on business. That he should know his own business best never occurs to these simple souls.

When buying books over the counter, the vendors will often favour the bookseller with a history of the books they are offering, their literary and monetary values, what they want for them, how soon they will sell, and the prices they will fetch. If the bookseller, after examination, forms a different estimate of them, they will argue the point with him, and in so many words insinuate that he does not know his own business and is too stupid or obstinate to learn. If worthless, and no offer made, they will look indignant and sternly demand "What's wrong with them?"

Those who know books best are the pleasantest and easiest to deal with, both in buying and selling, and generally regard the bookseller with kindly feelings. Ladies are harder to deal with than men, and are more regardless of the bookseller's time and feelings. When the working man or woman are book-lovers they are pleasant customers, but not much can be said in favour of the average sons and daughters of toil.

Many go hunting after a book all their lifetime, and are disappointed if they come across it. It's either too dear

THE CHINESE QUESTION.—THE BEGINNING OF THE BRITISH OCCUPATION OF WEI-HAI-WEI: THE DEPARTURE OF H.M.S. "NARCISSUS" AND THE DESTROYER "FAME" FROM CHEFOO ON MAY 20

From a Sketch by Mr. W. G. Littlejohns, H.M.S. "Centurion."

3　中国问题——英国开始占领威海卫，水仙号巡洋舰和费姆号驱逐舰（插图右侧）5 月 20 日驶离烟台芝罘岛。
The Chinese Question.—The beginning of the British occupation of Wei-Hai-Wei: the departure of H.M.S. "Narcissus" and the destroyer "Fame" from Chefoo on May 20.

中国国旗曾在前一天升起，两国国旗将以“双重控制”的名义共同飘扬三天。5 月 23 日，日本国旗在日军将领撤离时被降下。我们的插图（见此组报道图 2）呈现了日本三园子将军在撤离前为大英帝国和大清帝国举杯的仪式。爱德华·西摩尔元帅（英国海军驻华舰队司令——编者注）指派负责接收威海卫的代表是“水仙”号战舰的金霍尔舰长和烟台领事 L.C. 霍普金斯先生。中国方面的两位代表分别姓刘和严。这几位官员在三园子将军即将登船前为他举行了送行仪式。

——《中国事态 —— 英国占领威海卫的仪式》（选译）

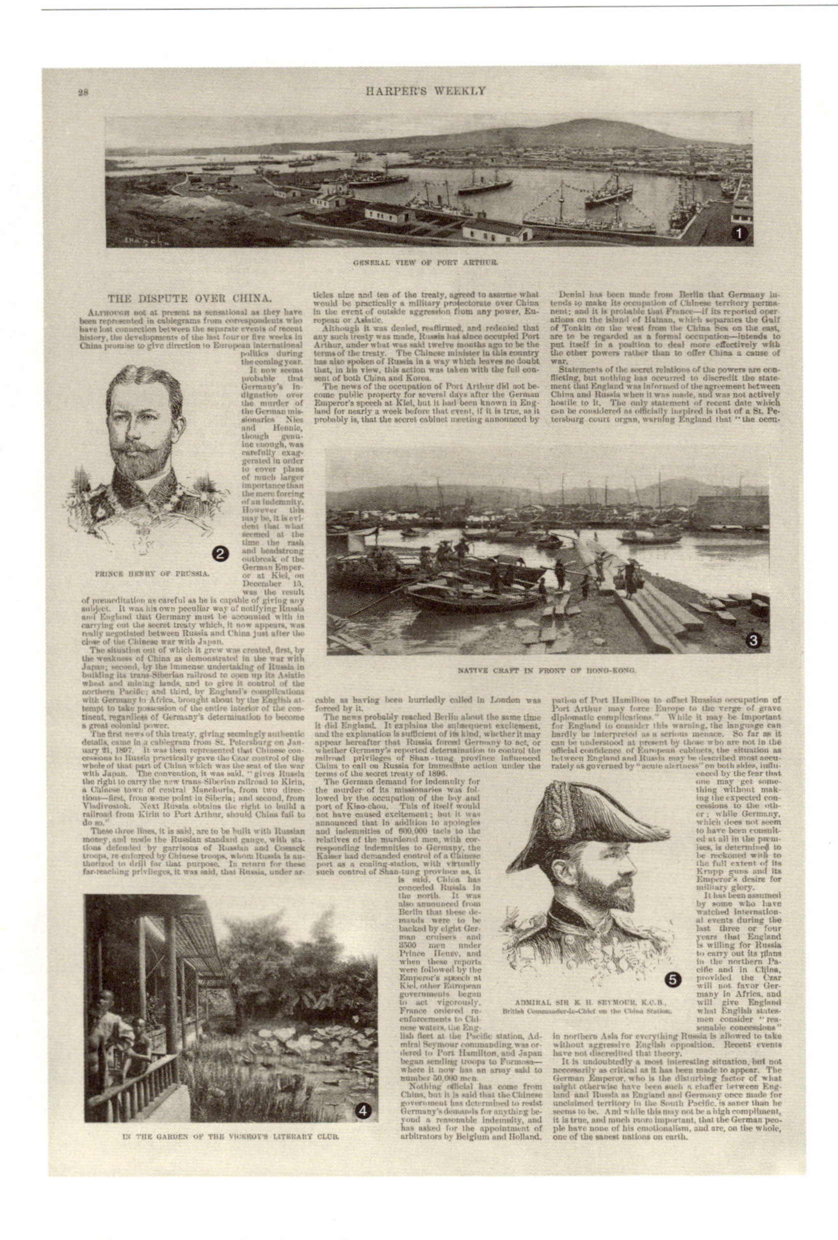
28 HARPER'S WEEKLY

GENERAL VIEW OF PORT ARTHUR.

THE DISPUTE OVER CHINA.

ALTHOUGH not at present as sensational as they have been represented in cablegrams from correspondents who have lost connection between the separate events of recent history, the developments of the last four or five weeks in China promise to give direction to European international politics during the coming year.

It now seems probable that Germany's indignation over the murder of the German missionaries Nies and Hennie, though genuine enough, was carefully exaggerated in order to cover plans of much larger importance than the mere forcing of an indemnity. However this may be, it is evident that what seemed at the time the rash and headstrong outbreak of the German Emperor at Kiel, on December 15, was the result of premeditation as careful as he is capable of giving any subject. It was his own peculiar way of notifying Russia and England that Germany must be accounted with in carrying out the secret treaty which, it now appears, was really negotiated between Russia and China just after the close of the Chinese war with Japan.

PRINCE HENRY OF PRUSSIA.

The situation out of which it grew was created, first, by the weakness of China as demonstrated in the war with Japan; second, by the immense undertaking of Russia in building its trans-Siberian railroad to open up its Asiatic wheat and mining lands, and to give it control of the northern Pacific; and third, by England's complications with Germany in Africa, brought about by the English attempt to take possession of the entire interior of the continent, regardless of Germany's determination to become a great colonial power.

The first news of this treaty, giving seemingly authentic details, came in a cablegram from St. Petersburg on January 21, 1897. It was then represented that Chinese concessions to Russia practically gave the Czar control of the whole of that part of China which was the seat of the war with Japan. The convention, it was said, "gives Russia the right to carry the new trans-Siberian railroad to Kirin, a Chinese town of central Manchuria, from two directions—first, from some point in Siberia; and second, from Vladivostok. Next Russia obtains the right to build a railroad from Kirin to Port Arthur, should China fail to do so."

These three lines, it is said, are to be built with Russian money, and made the Russian standard gauge, with stations defended by garrisons of Russian and Cossack troops, re-enforced by Chinese troops, whom Russia is authorized to drill for that purpose. In return for these far-reaching privileges, it was said, that Russia, under articles nine and ten of the treaty, agreed to assume what would be practically a military protectorate over China in the event of outside aggression from any power, European or Asiatic.

Although it was denied, reaffirmed, and redenied that any such treaty was made, Russia has since occupied Port Arthur, under what was said twelve months ago to be the terms of the treaty. The Chinese minister in this country has also spoken of Russia in a way which leaves no doubt that, in his view, this action was taken with the full consent of both China and Korea.

The news of the occupation of Port Arthur did not become public property for several days after the German Emperor's speech at Kiel, but it had been known in England for nearly a week before that event, if it is true, as it probably is, that the secret cabinet meeting announced by cable as having been hurriedly called in London was forced by it.

The news probably reached Berlin about the same time it did England. It explains the subsequent excitement, and the explanation is sufficient of its kind, whether it may appear hereafter that Russia forced Germany to act, or whether Germany's reported determination to control the railroad privileges of Shan-tung province influenced China to call on Russia for immediate action under the terms of the secret treaty of 1896.

The German demand for indemnity for the murder of its missionaries was followed by the occupation of the bay and port of Kiao-chou. This of itself would not have caused excitement; but it was announced that in addition to apologies and indemnities of 600,000 taels to the relatives of the murdered men, with corresponding indemnities to Germany, the Kaiser had demanded control of a Chinese port as a coaling-station, with virtually such control of Shan-tung province as, it is said, China has conceded Russia in the north. It was also announced from Berlin that these demands were to be backed by eight German cruisers and 3500 men under Prince Henry, and when these reports were followed by the Emperor's speech at Kiel, other European governments began to act vigorously. France ordered re-enforcements to Chinese waters, the English fleet at the Pacific station, Admiral Seymour commanding, was ordered to Port Hamilton, and Japan began sending troops to Formosa—where it now has an army said to number 50,000 men.

Nothing official has come from China, but it is said that the Chinese government has determined to resist Germany's demands for anything beyond a reasonable indemnity, and has asked for the appointment of arbitrators by Belgium and Holland.

Denial has been made from Berlin that Germany intends to make its occupation of Chinese territory permanent; and it is probable that France—if its reported operations on the island of Hainan, which separates the Gulf of Tonkin on the west from the China Sea on the east, are to be regarded as a formal occupation—intends to put itself in a position to deal more effectively with the other powers rather than to offer China a cause of war.

Statements of the secret relations of the powers are conflicting, but nothing has occurred to discredit the statement that England was informed of the agreement between China and Russia when it was made, and was not actively hostile to it. The only statement of recent date which can be considered as officially inspired is that of a St. Petersburg court organ, warning England that "the occupation of Port Hamilton to offset Russian occupation of Port Arthur may force Europe to the verge of grave diplomatic complications." While it may be important for England to consider this warning, the language can hardly be interpreted as a serious menace. So far as it can be understood at present by those who are not in the official confidence of European cabinets, the situation as between England and Russia may be described most accurately as governed by "acute alertness" on both sides, influenced by the fear that one may get something without making the expected concessions to the other; while Germany, which does not seem to have been consulted at all in the premises, is determined to be reckoned with to the full extent of its Krupp guns and its Emperor's desire for military glory.

NATIVE CRAFT IN FRONT OF HONG-KONG.

It has been assumed by some who have watched international events during the last three or four years that England is willing for Russia to carry out its plans in the northern Pacific and in China, provided the Czar will not favor Germany in Africa, and will give England what English statesmen consider "reasonable concessions" in northern Asia for everything Russia is allowed to take without aggressive English opposition. Recent events have not discredited that theory.

It is undoubtedly a most interesting situation, but not necessarily as critical as it has been made to appear. The German Emperor, who is the disturbing factor of what might otherwise have been such a chaffer between England and Russia as England and Germany once made for unclaimed territory in the South Pacific, is saner than he seems to be. And while this may not be a high compliment, it is true, and much more important, that the German people have none of his emotionalism, and are, on the whole, one of the sanest nations on earth.

IN THE GARDEN OF THE VICEROY'S LITERARY CLUB.

ADMIRAL SIR E. H. SEYMOUR, K.C.B.,
British Commander-in-Chief on the China Station.

1898年1月8日《哈珀斯周刊》

1 旅顺港鸟瞰	1 General view of Port Arthur.
2 普鲁士将军亨利亲王	2 Prince Henry of Prussia.
3 香港岸边的本土船只	3 Native craft in front of Hong-Kong.
4 在总督文学社的花园里	4 In the garden of the Viceroy's Literary Club.
5 爱德华·西摩尔爵士——英国海军驻华舰队司令	5 Admiral Sir E. H. Seymour, K.C.B., British Commander-in-Chief on the China Station.

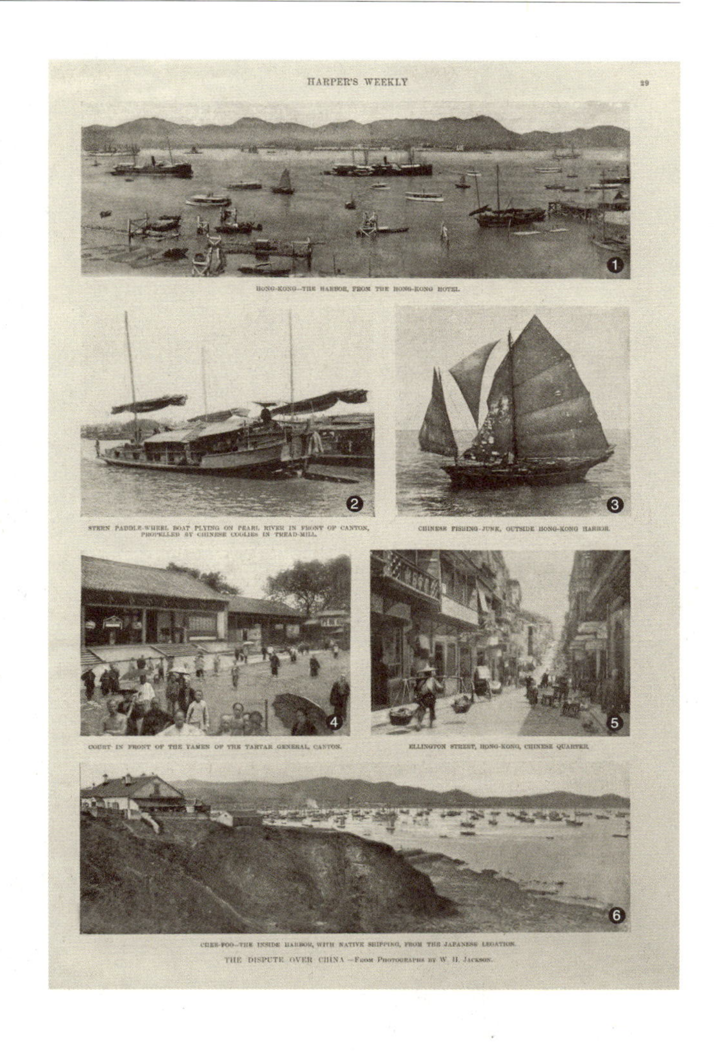
HARPER'S WEEKLY 29

HONG-KONG—THE HARBOR, FROM THE HONG-KONG HOTEL.

STERN PADDLE-WHEEL BOAT PLYING ON PEARL RIVER IN FRONT OF CANTON, PROPELLED BY CHINESE COOLIES IN TREAD-MILL.

CHINESE FISHING-JUNK, OUTSIDE HONG-KONG HARBOR.

COURT IN FRONT OF THE YAMEN OF THE TARTAR GENERAL, CANTON.

ELLINGTON STREET, HONG-KONG, CHINESE QUARTER.

CHEE-FOO—THE INSIDE HARBOR, WITH NATIVE SHIPPING, FROM THE JAPANESE LEGATION.

THE DISPUTE OVER CHINA.—FROM PHOTOGRAPHS BY W. H. JACKSON.

1898 年 1 月 8 日《哈珀斯周刊》

1　香港——从香港饭店望出去的港口

2　停在广州的中国脚踏轮船船尾，这种船在珠江上航行，由苦力脚踩前进

3　香港港口外的中国渔船

4　广州的衙门府

5　香港的灵顿街，中国人聚居区

6　烟台内港的本土船只，从日本领事馆望去

1　Hong-Kong—The harbor, from the Hong-Kong hotel.

2　Stern paddle-wheel boat plying on Pearl River in front of Canton, propelled by Chinese coolies in tread-mill.

3　Chinese fishing-junk, outside Hong-Kong harbor.

4　Court in front of the Yamen of the Tartar General, Canton.

5　Ellington street, Hong-Kong, Chinese Quarter.

6　Chee-Foothe inside harbor, with native shipping, from the Japanese Legation.

24 Supplément illustré du Petit Journal

EN CHINE
Le gâteau des Rois et... des Empereurs

1898 年 1 月 16 日《小日报》封底

亨利梅尔的政治漫画：在中国，各国帝王们的蛋糕

En Chine. Le gâteau des Rois et... des Empereurs.—Henri Meyer

一块名叫 Chine（法文：中国）的蛋糕旁坐着几位贵宾：英国的维多利亚女王、德皇威廉二世、俄国沙皇尼古拉二世和一个象征着日本的武士。在青年才俊的尼古拉二世身后是象征着法兰西共和精神的马丽安娜姑娘，她的一只手轻柔地搭在沙皇的肩膀上，伏下身子，希望和尼古拉共享一块写着 Port-Arthur（旅顺）的蛋糕。而维多利亚和威廉正怒目相斥，维多利亚用手紧捂着自己垂涎已久的最大一块，威廉干脆一刀切了下去，试图把 Kiao-Tchéou（胶州）一分为二,一半在英国那边（威海卫），一半留给自己（青岛）。只有日本武士的神情略显茫然，他的眼睛却在另一半蛋糕上打转。正在这时，一位头上扣着顶戴花翎、身上披着黄马褂的清朝大官（像是李鸿章）风风火火地冲来，明知自己已无能为力，却又张开手臂，嘴里像是在呼喊着："给我们留点儿……面子！"

日本《御国之誉》(浮世绘)

讽刺漫画《世界各国的儿童》

我国在日清战争中，通过胜利得到了领土辽东半岛，却又强忍泪水，饱含屈辱地还给清国。其中原因之一是为了保持远东的和平。然而向我们发出这种劝告（要求归还辽东半岛）的列国，随后又是怎么做的呢？

俄国获得了满洲的铁路建设权、矿山采掘权以及旅顺、大连的租借权等。在“北清事变”（八国联军侵华战争）后向满洲驻军的野心更加露骨地表现出来。德国以两位传教士被杀害为借口，突然占领了胶州湾，得到了这里99年的租借权，以及山东的铁路建设权和矿山采掘权。而英国逼迫着清国，在俄国租借旅顺期间，获得了威海卫的租借权，法国也成功租借到了广州湾。也就是说，（让我国）以“远东和平”为由归还辽东半岛，而列国的行动不是“搅乱东亚”又是什么呢？这张图就是对此进行讽刺的一幅滑稽画。

朝日太郎（代表日本）说：“喂，俄助（代表俄国），你们利用清吉（清国）的疏忽偷走了‘馒头’（利益）算怎么回事，快点还回来！”俄助说：“废话少说吧，傲慢的小子，你看见我庞大的身躯了吗？”法次（代表法国）说：“俄助，把馒头也分我一点吧。”德一（代表德国）说：“法次，如果你得到的话也应该分我一点啊。”美藏（代表美国）说：“这可真有趣，俄助说着不讲理的话，朝日不是受欺负了吗？”英子（代表英国）说：“俄助的样子真让人讨厌，有夫（代表阿根廷）啊，把两艘玩具船给太郎吧。”有夫说：“是啊，是啊，快给你吧太郎。”（指日本随后从阿根廷购入日进、春日两艘战舰。）韩坊（代表朝鲜）：“太郎哥，我好怕我好怕。”清吉：“呜……呜……”

——《世界各国的儿童》，日本《御国之誉》

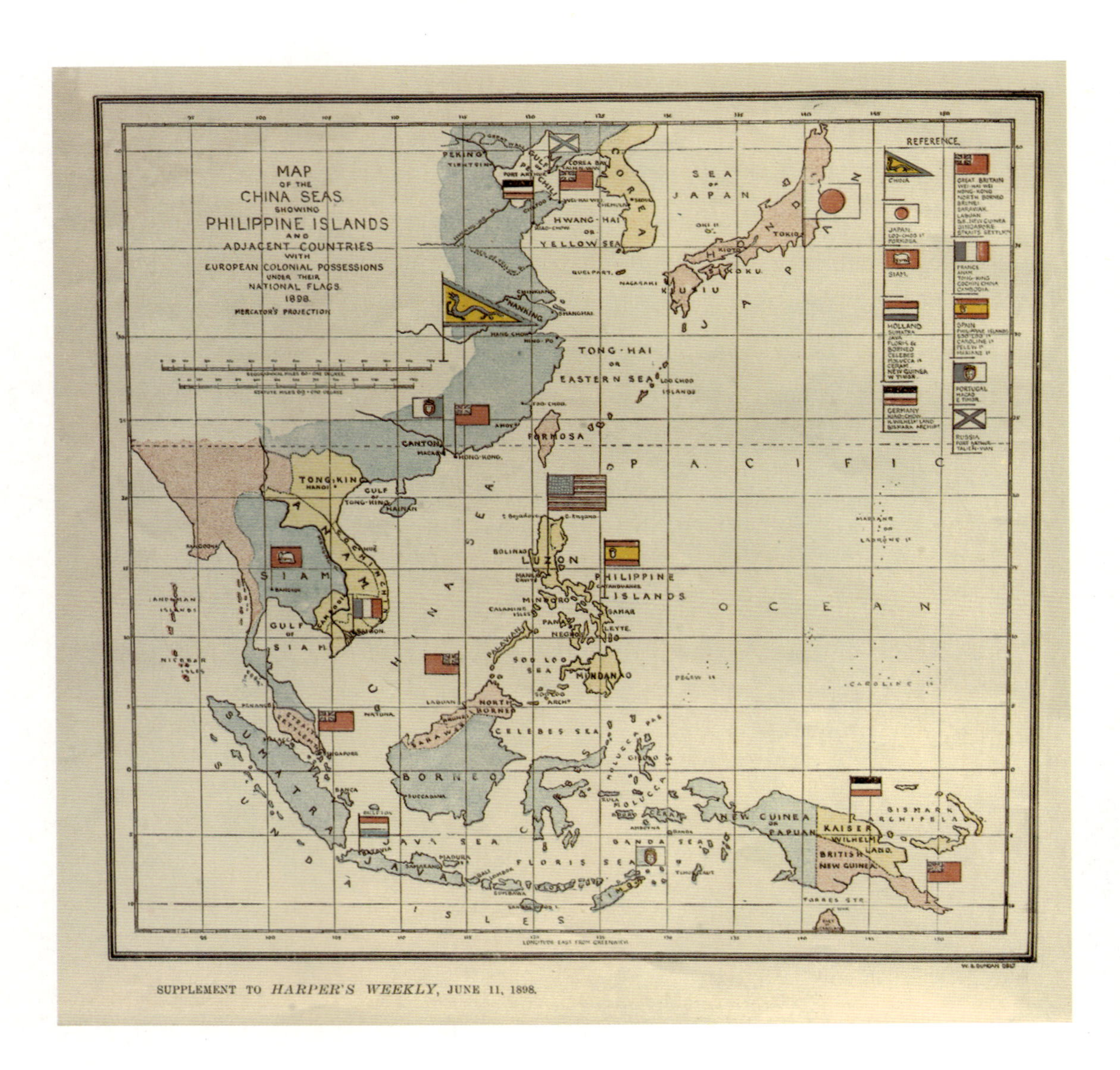

1898年6月11日《哈珀斯周刊》

西方国家在远东的势力范围图

1895 年 1 月 5 日《插图报》

列强瓜分中国的想象图

Carte du démembrement de la Chine.

《插图报》在对日本全国上下因战争的胜利而产生的狂热和民族自豪进行了报道后，转发了东京《时事新报》（日本主流政治思想家、“脱亚论”的鼓吹者福泽谕吉发起和主持的报纸）在 1894 年刊发的一张假想图——1904 年，10 年后中国解体后的地图：法、德、英、俄四个西方列强和日本瓜分了那时中国的大部分区域。记者因此写道：这张图之所以有趣不仅反映出日本人已经被胜利冲昏了头脑，更让欧洲人看到，近来传说日本社会流行的思想——在中国战败后与它建立攻守同盟联手对抗西方——看来并不像很多西方媒体的报道中所提到的那么邪乎。

"WIDE-OPEN" NEW YORK.—[See Page 1045.]

VOL. XLII.—No. 2183.

NEW YORK, SATURDAY, OCTOBER 22, 1898.

TEN CENTS A COPY.
FOUR DOLLARS A YEAR.

THE DISTURBANCES IN CHINA.

PEKING—THE FORBIDDEN CITY, AS SEEN FROM THE IMPERIAL CITY.

DRAWN BY HARRY FENN FROM THE ONLY PHOTOGRAPH KNOWN TO HAVE BEEN TAKEN OF THE PROHIBITED ENCLOSURE.—[SEE PAGE 1031.]

1898 年 10 月 22 日《哈珀斯周刊》

中国的动荡：从北京内城眺望紫禁城

The disturbances in China.Peking—the Forbidden City, as seen from the Imperial City.

根据我们所知唯一一张紫禁城照片绘制

Drawn by Harry Fenn from the only photograph known to have been taken of the prohibited Enclosures.

左上：光绪皇帝肖像（百日维新失败后，光绪皇帝的下落成了西方媒体追踪的焦点——编者注）

Kuang Hsu. Emperor of China. From a sketch from life.

如果要读懂最近关于中国皇帝逃跑、被刺或者自杀的报道，我们需要首先试着去理解一个在英文里完全不存在的中文俗语，这有助于我们分辨出真假，至少能帮我们从一堆不太可能发生的事情中挑拣出最可能发生的事情……这句俗语的字面意思就是“to save his face”（留面子）。大清帝国的任何高级官员在某些突发事件中也会把它用在自己身上，譬如当被威胁撤职时，他可能会认为维护自己或部门信用最好的途径就是自杀。但是对皇帝而言，礼仪和规则会让他别无选择。如果替代他的新皇帝人选已经敲定，或者至少是一个极有可能的新人选很快即将公布，他必须为了“保存帝国的脸面”而下台，但是也不一定是要刻意地谋杀他。

皇帝住的紫禁城虽被皇城包围，皇城外面还有蒙古城墙包围，但皇帝的安全感，却连最穷的广东渔民都不如；渔民至少可以预知自己的危险，但是皇帝，却无法控制自己生活的环境。

——《中国的动荡》（选译），1898 年 10 月 22 日《哈珀斯周刊》

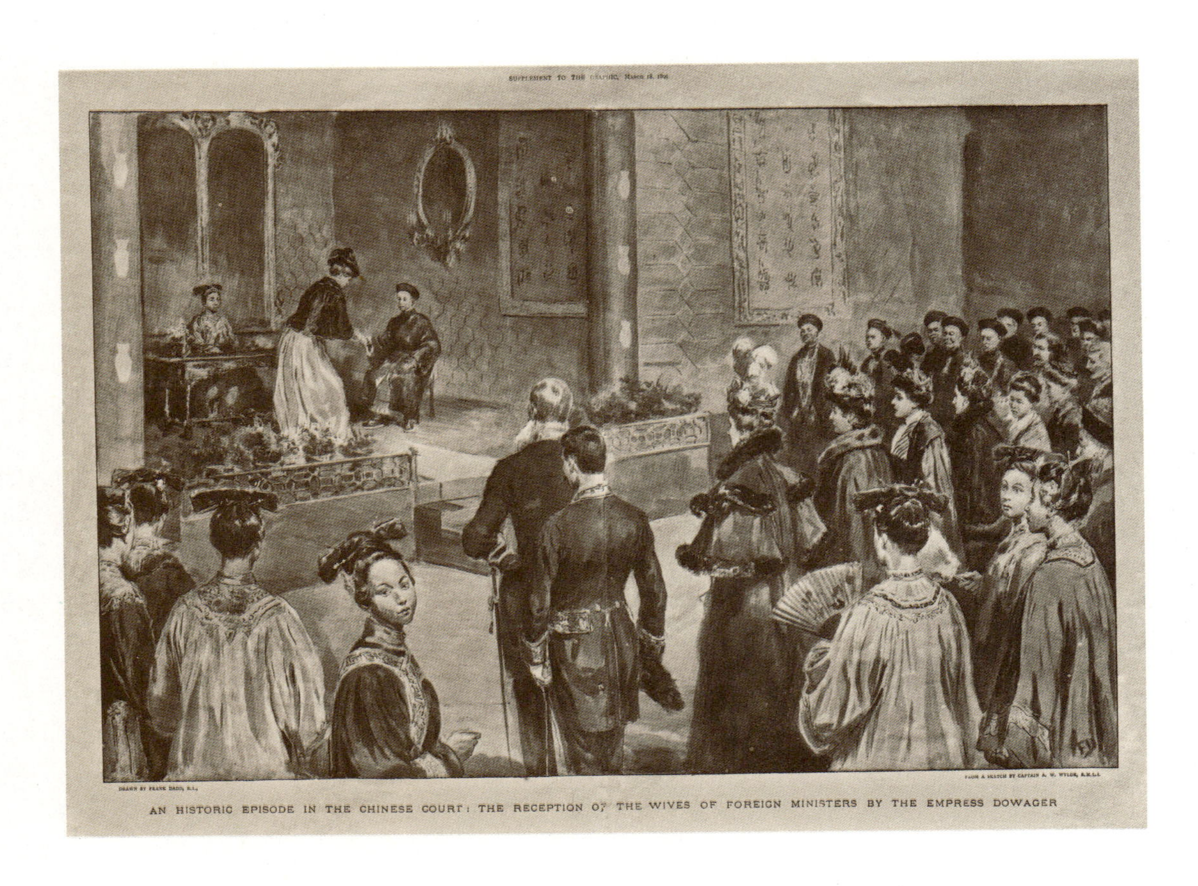

1899年3月18日《图片报》

中国宫廷里史无前例的一幕：慈禧太后举办外国公使夫人招待会

An historic episode in the Chinese Court: the reception of the wives of Foreign Ministers by the Empress Dowager.

结　语

上天加快了中国被瓜分的速度。中国遭此厄运，虽然表面看起来过于残酷，实则未然。天意难违，这一劫当属应天顺人。来自欧洲的这群血腥残暴的饿狼纷纷张牙舞爪地扑向一位老迈无力、风烛残年的耄耋老妪，就要把她撕个肢残体缺、肉光骨尽。尽管世人早已明知西方对此垂涎已久，但当这一幕丑陋上演之时，仍然让世人震惊得大跌眼镜。但中国“灭”不足惜，因为世道轮回，天理循环，劫数使然，此乃数之应也。无论有多少西方列强来瓜分这片锦绣河山、无论最后列强之间瓜分和割据的结果如何，除这个国家上层在全球都排得上名的极个别贪腐巨鳄之外，所有中国人都将在这次历史剧变中受益。中国人的统治理论、对公平正义的传统理解，以及对官民之间关系的传统观念，被全世界叹为“奇葩”。中国曾经是一个伟大的民族，它的聪明才智曾经让当时的东方迅速进入文明时代。但是，从此它因循守旧、抱残守缺，治理行径与上古盛世所推崇的善道初衷渐行渐远。较之于世界其他各大民族，中国人备受统治阶级的盘剥与摧残，终日为奴为隶，毫无尊严。

——朱利安·拉尔夫《中国的瓜分 》

1898 年 1 月 15 日　美国《哈珀斯周刊》

One of the principal events of Li Hung Chang's brief stay in Germany was his visit to Prince Bismarck. The visit lasted about two hours. Towards three o'clock Prince Bismarck, wearing a cuirassier appeared outside the Castle with Li Hung Chang, whom he afterwards conducted to his carriage. The two venerable statesmen shook hands warmly on parting. While in Berlin the Chinese statesman also vi Charlottenburg Polytechnic, when Professor Slaby showed a number of experiments with the Röntgen Rays. The Chinese Envoy consented to an attempt being made to discover, by means of the rays, the p the bullet fired at his head by the assassin at Shimonosaki last year. The image of the head which was obtained showed clearly the track of the bullet in the left cheek, and the bullet itself lodged in the tissues below. But more than by anything else Li Hung Chang would seem to have been impressed by his inspection of the Krupp Works at Essen.—Our illustration is from a photograph by the Neue Photographische Ges sent by Mr. Arthur Mennell

LI HUNG CHANG WITH PRINCE BISMARCK ON THE BALCONY OF THE CASTLE AT FRIEDRICHSRUHE

TWO VETERAN STATESMEN: A SCENE DURING THE CHINESE VICEROY'S GERMAN TOU

1896 年 7 月 4 日《图片报》

两位年迈的政治家：中国总督访德期间的一幕

李鸿章与俾斯麦在弗里德里希斯鲁庄园的阳台上

十二　媒体在战争中的作用

纵观甲午战争，除却黄海上的硝烟，还有一场看不见的战争：舆论战。

相比清朝政府对舆论宣传的漠视和放任，日本则是全面操纵了现代化传媒工具，在新闻通讯全球化初见端倪的时候，日本政府充分利用了木版与铜版印制手段、传统的素描、海报宣传画，以及刚刚在媒体中运用的摄影术等手段，全方位控制了舆论。反复的传播影响了社会公众和国际舆论，在这个战场上，他们占尽优势，一定程度上加速了清军的败局。

日本政府早在对朝鲜进行战略包围的时候，就已经将舆论宣传上升为国家战略，他们秘密聘请前《纽约论坛报》记者豪斯作为舆论战顾问，当《纽约世界报》记者克里曼揭露日本旅顺大屠杀事实后，日本政府勾结《华盛顿邮报》、《旧金山纪事》、《纽约时报》发表有利于日本的文章，从而质疑克里曼；清朝政府和媒体却在屠杀事件中集体保持沉默。日军在屠杀之后还公然打出“驱逐鞑虏、恢复中华”的口号，分裂满汉关系。

实际上清朝政府在新闻报道上是一贯采取极端保守的态度，甲午战争中拒绝外国记者随军采访，拒绝外国武官随军观战，清朝排斥媒体的做法，增加了清朝在战争立场中的不透明性，使国际社会只能听到日本的一面之词，诱导国际舆论向有利于日本的方向倾斜，例如丰岛海战，英籍运输船高升号被日本军舰击沉，1000多名清军士兵溺亡。旅顺大屠杀事件没有清朝政府和媒体强有力的声音，反而是《点石斋画报》、《上海新闻画报》等将清朝战争失利事件当成胜利，遭到国际媒体嘲讽。

日本在甲午战争中启动了所有的国家宣传机器：允许外国武官观战，允许外国新闻记者随军采访，允许国内的报刊记者、行军画师、照相师、僧侣、神官等人随军采访和工作，虽然在执行过程中军方设定了许多限制，但做法本身增加了战争透明性。据统计，甲午战争期间，日本共派出随军记者114名，还有15名画师、摄影师，并且多人在战争中丧生。战争爆发后仅一个月，有17名西方记者获得了随日军采访的许可。伊藤博文说，利用媒体攻势取得国民舆论的支持，就等于拿下了战争一半的胜利。

当然，蒸汽机时代的第一场海上战争也引起了当时的西方媒体的密切关注，毕竟甲午战争的结果将会改变西方势力在东亚的格局。英、法、美、德、俄等国家的媒体都给予了充分的报道，在这个报道过程中，日本政府不仅邀请西方记者采访，还为西方媒体提供采访素材，在本书收集的报道版面中有大量日本政府提供的版画和照片。

在为西方媒体提供采访便利的同时，日本政府还借助西方媒体进行舆论策划，在本章中，可以看到西方媒体对日本战地医院的大篇幅报道，正是在随军记者全程见证下，日方给受伤的清军"提供医疗服务"，治疗之后将他们释放。当北洋舰队提督丁汝昌自杀身亡后，伊东祐亨将他的遗体"以礼送还"。这些都成为日方舆论宣传的素材，以至于英国国际法专家胡兰德感慨：这是日本作为成熟的文明国家的标志性事件。

舆论战，日本全面获胜。

1896 年 8 月 29 日《纽约时报》

李鸿章——中国的总督，昨天以国宾身份到访

Li Hung Chang. The Chinese viceroy, who was received yesterday as the nation's guest.

李鸿章访美期间接受美国《纽约时报》记者的采访时说："中国办有报纸，但遗憾的是我们的编辑们不愿将真实情况告诉读者，他们不像你们的报纸讲真话，只讲真话。我国的编辑们在讲真话的时候十分吝啬，他们只讲部分的事实，而且他们的报纸也没有你们的报纸这么大的发行量。由于不能诚实地说明真相，我们的报纸就失去了新闻本身高贵的价值，失去了广泛传播文明的可能。"

"There are newspapers in China, but the Chinese editors, unfortunately, do not tell the truth. They do not , as your papers, tell 'the truth, the whole truth, and nothing but the truth.' The editors in China are great economizers of the truth; they tell only a part of it. They do not have , therefore, the great circulation that your papers have. Because of this economy of the truth, our papers fail in the mission of a great press, to be one of the means of civilization."

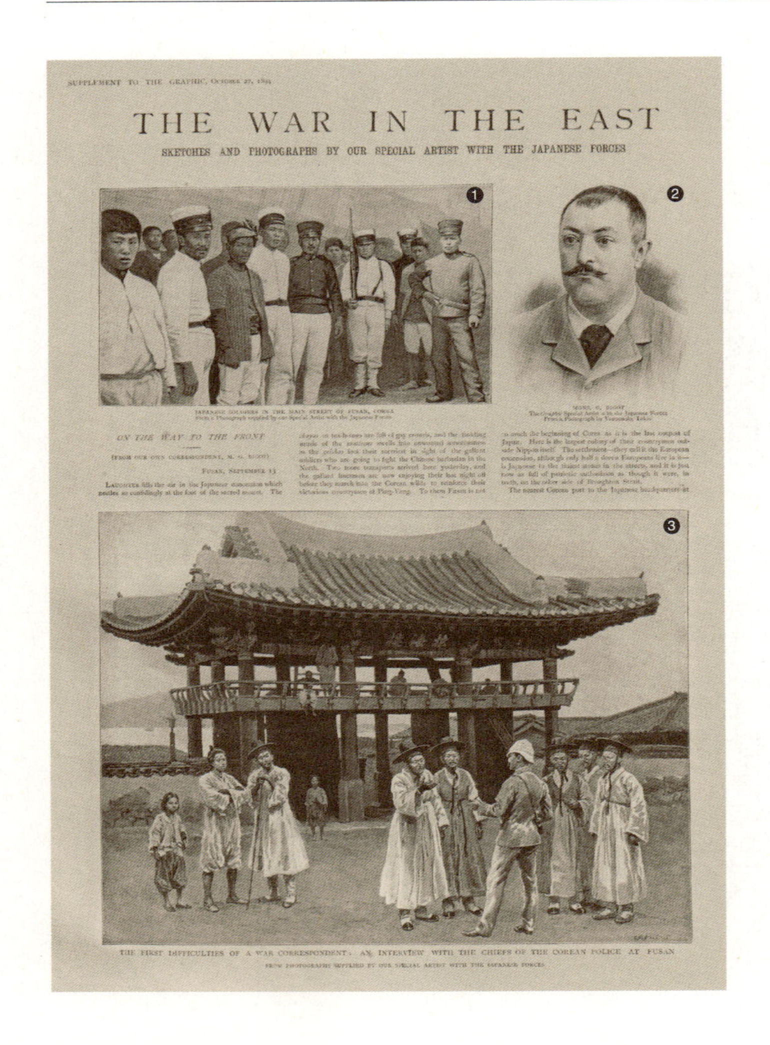

SUPPLEMENT TO THE GRAPHIC, OCTOBER 27, 1894

THE WAR IN THE EAST

SKETCHES AND PHOTOGRAPHS BY OUR SPECIAL ARTIST WITH THE JAPANESE FORCES

JAPANESE SOLDIERS IN THE MAIN STREET OF FUSAN, COREA

MONS. G. BIGOT

ON THE WAY TO THE FRONT

THE FIRST DIFFICULTIES OF A WAR CORRESPONDENT: AN INTERVIEW WITH THE CHIEFS OF THE COREAN POLICE AT FUSAN

1894 年 10 月 27 日《图片报》

1 日本士兵在朝鲜釜山的大街上

2 （《图片报》派驻日军的随军画师）毕高先生

3 战地记者遇到的第一个麻烦：在釜山采访时被朝鲜警察队长们盘问

1 Japanese soldiers in the main street of Fusan, Corea.

2 Mons. G. Bigot.

3 The first difficulties of a war correspondent: an interview with the chiefs of the Corean police at Fusan.

西方媒体为了争取第一手新闻和图片，向东亚派出了大批记者和各自优秀的画师。他们有的驻扎在上海、仁川、长崎等后方城市收集编纂各方信息发回欧美，有的跟随日军在前线采访、绘图。

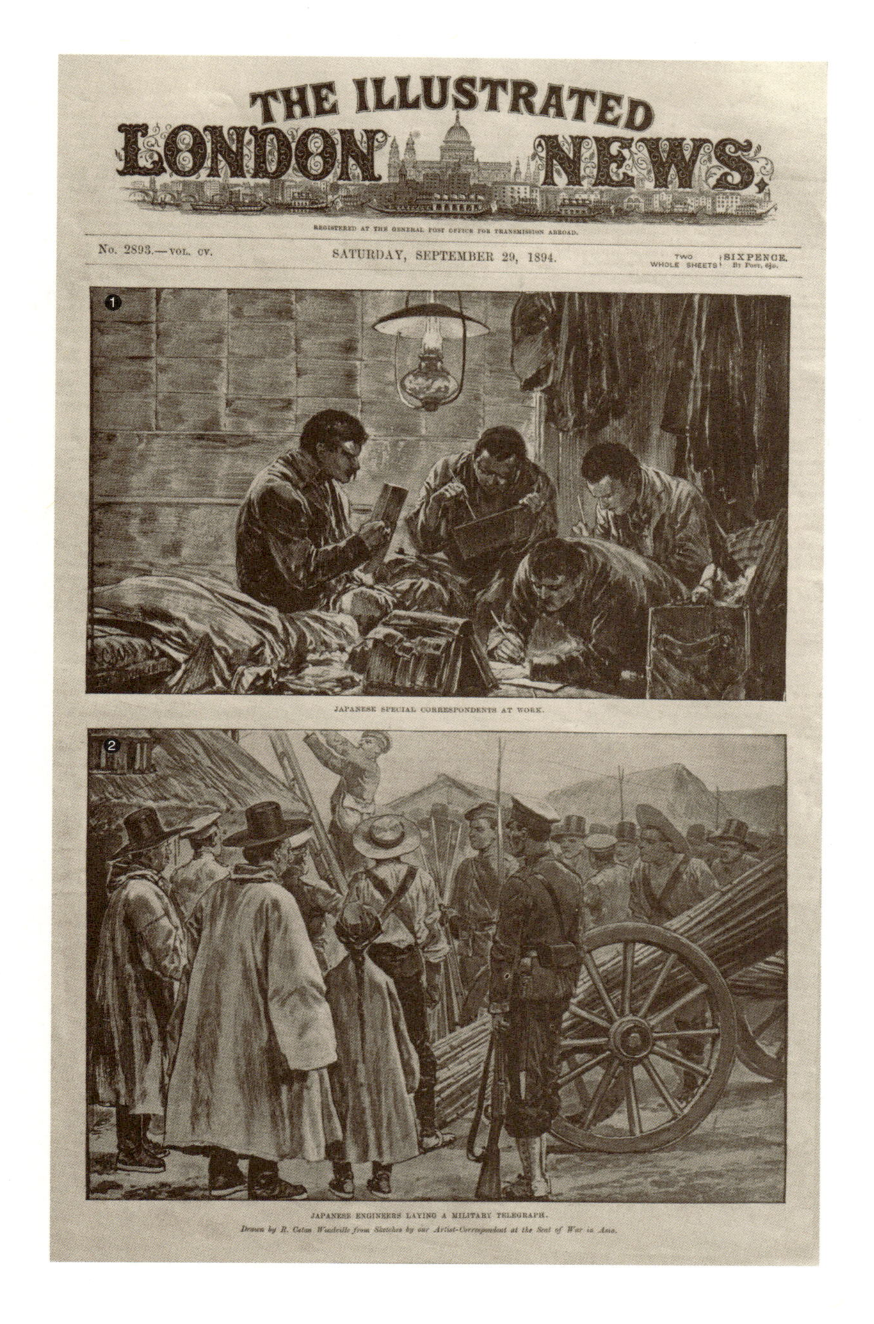

THE ILLUSTRATED LONDON NEWS

REGISTERED AT THE GENERAL POST OFFICE FOR TRANSMISSION ABROAD.

No. 2893.—VOL. CV. SATURDAY, SEPTEMBER 29, 1894. TWO WHOLE SHEETS | SIXPENCE. By Post, 6½d.

1

JAPANESE SPECIAL CORRESPONDENTS AT WORK.

2

JAPANESE ENGINEERS LAYING A MILITARY TELEGRAPH.

Drawn by R. Caton Woodville from Sketches by our Artist-Correspondent at the Seat of War in Asia.

1894 年 9 月 29 日《伦敦新闻画报》

1 日本随军记者在工作

2 日军（在朝鲜）架设军用电报电缆

1 Japanese special correspondents at work.

2 Japanese engineers laying a military telegraph.

战争开始后，日军在汉城和釜山之间铺设了 385 公里长的电报电缆。

THE ILLUSTRATED LONDON NEWS, Dec. 29, 1894.—804

HOW JAPANESE WAR PICTURES ARE MADE.

THE WAR IN THE SOUDAN.—THE BATTLE OF KERBEKAN, FEB. 10, 1885: GENERAL EARLE'S TROOPS ATTACKING THE ENEMY.

From a Sketch by Lieutenant Beverley W. R. Usher, 1st Battalion South Staffordshire Regiment.

THE ROUT OF CHIN-LEN-CHANG.

From the Private Collection of Mr. Lasenby Liberty (of Liberty and Co.), for Presentation to the Japan Society

OBVIOUSLY COPIED BY THE JAPANESE ARTIST FROM THE ABOVE.

1894 年 12 月 29 日《伦敦新闻画报》

日本战争宣传画是如何炼成的

1 苏丹战争——1885 年 2 月 10 日凯而巴肯战役：厄尔将军的部队攻打敌军

2 日本画家笔下的本次战争中的一个战役
日本画家显然拷贝了欧洲画师 10 年前的构图。

How Japanese war pictures are made.

1 The war in the Soudan.—The battle of Kerbekan, Feb. 10, 1885: General Earle's troops attacking the enemy.

2 The rout of Chin-Len-Chang.
Obviously copied by the Japanese artist from the above.

*THE FAR EAST**

THE globe-trotter is having a fine time of it nowadays, and nearly every man who has been in Eastern seas is publishing a book on Japan and the Far East. Mr. Henry Norman is, however, by no means a mere globe-trotter or special commissioner, bound to pick up a few facts in a hurry each time he touches a port, and to supplement his observations with the study of books already written on the subject, for he has spent three or four years in the countries he describes, and has made an intelligent study of the problems they offer for solution. His book is divided into sections, the first three dealing with the great European powers, England, France, and Russia, in the Far East, and the two next with Spain and Portugal, the representatives of the first Europeans who penetrated into these regions. Then he turns to the Eastern peoples, China, Corea, Japan (the two last being treated of shortly, as he has already published his appreciation of them), Siam and Malaya, winding up with an attempt to draw the horoscope of all these jarring interests as the matter stands now that Japan has shown herself the leading Power, and probably the most vital force in the future of the Far East. India is not touched upon, for that is an Empire in itself; but even putting the great dependency aside, England's interests in the Far East are far greater than those of all the other Powers. In the China seas, as elsewhere all over the globe, the stake for which we are fighting is our command of the sea, and the commercial supremacy which is its accompaniment. For, as Mr. Norman remarks later on when summing up the position of the rival States, England's "ships plough every sea in an unending procession, her merchants do nine-tenths of the trade, her consuls hold the sway of kings, and her word is the primary condition of every change. An upheaval is now transmuting the conditions that have hitherto controlled the Far East. What is to come of it?"

It is clear from Mr. Norman's survey of the subject and protected States in the Far East that the same law holds that obtains in all other parts of the world. The English are the colonists and administrators who govern Eastern nations best. Wherever the English have got a footing there commerce thrives and the country is well governed. It is satisfactory to learn that the present craze for colonisation in France will in all probability not last for long. Its mainspring is jealousy of England; and were it not for this her decreasing population and the great expense of her colonies in the Far East would long since have warned France that her weak and ill-administered dependencies were a source of weakness, and that she had better set her house in order before adventuring further in Madagascar.

It is the fact, though it seems almost incredible, that after all these years of French administration, the scores of military expeditions, the spending of countless millions of francs, the loss of tens of thousands of lives, Tongking is only pacified so far as the delta is concerned. The rest of the country is not safe from one day to another, and almost every transport of valuables has to have a military convoy.

And again a little further on—

Instability is the dominant characteristic of French administration in the Far East. Does anybody seriously believe that the solid foundations of future prosperity can ever be laid in this shifting quicksand? For an Englishman who cares for France it is positively distressing to hear Frenchmen talk in Tongking. Fifty times during my two visits was it said to me, "Ah! if only you English had Tongking!" Matters have somewhat improved for them lately; and a new hostility to England has sprung up, but I seriously believe that if a secret ballot had been taken then, a majority of the French in Tongking would have voted, in spite of their undying love of country, to hand over Indo-China to England. Then at least they would have been able to buy and sell, manufacture and import, create and develop, with no one to hamper them, and no "Administration" to forbid. As it is, the French colonist's attitude to his Government is summed up in the exclamation that I heard fall from the lips of one of them when he saw an official approaching him on duty—"Nom de Dieu! Voilà encore l'Administration qui arrive!"

And the result of all this ineptitude is that Tongking has cost the French taxpayer 4,881*l*. a day—Sundays included—for every day that he has had it, and that the imports of the country are nearly four times as great as the exports. The true story of France and Siam is equally instructive reading.

Turning to Russia, whose base on the Pacific, Vladivostock, is, of course, purely military, Mr. Norman lays great stress on the political railway now being built across Siberia. This will enable her to convey any number of European troops to a port on the Pacific, and with a powerful Pacific fleet and sufficient transports, to descend irresistibly upon any part of the Far East except Japan. By this railway China is threatened territorially and Great Britain commercially, and almost the whole of the Far East will be at the mercy of Russia unless England casts off her confidence and indifference. China is now the key of the situation, and the destiny of this land of ragtag and pigtail is, thinks Mr. Norman, partition among other nations. In all the country north of the southern frontier of China there are virtually only three great interests—those of England, Russia, and Japan. Their interests do not clash, and the ends aimed at are to the injury of no other party. There should be a combination of the three.

Let us, therefore, consider first the case of Japan. By the terms of an Anglo-Russian-Japanese understanding she would receive in the first place the virtual suzerainty of Corea; second, whatever reasonable indemnity she chooses to impose upon China; third, the cession of Formosa; fourth, the Chinese navy which she may capture; fifth, there need be no hesitation in allowing her to collect the customs in the port of Shanghai until the indemnity is paid, and, finally, she would have the inestimable advantage of being free from fear of China in the future. Next, consider the case of Russia. Her share would be the triangle of territory around which her Siberian railway is at present planned to run. . . . . Second, she would have to be provided with a winter port at the terminus of her railway, and to this it would be necessary for Japan to consent. . . . . Third, Russia would be freed for ever from the fear of China along the three thousand miles of her weak and hardly defensible frontier. Finally, what would be the position of Great Britain under this arrangement? First, she would secure her indispensable northern naval base at Chusan, Wei-hai-wei, or elsewhere. Second, the great markets of the whole of China would be thrown open to the whole world, and she would have her customary predominance in them. Third, she would be allowed to construct a railway from British Kowloon to Hong Kong, and the development of the province of Kwangtung and the city of Canton would be placed under her charge. Fourth, the Government of India would be given a free hand in Thibet. Fifth, all anxieties—and they are many and heavy—with regard to her future in the Far East would be happily removed. To an arrangement of this kind the powerful sympathy of the United States would hardly be wanting.

This passage sums up very adequately Mr. Norman's opinions as to what should be the outcome of the crisis produced by the present war between China and Japan. But the book is so exhaustive that it is impossible in a small sphere to do more than give a general idea of its contents and to dwell a little more fully on the position of England beyond Singapore, and on the rivalry between England and France, which, though it now seems so important owing to the irritation of France, is evidently destined to be overshadowed in the near future by the far more serious competition of Russia and Japan, two nations whose ambition is as great as that of France, but whose capacities for rivalry are in reality far greater. The outbreak of the war has roused the East from its long sleep; the fiction of a powerful China has been abolished, and the reality of a young and ambitious Japan has taken its place, with the consequence that mighty changes in the political and commercial balance are taking place, and that England must be prepared to meet the new order of things unless she would see herself pushed aside by her ambitious rivals. And at the critical moment comes Mr. Norman's book, the work not of an official whose remarks might be pooh-poohed by Little Englanders, but of a trained observer from the party which is the successor of the "Perish India" school, though it seems to have sloughed the pernicious doctrine contained in that phrase. Fortunately the book is one which, from a variety of circumstances, will be read by the public. Mr. Norman is doing good service to the State at the present crisis, and it only remains for the great body of the public to profit by the result of his labours.

OFF TO THE WAR: A JAPANESE SOLDIER BIDDING FAREWELL TO HIS FAMILY

FACSIMILE OF A DRAWING BY OUR SPECIAL ARTIST IN JAPAN

* "The Peoples and Politics of the Far East." By Henry Norman. (T. Fisher Unwin.)

1895 年 4 月 6 日《图片报》

上战场前的场景：一个日本士兵与家人依依惜别

Off to the war: a Japanese soldier bidding farewell to his family.

图为日本政府发放给西方媒体的宣传画之一。

29 DÉCEMBRE 1894 L'ILLUSTRATION N° 2705 — 547

L'hôpital de la Croix-Rouge, à Tokio : vue générale des batiments.

L'HOPITAL DE TOKIO

Quand, il y a quelque quinze ans, par une révolution unique dans l'histoire, le Japon décida, par ordre impérial, de dépouiller sa civilisation propre pour embrasser celle des Européens, on put croire tout d'abord que ce mouvement inattendu ne dépasserait pas le port du chapeau haut de forme pour les hommes, et celui du corset pour les femmes de cet étrange pays. La guerre qu'il poursuit actuellement contre son colossal voisin a bien vite montré que la transformation était plus profonde qu'on ne l'avait prévu, et qu'en adoptant les uniformes des armées occidentales et leur armement, les officiers de l'armée japonaise en avaient également acquis la science militaire et les traditions. Il est vrai que la conscience des nécessités de la lutte pour l'existence devait fatalement opérer cette transformation. Les photographies que nous venons de recevoir de Tokio nous apportent cependant la preuve que la renaissance du Japon est plus complète encore, et que, poursuivie jusque sur le domaine d'institutions humanitaires organisées d'après les données les plus modernes des sciences médicales, elle place vraiment ce coin de l'Extrême-Orient au rang des civilisations européennes.

Dans cet Hôpital de la Croix-Rouge dont nous donnons une vue d'ensemble, — et où sont actuellement en traitement un certain nombre de prisonniers chinois blessés — il n'y a pas que le nom ou la façade qui soient à la dernière façon du jour. Autant que nous pouvons en juger par ces documents d'une sincérité irrécusable, tout semble y avoir été édifié et installé d'après les grands principes qui président aujourd'hui à l'hygiène hospitalière, tels que les a formulés la doctrine microbienne.

Dans un quartier éloigné de la ville proprement dite de Tokio, à Shibuya, s'élèvent, autour d'un monument central réservé à l'administration, toute une série de petits pavillons séparés, comportant au plus un étage, isolés au milieu d'un vaste emplacement bien dégagé, et qui réalisent à première vue le type parfait de l'hôpital moderne, de celui que nous autres, vieilles civilisations encombrées de vieux bâtiments, nous avons tant de peine à obtenir. Combien en effet seraient heureux nos médecins, si tous ils avaient ainsi, pour les diverses catégories de leurs blessés et de leurs malades, des locaux séparés, à l'abri de la contagion des voisins et du mortel encombrement!

Pénétrons maintenant dans un de ces pavillons, et nous ne tarderons pas à acquérir la certitude que nous sommes bien dans un de ces petits temples de l'antisepsie, édifiés par l'hygiène pastorienne: médecins, élèves, infirmiers et infirmières y apparaissent revêtus de blouses de toile aptes à la fréquente désinfection; le matériel, depuis les boîtes à instruments jusqu'aux lavabos, est du dernier modèle. Et même l'état d'âme du directeur de l'Hôpital, le très aimable docteur T. Iwai, s'y dévoile d'une modernité étonnante, à nous faire honte, dans cette mise en scène, d'un réalisme un peu lugubre, de son personnel hospitalier et de ses blessés. Mais enfin, c'est de la chirurgie de guerre que l'on fait maintenant au Japon, et ces photographies devaient prouver au Mikado, pour qui elles ont été faites, que l'on travaille aussi bien, dans son empire, le bistouri que le sabre à la main... D'ailleurs les opérations semblent si bien réglées, et pratiquées par un personnel d'une propreté si correcte, nous pourrions dire presque élégante, que vraiment l'on peut admettre le public à y assister.

Les détails valent d'ailleurs la peine d'être vus de près. Voici d'abord un moignon d'amputé qui a fort bon aspect, et sur le sort duquel nous pouvons être tranquilles. Ne voyons-nous pas la main de l'étudiant — nous dirions de l'*interne* — diriger sur lui, sous les yeux du chirurgien, le liquide assurément antiseptique qui coule, par un tube en caoutchouc, du *bock* classique que soutient, à hauteur voulue, une jeune infirmière? Que l'on veuille bien remarquer la position de la main de l'aide, soutenant les chairs par le dessous, à l'aide du bout des doigts : tout cela est chirurgicalement d'une correction absolue; et le bon Chinois, qui sourit sur son lit de douleur, peut se vanter d'être pansé suivant les règles de l'art le plus moderne. Aussi est-il à peine besoin d'insister sur la scène de petite chirurgie que l'on voit plus loin : il est manifeste que l'art d'appliquer bandes et appareils n'a plus de secrets pour les Japonais.

Cela nous suffirait déjà pour supposer que le Service de santé doit être organisé, aux armées qui guerroient en ce moment, avec une perfection assez comparable à celle que réalisent nos services européens similaires. Mais la preuve nous en est encore apportée par un autre document : il s'agit d'une ambulance qui s'est établie près d'une masure quelconque, où, bien entendu, l'on n'a rien trouvé pour étendre les blessés à hauteur des chirurgiens. Mais bien vite les cantines d'ambulance ont été vidées, mises debout, et reliées deux à deux par des planches prises dans les environs; et voilà installés des lits, où les blessés seront commodément visités, opérés et pansés. Que les chirurgiens militaires japonais pratiquent l'antisepsie sur le champ de bataille, il n'en faut d'ailleurs pas douter : car voici, dans les mains des aides, les longues boîtes de fer-blanc, remplies de gaz antiseptique, que nous connaissons bien.

Nous savons d'autre part que les sciences médicales sont maintenant cultivées, au Japon, avec le plus grand succès, et que maîtres et élèves y sont entièrement à la hauteur de leurs *anciens* de la vieille Europe.

Non loin de cet Hôpital de la Croix-Rouge s'élève, en effet, une Faculté de médecine installée à l'européenne, et dans cette Faculté on trouve des laboratoires où travaillent de véritables savants, dont quelques-uns ont une notoriété *européenne*, celle qui doit être évidemment surtout agréable à des Japonais. Pour en donner un exemple, il nous suffirait de citer M. Kitasato, qui fut le collaborateur de M. Behring dans sa découverte du traitement sérothérapique du tétanos et de la diphtérie. Deux autres Japonais, MM. Jasuhara et Ogata, ont même été les premiers, après la découverte de la sérothérapie en France, à l'appliquer au traitement du charbon, précédant ainsi M. Behring lui-même. On le voit, il s'agit là de travaux essentiellement modernes, qui placent les savants japonais dans les rangs des véritables pionniers de la science.

Nous n'avons qu'un regret, à énumérer tous ces progrès, c'est de ne pouvoir dire que des Français en ont été les initiateurs. C'est à Berlin, en effet, que le gouvernement du Mikado envoie ses médecins pour s'y perfectionner dans les cliniques et dans les laboratoires, et ce sont encore des professeurs allemands qui ont organisé la nouvelle Faculté de médecine de Tokio.

X.

Après une amputation.

1894 年 12 月 29 日《插图报》

东京的医院	L'hopital de tokio.
1　东京红十字医院远景	1　L'hôpital de la Croix-Rouge, à Tokio: vue générale des bâtiments.
2　受伤清兵的截肢手术	2　Après une amputation.

548 — N° 2705 L'ILLUSTRATION 29 DÉCEMBRE 1894

Blessés chinois traités à l'hôpital de Tokio : l'heure de la promenade.

L'HOPITAL DE LA CROIX-ROUGE, A TOKIO. — Les pansements.

3　被俘中国伤兵在东京医院内接受治疗——散步时间

4　东京红十字医院——包扎伤兵

3　Blessés chinois traités à l'hôpital de Tokio: l'heure de la promenade.

4　L'hôpital de la Croix-Rouge, à Tokio.—Les pansements.

5　被俘中国伤兵在平壤战役后，接受日军战地急救队的治疗

La guerre sino-japonaise.—Après la bataille de Pyeng-Yang: une ambulance.

在这家为我们提供了全景图的红十字医院里，一些受伤的中国囚犯正在接受治疗。这家医院从名字到门面都是现代的。从无法否认其真实性的资料里，我们能够看出，这里一切貌似已按照当今医疗卫生的基本原则建设并安排好，这些原则包括微生物学里列出的那些。

——《东京的战俘医院》(选译)，1894 年 12 月 29 日《插图报》

上述 5 幅图片由日本政府发放给西方多家媒体，当时流传甚广。

HARPER'S WEEKLY

A JOURNAL OF CIVILIZATION

Vol. XXXIX.—No. 2000.
Copyright, 1895, by Harper & Brothers.
All Rights Reserved.

NEW YORK, SATURDAY, APRIL 20, 1895.

TEN CENTS A COPY.
FOUR DOLLARS A YEAR.

THE WAR IN THE EAST—CHINESE POOR RECEIVING ALMS AT THE JAPANESE STAFF-OFFICE IN THE KINCHU CITADEL.

Drawn by C. S. Reinhart from an Official Photograph taken for the Japanese Government.

1895 年 4 月 20 日《哈珀斯周刊》

日军占领金州后，在参谋部门前向贫困的中国百姓发放救济食品

The war in the East—Chinese poor receiving alms at the Japanese staff-office in the Kinchu citadel.

此图根据日本政府发放给西方媒体的照片绘制

Drawn by C.S. Reinhart from an official, photograph taken for the Japanese government.

1894 年 10 月 6 日《哈珀斯周刊》

纽约的日侨俱乐部

New York's Japanese Club.

日本人的宣传战并不仅仅停留在朝鲜前线，也同样在欧美媒体的大后方展开。图为纽约日侨俱乐部，作为日本在美国宣传的桥头堡，时常组织有西方记者、政界人士、社会名流参加的晚宴。

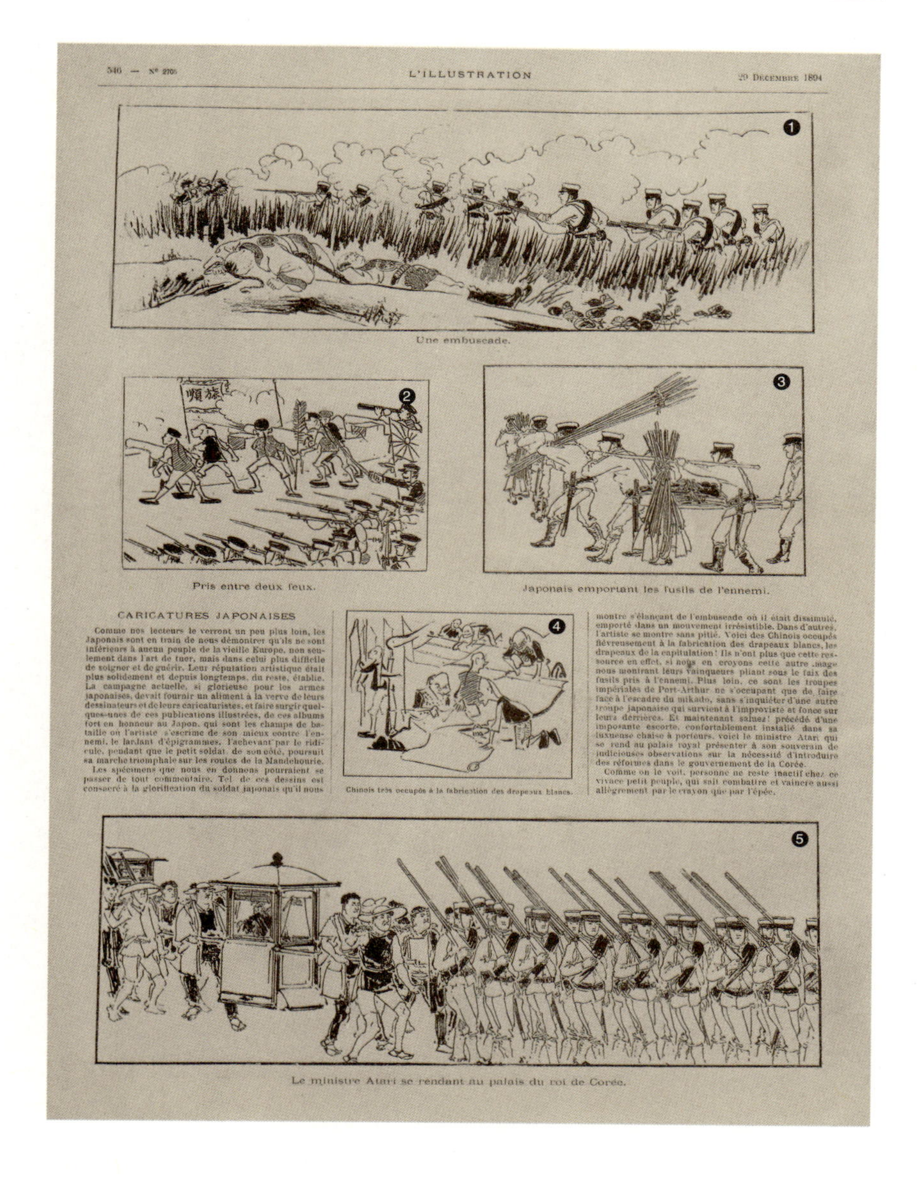

346 — N° 2705 L'ILLUSTRATION 29 DÉCEMBRE 1894

Une embuscade.

Pris entre deux feux.

Japonais emportant les fusils de l'ennemi.

CARICATURES JAPONAISES

Comme nos lecteurs le verront un peu plus loin, les Japonais sont en train de nous démontrer qu'ils ne sont inférieurs à aucun peuple de la vieille Europe, non seulement dans l'art de tuer, mais dans celui plus difficile de soigner et de guérir. Leur réputation artistique était plus solidement et depuis longtemps, du reste, établie. La campagne actuelle, si glorieuse pour les armes japonaises, devait fournir un aliment à la verve de leurs dessinateurs et de leurs caricaturistes, et faire surgir quelques-unes de ces publications illustrées, de ces albums fort en honneur au Japon, qui sont les champs de bataille où l'artiste s'escrime de son mieux contre l'ennemi, le lardant d'épigrammes, l'achevant par le ridicule, pendant que le petit soldat, de son côté, poursuit sa marche triomphale sur les routes de la Mandchourie.

Les spécimens que nous en donnons pourraient se passer de tout commentaire. Tel de ces dessins est consacré à la glorification du soldat japonais qu'il nous montre s'élançant de l'embuscade où il était dissimulé, emporté dans un mouvement irrésistible. Dans d'autres, l'artiste se montre sans pitié. Voici des Chinois occupés fiévreusement à la fabrication des drapeaux blancs, les drapeaux de la capitulation ! Ils n'ont plus que cette ressource en effet, si nous en croyons cette autre image nous montrant leurs vainqueurs pliant sous le faix des fusils pris à l'ennemi. Plus loin, ce sont les troupes impériales de Port-Arthur ne s'occupant que de faire face à l'escadre du mikado, sans s'inquiéter d'une autre troupe japonaise qui survient à l'improviste et fonce sur leurs derrières. Et maintenant saluez ! précédé d'une imposante escorte, confortablement installé dans sa luxueuse chaise à porteurs, voici le ministre Atari qui se rend au palais royal présenter à son souverain de judicieuses observations sur la nécessité d'introduire des réformes dans le gouvernement de la Corée.

Comme on le voit, personne ne reste inactif chez ce vivace petit peuple, qui sait combattre et vaincre aussi allègrement par le crayon que par l'épée.

Chinois très occupés à la fabrication des drapeaux blancs.

Le ministre Atari se rendant au palais du roi de Corée.

1894 年 12 月 29 日《插图报》

1　中了埋伏的清军
2　被前后夹击的清军
3　日军正运送从清军手里缴获的武器
4　忙着制造白旗的中国人
5　大鸟圭介公使前往朝鲜国王宫殿

1　Une ambuscade.
2　Pris entre deux feux.
3　Japonais emportant les fusils de l'ennemi.
4　Chinois très occupés à la fabrication des drapeaux blancs.
5　Le ministre Atari se rendant au palais du roi de Corée.

THE WAR IN EASTERN ASIA, AS DEPICTED BY A CHINESE ARTIST.

Skirmish between Chinese outposts and Japanese reconnaissance in force on the 25th of the 6th month (July 27).

The Gardner incident before the wall of Seoul. Observe the Japanese in the tent committing Seppuku or Hara-kiri; probably this, at least, is added by the Chinese Artist to give an appearance of verisimilitude to his sketch.

Naval skirmish between Japanese and Chinese men-of-war on the 23rd of the 6th month (July 25). The flags carried by the ships indicate their nationality—the square flag, white with red sun in the centre, the Japanese; and the pennant, yellow ground with a dragon, the Chinese.

The sinking of the *Kow-Shing* by Japanese men-of-war. The Chinese Artist, it will be observed, represents the Japanese as firing upon the Chinese in the water, while on the right a French man-of-war's boat is rescuing them struggling in the sea.

1894 年 10 月 6 日《伦敦新闻画报》

清朝画家笔下的东亚之战

The war in Eastern Asia, as depicted by a Chinese artist.

1　7月27日，中国士兵与日军侦察部队发生的冲突

1　Skirmish between Chinese outposts and Japanese reconnaissance in force on the 25th of the 6th month (July 27).

2　在汉城城墙前发生的加德纳事件，中国画师为了让图片更加生动，绘制了一个日本人在帐篷中剖腹自杀的场景

2　The Gardner incident before the wall of Seoul. Observe the Japanese in the tent committing Seppuku or Hara-Kiri; probably this, at least, is added by the Chinese artist to give an appearance of verisimilitude to his sketch.

3　7月25日的海上冲突，舰只的国别需要通过区分国旗才能知道

3　Naval skirmish between Japanese and Chinese men-of-war on the 23rd of the 6th month (July 25). The flags carried by the ships indicate their nationality—the square flag, white with red sun in the centre, the Japanese; and the pennant, yellow ground with a dragon, the Chinese.

4　日军战舰击沉高升号，中国画师描绘日本人向水中开枪射杀中国士兵，而在画面的右侧，法国的战船前来营救

4　The sinking of the Kow-shing by Japanese men-of-war. The Chinese artist, it will be observed, represents the Japanese as firing upon the Chinese in the water, while on the right a French man-of-war's boat is rescuing those struggling in the sea.

《点石斋画报》对甲午战争的假捷报——“牙山大胜”、“倭兵无状”、“海战捷音”、“形同海盗”。

《点石斋画报》是中国最早的旬刊画报，由上海《申报》附送，每期画页8幅，光绪十年（1884）创刊，光绪二十四年（1898）停刊。载大量时事和社会新闻内容，其中刊载的中日甲午战争中的石版画“牙山大胜”、“倭兵无状”、“海战捷音”、“形同海盗”完全是被清军谎报军情误导，颠倒了真相，国人还一时被虚假胜利蒙蔽，在国际上成为笑谈，造成恶劣影响；但就其画报本身而言还是担当了当时媒体先锋，更有当时著名画家奚友如、王钊、周慕乔等17人的参与，使此报风靡一时。

结　语

我在日本遇到的欧洲人都说，对于他们来说，最可靠、最有信息量的消息都来自于纽约和旧金山发行的报纸。出于各种原因，日本政府仅允许刊发对日方有利的新闻。这样一来，就不会有人信服在日本刊行媒体上的简短报道。在上海，差不多也是这样的情况，报纸只刊发获得中国政府首肯的消息。毋庸置疑的是，比起他们的敌人，中国人也更为宽容一些，或者说是更加地粗心大意，所以在中国报纸的字里行间总能看到军队打了败仗的消息。出于这样的现状，在中日两国，我只相信欧洲媒体的报纸。顺便说一句，我个人觉得日本横滨新闻社的消息很明显地在支持中国，反而上海的报纸是亲日的。在上海的欧洲人对当下的情形都很明白，如果中国战败了，那就意味着中国要进一步地对外开放，且这开放的力度与步伐与一百多年前的和平交易商贸往来相比，要大得多和快得多。这些想法也如实地在英文报纸上反映了出来。

在中日两国的报纸上，来自关于战场中心前线的消息，除了能供读者自行猜测解读之外，没有任何什么其他价值。比如，当我在长崎的时候，就在平壤之战前得到了战争的消息，报道说日军战死了36人，并俘获了3艘中方战舰，而中方死了2000人。读者看到这条消息时，他们会说，这场战争的细节的确有些荒唐，但看上去似乎那里真的发生了一场恶战，而且日本军队好像获得了完胜。但当我抵达上海时，关于这场战争，英文报纸已刊登了一篇500字的消息，报道中确认了平壤之战的失败，对海战的惨烈也进行了描述，中国海军将领战死。欧洲人对这篇报道不甚理解，只能将报纸翻来翻去，以求获得更多的信息。最后他们臆测：中国方面的伤亡一定非常惨重，否则中方就会将这场战争称做是胜仗。他们都一致认为中日双方各损失了3艘战舰，中国海军撤退并且逃跑了，中方用作运输的精美客船落入日军手中。这样的情况事实上是因为在中日两国关于战事所发的电报微乎其微，也只能写成这样不确定的消息。身在美国的民众们，关于朝鲜发生了什么，你们远比中日两国人民知道得更多，即便这些美国的报道因为战地记者被警告远离战场，而内容不得不写得如小说般夸张。

据说在日本，当局坚持对战事要绝对保密，以防革命的发生。但如果他们确信能够痛击中国，他们就竭力以求公开消息，因为没有任何成功能够比战争更加鼓舞人心，从而提升政府形象。战争的失败只能让人民转向支持革命的反欧洲排外政党。这样我们就不难发现，中日两国的改良进步运动都和日本军队的胜利息息相关。我们也看到日军是多么地肆无忌惮，那是对文明的泯灭，基督教徒一定会尽全力帮助中国。日本方面之所以抑制关于战事报道的另外一个原因是他们不愿意人民看到人员伤亡，这是日本的第一次对外战争，他们的武士以往都是赤手空拳进行搏斗，人们不会理解现代战争中必要的人员伤亡。在整个日本境内，人们都能看到彩色的宣传画，画面中大多都是日本人骑在中国人身上，击沉中国的船只，或者中国军队中烟雾四起，火光连天。在日本随处可见那些稍有知识的人如饥似渴地看着那些不过是薄棉纸上印刷了几行文字的所谓的报纸。

——朱利安·拉尔夫，1894 年 11 月 10 日　美国《哈珀斯周刊》

LI HUNG CHANG RECEIVING A VISITOR AT CARLTON HOUSE TERRACE

DRAWN FROM LIFE BY W. HATHERELL, R.I.

1896年8月22日《图片报》

李鸿章访英期间，在卡尔顿府接见前来拜会的《伦敦泰晤士报》前驻华特派记者柯乐洪

后记　西方的画报

19 世纪，西方列强的殖民进程和贸易全球化如火如荼；

19 世纪，工业革命为世界带来了火车、电报和坚船利炮；

19 世纪，古老的东亚在隆冬中惊蛰，扼腕地球的中心已随波西去；

19 世纪，欧美农民快步迈入城市，人口数量的攀升伴随着教育的飞跃；

19 世纪，邻里矛盾幻化成了国际争端，人们关注的焦点从自家门前的两亩三分地移向被列强角逐的全球资源。

19 世纪，无论是旧大陆还是新世界，无论是车夫还是富商，再也不可能回到两耳不闻窗外事的桃花源。当政治、金融、文化领域中的各方势力激烈博弈，支配社会的力量也渐渐从专制君主的手中旁落，无冕之王应运而生。文字在人类历史上首次变成了日用消费品，它们从大学图书馆尘封的典籍里挣脱出来，钻进了名目繁多的报纸杂志，和牛奶面包一起被摆上了城市居民的早餐桌。

1842 年 5 月 14 日周六，在英国诞生了一张名为《伦敦新闻画报》（*The Illustrated London News*）的周刊。无独有偶，九个月后的另一个周六，英吉利海峡对岸，一份法文的周末画报《插图报》（*L'Illustration*）在巴黎创刊。虽然这两份周刊的问世比英法两份最老资格的时政类日报《泰晤士报》（*The Times*）和《费加罗报》（*Le Figaro*）分别晚了 57 年和 16 年，但这并不能抹杀它们存在的意义。《伦敦新闻画报》和《插图报》的读者们看报时再也不必用力把双眼挤成一条缝，在密密麻麻的文字中和豆腐块文章里大海捞针般地寻找自己感兴趣的内容，因为它们的创办人明白了下面这个道理：一个新兴的读者群已经崛起，他们渴求通过更直观、更快速的方法了解世界，读图的时代正在到来！《插图报》的总编则撰写了《我们的目标》一文刊发在创刊号上，文章以此开头：“既然本世纪最流行‘插

L'ILLUSTRATION,

JOURNAL UNIVERSEL.

Ab. pour Paris. — 3 mois, 8 fr. — 6 mois, 16 fr. — Un an, 30 fr.
Prix de chaque N°, 75 c. — La collection mensuelle br., 2 fr. 75.

N° 1. VOL. I. — SAMEDI 4 MARS 1843.
Bureaux, rue de Seine, 33. — Réimprimé.

Ab. pour les Dep. — 3 mois, 9 fr. — 6 mois, 17 fr. — Un an, 32 fr.
pour l'étranger. — 10 — 20 — 40

SOMMAIRE.

Notre but. — Le Gouverneur des îles Marquises. *Portrait du capitaine Bruat; Maison en bois qui doit être transportée aux îles Marquises.* — Le Curé médecin, nouvelle, par E. Legouvé. — Nouvelles diverses. *Trois Gravures.* — Sauvetage du Télémaque. *Deux Gravures.* — Revue des Tribunaux. *Quatre Gravures.* — Chronique musicale. — Une Fleur, romance. — La duchesse d'Orléans. *Portrait.* — Espartero. — Promenade du Bœuf-Gras. *Une Gravure.* — Revue des Théâtres. Une scène des *Deux-Ânes.* — Bulletin bibliographique. — Université. — Annonces. Manuscrits de Napoléon. — Modes. *Une Gravure.* — Bulletin commercial. — Rébus.

NOTRE BUT.

Puisque le goût du siècle a relevé le mot *Illustration*, prenons-le! nous nous en servirons pour caractériser un nouveau mode de la presse nouvelliste.

Ce que veut ardemment le public aujourd'hui, ce qu'il demande avant tout le reste, c'est d'être mis aussi clairement que possible ...

tel bagage. Loin de craindre la disette, nous craindrions plutôt l'encombrement et la surcharge.

La plupart du temps il est impossible, en lisant un journal, de se faire une idée nette de ce dont il est question, parce qu'il serait nécessaire pour cela d'avoir sous les yeux une carte géographique et qu'il serait trop long d'en chercher une. Que l'on m'imprime dix colonnes sur les terrains en litige entre l'Angleterre et les États-Unis, j'aurai plutôt compris avec dix lignes, si l'on a eu soin d'y accoler une carte précise du pays. Cette carte est la pièce essentielle du procès, et faute de la posséder, tout demeure confus. Il faut en dire autant de toutes les nouvelles politiques qui se rapportent à des contrées éloignées. Qui ferait profession d'être assez versé dans la géographie pour suivre sans difficulté, sur les récits abrégés des journaux, les mouvements des armées de l'Afghanistan, dans l'Inde, dans la Chine, dans le Caucase, même dans l'Algérie? Nous compléterons donc notre texte par des cartes toutes les fois que les cartes lui seront utiles. Voilà un genre d'illustration dont personne ne contestera la convenance : mais ce n'est pas assez; les cartes ont par elles-mêmes quelque chose de trop sec et de trop peu vivant. Au moyen de correspondances, et, quand il le faudra, de voyages, nous les soutiendrons par les vues des villes, des marches d'armées, des flottes, des batailles. Qui n'éprouvera une joie plus vive en voyant les faits d'armes de nos frères d'Algérie retracés d'après nature, au milieu de ces sauvages montagnes, devant ces hordes barbares, au pied de ces ruines romaines, qu'en les lisant simplement dans les bulletins?

La Biographie nous offre une large scène. Nous voulons qu'avant peu il n'y ait pas en Europe un seul personnage, ministre, orateur, poète, général, d'un nom capable, à quelque titre que ce soit, de retentir dans le public, qui n'ait payé à notre journal le tribut de son portrait. ...

sur les points où elle présentera aux regards quelque chose soit de singulier, soit de grandiose.

Nous terminerons notre programme par un mot sur les modes. Il ne s'agit pas seulement de celles du costume, que nous ne négligerons cependant pas : il s'agit aussi pour nous de ces modes d'ameublement qui tiennent de si près à l'art et qui ont porté si haut la gloire de la France ; bronzerie, carrosserie, ébénisterie, orfèvrerie, bijouterie, toutes ces branches brillantes de l'industrie parisienne occuperont dans nos colonnes la place qui leur est due, et nous servirons peut-être à accélérer la dispersion dans le monde de ces innombrables essaims de formes riches, élégantes, destinées à l'embellissement de tout d'usages de la vie, et qui étendent sur le monde l'empire de notre patrie comme il s'y est longtemps étendu par la seule forme du langage.

En voilà assez pour marquer ce que nous voulons faire, et peut-être pour inspirer le désir de le voir. Concluons donc cette préface, et commençons notre œuvre en priant le public, qui vient d'en entrevoir les difficultés, de ne point s'étonner si nous ne nous élevons que progressivement à la hauteur du service nouveau que nous ne craignons pas d'embrasser.

Le Gouverneur des îles Marquises.

(Le capitaine Bruat, gouverneur des îles Marquises.)

Armand Bruat, né en Alsace, doit avoir de quarante-cinq à quarante-six ans. Il entra au service en 1811, à bord

《插图报》1843 年 3 月 4 日创刊号

图’这个词，那我们就用它！我们就用它来开启新闻传媒的一个新篇章。今天，公众最需要的是什么？他们要求被最明白地告知世界上到底发生了什么。那些只能刊发简讯的日报还能满足得了这个需求吗？恐怕不能了。它们能做到的，只不过是把故事讲个大概其罢了，而真正应该做的，是让人们仿佛亲眼目睹整个事件发生的全过程。难道今天的新闻媒体面对这样的目标真的束手无策吗？不，办法有一个！是一个被我们长期忽略了的古老办法，正是这个办法，将成为我们办报的主要特色，没错，您说对了——木刻版画！”

《伦敦新闻画报》和《插图报》是世界上最早的以图画内容为主的周报，它们以细腻生动的密线木刻版画，以 19 世纪的技术条件所能达到的最快速度，再现

《伦敦新闻画报》
1873年11月22日

上海的乌篷船内壁上居然贴满了《伦敦新闻画报》

世界各地的重大事件。《伦敦新闻画报》创刊号，售价6便士，在16个版面和32张插图中，人们读到了阿富汗战争、法国火车出轨、美国总统候选人的民意测验结果、白金汉宫里盛装舞会的场景、新剧和新书介绍，以及不少类似于"法制进行时"的案件侦破纪实，26,000份旋即售罄。1842年年底发行量就已经达到了80,000份，1851年突破了130,000份，1863年则达到了300,000份。《插图报》售价75生丁，创刊号发行了16,000份，1929年《插图报》更创下了650,000份的纪录。

这两份周末画报的成功轰动了整个西方世界，一大批类似的刊物跟风效仿：1843年《新闻画报》(*Illustrirte Zeitung*)在莱比锡创刊，1850年《哈珀斯月刊》

（*Haper's Monthly*）、1857年《哈珀斯周刊》（*Haper's Weekly*）在纽约创刊，1873年《意大利画报》（*L'Illustrazione Italiana*）在米兰问世。这些世界各地的画报周刊在创刊的那一刻就开宗明义地瞄准了《伦敦新闻画报》和《插图报》的模式。

而《伦敦新闻画报》为了争抢美国市场，又推出了纽约版，我们在本书中为大家展示了几份，它们比伦敦版整整晚两周印刷，因为这些版画的模具需要从伦敦穿越大西洋送到纽约的印厂。

有趣的是，1858年，在半句洋文也不通的中国，在广州采访的《伦敦新闻画报》的特派画家沃格曼（Charles Wirgman）惊讶地写道："中国人喜欢用《伦敦新闻画报》来装饰他们的墙壁和平底船！"而在1873年11月22日的《伦敦新闻画报》刊出了另一位特派画家辛普森（William Simpson）的速写和信件，他发现上海的乌篷船内壁上居然贴满了《伦敦新闻画报》！

市场竞争不仅存在于海外，也来自本土。1869年12月4日在伦敦创刊的《图片报》（*The Graphic*）给《伦敦新闻画报》带来不小的挑战。《图片报》的政治立场比保守的《伦敦新闻画报》偏左，社会改良主义的编辑方针配以更加精美的图片质量和更加活泼的版面风格，为《图片报》迅速赢得了大量对社会底层富有同情心的知识界的年轻读者。这一点，在我们收藏的关于"高升号被日军击沉"和"旅顺大屠杀"的报章中表现得最明显，《图片报》的图文报道对真相的揭露更为直接和深刻。当然，我们不能完全期盼一份生存在那个时代的媒体彻底摒弃强盗逻辑和殖民者的傲慢，但至少，我们可以从编辑方针的反差中解读出，在120年前的世纪之交，大英帝国并非铁板一块，在它内部存在着不同的阶层和不同的政治主张。《图片报》取得了巨大的成功，1869年起步时，编辑部设在租来的民宅里，1882年报社已经在纽约拥有3栋大楼、20多份出版物、1000名员工，且报刊大量销往北美。

而北美土生土长的《哈珀斯周刊》诞生于1857年的纽约，南北战争的前夕。从表现形式和编辑策略上而言，它更多地效仿了巴黎的《插图报》：不仅提供插图，还配以社会名家撰写的严谨的长篇文章，力求把周刊的优势发挥到极致，全面、深入地挖掘素材，为社会意见领袖和高端人群提供更精准、严肃的决策依据。1860年《哈珀斯周刊》的发行量就已经达到200,000份。从1862年起的20年中，"美国政治漫画之父"托马斯·纳斯特（Thomas Nast）的加盟为《哈珀斯周刊》增添了巨大的吸引力，纳斯特也依托《哈珀斯周刊》的巨大发行量，用自己的画笔推动了他个人的政治理想：反对奴隶制、维护黑人权利，帮助格兰特、海斯、克利夫兰等一个个候选人赢得总统选举，被誉为“总统制造者”。纳斯特还赋予美国以“人格化”，创造了“山姆大叔”的名字和形象。更为有趣的是，今天为亿万人所熟知的那个胖墩墩、笑眯眯的红鼻子圣诞老人也是他通过《哈珀斯周刊》带到这个世界上的。

我们收藏的另一类西方插图报刊是以法国《小日报》(*Le Petit Journal*)和《小巴黎人》(*Le Petit Parisien*)的周末增刊为代表的，它们与前面提到的几份周刊有较大的区别：它们瞄准的读者群体是社会底层的劳动人民，所以售价低廉，文字口语化，热衷于挖掘娱乐大众的新闻内容，插图幅面大，追求视觉刺激，《小日报》周末插图增刊甚至在1890年前后开始使用六彩套色滚筒印刷封面和封底。市场定位的不同使得它们的发行量极其可观，《小日报》周末增刊在1895年就达到了1,000,000份，在20世纪初又被《小巴黎人》的周末增刊超过。

无论是严肃的时政类报刊还是面向大众的街头小报，它们承载的那些笔法细腻的版画插图现在看起来都堪称是价值和品位甚高的艺术品。《插图报》从1891年起、《伦敦新闻画报》从1892年起就开始采用最先进的照片印刷技术，用越来越多的相片取代版画插图。120年前的甲午战争为摄影作品在画报上的普及提供了更多的机会，然而通过分析我们的收藏，读者能感受到，那时的报刊编辑们为了获得更大更清晰的图片效果，还是倾向于选用版画做插图，特别是在制版上，他们已经掌握了将照片和画家们发回来的速写直接运用于版画制作的技术，这大大提高了版画插图的逼真程度和刊发速度。

20世纪的到来后，世界大战的接踵而至，加之经营不善等因素，逐渐消磨了插图周刊的生命力；又由于《泰晤士报》、《费加罗报》、《纽约时报》(*The New York Times*)等传统时政类日报的插图化和摄影技术的不断普及，插图周刊在图像方面的领先优势也慢慢消失了，读者群随之缩小。《图片报》于1932年停刊；《插图报》于1955年停刊；《哈珀斯周刊》于1957年停刊；《伦敦新闻画报》于1971年改为月刊、1989年改为双月刊，最后在互联网呱呱落地的1994年改为半年刊，苟延残喘9年后，于2003年停止发行。

然而，《哈珀斯周刊》的两个姊妹刊物仍然存活至今：1850年问世的《哈珀斯月刊》如今还在以双月刊和网刊形式发行，偏重于文学；诞生于1867年的全球第一本时尚类画报《哈珀斯芭莎》(*Harper's Bazaar*)虽然在1901年从周刊改为月刊，而且后来几易其主，今天依然是全世界发行量最大的时尚类杂志之一，在30个国家和地区受到读者们的追捧，在中国大陆，它被称作《时尚芭莎》。

致　谢

今天呈现给读者的这本书，是根据我们历时多年从十几个国家所搜集来的老报纸编译而成。这个搜集过程是漫长的，但也是充满乐趣的。感谢所有朋友们的关注和鼓励，尤其是万国报馆在英国、法国、美国、德国、俄罗斯和日本的朋友们，他们为此付出了宝贵的时间和精力，难以一一致谢，但也要借此对Daniel Blasize先生、汪华先生、老若先生、李三先生、黄元龙先生、王兆南先生、刘艳民先生、李雪东先生、金妍女士、徐伟女士说声："谢谢！"过去几年里，没有你们的支持和帮助，万国报馆无法达到今天的规模；也要请你们原谅，在报纸搜集和运输过程中我们的万般叮嘱和啰嗦，使你们深受其扰。还要感谢我们的好友米川先生，把他的工作室变成120年前的故纸堆，让我们得以整理和研究。

在此还要特别感谢王怀庆先生、杨迎明先生、晓春女士和陈徒手先生，没有你们的引领，我们还在收藏的路上徘徊。

另外，在老报刊图片数字化过程中，我们得到了石利洛中国公司洪亮先生、徽州摄影家张建平先生，以及肖登标先生的大力协助，他们用21世纪最先进的哈苏数码摄影器材把百年前珍贵的老报刊变成了读者眼前细腻的图片，在此一并致以深深的谢意！

同时，也向我们的翻译团队致以最真挚的感谢！英、法、德、日、俄，多种文字的翻译为我们带来了志同道合的朋友们，谢谢你们：姜霞女士、朱强先生、肖振彪先生、刘心怡女士、贺靖女士、纪娜女士、潘文捷女士、温楷先生、张毅豪先生、夏然女士、王秋艳女士、张亚迟先生、邢成先生、朴美花女士。谢谢你们，被那些军舰型号和人物的名字折磨了一年多！

最后，感谢三联书店和本书的责任编辑唐明星女士，谢谢她的耐心和细心，促使我们完成这个功课，让我们得以在甲子之年实现回望之路。

万国报馆

2014年6月